Data Mining

Practical Machine Learning Tools and Techniques
with Java Implementations

The Morgan Kaufmann Series in Data Management Systems

Series Editor, Jim Gray

Data Mining

Practical Machine Learning Tools and Techniques
with Java Implementations

Ian H. Witten

Department of Computer Science
University of Waikato

Eibe Frank

Department of Computer Science
University of Waikato

MORGAN KAUFMANN PUBLISHERS

AN IMPRINT OF ACADEMIC PRESS
A Harcourt Science and Technology Company

SAN FRANCISCO   SAN DIEGO   NEW YORK   BOSTON
LONDON   SYDNEY   TOKYO

Senior Editor	Diane D. Cerra
Director of Production and Manufacturing	Yonie Overton
Senior Production Editor	Elisabeth Beller
Cover Design	Ross Carron
Cover Images	image copyright © 2000 Photodisc, Inc.
Text Design	Mark Ong, Side by Side Studios
Copyeditor	Carol Leyba
Proofreader	Beth Berkelhammer
Composition	Susan Riley, Side by Side Studios
Illustration	Cherie Plumlee Computer Illustration
Indexer	Western Indexing Services
Printer	Courier Corporation

Designations used by companies to distinguish their products are often claimed as trademarks or registered trademarks. In all instances where Morgan Kaufmann Publishers is aware of a claim, the product names appear in initial capital or all capital letters. Readers, however, should contact the appropriate companies for more complete information regarding trademarks and registration.

The *weka,* depicted on the cover, is an inquisitive bird found only in New Zealand (also shown). Weka (Waikato Environment for Knowledge Analysis) is a comprehensive software resource implementing techniques covered in this book and available as source code via *www.mkp.com/datamining* or at *www.cs.waikato.ac.nz/ml/weka.*

ACADEMIC PRESS
A Harcourt Science and Technology Company
525 B Street, Suite 1900, San Diego, CA 92101-4495, USA
http://www.academicpress.com

Academic Press
Harcourt Place, 32 Jamestown Road, London NW1 7BY, United Kingdom
http://www.hbuk.co.uk/ap/

Morgan Kaufmann Publishers
340 Pine Street, Sixth Floor, San Francisco, CA 94104-3205, USA
http://www.mkp.com

Library of Congress Cataloging-in-Publication Data

Witten, I. H. (Ian H.)
    Data mining: practical machine learning tools and techniques with Java
    implementations/Ian H. Witten, Eibe Frank.
        p. cm.
    Includes bibliographical references and index.
    ISBN 1-55860-552-5
        1. Data mining   2. Java (Computer program language)   I. Frank, Eibe.   II. Title.
QA76.9.D343 W58 1999
006.3--dc21

99-046067

Foreword

Jim Gray, Series Editor
Microsoft Research

Technology now allows us to capture and store vast quantities of data. Finding and summarizing the patterns, trends, and anomalies in these data sets is one of the grand challenges of the information age.

There has been stunning progress in data mining and machine learning in the last decade. The marriage of statistics, machine learning, information theory, and computing has created a solid science with a firm mathematical base and very powerful tools. Witten and Frank present much of this progress in their book and in the Java implementations of the key algorithms. This is a milestone in the synthesis of data mining, data analysis, information theory, and machine learning.

The authors present the basic theory of automatically extracting models from data and then validating those models. The book does an excellent job of explaining the various models (decision trees, rules, and linear models) and how to apply them in practice. With this foundation, the book then walks the reader through the steps and pitfalls of various approaches. Most of the book is tutorial, but one chapter broadly describes how commercial systems work, and another does a walkthrough of the Java tools that the authors provide through a website.

This book presents this new discipline in a very accessible form: suitable both to train the next generation of practitioners and researchers and to inform lifelong learners like myself. Witten and Frank have a passion for simple and elegant solutions. They approach each topic with this mindset, grounding all concepts in concrete examples and urging the reader to consider the simple techniques first and then to progress to the more sophisticated ones if the simple ones prove inadequate.

If you are interested in databases and have not been following the machine learning field for the last decade, this book is a great way to catch up on this exciting progress.

Contents

Figures

Tables

Preface

The convergence of computing and communication has produced a society that feeds on information. Yet most of the information is in its raw form: data. If *data* is characterized as recorded facts, then *information* is the set of patterns, or expectations, that underlie the data. There is a huge amount of information locked up in databases—information that is potentially important but has not yet been discovered or articulated. Our mission is to bring it forth.

Data mining is the extraction of implicit, previously unknown, and potentially useful information from data. The idea is to build computer programs that sift through databases automatically, seeking regularities or patterns. Strong patterns, if found, will likely generalize to make accurate predictions on future data. Of course, there will be problems. Many patterns will be banal and uninteresting. Others will be spurious, contingent on accidental coincidences in the particular dataset used. And real data is imperfect: some parts are garbled, some missing. Anything that is discovered will be inexact: there will be exceptions to every rule and cases not covered by any rule. Algorithms need to be robust enough to cope with imperfect data and to extract regularities that are inexact but useful.

Machine learning provides the technical basis of data mining. It is used to extract information from the raw data in databases—information that is expressed in a comprehensible form and can be used for a variety of purposes. The process is one of abstraction: taking the data, warts and all, and inferring whatever structure underlies it. This book is about the tools and techniques of machine learning that are used in practical data mining for finding, and describing, structural patterns in data.

As with any burgeoning new technology that enjoys intense commercial attention, the use of data mining is surrounded by a great deal of hype in the technical—and sometimes the popular—press. Exaggerated reports appear of the secrets that can be uncovered by setting learning algorithms loose on oceans of data. But there is no magic in machine learning, no hidden power, no alchemy. Instead there is an identifiable body of simple and practical techniques that can often extract useful information from raw data. This book describes these techniques and shows how they work.

We interpret machine learning as the acquisition of structural descriptions from examples. The kind of descriptions that are found can be used for prediction, explanation, and understanding. Some data mining applications focus on prediction: forecasting what will happen in new situations from data that describe what happened in the past, often by guessing the classification of new examples. But we are equally—perhaps more—interested in applications where the result of "learning" is an actual description of a structure that can be used to classify examples. This structural description supports explanation and understanding as well as prediction. In our experience, insights gained by the user are of most interest in the majority of practical data mining applications; indeed, this is one of machine learning's major advantages over classical statistical modeling.

The book explains a wide variety of machine learning methods. Some are pedagogically motivated: simple schemes designed to explain clearly how the basic ideas work. Others are practical: real systems that are used in applications today. Many are contemporary and have been developed only in the last few years.

A comprehensive software resource, written in the Java language, has been created to illustrate the ideas in the book. Called the Waikato Environment for Knowledge Analysis, or Weka[1] for short, this utility is available as source code on the World Wide Web via *www.mkp.com/datamining* or at *www.cs.waikato. ac.nz/ml/weka*. It is a full, industrial-strength implementation of essentially all the techniques that are covered in this book. It includes illustrative code and working implementations of machine learning methods. It offers clean, spare implementations of the simplest techniques, designed to aid understanding of the mechanisms involved. It also provides a workbench that includes full, working, state-of-the-art implementations of many popular learning schemes that can be used for practical data mining or for research. Finally, it contains a framework, in the form of a Java class library, that supports applications that use embedded machine learning and even the implementation of new learning schemes.

The objective of this book is to introduce the tools and techniques for machine learning that are used in data mining. After reading it, you will understand what these techniques are and appreciate their strengths and applicability. If you wish to experiment with your own data, you will be able to do this with the Weka software.

---

[1] Found only on the islands of New Zealand, the *weka* (pronounced to rhyme with "Mecca") is a flightless bird with an inquisitive nature.

The book spans the gulf between the intensely practical approach taken by trade books that provide case studies on data mining and the more theoretical, principle-driven exposition found in current textbooks on machine learning. (A brief description of these books appears in the *Further reading* section at the end of Chapter 1.) This gulf is rather wide. In order to apply machine learning techniques productively, you need to understand something about how they work; this is not a technology that you can apply blindly and expect to get good results. Different problems yield to different techniques, but these are early days for data mining, and it is never clear which techniques are suitable for a given situation: you need to know something about the range of possible solutions. And we cover an extremely wide range of techniques. We can do this because, unlike many trade books, this volume does not promote any particular commercial software or approach. The book contains a large number of examples, but they use illustrative datasets that are small enough to allow you to follow what is going on. Real datasets are far too large to show this (and in any case are invariably company confidential). Our datasets are chosen not to illustrate actual large-scale practical problems, but to help you understand what the different techniques do, how they work, and what their range of application is.

The book is aimed at the technically aware general reader who is interested in the principles and ideas underlying the current practice of data mining. It will also be of interest to information professionals who need to become acquainted with this new data mining technology, and to all those who wish to gain a detailed technical understanding of what machine learning involves. It is written for an eclectic audience of information systems practitioners, programmers, consultants, developers, information technology managers, specification writers, patent examiners, curious lay people—as well as students and professors—who need an easy-to-read book with lots of illustrations that describes what the major machine learning techniques are, what they do, how they are used, and how they work. It is practically oriented, with a strong "how to" flavor, and includes algorithms, code, and implementations. All those involved in practical data mining will benefit directly from the techniques described. The book is also aimed at people who want to cut through to the reality that underlies the hype about machine learning and who seek a practical, non-academic, unpretentious approach. We have avoided requiring any specific theoretical or mathematical knowledge, except in some sections that are marked by a light gray bar in the margin. These passages contain material for the more technical or theoretically inclined reader and may be skipped without loss of continuity.

The book is organized in layers that make the ideas accessible to readers who are interested in grasping the basics, as well as to those who would like more depth of treatment, along with full details on the techniques covered. We believe that consumers of machine learning need to have some idea of how the algorithms they use work. It is often observed that data models are only as good as the person who interprets them, and that person needs to know something about how the models are produced in order to appreciate the strengths, and limitations, of the technology. However, it is not necessary for all users to have a deep understanding of the finer details of the algorithms.

We address this situation by describing machine learning methods at successive levels of detail. The reader will learn the basic ideas, the topmost level, by reading the first three chapters. Chapter 1 describes, through examples, what machine learning is and where it can be used; it also provides actual practical applications. Chapters 2 and 3 cover the different kinds of input and output—or *knowledge representation*—that are involved. Different kinds of output dictate different styles of algorithm, and at the next level, Chapter 4 describes the basic methods of machine learning, simplified to make them easy to comprehend. Here the principles involved are conveyed in a variety of algorithms without getting bogged down in intricate details or tricky implementation issues. To make progress in the application of machine learning techniques to particular data mining problems, it is essential to be able to measure how well you are doing. Chapter 5, which can be read out of sequence, equips the reader to evaluate the results that are obtained from machine learning, addressing the sometimes complex issues involved in performance evaluation.

At the lowest and most detailed level, Chapter 6 exposes in naked detail the nitty-gritty issues of implementing a spectrum of machine learning algorithms, including the complexities that are necessary for them to work well in practice. Although many readers may want to ignore this detailed information, it is at this level that the full, working, tested Java implementations of machine learning schemes are written. Chapter 7 discusses practical topics involved with engineering the input to machine learning—for example, selecting and discretizing attributes—and covers several more advanced techniques for refining and combining the output from different learning techniques. Chapter 8 describes the Java code that accompanies the book. You can skip to this chapter directly from Chapter 4 if you are in a hurry to get on with analyzing your data and don't want to be bothered with the technical details. Finally, Chapter 9 looks to the future.

The book does not cover all machine learning methods. In particular, we do not discuss neural nets because this technique produces predictions rather than structural descriptions; also, it is well described in some recent books on data mining. Nor do we cover reinforcement learning since it is rarely applied in practical data mining; nor genetic algorithm approaches since these are really just an optimization technique; nor Bayesian networks because algorithms for learning them are not yet robust enough to be deployed; nor relational learning and inductive logic programming since they are rarely used in mainstream data mining applications.

Java has been chosen for the implementations of machine learning techniques that accompany this book because, as an object-oriented programming language, it allows a uniform interface to learning schemes and methods for pre- and post-processing. We have chosen Java instead of C++, Smalltalk, or other object-oriented languages because programs written in Java can be run on almost any computer without having to be recompiled, or having to go through complicated installation procedures, or—worst of all—having to change the code itself. A Java program is compiled into byte-code that can be executed on any computer equipped with an appropriate interpreter. This interpreter is called the *Java virtual machine*. Java virtual machines—and, for that matter, Java compilers—are freely available for all important platforms.

Like all widely used programming languages, Java has received its share of criticism. Although this is not the place to elaborate on such issues, in several cases the critics are clearly right. However, of all currently available programming languages that are widely supported, standardized, and extensively documented, Java seems to be the best choice for the purpose of this book. Its main disadvantage is speed of execution—or lack of it. Executing a Java program is several times slower than running a corresponding program written in C because the virtual machine has to translate the byte-code into machine code before it can be executed. In our experience the difference is a factor of three to five if the virtual machine uses a *just-in-time compiler*. Instead of translating each byte-code individually, a just-in-time compiler translates whole chunks of byte-code into machine code, thereby achieving significant speedup. However, if this is still too slow for your application, there are compilers that translate Java programs directly into machine code, bypassing the byte-code step. Of course, this code cannot be executed on other platforms, thereby sacrificing one of Java's most important advantages.

Teaching materials on the Web

There are teaching materials available online at *www.mkp.com/books_catalog/ bookpage1.asp#Extras* consisting of

- Powerpoint slides
    Powerpoint presentation containing all the figures from the book that can be downloaded
- exams
    an exam and the corresponding answers; available for instructors only
- assignments
    Assignment 1
    Assignment 2
    Assignment 3

Assignment 4
Assignment 5
Assignment 6
- quizzes
Quiz 1
Quiz 2
Quiz 3
Quiz 4
Quiz 5
Quiz 6
Quiz 7
Quiz 8
Quiz 9

Acknowledgments

Writing the acknowledgments is always the nicest part! A lot of people have helped us, and we relish this opportunity to thank them. This book has arisen out of the machine learning research project in the Computer Science Department at the University of Waikato, New Zealand. We have received generous encouragement and assistance from the academic staff members on that project: John Cleary, Sally Jo Cunningham, Matt Humphrey, Lyn Hunt, Bob McQueen, Lloyd Smith, and above all, Geoff Holmes, the project leader and source of inspiration. All who have worked on the machine learning project here have contributed to our thinking: we would particularly like to mention Steve Garner, Stuart Inglis, and Craig Nevill-Manning for helping us to get the project off the ground in the beginning when success was less certain and things were more difficult.

The Weka system that illustrates the ideas in this book forms a crucial component of it. It was conceived by the authors and designed and implemented by Eibe Frank, along with Len Trigg and Mark Hall. Many people in the machine learning laboratory at Waikato have made significant contributions, especially Yong Wang, who provided the implementation of M5′.

Tucked away as we are in a remote (but very pretty) corner of the southern hemisphere, we greatly appreciate the visitors to our department who play a crucial role in acting as sounding boards and helping us to develop our thinking in diverse ways. We would like to mention in particular Rob Holte, Bernhard Pfahringer, Carl Gutwin, and Russell Beale, each of whom visited us for several months; David Aha, who although he only came for a few days did so at an early and fragile stage of the project and performed a great service by his enthusiasm and encouragement; and Kai Ming Ting, who worked with us for two years on many of the topics discussed in Chapter 7 and helped to bring us into the mainstream of machine learning.

Past students at Waikato have played a significant role in the development of the project. Jamie Littin worked on ripple-down rules and relational learning. Brent Martin explored instance-based learning and nested instance-based representations. Murray Fife slaved over relational learning. Nadeeka Madapathage investigated the use of functional languages for expressing machine learning algorithms. Other graduate students have influenced us in numerous ways, particularly Gordon Paynter, who has been deeply involved with the keyphrase extraction scheme described in Section 9.4, and Zane Bray, who worked on the text mining scheme outlined in the same section. Colleagues Steve Jones, Tony Smith, and Malika Mahoui have also made great and far-reaching contributions to these and other machine learning projects.

Ian Witten would like to acknowledge the formative role of his former students at Calgary, particularly Brent Krawchuk, Dave Maulsby, Thong Phan, and Tanja Mitrovic, all of whom helped him develop his early ideas in machine learning, as did faculty members Bruce MacDonald, Brian Gaines, and David Hill at Calgary, and John Andreae at the University of Canterbury. Eibe Frank is particularly indebted to his former supervisor at the University of Karlsruhe, Klaus-Peter Huber (now with SAS Institute), who infected him with the fascination of machines that learn.

Diane Cerra and Belinda Breyer of Morgan Kaufmann have worked hard to shape this book, and Elisabeth Beller, our production editor, has made the process go very smoothly for us. Bronwyn Webster has provided excellent support at the Waikato end.

We gratefully acknowledge the unsung efforts of the anonymous reviewers, one of whom in particular made a great number of pertinent and constructive comments that helped us to improve this book very significantly. In addition, we would like to thank the librarians of the Repository of Machine Learning Databases at the University of California, Irvine, whose carefully collected datasets have been invaluable in our research.

Our research has been funded by the New Zealand Foundation for Research, Science, and Technology and the Royal Society of New Zealand Marsden Fund. The Department of Computer Science at the University of Waikato has generously supported us in all sorts of ways, and we owe a particular debt of gratitude to Mark Apperley for his enlightened leadership and warm encouragement. Part of this book was written while both authors were visiting the University of Calgary, Canada, and the support of the Computer Science department there is gratefully acknowledged—as is the positive and helpful attitude of the long-suffering students in the machine learning course, on whom we experimented.

Last, and most of all, we are grateful to our families and partners. Pam, Anna, and Nikki were all too well aware of the implications of having an author in the house ("not again!") but let Ian go ahead and write the book anyway. Julie was always supportive, even when Eibe had to burn the midnight oil in the machine learning lab. The six of us hail from Canada, England, Germany, Ireland, and Samoa: New Zealand has brought us together and provided an ideal, even idyllic, place to write this book.

chapter one

What's it all about?

Human *in vitro* fertilization involves collecting several eggs from a woman's ovaries, which, after fertilization with partner or donor sperm, produce several embryos. Some of these are selected and transferred to the woman's uterus. The problem is to select the "best" embryos to use—the ones that are most likely to survive. Selection is based on around sixty recorded features of the embryos—characterizing their morphology, oocyte, follicle, and the sperm sample. The number of features is sufficiently large that it is difficult for an embryologist to assess them all simultaneously and correlate historical data with the crucial outcome of whether that embryo did or did not result in a live child. In a research project in England, machine learning is being investigated as a technique for making the selection, using as training data historical records of embryos and their outcome.

Every year, dairy farmers in New Zealand have to make a tough business decision: which cows to retain in their herd and which to sell off to an abattoir. Typically, one fifth of the cows in a dairy herd are culled each year near the end of the milking season as feed reserves dwindle. Each cow's breeding and milk production history influences this decision. Other factors include age (a cow is nearing the end of its productive life at eight years), health problems, history of difficult calving, undesirable temperament traits (kicking, jumping fences), and not being in calf for the following season. About seven hundred attributes for each of several million cows have been recorded over the years. Machine learning is being investigated as a way of ascertaining what factors are taken into account by successful farmers—not to automate the decision but to propagate their skills and experience to others.

Life and death. From Europe to the antipodes. Family and business. Machine learning is a burgeoning new technology for mining knowledge from data, a technology that a lot of people are starting to take seriously.

1.1 Data mining and machine learning

We are overwhelmed with data. The amount of data in the world, in our lives, seems to go on and on increasing—and there's no end in sight. Omnipresent personal computers make it too easy to save things that previously we would have trashed. Inexpensive multi-gigabyte disks make it too easy to postpone decisions about what to do with all this stuff—we simply buy another disk and keep it all. Ubiquitous electronics record our decisions, our choices in the supermarket, our financial habits, our comings and goings. We swipe our way through the world, every swipe a record in a database. The World Wide Web overwhelms us with information; meanwhile, every choice we make is recorded. And all these are just personal choices: they have countless counterparts in the world of commerce and industry. We would all testify to the growing gap between the *generation* of data and our *understanding* of it. As the volume of data increases, inexorably, the proportion of it that people "understand" decreases, alarmingly. Lying hidden in all this data is information, potentially useful information, that is rarely made explicit or taken advantage of.

This book is about looking for patterns in data. There is nothing new about this. People have been seeking patterns in data ever since human life began. Hunters seek patterns in animal migration behavior, farmers seek patterns in crop growth, politicians seek patterns in voter opinion, lovers seek patterns in their partners' responses. A scientist's job (like a baby's) is to make sense of data, to discover the patterns that govern how the physical world works and encapsulate them in theories that can be used for predicting what will happen in new situations. The entrepreneur's job is to identify opportunities, that is, patterns in behavior that can be turned into a profitable business, and exploit them.

In *data mining*, the data is stored electronically and the search is automated—or at least augmented—by computer. Even this is not particularly new. Economists, statisticians, forecasters, and communication engineers have long worked with the idea that patterns in data can be sought automatically, identified, validated, and used for prediction. What is new is the staggering increase in opportunities for finding patterns in data. The unbridled growth of databases in recent years, databases on such everyday activities as customer choices, brings data mining to the forefront of new business technologies. It has been estimated that the amount of data stored in the world's databases doubles every twenty months, and although it would surely be difficult to justify this figure in any quantitative sense, we can all relate to the pace of growth qualitatively. As the flood of data swells and machines that can undertake the searching become commonplace, the opportunities for data mining increase. As the world grows in complexity, overwhelming us with the data it generates, data mining becomes our only hope for elucidating the patterns that underlie it. Intelligently analyzed data is a valuable resource. It can lead to new insights and, in commercial settings, to competitive advantages.

Data mining is about solving problems by analyzing data already present in databases. Suppose, to take a well-worn example, the problem is fickle customer loyalty in a highly competitive marketplace. A database of customer choices, along with customer profiles, holds the key to this problem. Behavior patterns of former customers can be analyzed to identify distinguishing characteristics of those likely to switch products and those likely to remain loyal. Once such characteristics are found, they can be put to work to identify present customers who are likely to jump ship—and this group can be targeted for special treatment, treatment too costly to apply to the customer base as a whole. More positively, the same techniques can be used to identify customers who might be attracted to another service the enterprise provides, one they are not presently enjoying, to target them for special offers that promote this service. In today's highly competitive, customer-centered, service-oriented economy, data is the raw material that fuels business growth—if only it can be mined.

Data mining is defined as the process of discovering patterns in data. The process must be automatic or (more usually) semi-automatic. The patterns discovered must be meaningful in that they lead to some advantage, usually an economic advantage. The data is invariably present in substantial quantities.

And how are the patterns expressed? Useful patterns allow us to make nontrivial predictions on new data. There are two extremes for the expression of a pattern: as a black box whose innards are effectively incomprehensible and as a transparent box whose construction reveals the structure of the pattern. Both, we are assuming, make good predictions. The difference is whether or not the patterns that are mined are represented in terms of a structure that can be examined, reasoned about, and used to inform future decisions. Those that are we call *structural* patterns because they capture the decision structure in an explicit way. In other words, they help to explain something about the data.

Now, finally, we can say what this book is about. It is about techniques for finding and describing structural patterns in data. And most of the techniques that we cover have developed within a field known as *machine learning*. But first let us look at what structural patterns are.

Describing structural patterns

What is meant by "structural patterns"? How do you describe them? And what form does the input take? We will answer these questions by way of illustration rather than by attempting formal, and ultimately sterile, definitions. There will be plenty of examples later in this chapter, but let's examine one right now to get a feeling for what we're talking about.

Look at the contact lens data in Table 1.1. This gives the conditions under which an optician might want to prescribe soft contact lenses, hard contact

Table 1.1	The contact lens data.			
age	spectacle prescription	astigmatism	tear production rate	recommended lenses
young	myope	no	reduced	none
young	myope	no	normal	soft
young	myope	yes	reduced	none
young	myope	yes	normal	hard
young	hypermetrope	no	reduced	none
young	hypermetrope	no	normal	soft
young	hypermetrope	yes	reduced	none
young	hypermetrope	yes	normal	hard
pre-presbyopic	myope	no	reduced	none
pre-presbyopic	myope	no	normal	soft
pre-presbyopic	myope	yes	reduced	none
pre-presbyopic	myope	yes	normal	hard
pre-presbyopic	hypermetrope	no	reduced	none
pre-presbyopic	hypermetrope	no	normal	soft
pre-presbyopic	hypermetrope	yes	reduced	none
pre-presbyopic	hypermetrope	yes	normal	none
presbyopic	myope	no	reduced	none
presbyopic	myope	no	normal	none
presbyopic	myope	yes	reduced	none
presbyopic	myope	yes	normal	hard
presbyopic	hypermetrope	no	reduced	none
presbyopic	hypermetrope	no	normal	soft
presbyopic	hypermetrope	yes	reduced	none
presbyopic	hypermetrope	yes	normal	none

lenses, or no contact lenses at all; we will say more about what the individual features mean later. Each line of the table is one of the examples. Part of a structural description of this information might be as follows:

```
If tear production rate = reduced then recommendation = none
Otherwise, if age = young and astigmatic = no
             then recommendation = soft
```

Structural descriptions need not necessarily be couched as rules like this. Decision trees, which specify the sequences of decisions that need to be made along with the resulting recommendation, are another popular means of expression.

This example is a very simplistic one. For a start, all combinations of possible values are represented in the table. There are 24 rows, representing three possible values of age, and two for each of spectacle prescription, astigmatism, and tear production rate ($3 \times 2 \times 2 \times 2 = 24$). The rules do not really generalize from the data; they merely summarize it. In most learning situations, the set of examples given as input is far from complete, and part of the job is to generalize to other, new examples. You can imagine omitting some of the rows in the table for which tear production rate is *reduced*, and still coming up with the rule

```
If tear production rate = reduced then recommendation = none
```

—which would generalize to the missing rows and fill them in correctly. Second, values are specified for all the features in all the examples. Real-life datasets invariably contain examples in which the values of some features, for some reason or other, are unknown—measurements were not taken, were lost, or whatever. Third, the rules above classify the examples correctly; whereas often, because of errors or "noise" in the data, misclassifications occur even on the data that is used to train the classifier.

Machine learning

Now that we have some idea of the inputs and outputs, let's turn to machine learning. What is learning, anyway? What is *machine learning*? These are philosophical questions, and we will not be much concerned with philosophy in this book; our emphasis is firmly on the practical. However, it is worth spending a few moments at the outset on fundamental issues, just to see how tricky they are, before rolling up our sleeves and looking at machine learning in practice. Our dictionary defines "to learn" as

to get knowledge of by study, experience, or being taught;
to become aware by information or from observation;
to commit to memory;
to be informed of, ascertain; to receive instruction.

These meanings have some shortcomings when it comes to talking about computers. For the first two, it is virtually impossible to test if learning has been achieved or not. How do you know whether a machine has "got knowledge of . . . "? You probably can't just ask it questions; even if you could, you wouldn't be testing its ability to learn but its ability to answer questions. How do you know whether it has "become aware . . . "? The whole question of whether computers can be aware, or conscious, is a burning philosophical issue. As for the last two meanings, while we can see what they denote in human terms, merely "committing to memory" and "receiving instruction" seem to fall far short of what we might mean by machine learning. They are too passive, and we know that computers find these tasks trivial. Instead, we are interested in improvements in performance, or at least in the potential for performance, in new situations. You can "commit to memory" or "be informed of" by rote learning without being able to apply the new knowledge to new situations. You can receive instruction without benefiting from it at all.

Earlier we defined data mining operationally, as the process of discovering patterns, automatically or semi-automatically, in large quantities of data—and the patterns must be useful. An operational definition can be formulated in the same way for learning. How about

> things learn when they change their behavior in a way that makes them perform better in the future.

This ties learning to *performance* rather than *knowledge*. You can test learning by observing the behavior and comparing it with past behavior. This is a much more objective kind of definition and appears to be far more satisfactory.

But still there's a problem. Learning is a rather slippery concept. Lots of things change their behavior in ways that make them perform better in the future, yet we wouldn't want to say that they have actually *learned*. A good example is a comfortable slipper. Has it *learned* the shape of your foot? It has certainly changed its behavior to make it perform better as a slipper! Yet we would hardly want to call this *learning*. In everyday language, we often use the word "training" to denote a mindless kind of learning. We train animals and even plants, though it would be stretching the word a bit to talk of training objects like slippers that are not in any sense alive. But learning is different. Learning implies thinking. Learning implies purpose. Something that learns has to do so *intentionally*. That is why we wouldn't say that a vine has learned to grow around a trellis in a vineyard—we'd say it has been *trained*. Learning without purpose is merely training. Or, more to the point, in learning the purpose is the learner's, whereas in training it is the teacher's.

Thus on closer examination the second definition of learning, in operational, performance-oriented terms, has its own problems when it comes to talking about computers. To decide whether something has actually learned, you need to see if it intended to, whether there was any purpose involved. And that makes the concept moot when applied to machines because whether artifacts can behave purposefully is unclear. Philosophical discussions of what is *really* meant by "learning," like discussions of what is *really* meant by "intention" or "purpose," are fraught with difficulty. Even the law courts find intention hard to grapple with.

Data mining

Fortunately the kind of learning techniques explained in this book do not present these conceptual problems—they are called *machine learning* without really presupposing any particular philosophical stance about what learning actually is. Data mining is a practical topic and involves learning in a practical, not a theoretical, sense. We are interested in techniques for finding and describing structural patterns in data, as a tool for helping to explain that data and make predictions from it. The data will take the form of a set of examples—examples of customers who have switched loyalties, for instance, or situations in which certain kinds of contact lenses can be prescribed. The output takes the form of predictions on new examples—a prediction of whether a particular customer will switch or a prediction of what kind of lens will be prescribed under given circumstances. But because this book is about finding *and describing* patterns in data, the output must also include an actual description of a structure that can be used to classify unknown examples in order that the decision can be explained. As well as *performance*, we also require an explicit representation of the *knowledge* that is acquired. In essence, we are invoking both of the definitions of learning considered above: the acquisition of knowledge and the ability to use it.

Many learning techniques look for structural descriptions of what is learned, descriptions that can become fairly complex and are typically expressed as sets of rules like the ones above or the decision trees described below. Because they can be understood by people, these descriptions serve to explain what has been learned, to explain the basis for new predictions. In this book we focus on the use of methods that produce easily understood structural descriptions. Some popular machine learning methods do not produce such descriptions. Neural nets, for example, learn to classify examples in ways that do not involve explicit structural descriptions of the knowledge that is learned. Neural nets are deliberately excluded from the scope of this book—even though they are certainly a useful technique for some data mining applications—because they do not produce a comprehensible model that accounts for the predictions they make.

Experience shows that in many applications of machine learning to data mining, the explicit knowledge structures that are acquired, the structural descriptions, are at least as important, and often very much more important, than the ability to perform well on new examples. People frequently use data mining to gain knowledge, not just predictions. Gaining knowledge from data certainly sounds like a good idea if you can do it. To find out how, read on!

1.2 Simple examples: The weather problem and others

We will be using a lot of examples in this book, which seems particularly appropriate considering that the book is all about learning from examples! There are several standard datasets that we will come back to again and again. Different datasets tend to expose new issues and challenges, and it is interesting and instructive to have in mind a variety of problems when considering learning methods. In fact, the need to work with different datasets is so important that a corpus containing around a hundred example problems has been gathered together so that different algorithms can be tested and compared on the same set of problems.

The illustrations in this section are all unrealistically simple. Serious application of data mining involves thousands, or hundreds of thousands—even millions—of individual cases. But when explaining what algorithms do and how they work, we need simple examples that capture the essence of the problem but are small enough to be comprehensible in every detail. We will be working with the illustrations in this section throughout the book, and they are intended to be "academic" in the sense that they will help us to understand what is going on. Some actual fielded applications of learning techniques are discussed in Section 1.3, and many are covered in the books mentioned in the *Further reading* section at the end of the chapter.

Another problem with actual real-life datasets is that they are often proprietary. No one is going to share customer and product choice datasets with you so that you can understand the details of a data mining application and how it works. Corporate data is a valuable asset, one whose value has increased enormously with the development of data mining techniques such as those described in this book. And yet we are concerned here with understanding how the methods used for data mining work, understanding the details of these methods so that we can trace their operation on actual data. That is why our illustrations are simple ones. But they are not simplistic: they exhibit the features of real datasets.

The weather problem

The weather problem is a tiny dataset that we will use again and again to illustrate machine learning methods. Entirely fictitious, it supposedly concerns the conditions that are suitable for playing some unspecified game. In general,

Table 1.2	The weather data.			
outlook	temperature	humidity	windy	play
sunny	hot	high	false	no
sunny	hot	high	true	no
overcast	hot	high	false	yes
rainy	mild	high	false	yes
rainy	cool	normal	false	yes
rainy	cool	normal	true	no
overcast	cool	normal	true	yes
sunny	mild	high	false	no
sunny	cool	normal	false	yes
rainy	mild	normal	false	yes
sunny	mild	normal	true	yes
overcast	mild	high	true	yes
overcast	hot	normal	false	yes
rainy	mild	high	true	no

instances in a dataset are characterized by the values of features, or *attributes*, that measure different aspects of the instance. In this case there are four attributes, outlook, temperature, humidity, and wind; and the outcome is whether to play or not.

In its simplest form, shown in Table 1.2, all four attributes have values that are symbolic categories rather than numbers. Outlook can be sunny, overcast, or rainy; temperature can be hot, mild, or cool; humidity can be high or normal; and windy can be true or false. This creates 36 possible combinations ($3 \times 3 \times 2 \times 2 = 36$), of which 14 are present in the set of input examples.

A set of rules learned from this information—not necessarily a very good one—might look like this:

```
If outlook = sunny and humidity = high then play = no
If outlook = rainy and windy = true    then play = no
If outlook = overcast                  then play = yes
If humidity = normal                   then play = yes
If none of the above                   then play = yes
```

These rules are meant to be interpreted in order: the first one first, then if it doesn't apply, the second, and so on. A set of rules to be interpreted in sequence is often called a *decision list*. Interpreted as a decision list, the rules correctly classify all of the examples in the table, whereas taken individually, out of context,

Table 1.3	Weather data with some numeric attributes.			
outlook	temperature	humidity	windy	play
sunny	85	85	false	no
sunny	80	90	true	no
overcast	83	86	false	yes
rainy	70	96	false	yes
rainy	68	80	false	yes
rainy	65	70	true	no
overcast	64	65	true	yes
sunny	72	95	false	no
sunny	69	70	false	yes
rainy	75	80	false	yes
sunny	75	70	true	yes
overcast	72	90	true	yes
overcast	81	75	false	yes
rainy	71	91	true	no

some of the rules are incorrect. For example, the rule `if humidity = normal then play = yes` gets one of the examples wrong (check which one). The meaning of a set of rules depends on how it is interpreted—not surprisingly!

In the slightly more complex form shown in Table 1.3, two of the attributes—`temperature` and `humidity`—have numeric values. This means that any learning scheme must create inequalities involving these attributes, rather than simple equality tests as in the former case. This is called a *numeric-attribute problem*—in this case, a *mixed-attribute problem* since not all the attributes are numeric.

Now the first rule above might take the form:

```
If outlook = sunny and humidity > 83 then play = no
```

A slightly more complex process is required to come up with rules that involve numeric tests.

The rules we have seen so far are *classification rules:* they predict the classification of the example in terms of whether to play or not. It is equally possible to disregard the classification and just look for any rules that strongly associate different attribute values. These are called *association rules.* Many association rules can be derived from the weather data in Table 1.2. Some good ones are

```
If temperature = cool                    then humidity = normal
If humidity = normal and windy = false   then play = yes
```

```
If outlook = sunny and play = no          then humidity = high
If windy = false and play = no            then outlook = sunny
   and humidity = high
```

All these rules are 100% correct on the given data; they make no false predictions. The first two apply to four examples in the dataset, the next to three examples, and the fourth to two examples. And there are many other rules: in fact, nearly sixty association rules can be found that apply to two or more examples of the weather data and are completely correct on this data. And if you look for rules that are less than 100% correct, then you will find very many more. There are so many because unlike classification rules, association rules can "predict" any of the attributes, not just a specified class, and can even predict more than one thing. For example, the fourth rule above predicts both that outlook will be sunny and that humidity will be high.

Contact lenses: An idealized problem

The contact lens data introduced earlier tells you the kind of contact lens to prescribe, given certain information about a patient. Note that this example is intended for illustration only: it grossly oversimplifies the problem and should certainly not be used for diagnostic purposes!

The first column of Table 1.1 gives the age of the patient. In case you're wondering, *presbyopia* is a form of long-sightedness that accompanies the onset of middle age. The second column gives the spectacle prescription: *myope* means short-sighted and *hypermetrope* means long-sighted. The third column shows whether the patient is astigmatic, while the fourth relates to the rate of tear production, which is important in this context because tears lubricate contact lenses. The final column shows which kind of lenses to prescribe, whether *hard, soft,* or *none.* All possible combinations of the attribute values are represented in the table.

A sample set of rules learned from this information is shown in Figure 1.1. This is a rather large set of rules—but it does correctly classify all the examples. These rules are complete and deterministic: they give a unique prescription for every conceivable example. Generally this is not the case. Sometimes there are situations in which no rule applies, other times more than one rule may apply, resulting in conflicting recommendations. Sometimes probabilities or weights may be associated with the rules themselves to indicate that some are more important, or more reliable, than others.

You may be wondering whether there is a smaller rule set that performs as well, and, if so, whether you would not be better off using the smaller rule set, and, if so, why? These are exactly the kinds of questions that will occupy us in this book. Because the examples form a complete set for the problem space, the rules do no more than summarize all the information that is given, expressing it in a different and more concise way. Even though it involves no generalization, this is often a very useful thing to do! People frequently use machine learning techniques to gain insight into the structure of their data rather than to make predictions for new cases. In fact, a prominent and successful line of research in machine learning began as an attempt to compress a huge database of possible chess endgames and their outcomes into a data structure of reasonable size. The data structure chosen for this enterprise was not a set of rules but a decision tree.

Figure 1.2 shows a structural description for the contact lens data in the form of a decision tree, which for many purposes is a more concise and perspicuous representation of the rules and has the advantage that it can be visualized more easily. (However, this decision tree—in contrast to the rule set given in Figure 1.1—classifies two examples incorrectly.) The tree calls first for a test on tear production rate, and the first two branches correspond to the two possible outcomes. If tear production rate is reduced (the left branch), the outcome is none. If it is normal (the right branch), a second test is made, this time on astigmatism. Eventually, whatever the outcome of the tests, a leaf of the tree is reached that dictates the contact lens recommendation for that case. The question of

```
If tear production rate = reduced then recommendation = none
If age = young and astigmatic = no and
   tear production rate = normal then recommendation = soft
If age = pre-presbyopic and astigmatic = no and
   tear production rate = normal then recommendation = soft
If age = presbyopic and spectacle prescription = myope and
   astigmatic = no then recommendation = none
If spectacle prescription = hypermetrope and astigmatic = no and
   tear production rate = normal then recommendation = soft
If spectacle prescription = myope and astigmatic = yes and
   tear production rate = normal then recommendation = hard
If age = young and astigmatic = yes and
   tear production rate = normal then recommendation = hard
If age = pre-presbyopic and
   spectacle prescription = hypermetrope and astigmatic = yes
   then recommendation = none
If age = presbyopic and spectacle prescription = hypermetrope
   and astigmatic = yes then recommendation = none
```

Figure 1.1 Rules for the contact lens data.

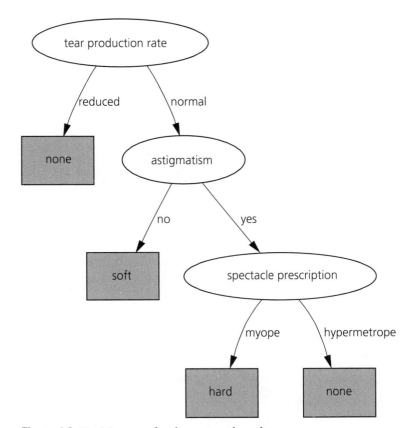

Figure 1.2 Decision tree for the contact lens data.

what is the most natural and easily understood format for the output from a machine learning scheme is one that we will return to in Chapter 3.

Irises: A classic numeric dataset

The Iris dataset, which dates back to seminal work by the eminent statistician R.A. Fisher in the mid-1930s and is arguably the most famous dataset used in data mining, contains fifty examples each of three types of plant: *Iris setosa, Iris versicolor,* and *Iris virginica.* It is excerpted in Table 1.4. There are four attributes: sepal length, sepal width, petal length, and petal width (all measured in cm). Unlike previous datasets, all attributes have values that are numeric.

The following set of rules might be learned from this dataset:

```
If petal-length < 2.45 then Iris-setosa
If sepal-width < 2.10 then Iris-versicolor
If sepal-width < 2.45 and petal-length < 4.55 then Iris-versicolor
```

```
If sepal-width < 2.95 and petal-width < 1.35 then Iris-versicolor
If petal-length ≥ 2.45 and petal-length < 4.45 then Iris-versicolor
If sepal-length ≥ 5.85 and petal-length < 4.75 then Iris-versicolor
If sepal-width < 2.55 and petal-length < 4.95 and
   petal-width < 1.55 then Iris-versicolor
If petal-length ≥ 2.45 and petal-length < 4.95 and
   petal-width < 1.55 then Iris-versicolor
If sepal-length ≥ 6.55 and petal-length < 5.05 then Iris-versicolor
If sepal-width < 2.75 and petal-width < 1.65 and
   sepal-length < 6.05 then Iris-versicolor
If sepal-length ≥ 5.85 and sepal-length < 5.95 and
   petal-length < 4.85 then Iris-versicolor
If petal-length ≥ 5.15 then Iris-virginica
If petal-width ≥ 1.85 then Iris-virginica
If petal-width ≥ 1.75 and sepal-width < 3.05 then Iris-virginica
If petal-length ≥ 4.95 and petal-width < 1.55 then Iris-virginica
```

These rules are very cumbersome, and we will see in Chapter 3 how more compact rules can be expressed that convey the same information.

Table 1.4		The Iris data.			
	sepal length	sepal width	petal length	petal width	type
1	5.1	3.5	1.4	0.2	*Iris setosa*
2	4.9	3.0	1.4	0.2	*Iris setosa*
3	4.7	3.2	1.3	0.2	*Iris setosa*
4	4.6	3.1	1.5	0.2	*Iris setosa*
5	5.0	3.6	1.4	0.2	*Iris setosa*
...					
51	7.0	3.2	4.7	1.4	*Iris versicolor*
52	6.4	3.2	4.5	1.5	*Iris versicolor*
53	6.9	3.1	4.9	1.5	*Iris versicolor*
54	5.5	2.3	4.0	1.3	*Iris versicolor*
55	6.5	2.8	4.6	1.5	*Iris versicolor*
101	6.3	3.3	6.0	2.5	*Iris virginica*
102	5.8	2.7	5.1	1.9	*Iris virginica*
103	7.1	3.0	5.9	2.1	*Iris virginica*
104	6.3	2.9	5.6	1.8	*Iris virginica*
105	6.5	3.0	5.8	2.2	*Iris virginica*

CPU performance: Introducing numeric prediction

Although the Iris dataset involves numeric attributes, the outcome—the type of iris—is a category, not a numeric value. Table 1.5 shows some data for which the outcome is numeric, as well as the attributes. It concerns the relative performance of computer processing power on the basis of a number of relevant attributes; each row represents one of 209 different computer configurations.

The classical way of dealing with continuous prediction is to write the outcome as a linear sum of the attribute values with appropriate weights, for example,

$$\text{PRP} = -55.9 + 0.0489\,\text{MYCT} + 0.0153\,\text{MMIN} + 0.0056\,\text{MMAX}$$
$$+ 0.6410\,\text{CACH} - 0.2700\,\text{CHMIN} + 1.480\,\text{CHMAX}.$$

(The abbreviated variable names are given in the second row of the table.) This is called a *regression equation,* and the process of determining the weights is called *regression,* a well-known procedure in statistics which we will review in Chapter 4. However, the basic regression method is incapable of discovering nonlinear relationships (although variants do exist—indeed, one will be described in Section 6.3), and in Chapter 3 we will examine different representations that can be used for predicting numeric quantities.

In the Iris and CPU performance data, all the attributes have numeric values. Practical situations frequently present a mixture of numeric and non-numeric attributes.

Table 1.5	The CPU performance data.						
	cycle time (ns)	main memory (Kb) min	main memory (Kb) max	cache (Kb)	channels min	channels max	performance
	MYCT	MMIN	MMAX	CACH	CHMIN	CHMAX	PRP
1	125	256	6000	256	16	128	198
2	29	8000	32000	32	8	32	269
3	29	8000	32000	32	8	32	220
4	29	8000	32000	32	8	32	172
5	29	8000	16000	32	8	16	132
...							
207	125	2000	8000	0	2	14	52
208	480	512	8000	32	0	0	67
209	480	1000	4000	0	0	0	45

Labor negotiations: A more realistic example

The labor negotiations dataset in Table 1.6 summarizes the outcome of Canadian contract negotiations in 1987–88. It includes all collective agreements reached in the business and personal services sector for organizations with at least 500 members (teachers, nurses, university staff, police, etc.). Each case concerns one contract, and the outcome is whether the contract is deemed to be *acceptable* or *unacceptable*. The acceptable contracts are ones where agreements were accepted by both labor and management. The unacceptable ones are either known offers that fell through because one party would not accept them or acceptable contracts that had been significantly perturbed to the extent that, in the view of experts, they would not have been accepted.

There are 40 examples in the dataset (plus another 17 which are normally reserved for test purposes). Unlike the other tables here, Table 1.6 presents the examples as columns rather than as rows because otherwise it would have to be

Table 1.6	The labor negotiations data.					
attribute	type	1	2	3	...	40
duration	(number of years)	1	2	3		2
wage increase first year	percentage	2%	4%	4.3%		4.5
wage increase second year	percentage	?	5%	4.4%		4.0
wage increase third year	percentage	?	?	?		?
cost of living adjustment	{none, tcf, tc}	none	tcf	?		none
working hours per week	(number of hours)	28	35	38		40
pension	{none, ret-allw, empl-cntr}	none	?	?		?
standby pay	percentage	?	13%	?		?
shift-work supplement	percentage	?	5%	4%		4
education allowance	{yes, no}	yes	?	?		?
statutory holidays	(number of days)	11	15	12		12
vacation	{below-avg, avg, gen}	avg	gen	gen		avg
long-term disability assistance	{yes, no}	no	?	?		yes
dental plan contribution	{none, half, full}	none	?	full		full
bereavement assistance	{yes, no}	no	?	?		yes
health plan contribution	{none, half, full}	none	?	full		half
acceptability of contract	{good, bad}	bad	good	good		good

stretched over several pages. Many of the values are unknown or missing, as indicated by question marks.

This is a much more realistic dataset than the others we have seen. It contains many missing values, and it seems unlikely that an exact classification can be obtained.

Figure 1.3 shows two decision trees that represent the dataset. Figure 1.3a is simple and approximate: it doesn't represent the data exactly. For example, it will predict bad for some contracts that are actually marked good. But it does make intuitive sense: a contract is bad (for the employee!) if the wage increase in the first year is too small (less than 2.5%). If the first-year wage increase is larger than this, it is good if there are lots of statutory holidays (more than 10 days). Even if there are fewer statutory holidays, it is good if the first-year wage increase is large enough (more than 4%).

Figure 1.3b is a more complex decision tree that represents the same dataset. In fact, this is a more accurate representation of the actual dataset that was used to create the tree. But it is not necessarily a more accurate representation of the underlying concept of good versus bad contracts. Look down the left branch. It doesn't seem to make sense intuitively that, if the working hours exceed 36, a contract is bad if there is no health-plan contribution or a full health-plan contribution but is good if there is half health-plan contribution. It is certainly reasonable that the health-plan contribution plays a role in the decision but not in this half-is-good, both-full-and-none-are-bad way. It seems likely that this is an artifact of the actual values used to create the decision tree rather than a genuine feature of the good versus bad distinction.

The tree in Figure 1.3b is more accurate on the data that was used to train the classifier but will probably perform less well on an independent set of test data. It is "overfitted" to the training data—it follows it too slavishly. The tree in Figure 1.3a is obtained from the one in Figure 1.3b by a process of pruning, which we will learn more about in Chapter 6.

Soybean classification: A classic machine learning success

An often quoted early success story in the application of machine learning to practical problems is the identification of rules for diagnosing soybean diseases. The data is taken from questionnaires describing plant diseases. There are about 680 examples, each representing a diseased plant. Plants were measured on 35 attributes, each one having a small set of possible values. Examples are labeled with the diagnosis of an expert in plant biology. There are 17 disease categories altogether—horrible-sounding diseases like diaporthe stem canker, rhizoctonia root rot, and bacterial blight, to mention just a few.

Table 1.7 gives the attributes, the number of different values that each can have, and a sample record for one particular plant. The attributes are placed into different categories just to make them easier to read.

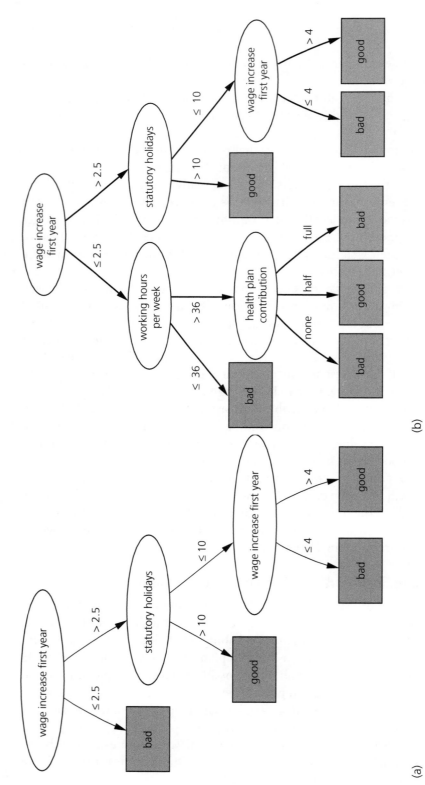

(a)

(b)

Figure 1.3 Decision trees for the labor negotiations data.

Table 1.7	The soybean data.		
	attribute	number of values	sample value
environment	time of occurrence	7	July
	precipitation	3	above normal
	temperature	3	normal
	cropping history	4	same as last year
	hail damage	2	yes
	damaged area	4	scattered
	severity	3	severe
	plant height	2	normal
	plant growth	2	abnormal
	seed treatment	3	fungicide
	germination	3	less than 80%
seed	condition	2	normal
	mold growth	2	absent
	discoloration	2	absent
	size	2	normal
	shriveling	2	absent
fruit	condition of fruit pods	4	normal
	fruit spots	5	—
leaves	condition	2	abnormal
	leaf spot size	3	—
	yellow leaf spot halo	3	absent
	leaf spot margins	3	—
	shredding	2	absent
	leaf malformation	2	absent
	leaf mildew growth	3	absent
stem	condition	2	abnormal
	stem lodging	2	yes
	stem cankers	4	above soil line
	canker lesion color	4	—
	fruiting bodies on stems	2	present
	external decay of stem	3	firm and dry
	mycelium on stem	2	absent
	internal discoloration	3	none
	sclerotia	2	absent
roots	condition	3	normal
diagnosis		19	diaporthe stem canker

Here are two example rules, learned from this data:

```
If   [leaf condition is normal and
      stem condition is abnormal and
      stem cankers is below soil line and
      canker lesion color is brown]
then
      diagnosis is rhizoctonia root rot

If   [leaf malformation is absent and
      stem condition is abnormal and
      stem cankers is below soil line and
      canker lesion color is brown]
then
      diagnosis is rhizoctonia root rot
```

These rules nicely illustrate the potential role of prior knowledge—often called *domain knowledge*—in machine learning, for in fact the only difference between the two descriptions is `leaf condition is normal` versus `leaf malformation is absent`. Now in fact, in this domain, if the leaf condition is normal then leaf malformation is necessarily absent, so one of these conditions happens to be a special case of the other. Thus if the first rule is true, then the second is necessarily true as well. The only time the second rule comes into play is when leaf malformation is absent but leaf condition is *not* normal, that is, when there is something other than malformation wrong with the leaf. This is certainly not apparent from a casual reading of the rules.

Research on this problem in the late 1970s found that these diagnostic rules could be generated by a machine learning algorithm, along with rules for every other disease category, from about 300 training examples. These training examples were carefully selected from the corpus of cases as being quite different from each other—"far apart" in the example space. At the same time, the plant pathologist who had produced the diagnoses was interviewed, and his expertise was translated into diagnostic rules. Surprisingly, the computer-generated rules outperformed the expert-derived rules on the remaining test examples. They gave the correct disease top ranking 97.5% of the time, compared to only 72% for the expert-derived rules. Furthermore, not only did the learning algorithm find rules that outperformed those of the expert collaborator, but the same expert was so impressed that he allegedly adopted the discovered rules in place of his own!

1.3 Fielded applications

The examples that we opened with are speculative research projects, not production systems. And the illustrations above are toy problems: they are deliberately chosen to be small so that we can use them to work through algorithms later in the book. Where's the beef? Here are some applications of machine learning that have actually been put into use.

Being fielded applications, the illustrations below tend to stress the use of learning in performance situations, in which the emphasis is on ability to perform well on new examples. However, this book is about the use of learning systems to gain knowledge from decision structures that are inferred from the data. We believe that this is as important—probably even more important in the long run—a use of the technology as merely making high-performance predictions. Still, it will tend to be underrepresented in fielded applications because when learning techniques are used to gain insight, the result is not normally a system that is put to work as an application in its own right. Nevertheless, in three of the examples below, the fact that the decision structure is comprehensible is a key feature in the successful adoption of the scheme.

Decisions involving judgment

When you apply for a loan, you have to fill out a questionnaire asking for relevant financial and personal information. This information is used by the loan company as the basis for its decision as to whether to lend you money. Such decisions are typically made in two stages. First, statistical methods are used to determine clear "accept" and "reject" cases. The remaining borderline cases are more difficult and call for human judgment. For example, one loan company uses a statistical decision procedure to calculate a numeric parameter based on the information supplied in the questionnaire. Applicants are accepted if this parameter exceeds a preset threshold and rejected if it falls below a second threshold. This accounts for 90% of cases, and the remaining 10% are referred to loans officers for a decision. On examining historical data on whether applicants did indeed repay their loans, however, it turned out that half of the borderline applicants who were granted loans actually defaulted. While it would be tempting simply to deny credit to borderline customers, credit industry professionals pointed out that if only their repayment future could be reliably determined it is precisely these customers whose business should be wooed, for they tend to be active customers of a credit institution because their finances remain in a chronically volatile condition. A suitable compromise must be reached between the viewpoint of a company accountant, who dislikes bad debt, and a sales executive, who dislikes turning business away.

Enter machine learning. The input was 1,000 training examples of borderline cases for which a loan had been made, specifying whether the borrower had finally paid off or defaulted. For each training example, about 20 attributes were extracted from the questionnaire, such as age, years with current employer, years at current address, years with the bank, other credit cards possessed. A machine learning procedure was used to produce a small set of classification rules that made correct predictions on two-thirds of the borderline cases in an independently chosen test set. Not only did these rules improve the success rate of the loan decisions, but the company also found them attractive because they could be used to explain to applicants the reasons behind the decision. Although the project was an exploratory one that took only a small development effort, the loan company was apparently so pleased with the result that the rules were put into use immediately.

Screening images

Since the early days of satellite technology, environmental scientists have been trying to detect oil slicks from satellite images to give early warning of ecological disasters and deter illegal dumping. Radar satellites provide an opportunity for monitoring coastal waters day and night, regardless of weather conditions. Oil slicks appear as dark regions in the image whose size and shape evolve depending on weather and sea conditions. However, other lookalike dark regions can be caused by local weather conditions such as high wind. Detecting oil slicks is an expensive manual process requiring highly trained personnel who assess each region in the image.

A hazard detection system has been developed to screen images for subsequent manual processing. Intended to be marketed worldwide to a wide variety of end users—government agencies and companies—with different objectives, applications, and geographical areas, it needs to be highly customizable to individual circumstances. Machine learning allows the system to be trained on examples of spills and nonspills supplied by the user and lets the user control the tradeoff between undetected spills and false alarms. Unlike other machine learning applications, which generate a classifier that is then deployed in the field, here it is the learning scheme itself that will be deployed.

The input is a set of raw pixel images from a radar satellite, and the output is a much smaller set of images with putative oil slicks marked with a colored border. First, standard image processing operations are applied to normalize the image. Then suspicious dark regions are identified. Several dozen attributes are extracted from each region characterizing its size, shape, area, intensity, sharpness and jaggedness of the boundaries, proximity to other regions, and information about the background in the vicinity of the region. Finally, standard learning techniques are applied to the resulting attribute vectors.

Several interesting problems were encountered. One is the scarcity of training data. Oil slicks are (fortunately) very rare, and manual classification is extremely costly. Another is the unbalanced nature of the problem: of the many dark regions in the training data, only a very small fraction are actual oil slicks. A third is that the examples group naturally into batches, with regions drawn from each image forming a single batch; and background characteristics vary from one batch to another. Finally, the performance task is to serve as a filter, and the user must be provided with a convenient means of varying the false-alarm rate.

Load forecasting

In the electricity supply industry, it is important to determine future demand for power as far in advance as possible. If accurate estimates can be made for the maximum and minimum load for each hour, day, month, season, and year, utility companies can make significant economies in areas such as setting the operating reserve, maintenance scheduling, and fuel inventory management.

An automated load forecasting assistant has been operating at a major utility supplier over the past decade to generate hourly forecasts two days in advance. The first step was to use data collected over the previous 15 years to create a sophisticated load model manually. This model has three components: base load for the year, load periodicity over the year, and the effect of holidays. To normalize for the base load, the data for each previous year is standardized by subtracting the average load for that year from each hourly reading and dividing by the standard deviation over the year. Electric load shows periodicity at three fundamental frequencies: diurnal, where usage has an early morning minimum and midday and afternoon maxima; weekly, where demand is lower on weekends; and seasonal, where increased demand during winter and summer for heating and cooling respectively creates a yearly cycle. Major holidays such as Thanksgiving, Christmas, and New Year's Day show significant variation from the normal load and are each modeled separately by averaging hourly loads for that day over the past 15 years. Minor official holidays, such as Columbus Day, are lumped together as School Holidays and treated as an offset to the normal diurnal pattern. All of these effects are incorporated by reconstructing a year's load as a sequence of typical days, fitting the holidays in their correct position, and denormalizing the load to account for overall growth.

Thus far, the load model is a static one, constructed manually from historical data, and implicitly assumes "normal" climatic conditions over the year. The final step was to take weather conditions into account, using a technique that locates the previous day most similar to the current circumstances and using the historical information from that day as a predictor. In this case the prediction is treated as an additive correction to the static load model. To guard against outliers, the eight most similar days are located and their additive corrections averaged. A database was constructed of temperature, humidity, wind speed, and cloud cover at three local weather centers for each hour of the 15-year historical record, along with the difference between the actual load and that predicted by the static model. A linear regression analysis was performed to determine the relative effects of these parameters on load, and the coefficients were used to weight the distance function used to locate the most similar days.

The resulting system yielded the same performance as trained human fore-casters, but was far quicker—taking seconds rather than hours to generate a daily forecast. Human operators can analyze the forecast's sensitivity to simu-lated changes in weather and bring up for examination the "most similar" days that the system used for weather adjustment.

Diagnosis

Diagnosis is one of the principal application areas of expert systems. While the hand-crafted rules used in expert systems often perform well, machine learning can be useful in situations where producing rules manually is too labor-intensive.

Preventative maintenance of electromechanical devices such as motors and generators can forestall failures that disrupt industrial processes. Technicians regularly inspect each device, measuring vibrations at various points to deter-mine whether the device needs servicing. Typical faults include shaft misalign-ment, mechanical loosening, faulty bearings, and unbalanced pumps. A partic-ular chemical plant uses over a thousand different devices, ranging from small pumps to very large turbo-alternators, which until recently were diagnosed by a human expert with twenty years' experience. Faults are identified by measuring vibrations at different places on the device's mounting and using Fourier analy-sis to check the energy present in three different directions at each harmonic of the basic rotation speed. This information, which is very noisy because of limi-tations in the measurement and recording procedure, is studied by the expert in order to arrive at a diagnosis. Although hand-crafted expert system rules had been developed for some situations, the elicitation process would have had to be repeated several times for different types of machinery, and so a learning approach was investigated.

Six hundred faults, each comprising a set of measurements along with the expert's diagnosis, were available, representing twenty years' experience in the field. About half were unsatisfactory for various reasons and had to be dis-carded; the remainder were used as training examples. The goal was not to determine whether or not a fault existed, but to diagnose the kind of fault, given that one was there. Thus there was no need to include fault-free cases in the training set. The measured attributes were rather low level and had to be aug-mented by intermediate concepts, that is, functions of basic attributes, which were defined in consultation with the expert and embodied some causal domain knowledge. The derived attributes were run through an induction algorithm to produce a set of diagnostic rules. Initially, the expert was not satisfied with the rules because he could not relate them to his own knowledge and experience. For him, mere statistical evidence was not, by itself, an adequate explanation. Further background knowledge had to be used before satisfactory rules were generated. Although the resulting rules were quite complex, the expert liked them because he could justify them in light of his mechanical knowledge. He was pleased that a third of the rules coincided with ones he used himself and was delighted to gain new insight from some of the others.

Performance tests indicated that the learned rules were slightly superior to the hand-crafted ones that had previously been elicited from the expert, and this result was confirmed by subsequent use in the chemical factory. It is interesting to note, however, that the system was put into use not because of its good performance but because the domain expert approved of the rules that had been learned.

Marketing and sales

Some of the most active applications of data mining have been in the area of marketing and sales. These are domains where companies possess massive volumes of precisely recorded data, data which—it has only recently been realized—is potentially extremely valuable. In these applications, the predictions themselves are the chief interest; the structure of how decisions are made is often completely irrelevant. Although this means that such applications do not use a key feature of the data mining methods described in this book, namely the transparency of the decision structure, the methods we describe have met with success in many marketing and sales applications.

We have already mentioned the problem of fickle customer loyalty and the challenge of detecting customers who are likely to defect so they can be wooed back into the fold by giving them special treatment. Banks were early adopters of data mining technology because of their successes in the use of machine learning for credit assessment. Data mining is now being used to reduce customer attrition by detecting changes in individual banking patterns that may herald a change of bank, or even life changes—such as a move to another city—that could result in a different bank being chosen. It may reveal, for example, a group of customers with an above-average attrition rate who do most of their banking by phone after hours when telephone response is slow. Data mining may determine groups for whom new services are appropriate, such as a cluster of profitable, reliable customers who rarely get cash advances from their credit cards except in November and December, when they are prepared to pay exorbitant interest rates to see them through the holiday season. In another domain, cellular phone companies fight "churn" by detecting patterns of behavior that could benefit from new services, and then advertising such services to retain their customer base. Incentives provided specifically to retain existing customers can be expensive, and successful data mining allows them to be precisely targeted to those customers where they are likely to yield maximum benefit.

Market basket analysis is the use of association techniques to find groups of items that tend to occur together in transactions, typically supermarket checkout data. For many retailers this is the only source of sales information available for data mining. For example, automated analysis of checkout data may uncover the fact that customers who buy beer also buy chips, a discovery that could be significant from the supermarket operator's point of view (although rather an obvious one that probably does not need a data mining exercise to discover). Or it may come up with the fact that on Thursdays, customers often purchase diapers and beer together, an initially surprising result that, on reflection, makes some sense as young parents stock up for a weekend at home. Such information could be used for many purposes: planning store layouts, limiting special discounts to just one of a set of items that tend to be purchased together, offering coupons for a matching product when one of them is sold alone, and so on. There is enormous added value in being able to identify individual customer's sales histories. In fact, this value is leading to a proliferation of discount or "loyalty" cards that allow retailers to identify individual customers whenever they make a purchase; the personal data that results will be far more valuable than the cash value of the discount. Identification of individual customers not only allows historical analysis of purchasing patterns, but also permits precisely targeted special offers to be mailed out to prospective customers.

This brings us to direct marketing, another popular domain for data mining. Promotional offers are expensive and have a very low—but highly profitable—response rate. Any technique that allows a promotional mailout to be more tightly focused, achieving the same or nearly the same response from a much smaller sample, is valuable. Commercially available databases containing demographic information based on zip codes that characterize the associated neighborhood can be correlated with information on existing customers to find a socioeconomic model that predicts what kind of people will turn out to be actual customers. This model can then be used on information gained in response to an initial mailout, where people send back a response card or call an 800 number for more information, to predict likely future customers. Direct mail companies have the advantage over shopping-mall retailers of having complete purchasing histories for each individual customer and can use data mining to determine those likely to respond to special offers. Targeted campaigns are less expensive than mass-marketed campaigns because companies save money by sending offers only to those likely to want the product. And machine learning can help find the targets.

1.4 Machine learning and statistics

What's the difference between machine learning and statistics? Cynics, looking wryly at the explosion of commercial interest (and hype) in this area, equate data mining to statistics plus marketing. In truth, you should not look for a dividing line between machine learning and statistics, for there is a continuum—and a multidimensional one at that—of data analysis techniques. Some derive from the skills taught in standard statistics courses, and others are more closely associated with the kind of machine learning that has arisen out of computer science. Historically, the two sides have had rather different traditions. If forced to point to a single difference of emphasis, it might be that statistics has been more concerned with testing hypotheses, whereas machine learning has been more concerned with formulating the process of generalization as a search through possible hypotheses. But this is a gross oversimplification: statistics comprises far more than just hypothesis-testing, and many machine learning techniques do not involve any searching at all.

In the past, very similar schemes have developed in parallel in machine learning and statistics. One is decision tree induction. Four statisticians (Breiman et al. 1984) published a book on *Classification and Regression Trees* in the mid-1980s, while throughout the 1970s and early 1980s a prominent machine learning researcher, J. Ross Quinlan, was developing a system for inferring classification trees from examples. These two independent projects produced quite similar schemes for generating trees from examples, and the researchers only became aware of each other's work much later. A second area where similar methods have arisen involves the use of nearest-neighbor methods for classification. These are standard statistical techniques that have been extensively adapted by machine learning researchers, both to improve classification performance and to make the procedure more efficient computationally. We will examine decision tree induction and nearest-neighbor methods in Chapter 4.

But now the two perspectives have converged. The techniques we will examine in this book incorporate a great deal of statistical thinking. Right from the beginning, when constructing and refining the initial example set, standard statistical methods apply: visualization of data, selection of attributes, discarding outliers, and so on. Most learning algorithms use statistical tests when constructing rules or trees and for correcting models that are "overfitted" in that they depend too strongly on the details of the particular examples used to produce them (we have already seen an example of this in the two decision trees of Figure 1.3 for the labor negotiations problem). Statistical tests are used to validate machine learning models and to evaluate machine learning algorithms. In our study of practical techniques for data mining, we will learn a great deal about statistics.

1.5   Generalization as search

One way of visualizing the problem of learning—and one that distinguishes it from statistical approaches—is to imagine a search through a space of possible concept descriptions for one that fits the data. While the idea of generalization as search is a powerful conceptual tool for thinking about machine learning, it is not essential for understanding the practical schemes described in this book; that is why this section is marked "optional," as indicated by the gray bar in the margin.

Suppose, for definiteness, that *concepts*—the result of learning—are expressed as rules like the ones given for the weather problem in Section 1.2 (though other concept description languages would do just as well). Suppose that we list all possible sets of rules and then look for ones that satisfy a given set of examples. A big job? Yes. An *infinite* job? At first sight it seems so because there is no limit to the number of rules there might be. But actually the number of possible rule sets is finite. Note first that each individual rule is no greater than a fixed maximum size, with at most one term for each attribute: for the weather data of Table 1.2 this involves four terms in all. And because the number of possible rules is finite, the number of possible rule *sets* is finite too, though extremely large. However, we'd hardly be interested in sets that contained a very large number of rules. In fact, we'd hardly be interested in sets that had more rules than there are examples because it is hard to imagine needing more than one rule for each example. So if we were to restrict consideration to rule sets smaller than that, the problem would be substantially reduced, though still very large.

The threat of an infinite number of possible concept descriptions seems more serious for the second version of the weather problem in Table 1.3 because these rules contain numbers. If they are real numbers, you can't enumerate them, even in principle. However, on reflection the problem again disappears because the numbers really just represent breakpoints in the numeric values that appear in the examples. For instance, consider the temperature attribute in Table 1.3. It involves the numbers 64, 65, 68, 69, 70, 71, 72, 75, 80, 81, 83, and 85—12 different numbers. And there are 13 possible places in which we might want to put a breakpoint for a rule involving temperature. The problem isn't infinite after all.

So the process of generalization can be regarded as a search through an enormous, but finite, search space. In principle, the problem can be solved by enumerating descriptions and striking out those that do not fit the examples presented. A positive example eliminates all descriptions that it does not match, while a negative one eliminates those it does match. With each example the set of remaining descriptions shrinks (or stays the same). If only one is left, it is the target description—the target concept.

If several descriptions are left, they may still be used to classify unknown objects. An unknown object that matches all remaining descriptions should be classified as matching the target; if it fails to match any one, it should be classified as being outside the target concept. Only when it matches some descriptions but not others is there ambiguity. In this case if the classification of the unknown object were revealed, it would cause the set of remaining descriptions to shrink because rule sets that classified the object the wrong way would be rejected.

Enumerating the concept space

Regarding it as search is a good way of looking at the learning process. However, the search space, while finite, is extremely big, and it is generally quite impractical to enumerate all possible descriptions and then see which ones fit. In the weather problem there are $4 \times 4 \times 3 \times 3 \times 2 = 288$ possibilities for each rule. There are four possibilities for the `outlook` attribute: `sunny`, `overcast`, `rainy`, or it may not participate in the rule at all. Similarly, there are four for `temperature`, three for `weather` and `humidity`, and two for the class. If we restrict the rule set to contain no more than 14 rules (for there are 14 examples in the training sets of Tables 1.2 and 1.3), there are around 2.7×10^{34} possible different rule sets. That's a lot to enumerate, especially for such a patently trivial problem.

Although there are ways of making the enumeration procedure more feasible, a serious problem remains: in practice, it is rare for the process to converge on a unique acceptable description. Either a large number of descriptions are still in the running after the examples are processed, or the descriptors are all eliminated. The first case arises when the examples are not sufficiently comprehensive to eliminate all possible descriptions except for the "correct" one. In practice, people often want a single "best" description, and it is necessary to apply some other criteria to select the best one from the set of remaining descriptions. The second problem arises either because the description language is not expressive enough to capture the actual concept, or because of noise in the examples. If an example comes in with the "wrong" classification due to an error in some of the attribute values or in the class that is assigned to it, this will likely eliminate the correct description from the space. The result is that the set of remaining descriptions becomes empty. This situation is very likely to happen if the examples contain any noise at all, which inevitably they do, except in artificial situations.

Another way of looking at generalization as search is to imagine it not as a process of enumerating descriptions and striking out those that don't apply, but as a kind of hill-climbing in description space to find the description that best matches the set of examples according to some prespecified matching criterion. This is the way that most practical machine learning methods work. However, except in the most trivial cases, it is completely impractical to search the whole space exhaustively; all practical algorithms involve heuristic search and cannot guarantee to find the optimal description.

Bias

Viewing generalization as a search in a space of possible concepts makes it clear that the most important decisions in a machine learning system are

- the concept description language
- the order in which the space is searched
- the way that overfitting to the particular training data is avoided

These three properties are generally referred to as the *bias* of the search and are called *language bias*, *search bias*, and *overfitting-avoidance bias*. You bias the learning scheme by choosing a language in which to express concepts, by searching in a particular way for an acceptable description, and by deciding when the concept has become so complex that it needs to be simplified.

Language bias

The most important question for language bias is whether the concept description language is universal or whether it imposes constraints on what concepts can be learned. If you consider the set of all possible examples, a concept is really just a division of it into subsets. In the weather example, if you were to enumerate all possible weather conditions, the *play* concept is a subset of possible weather conditions. A "universal" language is one that is capable of expressing each and every possible subset of examples. In practice, the set of possible examples is generally huge, and in this respect our perspective is a theoretical, not a practical, one.

If the concept description language permits statements involving logical *or,* that is, *disjunctions,* then any subset can be represented. If the description language is rule-based, disjunction can be achieved by using separate rules. For example, one possible concept representation is simply to enumerate the examples:

```
If outlook = overcast and temperature = hot and humidity = high
   and windy = false then play = yes
If outlook = rainy and temperature = mild and humidity = high
   and windy = false then play = yes
If outlook = rainy and temperature = cool and humidity = normal
   and windy = false then play = yes
If outlook = overcast and temperature = cool and humidity = normal
   and windy = true then play = yes
...
If none of the above then play = no
```

This is not a particularly enlightening concept description: it simply records the positive examples that have been observed and assumes that all the rest are negative. Each positive example is given its own rule, and the concept is the disjunction of the rules. Alternatively, you could imagine having individual rules for each of the negative examples, too—an equally uninteresting concept. In either case the concept description does not perform any generalization; it simply records the original data.

On the other hand, if disjunction is *not* allowed, some possible concepts—sets of examples—may not be able to be represented at all. In that case, a machine learning scheme may simply be unable to achieve good performance.

Another kind of language bias is that obtained from knowledge of the particular domain being used. For example, it may be that some combinations of attribute values can never happen. This would be the case if one attribute implied another. We saw an example of this when considering the rules for the soybean problem on page 17. Then, it would be pointless even to consider concepts that involved redundant or impossible combinations of attribute values. Domain knowledge can be used to cut down the search space. Knowledge is power: a little goes a long way, and even a small hint can reduce the search space dramatically.

Search bias

In realistic data mining problems, there are many alternative concept descriptions that fit the data, and the problem is to find the "best" one according to some criterion—usually simplicity. We use the term *fit* in a statistical sense; we seek the best description that fits the data reasonably well. Moreover, it is computationally infeasible to search the whole space and guarantee that the description found really is the best. Consequently the search procedure is heuristic, and no guarantees can be made about the optimality of the final result. This leaves plenty of room for "bias": different search heuristics bias the search in different ways.

For example, a learning algorithm might adopt a "greedy" search for rules by trying to find the best rule at each stage and adding it in to the rule set. However, it may be that the best *pair* of rules is not just the two rules that are individually found best. Or when building a decision tree, a commitment to split early on using a particular attribute might turn out later to be ill-considered in the light of how the tree develops below that node. To get around these problems, a "beam search" could be used where irrevocable commitments are not made, but instead a set of several active alternatives—whose number is the "beam width"—are pursued in parallel. This will complicate the learning algorithm quite considerably but has the potential to avoid the myopia associated with a greedy search. Of course, if the beam width is not large enough, myopia may still occur. There are more complex search strategies that help overcome this problem.

A more general and higher-level kind of search bias concerns whether the search is done by starting with a general description and refining it, or by starting with a specific example and generalizing it. The former is called a *general-to-specific* search bias; the latter a *specific-to-general* one. Many learning algorithms adopt the former policy, starting with an empty decision tree, or a very general rule, and specializing it to fit the examples. However, it is perfectly possible to work in the other direction. Instance-based methods start with a particular example and see how it can be generalized to cover other nearby examples in the same class.

Overfitting-avoidance bias

Overfitting-avoidance bias can be seen as just another kind of search bias. But because it addresses a rather special problem, we treat it separately. Recall the disjunction problem discussed above. The problem is that if disjunction is allowed, useless concept descriptions that merely summarize the data become possible, whereas if it is prohibited, some concepts are unlearnable. To get around this problem, it is common to search the concept space starting with the simplest concept descriptions and proceeding to more complex ones later: simplest-first ordering. This biases the search in favor of simple concept descriptions.

Using a simplest-first search and stopping when a sufficiently complex concept description is found is a good way of avoiding overfitting. It is sometimes called *forward pruning* or *prepruning* because complex descriptions are pruned away before they are reached. The alternative, *backward pruning* or *postpruning*, is also viable. Here we first find a description that fits the data well and then prune it back to a simpler description that also fits the data. This is not as redundant as it sounds. Often the only way to arrive at a simple theory is to find a complex one and then simplify it. Forward and backward pruning are both a kind of overfitting-avoidance bias.

In summary, while generalization as search is a nice way to think about the learning problem, bias is the only way to make it feasible in practice. Different learning algorithms correspond to different concept description spaces, searched with different biases. And this is what makes it interesting: different description languages and biases serve some problems well and other problems badly. There is no universal "best" learning method—as every teacher knows!

1.6 Data mining and ethics

The use of data—particularly data about people—for data mining has serious ethical implications, and practitioners of data mining techniques must act responsibly by making themselves aware of the ethical issues that surround their particular application.

When applied to people, data mining is frequently used to discriminate—who gets the loan, who gets the special offer, and so on. Certain kinds of discrimination—racial, sexual, religious, and so on—are not only unethical, but also illegal. However, the situation is complex: everything depends on the application. Using sexual and racial information for medical diagnosis is certainly ethical, but using the same information when mining loan payment behavior is not. Even when sensitive information is discarded, there is a risk that models will be built that rely on variables that can be shown to substitute for racial or sexual characteristics. For example, people frequently live in areas that are associated with particular ethnic identities, and so using an area code in a data mining study runs the risk of building models that are based on race—even though racial information has been explicitly excluded from the data.

It is widely accepted that before people make a decision to provide personal information, they need to know how it will be used and what it will be used for, what steps will be taken to protect its confidentiality and integrity, what the consequences of supplying or withholding the information are, and any rights of redress they may have. Whenever such information is collected, individuals should be told these things, not in legalistic small print but straightforwardly in plain language they can understand.

The potential use of data mining techniques means that the ways in which a repository of data can be used may stretch far beyond what was conceived when the data was originally collected. This creates a serious problem: it is necessary to determine the conditions under which the data was collected and for what purposes it may be used. Does the ownership of data bestow the right to use it in ways other than those purported when it was originally recorded? Clearly in the case of explicitly collected personal data it does not. But in general the situation is complex.

Surprising results can emerge from data mining. For example, it has been reported that one of the leading consumer groups in France has found that people with red cars are more likely to default on their car loans. What is the significance of such a "discovery"? What information is it based on? Under what conditions was that information collected? In what ways is it ethical to use it? Clearly insurance companies are in the business of discriminating among people based on stereotypes—young males pay heavily for automobile insurance—but such stereotypes are not based solely on statistical correlations; rather they involve common-sense knowledge about the world as well. Whether the finding above says something about the kind of person who chooses a red car, or whether it should be discarded as an irrelevancy, is a matter for human judgment based on knowledge of the world rather than on purely statistical criteria.

When presented with data, you need to ask who is permitted access to it, for what purpose it was collected, and what kind of conclusions is it legitimate to draw from it. The ethical dimension raises tough questions for those involved in practical data mining. It is necessary to consider the norms of the community that is used to dealing with the kind of data involved, standards that may have evolved over decades or centuries but ones that may not be known to the information specialist. For example, did you know that in the library community, it is taken for granted that the privacy of readers is a right that is jealously protected? If you call up your university library and ask who has such-and-such a textbook out on loan, they will not tell you. This prevents a student from being subjected to pressure from an irate professor to yield access to a book that he desperately needs for his latest grant application. It also prohibits inquiry into the dubious recreational reading tastes of the university ethics committee chairperson. Those who build, say, digital libraries may not be aware of these sensitivities and might incorporate data mining systems that analyze and compare individuals' reading habits in order to recommend new books—perhaps even selling the results to publishers!

In addition to community standards for the use of data, logical and scientific standards must be adhered to as well when drawing conclusions from it. If you do come up with conclusions (such as red car owners being greater credit risks), you need to attach caveats to them and to back them up with arguments other than purely statistical ones. The point is that data mining is just a tool in the whole process: it is people who take the results, along with other knowledge, and decide what action to apply.

Data mining prompts another question, which is really a political one, concerning the use to which society's resources are being put. We mentioned above the application of data mining to basket analysis, where supermarket checkout records are analyzed to detect associations between items that people purchase. What use should be made of the resulting information? Should the supermarket manager place the beer and chips together, to make it easier for shoppers, or farther apart, making it less convenient for them, and maximizing their time in the store and therefore their likelihood of being drawn into unplanned further purchases? Should the manager move the most expensive, most profitable diapers near the beer, increasing sales to harried fathers of a high-margin item, and add further luxury baby products nearby?

Of course, anyone who uses advanced technologies should consider the wisdom of what they are doing. If *data* is characterized as recorded facts, then *information* is the set of patterns, or expectations, that underlie the data. You could go on to define *knowledge* as the accumulation of your set of expectations, and *wisdom* as the value attached to knowledge. Although we will not pursue it further here, this issue is worth pondering.

As we saw at the very beginning of this chapter, the techniques described in this book may be called upon to help make some of the most profound and intimate decisions that life presents. Data mining is a technology that we need to take seriously.

1.7 Further reading

To avoid breaking up the flow of the main text, all references are collected in a section at the end of each chapter. This first *Further reading* section describes papers, books, and other resources relevant to the material covered in Chapter 1. The human *in vitro* fertilization research mentioned in the opening to this chapter is being undertaken by the Oxford University Computing Laboratory, while the research on cow culling is being performed in the Computer Science Department at Waikato University, New Zealand.

The example of the weather problem is from Quinlan (1986) and has been widely used to explain machine learning schemes. The corpus of example problems mentioned in the introduction to Section 1.2 is available from Blake et al. (1998). The contact lens example is from Cendrowska (1997), who introduced the PRISM rule-learning algorithm that we will encounter in Chapter 4. The Iris dataset was discussed in a classic early paper on statistical inference (Fisher 1936). The labor negotiations data is from the *Collective Bargaining Review*, a publication of Labour Canada issued by the Industrial Relations Information Service (BLI 1988), while the soybean problem was first described by Michalski and Chilausky (1980).

Some of the applications in Section 1.3 are covered in an excellent paper that gives plenty of other applications of machine learning and rule induction (Langley and Simon 1995); another source of fielded applications is a special issue of the *Machine Learning Journal* (Kohavi and Provost 1998). The loan company application is described in more detail by Michie (1989); the oil slick detector is from Kubat et al. (1998); the electric load forecasting work is by Jabbour et al. (1988); while the application to preventative maintenance of electromechanical devices is due to Saitta and Neri (1998).

The book *Classification and Regression Trees* mentioned in Section 1.4 is by Breiman et al. (1984), while the independently derived but similar scheme of Ross Quinlan was described in a series of papers that eventually led to a book (Quinlan 1993).

The first book on data mining appeared in 1991 (Piatetsky-Shapiro and Frawley 1991), a collection of papers presented at a workshop on knowledge discovery in databases in the late 1980s, and another book from the same stable has appeared more recently (Fayyad et al. 1996) from a 1994 workshop. Very recently a rash of business-oriented books on data mining have been published, focusing mainly on practical aspects of how data mining can be put into practice with only rather superficial descriptions of the technology that underlies the methods used. They are valuable sources of applications and inspiration. For example, Adriaans and Zantige (1996) from Syllogic, a European systems and database consultancy, is an early introduction to data mining. Berry and Linoff (1997), from a Pennsylvania-based firm specializing in data warehousing and data mining, give an excellent and example-studded review of data mining techniques for marketing, sales, and customer support. Cabena et al. (1998), written by people from five international IBM laboratories, give an overview of the data mining process with many examples of real-world applications. Dhar and Stein (1997) give a business perspective on data mining and include broad-brush, popularized reviews of many of the technologies involved. Groth (1998), working for a provider of data mining software, gives a brief introduction to data mining and then a fairly extensive review of data mining software products; the book includes a CD-ROM containing a demo version of his company's product. Finally, Weiss and Indurkhya (1998) look at a wide variety of statistical techniques for making predictions from what they call "big data."

Books on machine learning, on the other hand, tend to be academic texts suited for use in university courses rather than practical guides. Mitchell (1997) is an excellent book that covers many techniques of machine learning, including some—notably neural networks, genetic algorithms, and reinforcement—that are not covered here. Langley (1996) is another good text. Though the above-mentioned book by Quinlan (1993) concentrates on a particular learning algorithm, C4.5, which we will cover in detail in Chapters 4 and 6, it is an excellent introduction to some of the problems and techniques of machine learning.

This book does not cover the topic of data mining with neural networks. That is the subject of a book by Bigus (1996) of IBM, which features the IBM Neural Network Utility Product that he developed. Neither do we cover genetic algorithms, a popular optimization technique associated with machine learning, which is the subject of an excellent text by Goldberg (1989).

Input: Concepts, instances, attributes

Before delving into the question of how machine learning schemes operate, we begin by looking at the different forms the input might take and, in the next chapter, the different kinds of output that might be produced. With any software system, understanding what the inputs and outputs are is far more important than knowing what goes on in between, and machine learning is no exception.

The input takes the form of *concepts, instances,* and *attributes.* We call the thing that is to be learned a *concept description.* The idea of a concept, like the very idea of learning in the first place, is hard to pin down precisely, and we won't spend time philosophizing about just what it is and isn't. In a sense, what we are trying to find—the result of the learning process—is a description of the concept that is *intelligible* in that it can be understood, discussed, and disputed, and *operational* in that it can be applied to actual examples. The next section explains some distinctions between different kinds of learning problems, distinctions that are very concrete and very important in practical data mining.

The information that the learner is given takes the form of a set of *instances.* In the illustrations discussed in Chapter 1, each instance was an individual, independent example of the concept to be learned. Of course there are many things you might like to learn for which the raw data cannot be expressed as individual, independent instances. Perhaps background knowledge should be taken into account as part of the input. Perhaps the raw data is an agglomerated mass that cannot be fragmented into individual instances. Perhaps it is a single sequence, say a time sequence, that cannot meaningfully be cut into pieces. However, this book is about simple, practical methods of data mining, and we focus on situations where the information can be supplied in the form of individual examples.

Each instance is characterized by the values of attributes that measure different aspects of the instance. There are many different types of attribute, although typical data mining schemes deal only with numeric and *nominal*, or categorical, ones.

Finally, we examine the question of preparing input for data mining and introduce a simple format—the one that is used by the Java code that accompanies this book—for representing the input information as a text file.

2.1 What's a concept?

Four basically different styles of learning appear in data mining applications. In *classification learning*, a learning scheme takes a set of classified examples from which it is expected to learn a way of classifying unseen examples. In *association learning*, any association between features is sought, not just ones that predict a particular *class* value. In *clustering*, groups of examples that belong together are sought. In *numeric prediction*, the outcome to be predicted is not a discrete class but a numeric quantity. Regardless of the type of learning involved, we call the thing to be learned the *concept*, and the output produced by a learning scheme the *concept description*.

Most of the examples in Chapter 1 are classification problems. The weather data (Tables 1.2 and 1.3) presents a set of days together with a decision for each as to whether to play the game or not, and the problem is to learn how to classify new days as `play` or `don't play`. Given the contact lens data (Table 1.1), the problem is to learn how to decide on a lens recommendation for a new patient—or more precisely, since every possible combination of attributes is present in the data, the problem is to learn a way of summarizing the given data. For the irises (Table 1.4), the problem is to learn how to decide whether a new iris flower is *setosa*, *versicolor*, or *virginica*, given its sepal length and width and petal length and width. For the labor negotiations data (Table 1.6), the problem is to decide whether a new contract is acceptable or not, on the basis of its duration, wage increase in the first, second, and third years, cost of living adjustment, and so forth.

Classification learning is sometimes called *supervised* because, in a sense, the scheme operates under supervision by being provided with the actual outcome for each of the training examples—the play/don't play judgment, the lens recommendation, the type of iris, the acceptability of the labor contract. This outcome is called the *class* of the example. The success of classification learning can be judged by trying out the concept description that is learned on an independent set of test data for which the true classifications are known but not made available to the machine. The success rate on test data gives an objective measure of how well the concept has been learned. In many practical data mining applications, success is measured more subjectively in terms of how acceptable the learned description—rules, decision tree, or whatever—are to a human user.

Most of the examples in Chapter 1 can be used equally well for association learning, where there is no specified class. Here, the problem is to discover any structure in the data that is "interesting." Some association rules for the weather data were given in Section 1.2. Association rules differ from classification rules in two ways: they can "predict" any attribute, not just the class, and they can predict more than one attribute's value at a time. Because of this there are far more association rules than classification rules, and the challenge is to avoid being swamped with them. For this reason, association rules are often limited to those that apply to a certain minimum number of examples—say 80% of the dataset—and have greater than a certain minimum accuracy level—say 95% accurate. Even then, there are usually lots of them, and they have to be examined manually to determine whether they are meaningful or not. Association rules usually involve only non-numeric attributes: thus you wouldn't normally look for association rules in the Iris dataset.

When there is no specified class, clustering is used to group items that seem to fall naturally together. Imagine a version of the Iris data in which the type of iris is omitted, as in Table 2.1. Then it is likely that the 150 instances fall into natural clusters corresponding to the three iris types. The challenge is to find these clusters and assign the instances to them—and to be able to assign new instances to the clusters as well. It may be that one or more of the iris types splits naturally into subtypes, in which case the data will exhibit more than three natural clusters. The success of clustering is measured subjectively in terms of how useful the result appears to be to a human user. It may be followed by a second step of classification learning where rules are learned that give an intelligible description of how new instances should be placed into the clusters.

Numeric prediction is a variant of classification learning where the outcome is a numeric value rather than a category. The CPU performance problem is one example. Another, shown in Table 2.2, is a version of the weather data in which what is to be predicted is not `play` or `don't play`, but rather the time (in minutes) to play. With numeric prediction problems, as with other machine learning situations, the predicted value for new instances is often of less interest than the structure of the description that is learned, expressed in terms of what the important attributes are and how they relate to the numeric outcome.

Table 2.1	Iris data as a clustering problem.			
	sepal length	sepal width	petal length	petal width
1	5.1	3.5	1.4	0.2
2	4.9	3.0	1.4	0.2
3	4.7	3.2	1.3	0.2
4	4.6	3.1	1.5	0.2
5	5.0	3.6	1.4	0.2
…				
51	7.0	3.2	4.7	1.4
52	6.4	3.2	4.5	1.5
53	6.9	3.1	4.9	1.5
54	5.5	2.3	4.0	1.3
55	6.5	2.8	4.6	1.5
…				
101	6.3	3.3	6.0	2.5
102	5.8	2.7	5.1	1.9
103	7.1	3.0	5.9	2.1
104	6.3	2.9	5.6	1.8
105	6.5	3.0	5.8	2.2

Table 2.2	Weather data with a numeric class.			
outlook	temperature	humidity	windy	play-time
sunny	85	85	false	5
sunny	80	90	true	0
overcast	83	86	false	55
rainy	70	96	false	40
rainy	68	80	false	65
rainy	65	70	true	45
overcast	64	65	true	60
sunny	72	95	false	0
sunny	69	70	false	70
rainy	75	80	false	45
sunny	75	70	true	50
overcast	72	90	true	55
overcast	81	75	false	75
rainy	71	91	true	10

2.2 What's in an example?

The input to a machine learning scheme is a set of instances. These instances are the things that are to be classified, or associated, or clustered. Although until now we have called them *examples,* henceforth we will use the more specific term *instances* to refer to the input. Each instance is an individual, independent example of the concept to be learned. And each one is characterized by the values of a set of predetermined attributes. This was the case in all the sample datasets discussed in the last chapter (the weather, contact lens, iris, and labor negotiation problems). Each dataset is presented as a matrix of examples versus attributes, which in database terms is a single relation, or a *flat file.*

Expressing the input data as a set of independent instances is by far the most common situation for practical data mining. However, it is a rather restrictive way of formulating problems, and it is worth spending some time reviewing why. Problems often involve relationships between objects, rather than separate, independent instances. Suppose, to take a specific situation, a family tree is given, and we want to learn the concept *sister*. Imagine your own family tree, with your relatives (and their genders) placed at the nodes. This tree is the input to the learning process, along with a list of pairs of people and an indication of whether they are sisters or not.

Figure 2.1 shows part of a family tree, below which are two tables that each define sisterhood in a slightly different way. A *yes* in the third column of the tables means that the person in the second column is a sister of the person in the first column (that's just an arbitrary decision we've made in setting up this example).

The first thing to notice is that there are a lot of *nos* in the third column of the table on the left—because there are twelve people and $12 \times 12 = 144$ pairs of people in all, and most pairs of people aren't sisters. The table on the right, which gives the same information, records only the positive examples and assumes that all others are negative. The idea of specifying only positive examples and adopting a standing assumption that the rest are negative is called the *closed world assumption.* It is frequently assumed in theoretical studies; however, it is not of much practical use in real-life problems because they rarely involve "closed" worlds where you can be certain that all cases are covered.

Neither of the tables in Figure 2.1 are of any use without the family tree itself. This tree can also be expressed in the form of a table, part of which is shown in Table 2.3. Now the problem is expressed in terms of two relationships. But these tables do not contain independent sets of instances because values in the name, parent1, and parent2 columns of the sister-of relation refer to rows of the family tree relation. We can make them into a single set of instances by collapsing the two tables into the single one of Table 2.4.

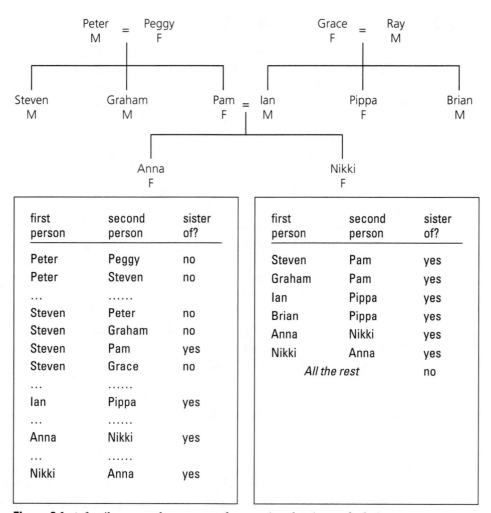

Figure 2.1 A family tree and two ways of expressing the sister-of relation.

We have at last succeeded in transforming the original relational problem into the form of instances, each of which is an individual, independent example of the concept to be learned. Of course, the instances are not really independent—there are plenty of relationships between different rows of the table!—but they are independent as far as the concept of sisterhood is concerned. Most machine learning schemes will still have trouble dealing with this kind of data, as we will see in Section 3.6, but at least the problem has been recast into the right form. A simple rule for the sister-of relation is

```
If second person's gender = female
   and first person's parent1 = second person's parent1
   then sister-of = yes
```

Table 2.3	Family tree represented as a table.		
name	gender	parent1	parent2
Peter	male	?	?
Peggy	female	?	?
Steven	male	Peter	Peggy
Graham	male	Peter	Peggy
Pam	female	Peter	Peggy
Ian	male	Grace	Ray

Table 2.4	The `sister-of` relation represented in a table.							
	first person				second person			sister of?
name	gender	parent1	parent2	name	gender	parent1	parent2	
Steven	male	Peter	Peggy	Pam	female	Peter	Peggy	yes
Graham	male	Peter	Peggy	Pam	female	Peter	Peggy	yes
Ian	male	Grace	Ray	Pippa	female	Grace	Ray	yes
Brian	male	Grace	Ray	Pippa	female	Grace	Ray	yes
Anna	female	Pam	Ian	Nikki	female	Pam	Ian	yes
Nikki	female	Pam	Ian	Anna	female	Pam	Ian	yes
			All the rest					no

This example shows how you can take a relationship between different nodes of a tree and recast it into a set of independent instances. In database terms, you take two relations and join them together to make one, a process of flattening that is technically called *denormalization*. It is always possible to do this with any (finite) set of (finite) relations.

The structure of Table 2.4 can be used to describe any relationship between two people—grandparenthood, second-cousin-twice-removed, or whatever. Relationships among more people require a larger table. Relationships where the maximum number of people is not specified in advance pose a more serious problem. If we want to learn the concept of *nuclear-family* (parents and their children), the number of people involved depends on the size of the largest nuclear family, and although we could guess at a reasonable maximum (ten? twenty?) the actual number can only be found by scanning the tree itself. Nevertheless, given a finite set of finite relations, we could, at least in principle, form a new "super-relation" that contained one row for *every* combination of people, and this would be enough to express any relationship between people no matter how many were involved. The computational and storage costs would, however, be prohibitive.

Another problem with denormalization is that it produces apparent regularities in the data that are completely spurious and are in fact merely reflections of the original database structure. For example, imagine a supermarket database with a *customers and the products they buy* relation, a *products and their supplier* relation, and a *suppliers and their address* relation. Denormalizing this will produce a flat file that contains, for each instance, *customer, product, supplier*, and *supplier address*. A database mining tool that seeks structure in the database may come up with the fact that customers who buy beer also buy chips, a discovery that could be significant from the supermarket manager's point of view. However, it may also come up with the fact that *supplier address* can be predicted exactly from *supplier*—a "discovery" that will not impress the supermarket manager at all. This fact masquerades as a significant discovery from the flat file but is present explicitly in the original database structure.

Many abstract computational problems involve relations that are not finite, although clearly any actual set of input examples must be finite. Concepts such as `ancestor-of` involve arbitrarily long paths through a tree, and although the human race, and hence its family tree, may be finite (though prodigiously large), many artificial problems generate data that truly is infinite. Although it may sound abstruse, this situation is the norm in areas such as list processing and logic programming and is addressed in a subdiscipline of machine learning called *inductive logic programming*. Computer science usually uses recursion to deal with situations in which the number of possible examples is infinite. For example,

```
If person1 is a parent of person2
    then person1 is an ancestor of person2
If person1 is a parent of person2
    and  person2 is an ancestor of person3
    then person1 is an ancestor of person3
```

is a simple recursive definition of `ancestor` that works no matter how distantly two people are related. Techniques of inductive logic programming can learn recursive rules like this from a finite set of instances such as those in Table 2.5.

The real drawback of such techniques, though, is that they do not cope well with noisy data, and they tend to be so slow as to be unusable on anything but small artificial datasets. They are not covered in this book; see Bergadano and Gunetti (1996) for a comprehensive treatment.

In summary, the input to a data mining scheme is generally expressed as a table of independent instances of the concept to be learned. Because of this it has been suggested, disparagingly, that we should really talk of *file mining* rather

Table 2.5   Another relation represented as a table.

first person				second person				ancestor of?
name	gender	parent1	parent2	name	gender	parent1	parent2	
Peter	male	?	?	Steven	male	Peter	Peggy	yes
Peter	male	?	?	Pam	female	Peter	Peggy	yes
Peter	male	?	?	Anna	female	Pam	Ian	yes
Peter	male	?	?	Nikki	female	Pam	Ian	yes
Pam	female	Peter	Peggy	Nikki	female	Pam	Ian	yes
Grace	female	?	?	Ian	male	Grace	Ray	yes
Grace	female	?	?	Nikki	female	Pam	Ian	yes
				Other examples here				yes
				All the rest				no

than *database mining*. Relational data is more complex than a flat file. A finite set of finite relations can always be recast into a single table, although often at enormous cost in space. Moreover, denormalization can generate spurious regularities in the data, and it is essential to check the data for such artifacts before applying a learning scheme. Finally, potentially infinite concepts can be dealt with by learning rules that are recursive, although that is beyond the scope of this book.

2.3   What's in an attribute?

Each individual, independent instance that provides the input to machine learning is characterized by its values on a fixed, predefined set of features or *attributes*. The instances are the rows of the tables that we have shown for the weather, contact lens, Iris, and CPU performance problems, and the attributes are the columns. (The contract negotiation data was an exception: we presented this with instances in columns and attributes in rows for space reasons.)

The use of a fixed set of features imposes another restriction on the kinds of problems generally considered in practical data mining. What if different instances have different features? If the instances were transportation vehicles, then number of wheels is a feature that applies to many vehicles but not to ships, for example, whereas number of masts might be a feature that applies to ships but not to land vehicles. The standard workaround is to make each possible feature an attribute and to use a special "irrelevant value" flag to indicate that a particular attribute is not available for a particular case. A similar situation arises when the existence of one feature (say, `spouse's name`) depends on the value of another (`married` or `not married`).

The value of an attribute for a particular instance is a measurement of the quantity that the attribute refers to. There is a broad distinction between quantities that are numeric and ones that are *nominal*. Numeric attributes, sometimes called *continuous* attributes, measure numbers—either real- or integer-valued. Note that the term *continuous* is routinely abused in this context: integer-valued attributes are certainly not continuous in the mathematical sense. Nominal attributes take on values in a prespecified, finite set of possibilities and are sometimes called *categorical*. But there are other possibilities. Statistics texts often introduce "levels of measurement" such as *nominal, ordinal, interval,* and *ratio.*

Nominal quantities have values that are distinct symbols. The values themselves serve only as labels or names—hence the term *nominal,* which comes from the Latin word for *name.* For example, in the weather data the attribute `outlook` has values `sunny`, `overcast`, and `rainy`. No relation is implied among these three—no ordering or distance measure. It certainly does not make sense to add the values together, or multiply them, or even compare their size. A rule using such an attribute can only test for equality or inequality, as in

```
outlook: sunny    ⇒ no
         overcast ⇒ yes
         rainy    ⇒ yes
```

Ordinal quantities are ones that make it possible to rank order the categories. However, although there is a notion of ordering, there is no notion of *distance.* For example, in the weather data the attribute `temperature` has values `hot`, `mild`, and `cool`. These are ordered. Whether you say that

```
hot > mild > cool  or  hot < mild < cool
```

is a matter of convention—it does not matter which is used so long as consistency is maintained. What is important is that `mild` lies between the other two. Although it makes sense to compare two values, it does not make sense to add or subtract them—the difference between `hot` and `mild` cannot be compared with the difference between `mild` and `cool`. A rule using such an attribute might involve a comparison, as in

```
temperature = hot ⇒ no
temperature < hot ⇒ yes
```

Notice that the distinction between nominal and ordinal quantities is not always straightforward and obvious. Indeed, the very example of an ordinal quantity that we used above, `outlook`, is not completely clear: you might argue that the three values *do* have an ordering—overcast being somehow intermediate between sunny and rainy as weather goes from good to bad.

Interval quantities have values that are not only ordered but measured in fixed and equal units. A good example is temperature, expressed in degrees (say, degrees Fahrenheit) rather than on the non-numeric scale implied by cool, mild and hot. It makes perfect sense to talk about the difference between two temperatures, say 46 and 48 degrees, and compare that with the difference between another two temperatures, say 22 and 24 degrees. Another example is dates. You can talk about the difference between the years 1939 and 1945 (6 years), or even the average of the years 1939 and 1945 (1942), but it doesn't make much sense to consider the sum of the years 1939 and 1945 (3684) or three times the year 1939 (5817), because the starting point, year 0, is completely arbitrary—indeed it has changed many times throughout the course of history. (Children sometimes wonder what the year 300 BC was called in 300 BC.)

Ratio quantities are ones for which the measurement scheme inherently defines a zero point. For example, when measuring distance from one object to others, the distance between the object and itself forms a natural zero. Ratio quantities are treated as real numbers: any mathematical operations are allowed. It certainly does make sense to talk about three times the distance, and even to multiply one distance by another to get an area.

However, the question of whether there is an "inherently" defined zero point can depend on our scientific knowledge—it's culture-relative. For example, Fahrenheit knew no lower limit to temperature and his scale is an interval one. Nowadays, however, we view temperature as a ratio scale based on absolute zero. Measurement of time in years since some culturally defined zero like AD 0 is not a ratio scale; years since the Big Bang is. Even the zero point of money—where we are usually quite happy to say that something cost twice as much as something else—may not be quite clearly defined for those of us who constantly max out our credit cards.

Most practical data mining systems accommodate just two of these four levels of measurement: nominal and ordinal. Nominal attributes are sometimes called *categorical, enumerated,* or *discrete. Enumerated* is the standard term used in computer science to denote a categorical data type; however, the strict definition of the term—namely, to put into one-to-one correspondence with the natural numbers—implies an ordering, which is specifically not implied in the machine learning context. *Discrete* also has connotations of ordering because you often discretize a continuous, numeric quantity. Ordinal attributes are generally called *numeric,* or perhaps *continuous,* but without the implication of mathematical continuity. A special case of the nominal scale is the *dichotomy,* which has only two members—often designated as *true* and *false,* or *yes* and *no* in the weather data. Such attributes are sometimes called *boolean.*

Machine learning systems can use a wide variety of other information about attributes. For instance, dimensional considerations could be used to restrict the search to expressions or comparisons that are dimensionally correct. Circular ordering could affect the kinds of tests that are considered. For example, in a temporal context, tests on a day attribute could involve next day, previous day, next weekday, same day next week. Partial orderings, that is, generalization/specialization relations, frequently occur in practical situations. Information of this kind is often referred to as *metadata,* data about data. However, the kind of practical schemes currently used for data mining are rarely capable of taking metadata into account, although it is likely that these capabilities will develop rapidly in the future. (We return to this in Chapter 9.)

2.4   Preparing the input

Preparing input for a data mining investigation usually consumes the bulk of the effort invested in the entire data mining process. While this book is not really about the problems of data preparation, we want to give you a feeling for the issues involved so that you can appreciate the complexities. Following that, we look at a particular input file format, the ARFF format, which is used in the Java package described in Chapter 8. Then we consider issues that arise when converting datasets to such a format, for there are some simple practical points to be aware of. Bitter experience shows that real data is often of disappointingly low quality, and careful checking—a process that has become known as *data cleaning*—pays off many times over.

Gathering the data together

When beginning work on a data mining problem, it is first necessary to bring all the data together into a set of instances. We explained the need to denormalize relational data when discussing the family tree example. Although it illustrates the basic issue, this self-contained and rather artificial example does not really convey what the process will be like in practice. In a real business application, it will be necessary to bring data together from different departments. For example, in a marketing study data will be needed from the sales department, the customer billing department, and the customer service department.

Integrating data from different sources usually presents many challenges—not deep issues of principle but nasty realities of practice. Different departments will use different styles of record keeping, different conventions, different time periods, different degrees of data aggregation, different primary keys, and will have different kinds of error. The data must be assembled, integrated, and cleaned up. The idea of enterprisewide database integration is known as *data warehousing.* Data warehouses provide a single consistent point of access to corporate or organizational data, transcending departmental divisions. They are the place where old data is published in a way that can be used to inform business decisions. The movement toward data warehousing is a recognition of the fact that the fragmented information that an organization uses to support day-to-day operations at a departmental level can have immense strategic value when brought together. Clearly the presence of a data warehouse is a very useful precursor to data mining, and if it is not available, many of the steps involved in data warehousing will have to be undertaken to prepare the data for mining.

Often even a data warehouse will not contain all the necessary data, and you may have to reach outside the organization to bring in data relevant to the problem at hand. For example, weather data had to be obtained in the load forecasting example in the last chapter, and demographic data for marketing and sales applications. Sometimes called *overlay data,* this is not normally collected by an organization but is clearly relevant to the data mining problem. And it too must be cleaned up and integrated with the other data that has been collected.

Another practical question when assembling the data is the degree of aggregation that is appropriate. When a dairy farmer decides which cows to sell off, the milk production records—which are recorded twice a day by an automatic milking machine—must be aggregated. Similarly, raw telephone call data is not much use when telecommunications firms study their clients' behavior: the data must be aggregated to the customer level. But do you want usage by month or by quarter, and for how many months or quarters in arrears? Selecting the right type and level of aggregation is usually critical for success.

Because so many different issues are involved, you can't expect to get it right the first time. This is why data assembly, integration, cleaning, aggregating, and general preparation take so long.

ARFF format

We now look at a standard way of representing datasets that consist of independent, unordered instances and does not involve relationships between instances, called an ARFF file.

Figure 2.2 shows an ARFF file for the weather data in Table 1.3, the version with some numeric features. Lines beginning with a % sign are comments. Following the comments at the beginning of the file are the name of the relation (weather) and a block defining the attributes (outlook, temperature, humidity, windy, play?). Nominal attributes are followed by the set of values they can take on, enclosed in curly braces. Numeric ones are followed by the keyword numeric.

Although the weather problem is to predict the class value play? from the values of the other attributes, the class attribute is not distinguished in any way in the data file. The ARFF format merely gives a dataset; it does not specify which of

```
% ARFF file for the weather data with some numeric features
%
@relation weather

@attribute outlook { sunny, overcast, rainy }
@attribute temperature numeric
@attribute humidity numeric
@attribute windy { true, false }
@attribute play? { yes, no }

@data
%
% 14 instances
%
sunny, 85, 85, false, no
sunny, 80, 90, true, no
overcast, 83, 86, false, yes
rainy, 70, 96, false, yes
rainy, 68, 80, false, yes
rainy, 65, 70, true, no
overcast, 64, 65, true, yes
sunny, 72, 95, false, no
sunny, 69, 70, false, yes
rainy, 75, 80, false, yes
sunny, 75, 70, true, yes
overcast, 72, 90, true, yes
overcast, 81, 75, false, yes
rainy, 71, 91, true, no
```

Figure 2.2 ARFF file for the weather data.

the attributes is the one that is supposed to be predicted. This means that the same file can be used for investigating how well each attribute can be predicted from the others, or to find association rules, or for clustering.

Following the attribute definitions is an @data line that signals the start of the instances in the dataset. Instances are written one per line, with values for each attribute in turn, separated by commas. If a value is missing it is represented by a single question mark (there are no missing values in this dataset). The attribute specifications in ARFF files allow the dataset to be checked to ensure that it contains legal values for all attributes, and programs that read ARFF files do this checking automatically.

Attribute types

The ARFF format accommodates the two basic data types, nominal and numeric. But how these data types are interpreted depends on the learning scheme being used. For example, most schemes treat numeric attributes as ordinal scales and only use less-than and greater-than comparisons between the values. However, some treat them as ratio scales and use distance calculations. You need to understand how machine learning schemes work before using them for data mining.

If a learning scheme treats numeric attributes as though they are measured on ratio scales, the question of normalization arises. Attributes are often normalized to lie in a fixed range, say from zero to one, by dividing all values by the maximum value encountered, or by subtracting the minimum value and dividing by the range between the maximum and minimum values. Another normalization technique is to calculate the statistical mean and standard deviation of the attribute values, subtract the mean from each value, and divide the result by the standard deviation. This process is called *standardizing* a statistical variable, and results in a set of values whose mean is zero and standard deviation is one.

Some learning schemes—for example, varieties of instance-based learning, and regression methods—deal only with ratio scales, because they calculate the "distance" between two instances based on the values of their attributes. If the actual scale is ordinal, a numeric distance function must be defined. One way of doing this is to use a two-level distance: 1 if the two values are different and 0 if they are the same. Any nominal quantity can be treated as numeric by using this distance function. However, it is rather a crude technique and conceals the true degree of variation between instances. Another possibility is to generate several synthetic binary attributes for each nominal attribute. We return to this in Chapter 6 (Section 6.5) when we look at the use of trees for numeric prediction.

Sometimes there is a genuine mapping between nominal quantities and numeric scales. For example, postal zip codes indicate areas that could be represented by geographical coordinates; the leading digits of telephone numbers may do so too, depending on where you live. The first two digits of a student's ID number may be the year in which they first enrolled.

It is very common for practical datasets to contain nominal values that are coded as integers. For example, an integer identifier may be used as a code for an attribute such as `part number`, yet such integers are not intended for use in less-than or greater-than comparisons. If this is the case, it is important to specify that the attribute is nominal rather than numeric.

It is quite possible to treat an ordinal quantity as though it were nominal. Indeed, some machine learning schemes only deal with nominal elements. For example, in the contact lens problem the age attribute is treated as nominal, and the rules generated included these:

```
If age = young and astigmatic = no and
   tear production rate = normal then recommendation = soft
If age = pre-presbyopic and astigmatic = no and
   tear production rate = normal then recommendation = soft
```

But in fact age, specified in this way, is really an ordinal quantity, with

```
young < pre-presbyopic < presbyopic
```

If it were treated as ordinal, the two rules could be collapsed into one:

```
If age ≤ pre-presbyopic and astigmatic = no and
   tear production rate = normal then recommendation = soft
```

which is a more compact, and hence more satisfactory, way of saying the same thing.

Missing values

Most datasets encountered in practice, like the labor negotiations data in Table 1.6, contain missing values. Missing values are frequently indicated by out-of-range entries, perhaps a negative number (e.g., −1) in a numeric field that is normally only positive, or a zero in a numeric field that can never normally be zero. For nominal attributes, missing values may be indicated by blanks or dashes. Sometimes different kinds of missing values are distinguished (e.g., unknown vs. unrecorded vs. irrelevant values) and perhaps represented by different negative integers (−1, −2, etc.).

You have to think carefully about the significance of missing values. They may occur for a number of reasons, such as malfunctioning measurement equipment, changes in experimental design during data collection, and collation of several similar but not identical datasets. Respondents in a survey may refuse to answer certain questions such as age or income. In an archaeological study, a specimen such as a skull may be damaged so that some variables cannot be measured. In a biological one, plants or animals may die before all variables have been measured. What do these things *mean* about the example under consideration? Might the skull damage have some significance in itself, or is it just due to some random event? Does the fact that the plants died early have some bearing on the case, or not?

Most machine learning schemes make the implicit assumption that there is no particular significance in the fact that a certain instance has an attribute value missing: the value is simply not known. However, there may be a good reason why the attribute's value is unknown—perhaps a decision was taken, on the evidence available, not to perform some particular test—and that might convey some information about the instance other than the fact that the value is simply missing. If this is the case, then it would be more appropriate to record *not tested* as another possible value for this attribute, or perhaps as another attribute in the dataset. As the examples above illustrate, only someone familiar with the data can make an informed judgment as to whether a particular value being missing has some extra significance, or whether it should simply be coded as an ordinary missing value. Of course, if there seem to be several types of missing value, that is prima facie evidence that something is going on that needs to be investigated.

If missing values mean that an operator has decided not to make a particular measurement, that may convey a great deal more than the mere fact that the value is unknown. For example, people analyzing medical databases have noticed that, in some circumstances, cases may be diagnosable strictly from the tests that a doctor decides to make, regardless of the outcome of the tests. Then a record of which values are "missing" is all that is needed for a full diagnosis—the actual values can be ignored completely!

Inaccurate values

It is important to check data mining files carefully for rogue attributes and attribute values. The data used for mining has almost certainly not been gathered expressly for that purpose. When originally collected, many of the fields probably didn't matter and were left blank or unchecked. Provided it does not affect the original purpose of the data, there is no incentive for correcting it. However, when the same database is used for mining, the errors and omissions suddenly start to assume great significance. For example, banks do not really need to know the age of their customers, so their databases may contain many missing or incorrect values. But age may be a very significant feature in mined rules.

Typographical errors in a dataset will obviously lead to incorrect values. Often the value of a nominal attribute is misspelled, creating an extra possible value for that attribute. Or perhaps it is not a misspelling but different names for the same thing, like Pepsi and Pepsi Cola. Obviously the point of a defined format such as ARFF is to allow data files to be checked for internal consistency. However, errors that occur in the original data file are often preserved through the conversion process into the file that is used for data mining; thus the list of possible values that each attribute takes on should be examined carefully.

Typographical or measurement errors in numeric values generally cause outliers that can be detected by graphing one variable at a time. Erroneous values often deviate significantly from the pattern that is apparent in the remaining values. Sometimes, of course, inaccurate values are hard to find, particularly without specialist domain knowledge.

Duplicate data presents another source of error. Most machine learning tools will produce different results if some of the instances in the data files are duplicated, because repetition gives them more influence on the result.

People often make deliberate errors when entering personal data into databases. They might make minor changes in the spelling of their street name to try to identify whether the information they have provided ends up being sold to advertising agencies that burden them with junk mail. They might adjust the spelling of their name when applying for insurance if they have had insurance refused in the past. Rigid computerized data entry systems often impose artificial restrictions that require imaginative workarounds. One story tells of a foreigner renting a vehicle in the U.S. Being from abroad, he had no zip code; yet the computer insisted on one, and in desperation the operator suggested that he use the zip code of the rental agency. If this is common practice, future data mining projects may notice a cluster of customers who apparently live in the same district as the agency! Similarly, supermarket checkout operators sometimes use their own frequent buyer card in situations where the customer does not supply one, either so that the customer can get a discount that would otherwise be unavailable, or simply to accumulate credit points in the cashier's account. Only a deep semantic knowledge of what is going on will be able to explain systematic data errors like these.

Finally, data goes stale. Many items change as circumstances change. For example, items in mailing lists—names, addresses, telephone numbers—change frequently. You need to consider whether the data you are mining is still current.

Getting to know your data

There is no substitute for getting to know your data. Simple tools that show histograms of the distribution of values of nominal attributes, and graphs of the values of numeric attributes (perhaps sorted, or simply graphed against instance number), are very helpful. These graphical visualizations of the data make it easy to identify outliers, which may well represent errors in the data file—or arcane conventions for coding unusual situations, like a missing year as 9999 or a missing weight as −1 kg, that no one has thought to tell you about. Domain experts need to be consulted to explain anomalies, missing values, the significance of integers that represent categories rather than numeric quantities, and so on. Pairwise plots of one attribute against another, or each attribute against the class value, can be extremely revealing.

Data cleaning is a time-consuming and labor-intensive procedure, but one that is absolutely necessary for successful data mining. With a large dataset, people often give up—how can they possibly check it all? Instead, you should sample a few instances and examine them carefully. You'll be surprised at what you find. Time looking at your data is always well spent.

2.5 Further reading

Although little has been written about the form of the input to machine learn-ing schemes, there is a great deal of current interest in data warehousing and the problems it entails. Kimball (1996) is the best introduction to these that we know of. Cabena et al. (1998) estimate that data preparation accounts for 60% of the effort involved in a data mining application, and they talk at some length about the problems involved.

The area of inductive logic programming, which deals with finite and infinite relations, is covered by Bergadano and Gunetti (1996). The different "levels of measurement" for attributes were introduced by Stevens (1946) and are well described in the manuals for statistical packages like SPSS (Nie et al. 1970).

chapter three

Output: Knowledge representation

This book is about techniques for discovering structural patterns in data. Before looking at how these techniques work, we have to see how structural patterns can be expressed. There are many different ways for representing the patterns that can be discovered by machine learning, and each one dictates the kind of technique that can be used to infer that output structure from data. Once you understand how the output is represented, you have come a long way toward understanding how it can be generated.

We saw many examples of data mining in Chapter 1. In these cases the output took the form of decision trees and classification rules, which are basic knowledge representation styles that many machine learning methods use. *Knowledge* is really too imposing a word for a decision tree or a collection of rules, and by using it we don't really mean to imply that these structures vie with the *real* kind of knowledge that we carry in our heads: it's just that we need some word to refer to the structures that learning methods produce. There are more complex varieties of rules that allow exceptions to be specified, and ones that can express relations between the values of the attributes of different instances. Special forms of trees can be used for numeric prediction too. Instance-based representations focus on the instances themselves rather than on rules that govern their attribute values. Finally, some learning schemes generate clusters of instances. These different knowledge representation methods parallel the different kinds of learning problems introduced in Chapter 2.

3.1 Decision tables

The simplest, most rudimentary way of representing the output from machine learning is to make it just like the input—a *decision table*. For example, Table 1.2 is a decision table for the weather data: you simply look up the appropriate conditions to decide whether or not to `play`. Less trivially, creating a decision table might involve selecting some of the attributes. If `temperature` is irrelevant to the decision, for example, a smaller, condensed table with that attribute missing would be a better guide. The problem is, of course, to decide which attributes to leave out without affecting the final decision.

3.2 Decision trees

A "divide-and-conquer" approach to the problem of learning from a set of independent instances leads naturally to a style of representation called a *decision tree*. We have seen some examples of decision trees, for the contact lens (Figure 1.2) and labor negotiations (Figure 1.3) datasets. Nodes in a decision tree involve testing a particular attribute. Usually, the test at a node compares an attribute value with a constant. However, some trees compare two attributes with each other, or utilize some function of one or more attributes. Leaf nodes give a classification that applies to all instances that reach the leaf, or a set of classifications, or a probability distribution over all possible classifications. To classify an unknown instance, it is routed down the tree according to the values of the attributes tested in successive nodes, and when a leaf is reached the instance is classified according to the class assigned to the leaf.

If the attribute that is tested at a node is a nominal one, the number of children is usually the number of possible values of the attribute. In this case, since there is one branch for each possible value, the same attribute will not be tested again further down the tree. Sometimes the attribute values are divided into two subsets, and the tree branches just two ways depending on which subset the value lies in; in that case, the attribute might be tested more than once in a path.

If the attribute is numeric, the test at a node usually determines whether its value is greater or less than a predetermined constant, giving a two-way split. Alternatively, a three-way split may be used, in which case there are several different possibilities. If *missing value* is treated as an attribute value in its own right, that will create a third branch. An alternative for an integer-valued attribute would be a three-way split into *less than*, *equal to*, and *greater than*. An alternative for a real-valued attribute, for which *equal to* is not such a meaningful option, would be to test against an interval rather than a single constant, again giving a three-way split: *below*, *within*, and *above*. A numeric attribute is often tested several times in any given path down the tree from root to leaf, each test involving a different constant. We return to this when discussing the handling of numeric attributes in Chapter 6 (Section 6.1).

Missing values pose an obvious problem. It is not clear which branch should be taken when a node tests an attribute whose value is missing. In some cases, *missing value* is treated as an attribute value in its own right. This assumes that the absence of a value may be of some significance. If this is not the case, missing values should be treated in a special way rather than being considered as just another possible value that the attribute might take. A simple solution is to record the number of elements in the training set that go down each branch and use the most popular branch if the value for a test instance is missing.

A more sophisticated solution is to notionally split the instance into pieces and send part of it down each branch and from there right on down to the leaves of the subtrees involved. The split is accomplished using a numeric weight between 0 and 1, and the weight for a branch is chosen to be proportional to the number of training instances going down that branch, all weights summing to one. A weighted instance may be further split at a lower node. Eventually the various parts of the instance will each reach a leaf node, and the decisions at these leaf nodes must be recombined using the weights that have percolated down to the leaves. We return to this in Section 6.1.

3.3 Classification rules

Classification rules are a popular alternative to decision trees, and we have already seen examples for the weather (pages 8–11), contact lens (pages 11–13), iris (pages 13–14) and soybean (pages 17–20) datasets. The *antecedent,* or precondition, of a rule is a series of tests just like the tests at nodes in decision trees, while the *consequent,* or conclusion, gives the class or classes that apply to instances covered by that rule, or perhaps a probability distribution over the classes. Generally, the preconditions are logically ANDed together, and all the tests must succeed if the rule is to fire. However, in some rule formulations the preconditions are general logical expressions rather than simple conjunctions. We often think of the individual rules as being effectively logically ORed together: if any one applies, the class (or probability distribution) given in its conclusion is applied to the instance. However, conflicts arise when several rules with different conclusions apply; we return to this shortly.

It is easy to read a set of rules directly off a decision tree. One rule is generated for each leaf. The antecedent of the rule includes a condition for every node on the path from the root to that leaf, and the consequent of the rule is the class assigned by the leaf. This procedure produces rules that are unambiguous in that the order in which they are executed is irrelevant. However, in general rules that are read directly off a decision tree are far more complex than necessary, and rules derived from trees are usually pruned to remove redundant tests.

Because decision trees cannot easily express the disjunction implied between the different rules in a set, transforming a general set of rules into a tree is not quite so straightforward. A good illustration of this occurs when the rules have the same structure but different attributes, like

```
If a and b then x
If c and d then x
```

Then it is necessary to break the symmetry and choose a single test for the root node. If, for example, a is chosen, the second rule must, in effect, be repeated twice in the tree, as shown in Figure 3.1. This is known as the *replicated subtree problem*.

The replicated subtree problem is sufficiently important that it is worth looking at a couple more examples. The diagram on the left of Figure 3.2 shows an *exclusive-or* function for which the output is a if $x = 1$ or $y = 1$ but not both. To make this into a tree, you have to split on one attribute first, leading to a structure like the one shown in the center. In contrast, rules can faithfully reflect the true symmetry of the problem with respect to the attributes, as shown on the right.

In this example the rules are not notably more compact than the tree. In fact, they are just what you would get by reading rules off the tree in the obvious way. But in other situations, rules are much more compact than trees, particularly if it is possible to have a "default" rule that covers cases not specified by the other rules. For example, to capture the effect of the rules in Figure 3.3, in a situation where there are four attributes, x, y, z, and w, which can each be 1, 2, or 3, requires the tree shown on the right. Each of the three small gray triangles to the upper right should actually contain the whole three-level subtree that is displayed in gray, a rather extreme example of the replicated subtree problem. This is a distressingly complex description of a rather simple concept.

One reason why rules are popular is that each rule seems to represent an independent "nugget" of knowledge. New rules can be added to an existing rule set without disturbing those already there, whereas to add to a tree structure may require reshaping the whole tree. However, this independence is something of an illusion, for it ignores the question of how the rule set is executed. We discussed earlier (on page 9) the fact that if rules are meant to be interpreted *in order* as a "decision list," some of them, taken individually and out of context, may be incorrect. On the other hand, if the order of interpretation is supposed

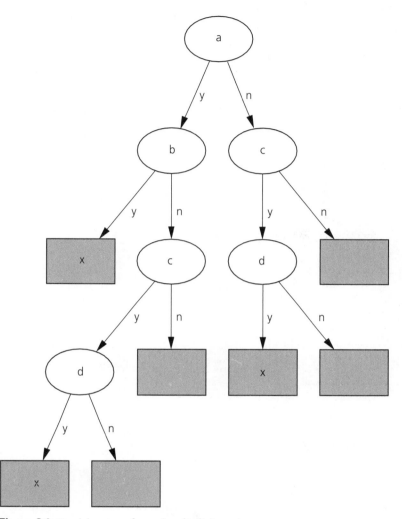

Figure 3.1 Decision tree for a simple disjunction.

to be immaterial, then it is not clear what to do when different rules lead to different conclusions for the same instance. This situation cannot arise for rules that are read directly off a decision tree, for the redundancy included in the structure of the rules prevents any ambiguity in interpretation. But it does arise when rules are generated in other ways.

If a rule set gives multiple classifications for a particular example, one solution is to give no conclusion at all. Another is to count how often each rule fires on the training data and go with the most popular one. These strategies can lead to radically different results. A different problem occurs when an instance is encountered that the rules fail to classify at all. Again, this cannot occur with decision trees, or with rules read directly off them, but it can easily happen with

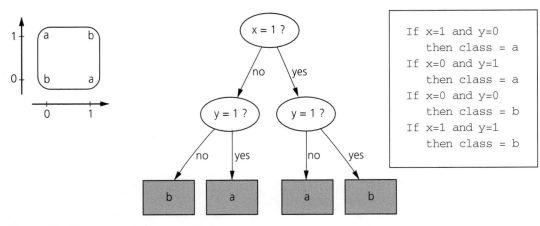

Figure 3.2 The exclusive-or problem.

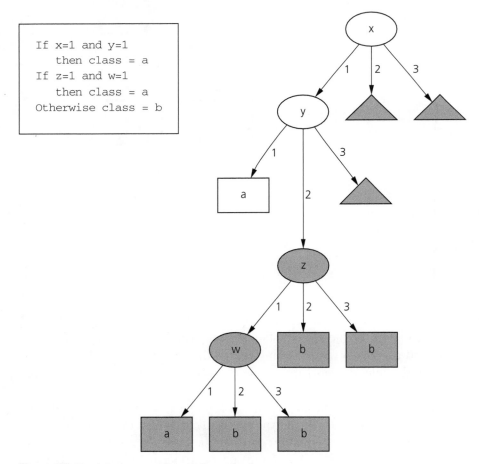

Figure 3.3 Decision tree with a replicated subtree.

general rule sets. One way of dealing with this situation is to fail to classify such an example; another is to choose the most frequently occurring class as a default. Again, radically different results may be obtained by these strategies. Individual rules are simple, and sets of rules seem deceptively simple—but given just a set of rules with no additional information, it is not clear how the rules should be interpreted.

A particularly straightforward situation occurs when rules lead to a class that is boolean (say, *yes* and *no*), and when only rules leading to one outcome (say, *yes*) are expressed. The assumption is that if a particular instance is not in class *yes,* then it must be in class *no*—a form of closed world assumption. If this is the case, then rules cannot conflict and there is no ambiguity in rule interpretation, any interpretation strategy will give the same result. Such a set of rules can be written as a logic expression in what is called *disjunctive normal form*: that is, as a disjunction (OR) of conjunctive (ANDed) conditions.

It is this simple special case that seduces people into assuming that rules are very easy to deal with, for here each rule really does operate as a new, independent piece of information that contributes in a straightforward way to the disjunction. Unfortunately it only applies to boolean outcomes and requires the closed-world assumption, and both these constraints are unrealistic in most practical situations. Machine learning algorithms that generate rules invariably produce ordered rule sets in multiclass situations, and this sacrifices any possibility of modularity because the order of execution is critical.

3.4 Association rules

Association rules are really no different from classification rules except that they can predict any attribute, not just the class, and this gives them the freedom to predict combinations of attributes too. Also, association rules are not intended to be used together as a set, as classification rules are. Different association rules express different regularities that underlie the dataset, and they generally predict different things.

Because so many different association rules can be derived from even a tiny dataset, interest is restricted to those that apply to a reasonably large number of instances and have a reasonably high accuracy on the instances they apply to. The *coverage* of an association rule is the number of instances for which it predicts correctly—this is often called its *support*. And its *accuracy*—often called *confidence*—is the number of instances that it predicts correctly, expressed as a proportion of all instances it applies to. For example, with the rule

```
If temperature = cool then humidity = normal
```

the coverage is the number of days that are both cool and have normal humidity (4 in the data of Table 1.2), and the accuracy is the proportion of cool days that have normal humidity (100% in this case). It is usual to specify minimum coverage and accuracy values and to seek only those rules whose coverage and accuracy are both at least these specified minima. In the weather data, for example, there are 58 rules whose coverage and accuracy are at least 2 and 95% respectively. (It may also be convenient to specify coverage as a percentage of the total number of instances instead.)

Association rules that predict multiple consequences must be interpreted rather carefully. For example, with the weather data in Table 1.2 we saw this rule:

```
If windy = false and play = no then outlook = sunny
                                  and humidity = high.
```

This is *not* just a shorthand expression for the two separate rules

```
If windy = false and play = no then outlook = sunny
If windy = false and play = no then humidity = high
```

It does indeed imply that these exceed the minimum coverage and accuracy figures—but it implies more. The original rule means that the number of examples that are non-windy, non-playing, with sunny outlook and high humidity, is at least as great as the specified minimum coverage figure. And it also means that the number of such days, expressed as a proportion of non-windy, non-playing days, is at least the specified minimum accuracy figure. This implies that the rule

```
If humidity = high and windy = false and play = no
   then outlook = sunny
```

also holds, because it has the same coverage as the original rule, and its accuracy must be at least as high as the original rule's because the number of high-humidity, non-windy, non-playing days is necessarily less than that of non-windy, non-playing days—which makes the accuracy greater.

As we have seen, there are relationships between particular association rules: some rules imply others. To reduce the number of rules that are produced, in cases where several rules are related it makes sense to present only the strongest one to the user. In the above example, only the first rule should be printed.

3.5 **Rules with exceptions**

Returning to classification rules, a natural extension is to allow them to have *exceptions*. Then incremental modifications can be made to a rule set by expressing exceptions to existing rules rather than by reengineering the entire set. For example, consider the iris problem discussed earlier. Suppose a new

Table 3.1	A new iris flower.			
sepal length	sepal width	petal length	petal width	type
5.1	3.5	2.6	0.2	?

flower was found with the dimensions given in Table 3.1, and an expert declared it to be an instance of *Iris setosa*. If this flower was classified by the rules given in Chapter 1 (page 13) for this problem, it would be misclassified by two of them:

```
If petal-length ≥ 2.45 and petal-length < 4.45 then Iris-versicolor
If petal-length ≥ 2.45 and petal-length < 4.95 and
    petal-width < 1.55 then Iris-versicolor
```

These rules require modification so that the new instance can be treated correctly. However, simply changing the bounds for the attribute-value tests in these rules may not suffice because the instances used to create the rule set may then be misclassified. Fixing up a rule set is not as simple as it sounds.

Instead of changing the tests in the existing rules, an expert might be consulted to explain why the new flower violates them, giving explanations that could be used to extend the relevant rules only. For example, the first of these two rules misclassifies the new *Iris setosa* as an instance of the genus *Iris versicolor*. Instead of altering the bounds on any of the inequalities in the rule, an exception can be made based on some other attribute:

```
If petal-length ≥ 2.45 and petal-length < 4.45 then
    Iris-versicolor EXCEPT if petal-width < 1.0 then Iris-setosa
```

This rule says that a flower is *Iris versicolor* if its petal length is between 2.45 cm and 4.45 cm *except* when its petal width is less than 1.0 cm, in which case it is *Iris setosa*.

Of course, we might have exceptions to the exceptions, exceptions to these, and so on, giving the rule set something of the character of a tree. As well as being used to make incremental changes to existing rule sets, rules with exceptions can be used to represent the entire concept description in the first place.

Figure 3.4 shows a set of rules that correctly classifies all examples in the Iris dataset given earlier (page 13). These rules are quite difficult to comprehend at first. Let's follow them through. A default outcome has been chosen, *Iris setosa*, and is shown in the first line. For this dataset, the choice of default is rather arbitrary because there are 50 examples of each type. Normally, the most frequent outcome is chosen as the default.

```
Default: Iris-setosa                                             1
except if petal-length ≥ 2.45 and petal-length < 5.355          2
           and petal-width < 1.75                               3
       then Iris-versicolor                                     4
           except if petal-length ≥ 4.95 and petal-width < 1.55 5
                  then Iris-virginica                           6
                  else if sepal-length < 4.95 and sepal-width ≥ 2.45  7
                       then Iris-virginica                      8
       else if petal-length ≥ 3.35                              9
            then Iris-virginica                                 10
               except if petal-length < 4.85 and sepal-length < 5.95  11
                      then Iris-versicolor                      12
```

Figure 3.4 Rules for the Iris data.

Subsequent rules give exceptions to this default. The first if ... then, on lines 2 through 4, gives a condition that leads to the classification *Iris versicolor*. However, there are two exceptions to this rule (lines 5 through 8), which we will deal with in a moment. If the conditions on lines 2 and 3 fail, the else clause on line 9 is reached, which essentially specifies a second exception to the original default. If the condition on line 9 holds, the classification is *Iris virginica* (line 10). Again, there is an exception to this rule (on lines 11 and 12).

Now return to the exception on lines 5 through 8. This overrides the *Iris versicolor* conclusion on line 4 if either of the tests on lines 5 and 7 holds. As it happens, these two exceptions both lead to the same conclusion, *Iris virginica* (lines 6 and 8). The final exception is the one on lines 11 and 12, which overrides the *Iris virginica* conclusion on line 10 when the condition on line 11 is met, and leads to the classification *Iris versicolor*.

You will probably need to ponder these rules for some minutes before it becomes clear how they are intended to be read. Although it takes some time to get used to reading them, sorting out the excepts and if ... then ... elses becomes easier with familiarity. People often think of real problems in terms of rules, exceptions, and exceptions to the exceptions, so it is often a good way to express a complex rule set. But the main point in favor of this way of representing rules is that it scales up well. Although the whole rule set is a little hard to comprehend, each individual conclusion, each individual then statement, can be considered just in the context of the rules and exceptions that lead to it; whereas with decision lists, all prior rules need to be reviewed to determine the precise effect of an individual rule. This locality property is crucial when trying to understand large rule sets. Psychologically, people familiar with the data think of a particular set of cases, or kind of case, when looking at any one conclusion in the exception structure, and when one of these cases turns out to be an exception to the conclusion, it is easy to add an except clause to cater for it.

It is worth pointing out that the default . . . except if . . . then . . . structure is logically equivalent to an if . . . then . . . else . . . , where the else is unconditional and specifies exactly what the default did. An unconditional else is, of course, a default. (Note that there are no unconditional *elses* in the above rules.) Logically speaking, the exception-based rules can very simply be rewritten in terms of regular if . . . then . . . else clauses. What is gained by the formulation in terms of exceptions is not *logical* but *psychological*. We assume that the defaults and the tests that occur early on apply more widely than the exceptions further down. If this is indeed true for the domain, and the user can see that it is plausible, the expression in terms of (common) rules and (rare) exceptions will be easier to grasp than a different, but logically equivalent, structure.

3.6   Rules involving relations

We have assumed implicitly that the conditions in rules involve testing an attribute value against a constant. Such rules are called *propositional* because the attribute-value language used to define them has the same power as what logicians call the *propositional calculus*. In many classification tasks, propositional rules are sufficiently expressive for concise, accurate concept descriptions. The weather, contact lens recommendation, iris type, and acceptability of labor contract datasets discussed above, for example, are well described by propositional rules. However, there are situations where a more expressive form of rule would provide a more intuitive and concise concept description, and these are situations that involve relationships between examples like those we encountered in Section 2.2.

Suppose, to take a concrete example, we have the set of eight building blocks of various shapes and sizes illustrated in Figure 3.5, and we wish to learn the concept of *standing up*. This is a classic two-class problem with classes standing and lying. The four shaded blocks are positive (standing) examples of the concept, and the unshaded blocks are negative (lying) examples. The only information the learning algorithm will be given is the width, height, and number of sides of each block. The training data is shown in Table 3.2.

A propositional rule set that might be produced for this data is

```
If width ≥ 3.5 and height < 7.0 then lying
If height ≥ 3.5 then standing
```

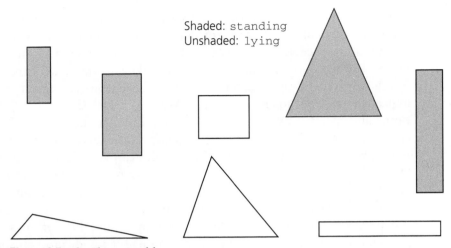

Shaded: standing
Unshaded: lying

Figure 3.5 The *shapes* problem.

Table 3.2	Training data for the *shapes* problem.		
width	height	sides	class
2	4	4	standing
3	6	4	standing
4	3	4	lying
7	8	3	standing
7	6	3	lying
2	9	4	standing
9	1	4	lying
10	2	3	lying

In case you're wondering, 3.5 is chosen as the breakpoint for width because it is halfway between the width of the thinnest lying block, namely 4, and the width of the fattest standing block whose height is less than 7, namely 3. Also, 7.0 is chosen as the breakpoint for height because it is halfway between the height of the tallest lying block, namely 6, and the shortest standing block whose width is greater than 3.5, namely 8. It is common to place numeric thresholds halfway between the values that delimit the boundaries of a concept.

Although these two rules work well on the examples given, they are not very good. Many new blocks would not be classified by either rule (for example, one with width 1 and height 2), and it is easy to devise many legitimate blocks that the rules would not fit.

A person classifying the eight blocks would probably notice that "standing blocks are those that are taller than they are wide." This rule does not compare attribute values with constants, it compares attributes with each other:

```
If width > height then lying
If height > width then standing
```

The actual values of the `height` and `width` attributes are not important, just the result of comparing the two. Rules of this form are called *relational*, because they express relationships between attributes, rather than *propositional*, which denotes a fact about just one attribute.

Standard relations include equality (and inequality) for nominal attributes, less-than and greater-than for numeric ones. Although relational nodes could be put into decision trees just as relational conditions can be put into rules, schemes that accommodate relations generally use the rule rather than the tree representation. However, most machine learning schemes do not consider relational rules, for there is a considerable cost in doing so. One way of allowing a propositional scheme to make use of relations is to add extra, secondary attributes that say whether two primary attributes are equal or not, or that give the difference between them if they are numeric. For example, we might add a binary attribute `is width < height?` to Table 3.2. Such attributes are often added as part of the data engineering process.

With a seemingly rather small further enhancement, the expressive power of the relational knowledge representation can be extended very greatly. The trick is to express rules in a way that makes the role of the instance explicit:

```
If width(block) > height(block) then lying(block)
If height(block) > width(block) then standing(block)
```

Although this does not seem like much of an extension, it is if instances can be decomposed into parts. For example, if a `tower` is a pile of blocks, one on top of the other, then the fact that the topmost block of the tower is standing can be expressed by

```
If height(tower.top) > width(tower.top) then standing(tower.top)
```

Here, `tower.top` is used to refer to the topmost block. So far, nothing has been gained. But if `tower.rest` refers to the rest of the tower, then the fact that the tower is composed *entirely* of standing blocks can be expressed by the rules:

```
If height(tower.top) > width(tower.top) and standing(tower.rest)
   then standing(tower)
```

The apparently minor addition of the condition `standing(tower.rest)` is a recursive expression that will turn out to be true only if the rest of the tower is composed of standing blocks. That will be tested by a recursive application of the same rule. Of course, it is necessary to ensure that the recursion "bottoms out" properly by adding a further rule like

```
If tower = empty then standing(tower.top)
```

With this addition, relational rules can express concepts that cannot possibly be expressed propositionally, because the recursion can take place over arbitrarily long lists of objects. Sets of rules like this are called *logic programs*, and this area of machine learning is called *inductive logic programming*. We will not be treating it further in this book.

3.7 Trees for numeric prediction

The kind of decision trees and rules that we have been looking at are designed for predicting categories rather than numeric quantities. When it comes to predicting numeric quantities, as with the CPU performance data in Table 1.5, the same kind of tree or rule representation can be used, but the leaf nodes of the tree, or the right-hand side of the rules, would contain a numeric value which is the average of all the training set values that the leaf, or rule, applies to. Because statisticians use the term *regression* for the process of computing an expression that predicts a numeric quantity, decision trees with averaged numeric values at the leaves are called *regression trees*.

Figure 3.6a shows a regression equation for the CPU performance data, and Figure 3.6b shows a regression tree. The leaves of the tree are numbers that represent the average outcome for instances that reach the leaf. The tree is much larger and more complex than the regression equation, and if we calculate the average of the absolute values of the errors between the predicted and actual CPU performance measures, it turns out to be significantly less for the tree than for the regression equation. The regression tree is more accurate because the data in this problem is not represented well by a simple linear model. However, the tree is cumbersome and difficult to interpret because of its large size.

It is possible to combine regression equations with regression trees. Figure 3.6c is a tree whose leaves contain linear expressions—that is, regression equations—rather than single predicted values. This is (slightly confusingly) called a *model tree*. To the right of Figure 3.6c are the six linear models that belong at the six leaves, labeled LM1 through LM6. The model tree approximates continuous functions by linear "patches," a more sophisticated representation than either linear regression or regression trees. Although the model tree is smaller and

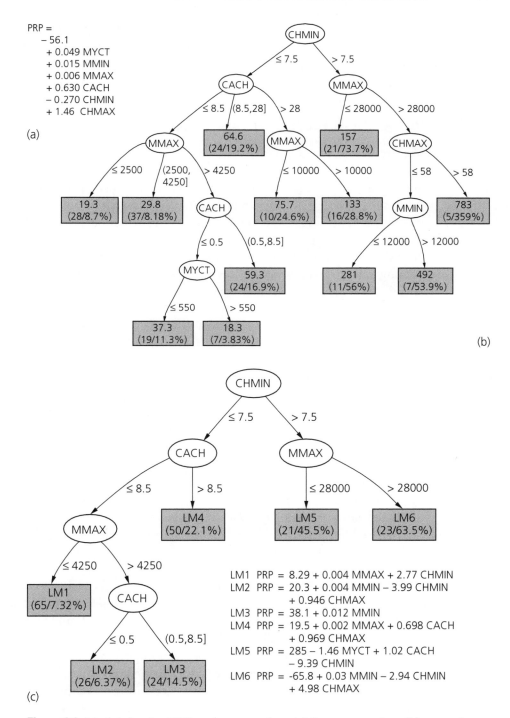

Figure 3.6 Models for the CPU performance data: (a) linear regression, (b) regression tree, and (c) model tree.

more comprehensible than the regression tree, the average error values on the training data are lower. (However, we will see in Chapter 5 that calculating the average error on the training set is not in general a good way of assessing the performance of models.)

3.8 Instance-based representation

The simplest form of learning is plain memorization, or *rote learning*. Once a set of training instances has been memorized, on encountering a new instance the memory is searched for the training instance that most strongly resembles the new one. The only problem is how to interpret "resembles": we will discuss that shortly. First, however, note that this is a completely different way of representing the "knowledge" extracted from a set of instances: just store the instances themselves and operate by relating new instances whose class is unknown to existing ones whose class is known. Instead of trying to create rules, work directly from the examples themselves. This is known as *instance-based* learning. In a sense all the other learning methods are "instance-based" too, for we always start with a set of instances as the initial training information. But the instance-based knowledge representation uses the instances themselves to represent what is learned, rather than inferring a rule set or decision tree and storing it instead.

In instance-based learning, all the real work is done when the time comes to classify a new instance, rather than when the training set is processed. In a sense, then, the difference between this method and the others that we have seen is the time at which the "learning" takes place: instance-based learning is lazy, deferring the real work as long as possible, whereas other methods are eager, producing a generalization as soon as the data has been seen. In instance-based learning, each new instance is compared with existing ones using a distance metric, and the closest existing instance is used to assign the class to the new one. This is called the *nearest-neighbor* classification method. Sometimes more than one nearest neighbor is used, and the majority class of the closest k neighbors (or the distance-weighted average, if the class is numeric) is assigned to the new instance: this is termed the *k-nearest-neighbor* method.

Computing the distance between two examples is trivial when examples have just one numeric attribute: it is just the difference between the two attribute values. It is almost as straightforward when there are several numeric attributes: generally the standard Euclidean distance is used. However, this assumes that the attributes are normalized and are of equal importance, and one of the main problems in learning is to determine which are the important features.

When nominal attributes are present, it is necessary to come up with a "distance" between different values of that attribute. What are the distances between, say, the values red, green, and blue? Usually a distance of 0 is assigned if the values are identical, otherwise the distance is 1. Thus the distance between red and red is 0 but that between red and green is 1. However, it may be desirable to use a more sophisticated representation of the attributes. For example, with more colors one could use a numeric measure of hue in color space, making yellow closer to orange than it is to green, and ocher closer still.

Some attributes will be more important than others, and this is usually reflected in the distance metric by some kind of attribute weighting. Deriving suitable attribute weights from the training set is a key problem in instance-based learning.

It may not be necessary, or desirable, to store *all* the training instances. For one thing, this may make the nearest neighbor calculation unbearably slow. For another, it may consume unrealistic amounts of storage. Generally some regions of attribute space are more stable with regard to class than others, and just a few exemplars are needed inside stable regions. For example, you might expect the required density of exemplars that lie well inside class boundaries to be much less than the density that is needed near class boundaries. Deciding which instances to save and which to discard is another key problem in instance-based learning.

An apparent drawback to instance-based representations is that they do not make explicit the structures that are learned. In a sense this violates the notion of "learning" that we presented at the beginning of this book; instances do not really "describe" the patterns in data. However, the instances combine with the distance metric to carve out boundaries in instance space that distinguish one class from another, and this is a kind of explicit representation of knowledge. For example, given a single instance of each of two classes, the nearest-neighbor rule effectively splits the instance space along the perpendicular bisector of the line joining the instances. Given several instances of each class, the space is divided by a set of lines that represent the perpendicular bisectors of selected lines joining an instance of one class to one of another class. Figure 3.7a illustrates a nine-sided polygon that separates the filled-circle class from the open-circle class. This polygon is implicit in the operation of the nearest-neighbor rule.

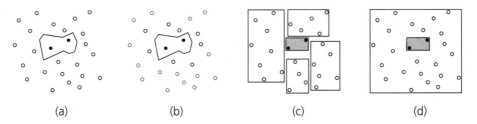

(a)   (b)   (c)   (d)

Figure 3.7 Different ways of partitioning the instance space.

When training instances are discarded, the result is to save just a few proto-typical examples of each class. Figure 3.7b shows only the examples that actually get used in nearest-neighbor decisions: the others (the light gray ones) can be discarded without affecting the result. These prototypical examples serve as a kind of explicit knowledge representation.

Some instance-based representations go further and explicitly generalize the instances. Typically this is accomplished by creating rectangular regions that enclose examples of the same class. Figure 3.7c shows the rectangular regions that might be produced. Unknown examples that fall within one of the rectangles will be assigned the corresponding class; ones that fall outside all rectangles will be subject to the usual nearest-neighbor rule. Of course this produces different decision boundaries from the straightforward nearest-neighbor rule, as can be seen by superimposing the polygon in Figure 3.7a onto the rectangles: any part of the polygon that lies within a rectangle will be chopped off and replaced by the rectangle's boundary.

Rectangular generalizations in instance space are just like rules with a special form of condition, one that tests a numeric variable against an upper and lower bound and selects the region in between. Different dimensions of the rectangle correspond to tests on different attributes being ANDed together. Choosing snugly fitting rectangular regions as tests leads to much more conservative rules than those generally produced by rule-based machine learning schemes, because for each boundary of the region, there is an actual instance that lies on (or just inside) that boundary, whereas tests like $x < a$ (where x is an attribute value and a is a constant) encompass an entire half plane—they apply no matter how small x is, so long as it is less than a. When doing rectangular generalization in instance space, you can afford to be conservative because if a new example is encountered that lies outside all regions, you can fall back on the nearest-neigh-bor metric, whereas with rule-based methods the example cannot be classified, or receives just a default classification, if no rules apply to it. And the advantage of more conservative rules is that, although incomplete, they may be more per-spicuous than a complete set of rules that covers all cases. Finally, ensuring that the regions do not overlap is tantamount to ensuring that at most one rule can apply to an example, eliminating another of the difficulties of rule-based sys-tems—what to do when several rules apply.

A more complex kind of generalization is to permit rectangular regions to nest one within another. Then a region that is basically all one class can contain an inner region of a different class, as illustrated in Figure 3.7d. It is possible to allow nesting within nesting, so that the inner region can itself contain its own inner region of a different class—perhaps the original class of the outer region. This is analogous to allowing rules to have exceptions, and exceptions to the exceptions, as in Section 3.5.

It is worth pointing out a slight danger to the technique of visualizing instance-based learning in terms of boundaries in example space: it makes the implicit assumption that attributes are numeric rather than nominal. If the various values that a nominal attribute can take on were laid out along a line, generalizations involving a segment of that line would make no sense: each test involves either one value for the attribute, or all values for it (or perhaps an arbitrary subset of values). Although you can more or less easily imagine extending the examples in Figure 3.7 to several dimensions, it is much harder to imagine how rules involving nominal attributes will look in multidimensional instance space. Many machine learning situations involve a large number of attributes, and our intuitions tend to lead us astray when extended to high-dimensional spaces.

3.9 Clusters

When clusters rather than a classifier is learned, the output takes the form of a diagram that shows how the instances fall into clusters. In the simplest case this involves associating a cluster number with each instance, which might be depicted by laying the instances out in two dimensions and partitioning the space to show each cluster, as illustrated in Figure 3.8a.

Some clustering algorithms allow one instance to belong to more than one cluster, so the diagram might lay the instances out in two dimensions and draw overlapping subsets representing each cluster—a Venn diagram. Some algorithms associate instances with clusters probabilistically rather than categorically. In this case, for every instance there is a probability or degree of member-

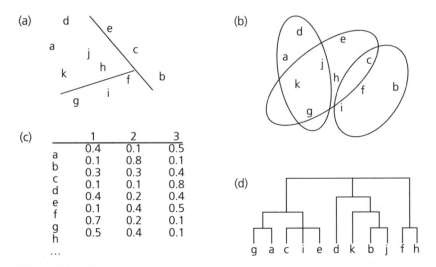

Figure 3.8 Different ways of representing clusters.

ship with which it belongs to each of the clusters. This is shown in Figure 3.8c. This particular association is meant to be a probabilistic one, so the numbers for each example sum to 1—though that is not always the case. Other algorithms produce a hierarchical structure of clusters, so that at the top level the instance space divides into just a few clusters, each of which divides into its own subclusters at the next level down, and so on. In this case a diagram like the one in Figure 3.8d is used, in which elements joined together at lower levels are more tightly clustered than ones joined together at higher levels. Diagrams like this are called *dendrograms*. This term means just the same thing as *tree diagrams* (the Greek word *dendron* means a tree), but in clustering the more exotic version seems to be preferred—perhaps because biological species are a prime application area for clustering techniques, and ancient languages are often used for naming in biology.

Clustering is often followed by a stage where a decision tree or rule set is inferred that allocates each instance to the cluster in which it belongs. Then, the clustering operation is just one step on the way to a structural description.

3.10 Further reading

Knowledge representation is a key topic in classical artificial intelligence and is well represented by a comprehensive series of papers edited by Brachman and Levesque (1985). However, these are about ways of representing hand-crafted, not learned knowledge, and the kind of representations that can be learned from examples are quite rudimentary in comparison. In particular, the shortcomings of propositional rules, which in logic are referred to as the *propositional calculus,* and the extra expressive power of relational rules, or the predicate calculus, is well described in introductions to logic such as that in Chapter 2 of Genesereth and Nilsson (1987).

We mentioned the problem of dealing with conflict between different rules. Various ways of doing this, called *conflict resolution strategies,* have been developed for use with rule-based programming systems. These are described in books on rule-based programming, such as Brownstown et al. (1985). Again, however, they are designed for use with hand-crafted rule sets rather than ones that have been learned. The use of rules with exceptions for a large hand-crafted dataset has been studied by Gaines and Compton (1995), and Richards and Compton (1998) discuss their role as an alternative to classic knowledge engineering.

Further information on the various styles of concept representation can be found in the papers that describe machine learning methods of inferring concepts from examples, and these are covered in the *Further reading* sections of Chapter 4 and the *Discussion* sections of Chapter 6.

chapter four

Algorithms: The basic methods

Now that we've seen how the inputs and outputs can be represented, it's time to look at the learning algorithms themselves. This chapter explains the basic ideas behind the techniques that are used in practical data mining. We will not delve too deeply into the trickier issues—advanced algorithms, optimizations that are possible, complications that arise in practice, details of how efficiency concerns can be addressed. These topics are deferred to Chapter 6, where we come to grips with real implementations of machine learning schemes like the ones included in data mining toolkits and used for real-world applications. It is important to understand these more advanced issues, so that you know what is really going on when you analyze a particular dataset.

In this chapter we look at the basic ideas. One of the most instructive lessons is that simple ideas often work very well, and we strongly recommend the adoption of a "simplicity-first" methodology when analyzing practical datasets. There are many different kinds of simple structure that datasets can exhibit. In one dataset, there might be a single attribute that does all the work, the others being irrelevant or redundant. In another dataset, the attributes might contribute independently and in equal measure to the final outcome. A third might have a simple logical structure, involving just a few attributes, which can be captured by a decision tree. In a fourth, there may be a few independent rules that govern the assignment of instances to different classes. A fifth might exhibit dependencies between different subsets of attributes. A sixth might involve linear dependence between numeric attributes, where what matters is a weighted sum of attribute values with appropriately chosen weights. And in a seventh, the classifications appropriate to particular regions of instance space might be governed by the distances between the instances themselves.

In the infinite variety of possible datasets there are many different *kinds* of structure that can occur, and a data mining tool—no matter how capable—that is looking for one class of structure may completely miss regularities of a different kind, regardless of how rudimentary those may be. The result: a baroque and opaque classification structure of one kind instead of a simple, elegant, immediately comprehensible structure of another.

Each of the seven examples of different kinds of datasets sketched above leads to a different machine learning scheme that is well suited to discovering it. The sections of this chapter look at each of these structures in turn.

4.1 Inferring rudimentary rules

Here's an easy way to find very simple classification rules from a set of instances. Called *1R* for "1-rule," it generates a one-level decision tree, which is expressed in the form of a set of rules that all test one particular attribute. 1R is a simple, cheap method that often comes up with quite good rules for characterizing the structure in data. It turns out that simple rules frequently achieve surprisingly high accuracy. Perhaps this is because the structure underlying many real-world datasets is quite rudimentary, and just one attribute is sufficient to determine the class of an instance quite accurately. In any event, it is always a good plan to try the simplest things first.

The idea is this: We make rules that test a single attribute and branch accordingly. Each branch corresponds to a different value of the attribute. It is obvious which is the best classification to give each branch: use the class that occurs most often in the training data. Then the error rate of the rules can easily be determined: just count the errors that occur on the training data, that is, the number of instances that do not have the majority class.

Each attribute generates a different set of rules, one rule for every value of the attribute. Evaluate the error rate for each attribute's rule set and choose the best. It's that simple. Figure 4.1 shows the algorithm in the form of pseudo-code.

To see the 1R method at work, consider the weather data of Table 1.2 (we will encounter it many times again when looking at how learning algorithms work).

```
For each attribute,
   For each value of that attribute, make a rule as follows:
      count how often each class appears
      find the most frequent class
      make the rule assign that class to this attribute-value.
   Calculate the error rate of the rules.
Choose the rules with the smallest error rate.
```

Figure 4.1 Pseudo-code for 1R.

To classify on the final column, `play`, 1R considers four sets of rules, one for each attribute. These rules are shown in Table 4.1. An asterisk indicates that a random choice has been made between two equally likely outcomes. The number of errors is given for each rule, along with the total number of errors for the rule set as a whole. 1R chooses the attribute that produces rules with the smallest number of errors—that is, the first and third rule sets. Arbitrarily breaking the tie between these two rule sets gives the following:

```
outlook: sunny    → no
         overcast → yes
         rainy    → yes
```

We said at the outset that the game for the weather data is unspecified. Oddly enough, it is apparently played when it is overcast or rainy but not when it is sunny. Perhaps it's an indoor pursuit.

Table 4.1   Evaluating the attributes in the weather data.

	attribute	rules	errors	total errors
1	outlook	sunny → no	2/5	4/14
		overcast → yes	0/4	
		rainy → yes	2/5	
2	temperature	hot → no*	2/4	5/14
		mild → yes	2/6	
		cool → yes	1/4	
3	humidity	high → no	3/7	4/14
		normal → yes	1/7	
4	windy	false → yes	2/8	5/14
		true → no*	3/6	

Missing values and numeric attributes

Although a very rudimentary learning scheme, 1R does accommodate both missing values and numeric attributes. It deals with these in simple but effective ways. Missing is treated as just another attribute value so that, for example, if the weather data had contained missing values for the outlook attribute, a rule set formed on outlook would specify four possible class values, one for each of sunny, overcast, rainy, and a fourth for missing.

Numeric attributes are converted into nominal ones using a simple discretization scheme. First, the training examples are sorted according to the values of the numeric attribute. This produces a sequence of class values. For example, sorting the numeric version of the weather data (Table 1.3) according to the values of temperature produces the sequence

64	65	68	69	70	71	72	72	75	75	80	81	83	85
yes	no	yes	yes	yes	no	no	yes	yes	yes	no	yes	yes	no

Discretization involves partitioning this sequence by placing breakpoints in it. One possibility is to place breakpoints wherever the class changes, producing eight categories:

yes | no | yes yes yes | no no | yes yes yes | no | yes yes | no

Choosing breakpoints halfway between the examples on either side places them at 64.5, 66.5, 70.5, 72, 77.5, 80.5, and 84. However, the two instances with value 72 cause a problem because they have the same value of temperature but fall into different classes. The simplest fix is to move the breakpoint at 72 up one example, to 73.5, producing a mixed partition in which *no* is the majority class.

A more serious problem is that this procedure tends to form a large number of categories. The 1R method will naturally gravitate toward choosing an attribute that splits into many categories, because this will partition the dataset into many classes, making it more likely that instances will have the same class as the majority in their partition. In fact, the limiting case is an attribute that has a different value for each instance—that is, an identification code attribute that pinpoints instances uniquely—and this will yield a zero error rate on the training set because each partition contains just one instance. Of course, highly branching attributes do not usually perform well on test examples; indeed the identification code attribute will never get any examples outside the training set correct. This phenomenon is known as *overfitting;* we have already discussed overfitting-avoidance bias in Chapter 1 (page 32), and we will encounter this problem again and again in subsequent chapters.

For 1R, overfitting is likely to occur whenever an attribute has a large number of possible values. Consequently, when discretizing a numeric attribute, a rule is adopted that dictates a minimum number of examples of the majority class in each partition. Suppose that minimum is set at three. This eliminates all but two of the above partitions. Instead, the partitioning process begins

```
yes no yes yes | yes …
```

ensuring that there are three occurrences of yes, the majority class, in the first partition. However, since the next example is also yes, nothing is lost by including that in the first partition too. This leads to a new division

```
yes no yes yes yes | no no yes yes yes | no yes yes no
```

where each partition contains at least three instances of the majority class, except the last one, which will usually have less. Partition boundaries always fall between examples of different classes.

Whenever adjacent partitions have the same majority class, as do the first two partitions above, they can be merged together without affecting the meaning of the rule sets. Thus the final discretization is

```
yes no yes yes yes no no yes yes yes | no yes yes no
```

which leads to the rule set

```
temperature: ≤ 77.5 → yes
             > 77.5 → no
```

The second rule involved an arbitrary choice; as it happens, no was chosen. If yes had been chosen instead, there would have been no need for any breakpoint at all—and as this example illustrates, it might have been better to use the adjacent categories to help with tie-breaking. In fact this rule generates five errors on the training set, and so is less effective than the above rule for outlook. However, the same procedure leads to this rule for humidity:

```
humidity: ≤ 82.5 → yes
          > 82.5 and ≤ 95.5 → no
          > 95.5 → yes
```

This generates only three errors on the training set and is the best "1-rule" for the data in Table 1.3.

Finally, if a numeric attribute has missing values, an additional category is created for them, and the above discretization procedure is applied just to the instances for which the attribute's value is defined.

Discussion

In a seminal paper entitled "Very simple classification rules perform well on most commonly used datasets" (Holte 1993), a comprehensive study of the performance of the 1R procedure was reported on sixteen datasets frequently used by machine learning researchers to evaluate their algorithms. *Cross-validation,* an evaluation technique that will be explained in Chapter 5, was used throughout to ensure that the results were representative of what would be obtained on independent test sets. After some experimentation, the minimum number of examples in each partition of a numeric attribute was set at six, not three as used for illustration above.

Surprisingly, despite its simplicity 1R did astonishingly—even embarrassingly—well in comparison with state-of-the-art learning schemes, and the rules it produced turned out to be just a few percentage points less accurate, on almost all of the datasets, than the decision trees produced by a state-of-the-art decision tree induction scheme. These trees were, in general, considerably larger than 1R's rules. Rules that test a single attribute are often a viable alternative to more complex structures, and this strongly encourages a "simplicity-first" methodology in which the baseline performance is established using simple, rudimentary techniques before progressing to more sophisticated learning schemes, which inevitably generate output that is harder for people to interpret.

4.2 Statistical modeling

The 1R method uses a single attribute as the basis for its decisions and chooses the one that works best. Another simple technique is to use all attributes and allow them to make contributions to the decision that are *equally important* and *independent* of one another, given the class. This is unrealistic, of course: what makes real-life datasets interesting is that the attributes are certainly not equally important, nor are they independent of one another. But it leads to a simple scheme that again works surprisingly well in practice.

Table 4.2 shows a summary of the weather data obtained by counting how many times each attribute-value pair occurs with each value (yes and no) for

Table 4.2		**The weather data, with counts and probabilities.**										
outlook			temperature			humidity			windy			play
	yes	*no*		*yes*	*no*		*yes*	*no*		*yes*	*no*	*yes*	*no*
sunny	2	3	hot	2	2	high	3	4	false	6	2	9	5
overcast	4	0	mild	4	2	normal	6	1	true	3	3		
rainy	3	2	cool	3	1								
sunny	2/9	3/5	hot	2/9	2/5	high	3/9	4/5	false	6/9	2/5	9/14	5/14
overcast	4/9	0/5	mild	4/9	2/5	normal	6/9	1/5	true	3/9	3/5		
rainy	3/9	2/5	cool	3/9	1/5								

Table 4.3	A new day.			
outlook	temperature	humidity	windy	play
sunny	cool	high	true	?

play. For example, you can see from Table 1.2 that outlook is sunny for five examples, two of which have play = yes and three having play = no. The cells in the first row of the new table simply count these occurrences for all possible values of each attribute, and the play figure in the final column counts the total number of occurrences of yes and no. In the lower part of the table, the same information is rewritten in the form of fractions, or observed probabilities. For example, of the nine days that play is yes, outlook is sunny for two, yielding a fraction of 2/9. For play the fractions are different: they are the proportion of days that play is yes and no respectively.

Now suppose we encounter a new example with the values in Table 4.3. We treat the five features in Table 4.2—outlook, temperature, humidity, windy, and the overall likelihood that play is yes or no—as equally important, independent pieces of evidence, and multiply the corresponding fractions. Looking at the outcome yes gives

likelihood of yes = 2/9 × 3/9 × 3/9 × 3/9 × 9/14 = 0.0053.

The fractions are taken from the yes entries in the table according to the values of the attributes for the new day, and the final 9/14 is the overall fraction representing the proportion of days on which play is yes. A similar calculation for the outcome no leads to

likelihood of no = 3/5 × 1/5 × 4/5 × 3/5 × 5/14 = 0.0206.

This indicates that for the new day, no is more likely than yes—four times more likely. The numbers can be turned into probabilities by normalizing them so that they sum to 1:

$$\text{probability of yes} = \frac{0.0053}{0.0053 + 0.0206} = 20.5\%,$$

$$\text{probability of no} = \frac{0.0206}{0.0053 + 0.0206} = 79.5\%.$$

This simple and intuitive method is based on Bayes's rule of conditional probability. Bayes's rule says that if you have a hypothesis H, and evidence E which bears on that hypothesis, then

$$\Pr[H|E] = \frac{\Pr[E|H]\,\Pr[H]}{\Pr[E]}.$$

We use the notation that $\Pr[A]$ denotes the probability of an event A, and $\Pr[A|B]$ denotes the probability of A conditional on another event B. The hypothesis H is that play will be, let's say, yes, and $\Pr[H|E]$ is going to turn out to be 20.5%, just as above. The evidence E is the particular combination of attribute values for the new day, outlook = sunny, temperature = cool, humidity = high, windy = true. Let's call these four pieces of evidence E_1, E_2, E_3, and E_4, respectively. Assuming that these pieces of evidence are independent (given the class), their combined probability is obtained by multiplying the probabilities, so

$$\Pr[yes|E] = \frac{\Pr[E_1|yes] \times \Pr[E_2|yes] \times \Pr[E_3|yes] \times \Pr[E_4|yes] \times \Pr[yes]}{\Pr[E]}.$$

Don't worry about the denominator: we will ignore it, and eliminate it in the final normalizing step when we make the probabilities of yes and no sum to 1, just as we did above. The $\Pr[yes]$ at the end is the probability of a yes outcome without knowing any of the evidence E, that is, without knowing anything about the particular day we're talking about—it's called the *prior probability* of the hypothesis H. In our case, it's just 9/14, since 9 of the 14 training examples had a yes value for play. Substituting the fractions in Table 4.2 for the appropriate evidence probabilities leads to

$$\Pr[yes|E] = \frac{2/9 \times 3/9 \times 3/9 \times 3/9 \times 9/14}{\Pr[E]},$$

just as we calculated above. Again, the $\Pr[E]$ in the denominator will disappear when we normalize.

This method goes by the name of *Naive Bayes,* because it's based on Bayes's rule and "naively" assumes independence—it is only valid to multiply probabilities when the events are independent. The assumption that attributes are independent (given the class) in real life certainly is a simplistic one. But despite the disparaging name, Naive Bayes works very well when tested on actual datasets, particularly when combined with some of the attribute selection procedures introduced in Chapter 7 that serve to eliminate redundant, and hence non-independent, attributes.

One thing that can go wrong with Naive Bayes is that if a particular attribute value does not occur in the training set in conjunction with *every* class value, things go badly awry. Suppose in the example that the training data was different and the attribute value outlook = sunny had always been associated with the outcome no. Then the probability of a yes given outlook = sunny, that is, $\Pr[yes|outlook = sunny]$, would be zero, and since the other probabilities are multiplied by this, the final probability of yes would be zero no matter how large they were. Probabilities that are zero hold a veto over the other ones. This is not a good idea. But the bug is easily fixed by minor adjustments to the method of calculating probabilities from frequencies.

For example, the upper part of Table 4.2 shows that for play = yes, outlook is sunny for two examples, overcast for four, and rainy for three, and the lower part gives these events probabilities of 2/9, 4/9, and 3/9 respectively. Instead we could add 1 to each numerator, and compensate by adding 3 to the denominator, giving probabilities of 3/12, 5/12, and 4/12 respectively. This will ensure that an attribute value that occurs zero times receives a probability which is nonzero, albeit small. The strategy of adding 1 to each count is a standard technique called the *Laplace estimator* after the great eighteenth-century French mathematician Pierre Laplace. Although it works well in practice, there is no particular reason for adding 1 to the counts: we could instead choose a small constant μ and use

$$\frac{2 + \mu/3}{9 + \mu}, \frac{4 + \mu/3}{9 + \mu}, \text{ and } \frac{3 + \mu/3}{9 + \mu}.$$

The value of μ, which was set to 3 above, effectively provides a weight that determines how influential the a priori values of 1/3, 1/3, and 1/3 are for each of the three possible attribute values: a large μ says that these priors are very important compared with the new evidence coming in from the training set, whereas a small one gives them less influence. Finally, there is no particular reason for dividing μ into three *equal* parts in the numerators: we could use

$$\frac{2 + \mu p_1}{9 + \mu}, \frac{4 + \mu p_2}{9 + \mu}, \text{ and } \frac{3 + \mu p_3}{9 + \mu}$$

instead, where p_1, p_2, and p_3 sum to 1. Effectively, these three numbers are a priori probabilities of the values of the outlook attribute being sunny, overcast, and rainy respectively.

This is now a fully Bayesian formulation where prior probabilities have been assigned to everything in sight. It has the advantage of being completely rigorous, but the disadvantage that it is not usually clear just how these prior probabilities should be assigned. In practice, the prior probabilities make little difference provided there are a reasonable number of training instances, and people generally just estimate frequencies using the Laplace estimator by initializing all counts to 1 instead of to 0.

Missing values and numeric attributes

One of the really nice things about the Bayesian formulation is that missing values are no problem at all. For example, if the value of outlook were missing in the example of Table 4.3 above, the calculation would simply omit this attribute, yielding

likelihood of yes = 3/9 × 3/9 × 3/9 × 9/14 = 0.0238,
likelihood of no = 1/5 × 4/5 × 3/5 × 5/14 = 0.0343.

These two numbers are individually a lot higher than they were before, because one of the fractions is missing. But that's not a problem because a fraction is missing in both cases, and these likelihoods are subject to a further normalization process. This yields probabilities of yes and no of 41% and 59% respectively.

If a value is missing in a training instance, it is simply not included in the frequency counts, and the probability ratios are based on the number of values that actually occur rather than on the total number of instances.

Numeric values are usually handled by assuming that they have a "normal" or "Gaussian" probability distribution. Table 4.4 gives a summary of the weather data with numeric features from Table 1.3. For nominal attributes, counts are calculated as before, while for numeric ones the values that occur are simply listed. Then, whereas the counts for the nominal attributes are normalized into probabilities, the mean and standard deviation are calculated for each class and each numeric attribute. Thus the mean value of temperature over the yes instances is 73, and its standard deviation is 6.2. The mean is simply the

Table 4.4		The numeric weather data with summary statistics.							
outlook		**temperature**		**humidity**		**windy**			**play**
yes	no	yes	no	yes	no		yes	no	yes	no
sunny	2	3	83	85	86	85	false	6	2	9	5
overcast	4	0	70	80	96	90	true	3	3	
rainy	3	2	68	65	80	70				
			64	72	65	95				
			69	71	70	91				
			75		80					
			75		70					
			72		90					
			81		75					
sunny	2/9	3/5	*mean* 73	74.6	*mean* 79.1	86.2	false	6/9	2/5	9/14	5/14
overcast	4/9	0/5	*std dev* 6.2	7.9	*std dev* 10.2	9.7	true	3/9	3/5	
rainy	3/9	2/5								

average of the values above, that is, the sum divided by the number of values. The standard deviation is the square root of the sample variance, which is calculated as follows: subtract the mean from each value, square the result, sum them together, and then divide by *one less than* the number of values. This is the standard way of calculating mean and standard deviation of a set of numbers (the "one less than" has to do with the number of degrees of freedom in the sample, a statistical notion that we don't want to get into here).

The probability density function for a normal distribution with mean μ and standard deviation σ is given by the rather formidable expression

$$f(x) \ = \ \frac{1}{\sqrt{2\pi}\sigma} e^{-\frac{(x-\mu)^2}{2\sigma^2}}.$$

But fear not! All this means is that if we are considering a yes outcome when temperature has value, say, 66, we just need to plug $x = 66$, $\mu = 73$, and $\sigma = 6.2$ into the formula. So the value of the probability density function is

$$f(temperature = 66 \mid yes) \ = \ \frac{1}{\sqrt{2\pi} \cdot 6.2} e^{-\frac{(66-73)^2}{2 \cdot 6.2^2}} \ = \ 0.0340.$$

And by the same token, the probability density of a yes outcome when humidity has value, say, 90, is calculated in the same way to be

$$f(humidity = 90 \mid yes) = 0.0221.$$

The probability density function for an event is very closely related to its probability. However, it is not quite the same thing. If temperature is a continuous scale, the probability of the temperature being *exactly* 66—or *exactly* any other value, like 63.14159262, is zero. The real meaning of the density function $f(x)$ is that the probability that the quantity lies within a small region around x, say between $x - \varepsilon/2$ and $x + \varepsilon/2$, is $\varepsilon \cdot f(x)$. What we have written above is correct if temperature is measured to the nearest degree and humidity is measured to the nearest percentage point. You might think we ought to factor in the accuracy figure ε when using these probabilities; but that's not necessary. The same ε would appear in both the yes and no likelihoods below and cancel out when the probabilities were calculated.

Using these probabilities for the new day in Table 4.5 yields

likelihood of yes $= 2/9 \times 0.0340 \times 0.0221 \times 3/9 \times 9/14 = 0.000036,$
likelihood of no $\ = 3/5 \times 0.0291 \times 0.0380 \times 3/5 \times 5/14 = 0.000136;$

which leads to probabilities

$$\text{Probability of yes} = \frac{0.000036}{0.000036 + 0.000136} = 20.9\%,$$

$$\text{Probability of } no = \frac{0.000136}{0.000036 + 0.000136} = 79.1\%.$$

These figures are very close to the probabilities calculated earlier for the new day in Table 4.3, because the `temperature` and `humidity` values of 66 and 90 yield similar probabilities to the `cool` and `high` values that we used before.

The normal-distribution assumption makes it easy to extend the Naive Bayes classifier to deal with numeric attributes. If the values of any numeric attributes are missing, the mean and standard deviation calculations are based on just the ones that are present.

Table 4.5	Another new day.			
outlook	temperature	humidity	windy	play
sunny	66	90	true	?

Discussion

Naive Bayes gives a simple approach, with clear semantics, to representing, using, and learning probabilistic knowledge. And impressive results can be achieved using it. It has many times been shown that Naive Bayes rivals, and indeed outperforms, more sophisticated classifiers on many datasets. The moral is, always try the simple things first. Over and over again in machine learning people have eventually, after an extended struggle, managed to obtain good results using sophisticated learning schemes, only to discover years later that simple methods like 1R and Naive Bayes do just as well—or even better.

There are many datasets for which Naive Bayes does not do so well, however, and it is easy to see why. Since attributes are treated as though they were completely independent, the addition of redundant ones skews the learning process. As an extreme example, if you were to include a new attribute with the same values as `temperature` to the weather data, the effect of the `temperature` attribute would be multiplied: all of its probabilities would be squared, giving it a great deal more influence on the decision. If you were to add ten such attributes, then the decisions would effectively be made on `temperature` alone. Dependencies between attributes inevitably reduce the power of Naive Bayes to discern what is going on. They can, however, be ameliorated by using a subset of the attributes in the decision procedure, making a careful selection of which ones to use. Chapter 7 shows how.

The normal-distribution assumption for numeric attributes is another restriction on Naive Bayes as we have formulated it here. Many features simply aren't normally distributed. However, there is nothing to prevent us from using other distributions for the numeric attributes: there is nothing magic about the normal distribution. If you know that a particular attribute is likely to follow some other distribution, standard estimation procedures for that distribution can be used instead. If you suspect it isn't normal but don't know the actual distribution, there are procedures for "kernel density estimation" that do not assume any particular distribution for the attribute values. Another possibility is simply to discretize the data first.

4.3 Divide and conquer: Constructing decision trees

The problem of constructing a decision tree can be expressed recursively. First, select an attribute to place at the root node and make one branch for each possible value. This splits up the example set into subsets, one for every value of the attribute. Now the process can be repeated recursively for each branch, using only those instances that actually reach the branch. If at any time all instances at a node have the same classification, stop developing that part of the tree.

The only thing left to decide is how to determine which attribute to split on, given a set of examples with different classes. Consider (again!) the weather data. There are four possibilities for each split, and at the top level they produce trees like those in Figure 4.2. Which is the best choice? The number of yes and no classes are shown at the leaves. Any leaf with only one class—yes or no—will not have to be split further, and the recursive process down that branch will terminate. Since we seek small trees, we would like this to happen as soon as possible. If we had a measure of the purity of each node, we could choose the attribute that produces the purest daughter nodes. Take a moment to look at Figure 4.2 and ponder which attribute you think is the best choice.

The measure of purity that we will use is called the *information* and is measured in units called *bits*. Associated with a node of the tree, it represents the expected amount of information that would be needed to specify whether a new instance should be classified yes or no, given that the example reached that node. Unlike the "bits" in computer memories, the expected amount of information usually involves fractions of a bit—and is often less than one! It is calculated based on the number of yes and no classes at the node; we will look at the details of the calculation shortly. But first let's see how it's used. When evaluating the first tree in Figure 4.2, the numbers of yes and no classes at the leaf nodes are [2, 3], [4, 0], and [3, 2] respectively, and the information values of these nodes are

$$\text{info}([2, 3]) = 0.971 \text{ bits}$$
$$\text{info}([4, 0]) = 0.0 \text{ bits}$$
$$\text{info}([3, 2]) = 0.971 \text{ bits}$$

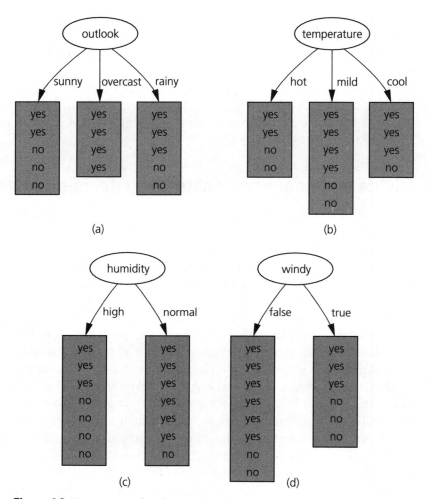

Figure 4.2 Tree stumps for the weather data.

We calculate the average information value of these, taking into account the number of instances that go down each branch; five down the first and third and four down the second:

$$\text{info}([2,3], [4,0], [3,2]) = (5/14) \times 0.971 + (4/14) \times 0 + (5/14) \times 0.971$$
$$= 0.693 \text{ bits.}$$

This average represents the amount of information that we expect would be necessary to specify the class of a new instance, given the tree structure in Figure 4.2a.

Now before any of the nascent tree structures in Figure 4.2 were created, the training examples at the root comprised nine yes and five no nodes, corresponding to an information value of

$$\text{info}([9, 5]) = 0.940 \text{ bits.}$$

Thus the tree in Figure 4.2a is responsible for an information gain of

$$\text{gain}(\texttt{outlook}) = \text{info}([9, 5]) - \text{info}([2, 3], [4, 0], [3, 2]) = 0.940 - 0.693$$
$$= 0.247 \text{ bits,}$$

which can be interpreted as the informational value of creating a branch on the outlook attribute.

The way forward is clear. We calculate the information gain for each attribute and choose the one that gains the most information to split on. In the situation of Figure 4.2,

$$\text{gain}(\texttt{outlook}) \quad\ = 0.247 \text{ bits}$$
$$\text{gain}(\texttt{temperature}) = 0.029 \text{ bits}$$
$$\text{gain}(\texttt{humidity}) \quad = 0.152 \text{ bits}$$
$$\text{gain}(\texttt{windy}) \quad\quad\ = 0.048 \text{ bits,}$$

so we select outlook as the splitting attribute at the root of the tree. Hopefully this accords with your intuition as the best one to select. It is the only choice for which one daughter node is completely pure, and this gives it a considerable advantage over the other attributes. Humidity is the next best choice, for it produces a larger daughter node that is almost completely pure.

Then we continue, recursively. Figure 4.3 shows the possibilities for a further branch at the node reached when outlook is sunny. Clearly, a further split on outlook will produce nothing new, so only the other three attributes are considered. The information gain for each turns out to be

$$\text{gain}(\texttt{temperature}) = 0.571 \text{ bits}$$
$$\text{gain}(\texttt{humidity}) \quad = 0.971 \text{ bits}$$
$$\text{gain}(\texttt{windy}) \quad\quad\ = 0.020 \text{ bits,}$$

so we select humidity as the splitting attribute at this point. There is no need to split these nodes any further, so this branch is finished.

Continued application of the same idea leads to the decision tree of Figure 4.4 for the weather data. Ideally the process terminates when all leaf nodes are pure, that is, when they contain instances that all have the same classification. However, it might not be possible to reach this happy situation, for there is nothing to stop the training set from containing two examples with identical sets of attributes but different classes. Consequently we stop when the data can't be split any further.

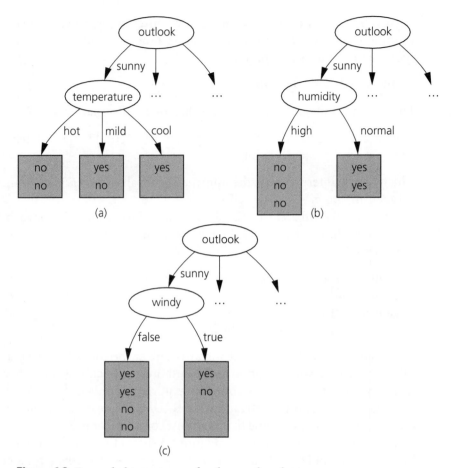

(a)

(b)

(c)

Figure 4.3 Expanded tree stumps for the weather data.

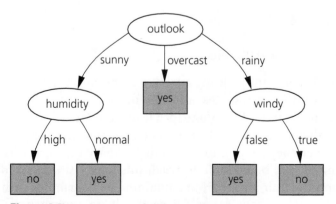

Figure 4.4 Decision tree for the weather data.

Calculating information

Now we will discuss how to calculate the information measure that is used as the basis for evaluating different splits. We describe the basic idea in this section, then in the next we examine a correction that is usually made to counter a bias toward selecting splits on attributes with large numbers of possible values.

Before examining the detailed formula for calculating the amount of information required to specify the class of an example given that it reaches a tree node with a certain number of yeses and nos, consider first the kind of properties we would expect this quantity to have:

- when the number of either yeses or nos is zero, the information is zero
- when the number of yeses and nos is equal, the information reaches a maximum

Moreover, the measure should be applicable to multiclass situations, not just to two-class ones.

The information measure relates to the amount of information obtained by making a decision, and a more subtle property of information can be derived by considering the nature of decisions. Decisions can be made in a single stage, or they can be made in several stages, and the amount of information involved is the same in both cases. For example, the decision involved in

$$\text{info}([2, 3, 4])$$

can be made in two stages. First decide whether it's the first case or one of the other two cases,

$$\text{info}([2, 7])$$

and then decide which of the other two cases it is:

$$\text{info}([3, 4])$$

In some cases the second decision will not need to be made, namely where the decision turns out to be the first one. Taking this into account leads to the equation

$$\text{info}([2, 3, 4]) = \text{info}([2, 7]) + (7/9) \times \text{info}([3, 4]).$$

Of course, there is nothing special about these particular numbers, and a similar relationship must hold regardless of the actual values. Thus we can add a further criterion to the list above:

- must obey the multistage property illustrated above

Remarkably, it turns out that there is only one function that satisfies all these properties, and it is known as the *information value* or *entropy*:

$$\text{entropy}\,(p_1, p_2, \ldots, p_n) \;=\; -p_1 \log p_1 - p_2 \log p_2 \ldots - p_n \log p_n.$$

The reason for the minus signs is that logarithms of the fractions $p_1, p_2, \ldots, p_n$ are negative, so the entropy is actually positive. Usually the logarithms are expressed in base 2, and then the entropy is in units called "bits"—just the usual kind of bits that we use with computers.

The arguments $p_1, p_2, \ldots$ of the entropy formula are expressed as fractions that add up to 1, so that, for example,

$$\text{info}([2, 3, 4]) \;=\; \text{entropy}(2/9, 3/9, 4/9).$$

Thus the multistage decision property can be written in general as

$$\text{entropy}(p, q, r) \;=\; \text{entropy}\,(p, q + r) \,+\, (q + r) \cdot \text{entropy}(\frac{q}{q + r}, \frac{r}{q + r}).$$

where $p + q + r = 1$.

Because of the way the log function works, you can calculate the information measure without having to work out the individual fractions. For example,

$$\begin{aligned}
\text{info}([2, 3, 4]) &= -2/9 \times \log 2/9 \,-\, 3/9 \times \log 3/9 \,-\, 4/9 \times \log 4/9 \\
&= [-2 \log 2 - 3 \log 3 - 4 \log 4 + 9 \log 9]/9.
\end{aligned}$$

This is the way that the information measure is usually calculated in practice.

Highly-branching attributes

When some attributes have a large number of possible values, giving rise to a multiway branch with many child nodes, a problem arises with the information gain calculation. The problem can best be appreciated in the extreme case when an attribute has a different value for each instance in the dataset—as, for example, an *identification code* attribute might.

Table 4.6 gives the weather data with this extra attribute. Branching on ID code produces the tree stump in Figure 4.5. The information required to specify the class given the value of this attribute is

$$\text{info}([0, 1]) \,+\, \text{info}([0, 1]) \,+\, \text{info}([1, 0]) \,+\ldots+\, \text{info}([1, 0]) \,+\, \text{info}([0, 1]),$$

which is zero because each of the 14 terms is zero. This is not surprising: the ID code attribute identifies the instance, which determines the class without any ambiguity—just as Table 4.6 shows. Consequently the information gain of this attribute is just the information at the root, $\text{info}([9, 5]) = 0.940$ bits. This is greater than the information gain of any other attribute, and so ID code will inevitably be chosen as the splitting attribute. But branching on the identification code is no good for predicting the class of unknown instances and tells

Table 4.6	The weather data with identification codes.				
ID code	outlook	temperature	humidity	windy	play
a	sunny	hot	high	false	no
b	sunny	hot	high	true	no
c	overcast	hot	high	false	yes
d	rainy	mild	high	false	yes
e	rainy	cool	normal	false	yes
f	rainy	cool	normal	true	no
g	overcast	cool	normal	true	yes
h	sunny	mild	high	false	no
i	sunny	cool	normal	false	yes
j	rainy	mild	normal	false	yes
k	sunny	mild	normal	true	yes
l	overcast	mild	high	true	yes
m	overcast	hot	normal	false	yes
n	rainy	mild	high	true	no

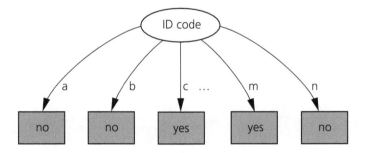

Figure 4.5 Tree stump for the ID code attribute.

nothing about the structure of the decision, which after all are the twin goals of machine learning.

The overall effect is that the information gain measure tends to prefer attributes with large numbers of possible values. To compensate for this, a modification of the measure called the *gain ratio* is widely used. The gain ratio is derived by taking into account the number and size of daughter nodes into which an attribute splits the dataset, disregarding any information about the class. In the situation shown in Figure 4.5, all counts have a value of 1, and so the information value of the split is

$$\text{info}([1, 1, \dots, 1]) = -1/14 \times \log 1/14 \times 14,$$

Table 4.7	Gain ratio calculations for the tree stumps of Figure 4.2.		
outlook		**temperature**	
info:	0.693	info:	0.911
gain: 0.940 − 0.693	0.247	gain: 0.940 − 0.911	0.029
split info: info([5, 4, 5])	1.577	split info: info([4, 6, 4])	1.362
gain ratio: 0.247/1.577	0.156	0.029/1.362	0.021
humidity		**windy**	
info:	0.788	info:	0.892
gain: 0.940 − 0.788	0.152	gain: 0.940 − 0.892	0.048
split info: info([7, 7])	1.000	split info: info([8, 6])	0.985
gain ratio: 0.152/1	0.152	gain ratio: 0.048/0.985	0.049

because the same fraction 1/14 appears 14 times. This amounts to log 14 or 3.807 bits, which is a very high value. This is because the information value of a split is the number of bits needed to determine which branch each instance is assigned to, and the more branches there are, the greater this value is. The gain ratio is calculated by dividing the original information gain, 0.940 in this case, by the information value of the attribute, 3.807—yielding a gain ratio value of 0.246 for the ID code attribute.

Returning to the tree stumps for the weather data in Figure 4.2, outlook splits the dataset into three subsets of size 5, 4, and 5, and thus has an intrinsic information value of

$$\text{info}([5, 4, 5]) = 1.577$$

without paying any attention to the classes involved in the subsets. As we have seen, this intrinsic information value is higher for a more highly branching attribute such as the hypothesized ID code. Again the information gain is corrected by dividing by the intrinsic information value to get the gain ratio.

The results of these calculations for the tree stumps of Figure 4.2 are summarized in Table 4.7. Outlook still comes out on top, but humidity is now a much closer contender because it splits the data into two subsets instead of three. In this particular example, the hypothetical ID code attribute, with a gain ratio of 0.246, would still be preferred to any of these four. However, its advantage is greatly reduced. In practical implementations, an ad hoc test is used to guard against splitting on such a useless attribute.

Unfortunately, in some situations the gain ratio modification overcompensates and can lead to preferring an attribute just because its intrinsic information is much lower than for the other attributes. A standard fix is to choose the attribute that maximizes the gain ratio, provided the information gain for that attribute is at least as great as the average information gain for all the attributes examined.

Discussion

The divide-and-conquer approach to decision tree induction, sometimes called *top-down induction of decision trees,* was developed and refined over many years by Ross Quinlan of the University of Sydney, Australia. Although others have worked on similar methods, Quinlan's research has always been at the very forefront of decision tree induction. The scheme that has been described using the information gain criterion is essentially the same as one known as ID3. The use of the gain ratio was one of many improvements that were made to ID3 over a number of years; Quinlan described it as robust under a wide variety of circumstances. Although a practical solution, it sacrifices some of the elegance and clean theoretical motivation of the information gain criterion.

A series of improvements to ID3 culminated in an influential and widely used system for decision tree induction called C4.5. These improvements include methods for dealing with numeric attributes, missing values, noisy data, and generating rules from trees, and are described in Chapter 6 (Section 6.1).

4.4 Covering algorithms: Constructing rules

As we have seen, decision tree algorithms are based on a divide-and-conquer approach to the classification problem. They work top-down, seeking at each stage an attribute to split on that best separates the classes, and then recursively processing the subproblems that result from the split. This strategy generates a decision tree, which can if necessary be converted into a set of classification rules—although if it is to produce effective rules, the conversion is not trivial.

An alternative approach is to take each class in turn and seek a way of covering all instances in it, at the same time excluding instances not in the class. This is called a *covering* approach because at each stage you identify a rule that "covers" some of the instances. By its very nature, this covering approach leads to a set of rules rather than to a decision tree.

The covering method can readily be visualized in a two-dimensional space of instances as shown in Figure 4.6a. We first make a rule covering the as. For the first test in the rule, split the space vertically as shown in the center picture. This gives the beginnings of a rule:

```
If x > 1.2 then class = a
```

However, the rule covers many bs as well as as, so a new test is added to the rule by further splitting the space horizontally as shown in the third diagram:

```
If x > 1.2 and y > 2.6 then class = a
```

This gives a rule covering all but one of the as. It's probably appropriate to leave it at that, but if it were felt necessary to cover the final a, another rule would be necessary—perhaps

```
If x > 1.4 and y < 2.4 then class = a
```

The same procedure leads to two rules covering the bs:

```
If x ≤ 1.2 then class = b
If x > 1.2 and y ≤ 2.6 then class = b
```

Again, one a is erroneously covered by these rules. If it were necessary to exclude it, more tests would have to be added to the second rule, and additional rules would need to be introduced to cover the bs that these new tests exclude.

Rules versus trees

A top-down divide-and-conquer algorithm operates on the same data in a manner that is, at least superficially, quite similar to a covering algorithm. It might first split the dataset using the x attribute, and would probably end up splitting it at the same place, x = 1.2. However, whereas the covering algorithm is concerned only with covering a single class, the division would take both classes into account, because divide-and-conquer algorithms create a single concept description that applies to all classes. The second split might also be at the same place, y = 2.6, leading to the decision tree in Figure 4.6b. This tree corresponds exactly to the set of rules, and in this case there is no difference in effect between the covering and divide-and-conquer algorithms.

But in many situations there *is* a difference between rules and trees, in terms of the perspicuity of the representation. For example, when we discussed the replicated subtree problem in Section 3.3, we noted that rules can be symmetric whereas trees must select one attribute to split on first, and this can lead to trees that are much larger than an equivalent set of rules. Another difference is that, in the multiclass case, a decision-tree split takes all classes into account, trying to maximize the purity of the split; whereas the rule-generating method concentrates on one class at a time, disregarding what happens to the other classes.

A simple covering algorithm

Covering algorithms operate by adding tests to the rule that is under construction, always striving to create a rule with maximum accuracy. In contrast,

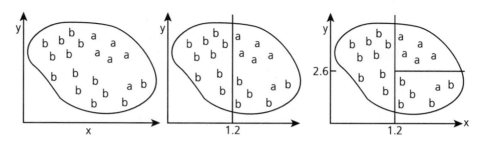

(a)

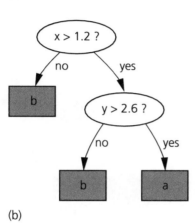

(b)

Figure 4.6 (a) Operation of a covering algorithm; (b) decision tree for the same problem.

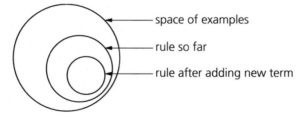

Figure 4.7. The instance space during operation of a covering algorithm.

divide-and-conquer algorithms operate by adding tests to the tree that is under construction, always striving to maximize the separation between the classes. Each of these involves finding an attribute to split on. But the criterion for the best attribute is different in each case. Whereas divide-and-conquer algorithms like ID3 choose an attribute to maximize the information gain, the covering algorithm we will describe chooses an attribute-value pair to maximize the probability of the desired classification.

Figure 4.7 gives a picture of the situation, showing the space containing all the instances, a partially constructed rule, and the same rule after a new term has been added. The new term restricts the coverage of the rule: the idea is to include as many instances of the desired class as possible and exclude as many instances of other classes as possible. Suppose the new rule will cover a total of t instances, of which p are positive examples of the class and $t-p$ are in other classes—that is, they are errors made by the rule. Then we choose the new term to maximize the ratio p/t.

An example will help. For a change, we use the contact lens problem of Table 1.1. We will form rules that cover each of the three classes hard, soft, and none in turn. To begin, we seek a rule

```
If ? then recommendation = hard
```

For the unknown term ?, we have nine choices:

age = young	2/8
age = pre-presbyopic	1/8
age = presbyopic	1/8
spectacle prescription = myope	3/12
spectacle prescription = hypermetrope	1/12
astigmatism = no	0/12
astigmatism = yes	4/12
tear production rate = reduced	0/12
tear production rate = normal	4/12

The numbers on the right show the fraction of "correct" instances in the set singled out by that choice. In this case, *correct* means that their recommendation is hard. For instance, age = young selects eight instances, two of which recommend hard contact lenses, so the first fraction is 2/8. (In order to follow this, you will need to look back at the contact lens data in Table 1.1 on page 4 and count up the entries in the table.) We select the largest fraction, 4/12, arbitrarily choosing between the seventh and the last choice in the list above, and create the rule:

```
If astigmatism = yes then recommendation = hard
```

This rule is not a very accurate one, getting only four instances correct out of the twelve that it covers, shown in Table 4.8. So we refine it further, to

```
If astigmatism = yes and ? then recommendation = hard
```

Considering the possibilities for the unknown term ? yields the seven choices:

age = young	2/4
age = pre-presbyopic	1/4
age = presbyopic	1/4

Table 4.8	Part of the contact lens data for which `astigmatism = yes`.			
age	spectacle prescription	astigmatism	tear production rate	recommended lenses
young	myope	yes	reduced	none
young	myope	yes	normal	hard
young	hypermetrope	yes	reduced	none
young	hypermetrope	yes	normal	hard
pre-presbyopic	myope	yes	reduced	none
pre-presbyopic	myope	yes	normal	hard
pre-presbyopic	hypermetrope	yes	reduced	none
pre-presbyopic	hypermetrope	yes	normal	none
presbyopic	myope	yes	reduced	none
presbyopic	myope	yes	normal	hard
presbyopic	hypermetrope	yes	reduced	none
presbyopic	hypermetrope	yes	normal	none

```
spectacle prescription = myope          3/6
spectacle prescription = hypermetrope   1/6
tear production rate = reduced          0/6
tear production rate = normal           4/6
```

(Again, count the entries in Table 4.8.) The last is a clear winner, getting four instances correct out of the six that it covers, and corresponds to the rule

```
If astigmatism = yes and tear production rate = normal
    then recommendation = hard
```

Should we stop here? Perhaps. But let's say we are going for exact rules, no matter how complex they become. Table 4.9 shows the cases that are covered by the rule so far. The possibilities for the next term are now

```
age = young                              2/2
age = pre-presbyopic                     1/2
age = presbyopic                         1/2
spectacle prescription = myope           3/3
spectacle prescription = hypermetrope    1/3
```

We need to choose between the first and fourth. So far we have treated the fractions numerically, but although these two are equal (both evaluate to 1), they have different coverage: one selects just two correct instances while the other

Table 4.9	Part of the contact lens data for which `astigmatism = yes` and `tear production rate = normal`.			
age	spectacle prescription	astigmatism	tear production rate	recommended lenses
young	myope	yes	normal	hard
young	hypermetrope	yes	normal	hard
pre-presbyopic	myope	yes	normal	hard
pre-presbyopic	hypermetrope	yes	normal	none
presbyopic	myope	yes	normal	hard
presbyopic	hypermetrope	yes	normal	none

selects three. In the event of a tie, we choose the rule with the greater coverage, giving the final rule:

```
If astigmatism = yes and tear production rate = normal
    and spectacle prescription = myope then recommendation = hard
```

This is indeed one of the rules given for the contact lens problem. But it only covers three out of the four `hard` recommendations. So we delete these three from the set of instances and start again, looking for another rule of the form:

```
If ? then recommendation = hard
```

Following the same process, we will eventually find that `age = young` is the best choice for the first term. Its coverage is one out of seven; the reason for the seven is that three instances have been removed from the original set, leaving 21 instances altogether. The best choice for the second term is `astigmatism = yes`, selecting 1/3 (actually, this is a tie); `tear production rate = normal` is the best for the third, selecting 1/1.

```
If age = young and astigmatism = yes and
    tear production rate = normal then recommendation = hard
```

This rule actually covers three of the original set of instances, two of which are covered by the previous rule—but that's all right since the recommendation is the same for each rule.

Now that all the hard-lens cases are covered, the next step is to proceed with the soft-lens ones in just the same way. Finally, rules are generated for the `none` case—unless we are seeking a rule set with a default rule, in which case explicit rules for the final outcome are unnecessary.

```
For each class C
  Initialize E to the instance set
  While E contains instances in class C
    Create a rule R with an empty left-hand side that predicts class C
    Until R is perfect (or there are no more attributes to use) do
      For each attribute A not mentioned in R, and each value v,
        Consider adding the condition A=v to the LHS of R
        Select A and v to maximize the accuracy p/t
          (break ties by choosing the condition with the largest p)
      Add A=v to R
    Remove the instances covered by R from E
```

Figure 4.8 Pseudo-code for a basic rule learner.

What we have just described is the PRISM method for constructing rules. It generates only correct or "perfect" rules. It measures the success of a rule by the accuracy formula p/t. Any rule with accuracy less than 100% is "incorrect" in that it assigns cases to the class in question that actually do not have that class. PRISM continues adding clauses to each rule until it is perfect: its accuracy is 100%. Figure 4.8 gives a summary of the algorithm. The outer loop iterates over the classes, generating rules for each class in turn. Note that we reinitialize to the full set of examples each time round. Then we create rules for that class and remove the examples from the set until there are none of that class left. Whenever we create a rule, we start with an empty rule (which covers all the examples), and then restrict it by adding tests until it covers only examples of the desired class. At each stage the most promising test is chosen, that is, the one that maximizes the accuracy of the rule. Finally, ties are broken by selecting the test with greatest coverage.

Rules versus decision lists

Consider the rules produced for a particular class, that is, the algorithm in Figure 4.8 with the outer loop removed. It seems clear from the way that these rules are produced that they are intended to be interpreted in order, that is, as a decision list, testing the rules in turn until one applies and then using that. This is because the instances covered by a new rule are removed from the instance set as soon as the rule is completed (in the third line from the end of the code in Figure 4.8): thus subsequent rules are designed for instances that are *not* covered by the rule. However, although it appears that the rules are supposed to be checked in turn, they do not have to be. Consider that any subsequent rules generated for this class will have the same effect—they all predict the same class. This means that it does not matter what order they are executed in: either a rule will be found that covers this instance, in which case the class in question is predicted, or no such rule is found, in which case the class is not predicted.

Now return to the overall algorithm. Each class is considered in turn, and rules are generated that distinguish instances in that class from the others. No ordering is implied between the rules for one class and those for another. Consequently the rules that are produced can be executed in an order-independent manner.

As discussed at the bottom of page 60, order-independent rules seem to provide more modularity by each acting as independent nuggets of "knowledge," but suffer from the disadvantage that it is not clear what to do when conflicting rules apply. With rules generated in this way, a test example may receive multiple classifications, that is, it may be accepted by rules that apply to different classes. Other test examples may receive no classification at all. A simple strategy to force a decision in these ambiguous cases is to choose, out of the classifications that are predicted, the one with the most training examples, and if no classification is predicted, to choose the category with the most training examples overall. These difficulties do not occur with decision lists, for they are meant to be interpreted in order, and execution stops as soon as one rule applies: the addition of a default rule at the end serves to ensure that any test instance receives a classification. It is possible to generate good decision lists for the multiclass case using a slightly different method, as we shall see in Chapter 6 (page 171).

Methods like Prism can be described as *separate-and-conquer* algorithms: you identify a rule that covers many instances in the class (and excludes ones not in the class), separate out the covered instances because they are already taken care of by the rule, and continue the process on those that are left. This contrasts nicely with the divide-and-conquer approach of decision trees. The "separate" step greatly increases the efficiency of the method because the instance set continually shrinks as the operation proceeds.

4.5 Mining association rules

Association rules are like classification rules. And you could find them in the same way, by executing a divide-and-conquer rule induction procedure for each possible expression that could occur on the right-hand side of the rule. However, any attribute might occur on the right-hand side with any possible value, and a single association rule can often predict the value of more than one attribute. To find such rules, you would have to execute the rule induction procedure once for every possible *combination* of attributes, with every possible combination of values, on the right-hand side. That would result in an enormous number of association rules, which would then have to be pruned down on the basis of their *coverage* (the number of instances they predict correctly)— and *accuracy* (the same number expressed as a proportion of the number of instances that the rule applies to). This approach is quite infeasible. (Note that, as we said in Section 3.4, what we are calling *coverage* is often called *support,* and what we are calling *accuracy* is often called *confidence.*)

Instead, we capitalize on the fact that we are only interested in association rules with high coverage. We ignore, for the moment, the distinction between the left- and right-hand sides of a rule, and seek combinations of attribute-value pairs that have a prespecified minimum coverage. These are called *item sets:* an attribute-value pair is an *item.* The terminology derives from market basket analysis, where the items are articles in your shopping cart and the supermarket manager is looking for associations among these purchases.

Item sets

The first column of Table 4.10 shows the individual items for the weather data of Table 1.2, with the number of times each item appears in the dataset given at the right. These are the one-item sets. The next step is to generate the two-item sets, by taking pairs of one-item sets. Of course, there is no point in generating a set containing two different values of the same attribute (like outlook = sunny and outlook = overcast), for that cannot occur in any actual instance.

Assume that we seek association rules with a minimum coverage of two: thus we discard any item sets that cover fewer than two instances. This leaves 47 two-item sets, some of which are shown in the second column along with the number of times they appear. The next step is to generate the three-item sets, of which 39 have a coverage of two or more. There are 6 four-item sets, and no five-item sets—for this data, a five-item set with coverage of two or more could only correspond to a repeated instance. The first row of the table, for example, shows that there are five days when outlook = sunny, two of which have temperature = mild and, in fact, on both of those days humidity = high and play = no as well.

Association rules

Shortly we will discuss how to generate these item sets efficiently. But first let's finish the story. Once all item sets with the required coverage have been generated, the next step is to turn each into a rule, or set of rules, with at least the specified minimum accuracy. Some item sets will produce more than one rule; others will produce none. For example, there is one three-item set with a coverage of four (row 38 of Table 4.10):

```
humidity = normal, windy = false, play = yes
```

Table 4.10   Item sets for the weather data with coverage of two or more.

	one-item sets	two-item sets	three-item sets	four-item sets
1	outlook = sunny (5)	outlook = sunny temperature = mild (2)	outlook = sunny temperature = hot humidity = high (2)	outlook = sunny temperature = hot humidity = high play = no (2)
2	outlook = overcast (4)	outlook = sunny temperature = hot (2)	outlook = sunny temperature = hot play = no (2)	outlook = sunny humidity = high windy = false play = no (2)
3	outlook = rainy (5)	outlook = sunny humidity = normal (2)	outlook = sunny humidity = normal play = yes (2)	outlook = overcast temperature = hot windy = false play = yes (2)
4	temperature = cool (4)	outlook = sunny humidity = high (3)	outlook = sunny humidity = high windy = false (2)	outlook = rainy temperature = mild windy = false play = yes (2)
5	temperature = mild (6)	outlook = sunny windy = true (2)	outlook = sunny humidity = high play = no (3)	outlook = rainy humidity = normal windy = false play = yes (2)
6	temperature = hot (4)	outlook = sunny windy = false (3)	outlook = sunny windy = false play = no (2)	temperature = cool humidity = normal windy = false play = yes (2)
7	humidity = normal (7)	outlook = sunny play = yes (2)	outlook = overcast temperature = hot windy = false (2)	
8	humidity = high (7)	outlook = sunny play = no (3)	outlook = overcast temperature = hot play = yes (2)	
9	windy = true (6)	outlook = overcast temperature = hot (2)	outlook = overcast humidity = normal play = yes (2)	
10	windy = false (8)	outlook = overcast humidity = normal (2)	outlook = overcast humidity = high play = yes (2)	
11	play = yes (9)	outlook = overcast humidity = high (2)	outlook = overcast windy = true play = yes (2)	

	one-item sets	two-item sets	three-item sets	four-item sets
12	play = no (5)	outlook = overcast windy = true (2)	outlook = overcast windy = false play = yes (2)	
13		outlook = overcast windy = false (2)	outlook = rainy temperature = cool humidity = normal (2)	
...	...	...	...	
38		humidity = normal windy = false (4)	humidity = normal windy = false play = yes (4)	
39		humidity = normal play = yes (6)	humidity = high windy = false play = no (2)	
40		humidity = high windy = true (3)		
...	...	...	...	
47		windy = false play = no (2)		

Table 4.10   (continued)

This set leads to seven potential rules:

```
If humidity = normal and windy = false then play = yes        4/4
If humidity = normal and play = yes then windy = false        4/6
If windy = false and play = yes then humidity = normal        4/6
If humidity = normal then windy = false and play = yes        4/7
If windy = false then humidity = normal and play = yes        4/8
If play = yes then humidity = normal and windy = false        4/9
If - then humidity = normal and windy = false and play = yes  4/12
```

The figures at the right show the number of instances for which all three conditions are true (that is, the coverage) divided by the number of instances for which the conditions in the antecedent are true. Interpreted as a fraction, they represent the proportion of instances on which the rule is correct—that is, its accuracy. Assuming that the minimum specified accuracy is 100%, only the first of these rules will make it into the final rule set. The denominators of the fractions are readily obtained by looking up the antecedent expression in Table 4.10.

The final rule above has no conditions in the antecedent, and its denominator is the total number of instances in the dataset.

Table 4.11 shows the final rule set for the weather data, with minimum coverage two and minimum accuracy 100%, sorted by coverage. There are 58 rules, 3 with coverage four, 5 with coverage three, and 50 with coverage two. Only 7 have two conditions in the consequent, and none has more than two. The first rule comes from the item set discussed above. Sometimes several rules arise from the same item set. For example, rules 9, 10, and 11 all arise from the four-item set in row 6 of Table 4.10:

```
temperature = cool, humidity = normal, windy = false, play = yes
```

which has coverage two. Three subsets of this item set also have coverage two:

```
temperature = cool, windy = false
temperature = cool, humidity = normal, windy = false
temperature = cool, windy = false, play = yes
```

and these lead to rules 9, 10, and 11, all of which are 100% accurate (on the training data).

Generating rules efficiently

We now consider in more detail an algorithm for producing association rules with specified minimum coverage and accuracy. There are two stages: generating item sets with the specified minimum coverage, and from each item set determining the rules that have the specified minimum accuracy.

The first stage proceeds by generating all one-item sets with the given minimum coverage (the first column of Table 4.10) and then using this to generate the two-item sets (second column), three-item sets (third column), and so on. Each operation involves a pass through the dataset to count the items in each set, and after the pass the surviving item sets are stored in a hash table—a standard data structure that allows elements stored in it to be found very quickly. From the one-item sets, candidate two-item sets are generated, and then a pass is made through the dataset, counting the coverage of each two-item set; at the end the candidate sets with less than minimum coverage are removed from the table. The candidate two-item sets are simply all of the one-item sets, taken in pairs, for a two-item set cannot have the minimum coverage unless both its constituent one-item sets have minumum coverage too. This applies in general: a three-item set can only have the minimum coverage if all three of its two-item subsets have minimum coverage as well, and similarly for four-item sets.

An example will help to explain how candidate item sets are generated. Suppose there are five three-item sets: (A B C), (A B D), (A C D), (A C E), and

Table 4.11   Association rules for the weather data.

	association rule			coverage	accuracy
1	humidity = normal windy = false	⇒	play = yes	4	100%
2	temperature = cool	⇒	humidity = normal	4	100%
3	outlook = overcast	⇒	play = yes	4	100%
4	temperature = cool play = yes	⇒	humidity = normal	3	100%
5	outlook = rainy windy = false	⇒	play = yes	3	100%
6	outlook = rainy play = yes	⇒	windy = false	3	100%
7	outlook = sunny humidity = high	⇒	play = no	3	100%
8	outlook = sunny play = no	⇒	humidity = high	3	100%
9	temperature = cool windy = false	⇒	humidity = normal play = yes	2	100%
10	temperature = cool humidity = normal windy = false	⇒	play = yes	2	100%
11	temperature = cool windy = false play = yes	⇒	humidity = normal	2	100%
12	outlook = rainy humidity = normal windy = false	⇒	play = yes	2	100%
13	outlook = rainy humidity = normal play = yes	⇒	windy = false	2	100%
14	outlook = rainy temperature = mild windy = false	⇒	play = yes	2	100%
15	outlook = rainy temperature = mild play = yes	⇒	windy = false	2	100%
16	temperature = mild windy = false play = yes	⇒	outlook = rainy	2	100%
17	outlook = overcast temperature = hot	⇒	windy = false play = yes	2	100%
18	outlook = overcast windy = false	⇒	temperature = hot play = yes	2	100%
19	temperature = hot play = yes	⇒	outlook = overcast windy = false	2	100%
20	outlook = overcast temperature = hot windy = false	⇒	play = yes	2	100%
21	outlook = overcast temperature = hot play = yes	⇒	windy = false	2	100%
22	outlook = overcast windy = false play = yes	⇒	temperature = hot	2	100%
23	temperature = hot windy = false play = yes	⇒	outlook = overcast	2	100%
...				...	
58	outlook = sunny temperature = hot	⇒	humidity = high	2	100%

(B C D)—where, for example, A is a feature like outlook = sunny. The union of the first two, (A B C D), is a candidate four-item set because its other three-item subsets (A C D) and (B C D) have greater than minimum coverage. If the three-item sets are sorted into lexical order, as they are in this list, then we need only consider pairs whose first two members are the same, because otherwise the resulting item set would contain more than four items. These are the pairs (A B C) and (A B D), which we have already discussed, and (A C D) and (A C E). This second pair leads to a set (A C D E) whose three-item subsets do not all have the minimum coverage, and so it is discarded. The hash table assists with this check: we need simply remove each item from the set in turn and check that the remaining three-item set is indeed present in the hash table. Thus in this example there is only one candidate four-item set, (A B C D). Whether or not it actually has minimum coverage can only be determined by checking the instances in the dataset.

The second stage of the procedure takes each item set and generates rules from it, checking that they have the specified minimum accuracy. If only rules with a single test on the right-hand side were sought, it would be simply a matter of considering each condition in turn as the consequent of the rule, deleting it from the item set, and dividing the coverage of the entire item set by the coverage of the resulting subset—obtained from the hash table—to yield the accuracy of the corresponding rule. Given that we are also interested in association rules with multiple tests in the consequent, it looks like we have to evaluate the effect of placing each *subset* of the item set on the right-hand side, leaving the remainder of the set as the antecedent.

This brute-force method will be excessively computation-intensive unless item sets are small, because the number of possible subsets grows exponentially with the size of the item set. However, there is a better way. We observed when discussing association rules in Section 3.4 that if the double-consequent rule

```
If windy = false and play = no then outlook = sunny
                                    and humidity = high
```

holds with a given minimum coverage and accuracy, then both single-consequent rules formed from the same item set must also hold:

```
If humidity = high and windy = false and play = no
   then outlook = sunny
If outlook = sunny and windy = false and play = no
   then humidity = high
```

Conversely, if one or other of the single-consequent rules does not hold, there is no point in considering the double-consequent one. This gives a way of building up from single-consequent rules to candidate double-consequent ones, from double-consequent rules to candidate triple-consequent ones, and so on. Of course, each candidate rule must be checked against the hash table to see if it really does have more than the specified minimum accuracy. But this generally involves checking far fewer rules than does the brute-force method. It is interesting that this way of building up candidate $(n + 1)$-consequent rules from actual n-consequent ones is really just the same as building up candidate $(n + 1)$-item sets from actual n-item sets, described earlier.

Discussion

Association rules are often sought for very large datasets, and efficient algorithms are highly valued. The method described above makes one pass through the dataset for each different size of item set. Sometimes the dataset is too large to read into main memory and must be kept on disk, and then it may be worthwhile reducing the number of passes by checking item sets of two consecutive sizes in one go. For example, once sets with two items have been generated, all sets of three items could be generated from them before going through the instance set to count the actual number of items in the sets. More three-item sets than necessary would be considered, but the number of passes through the entire dataset would be reduced.

In practice, the amount of computation needed to generate association rules depends critically on the minimum coverage specified. The accuracy has less influence because it does not affect the number of passes that must be made through the dataset. In many situations we would like to obtain a certain number of rules—say fifty—with the greatest possible coverage, at a prespecified minimum accuracy level. The best way to do this is to begin by specifying the coverage to be rather high and then to successively reduce it, re-executing the entire rule-finding algorithm for each coverage value and repeating until the desired number of rules have been generated.

The tabular input format that we use throughout this book, and in particular the ARFF format that is based on it, is very inefficient for many association-rule problems. Association rules are often used in situations where attributes are unary—either present or not—and most of the attribute values associated with a given instance are missing. For example, in supermarket basket analysis, an instance is a particular shopping cart, the attributes are all the items for sale, and attribute values are *present* if that item appears in the cart and *missing* (represented by ?) otherwise. Most carts contain far fewer items than there are in the supermarket, and it is more efficient to represent each instance as a list of the attributes whose value is present rather than a vector with one element for every possible item. However, this input representation makes no difference to algorithms for finding association rules.

4.6 Linear models

The methods we have been looking at for decision trees and rules work most naturally with nominal attributes. They can be extended to numeric attributes either by incorporating numeric-value tests directly into the decision tree or rule induction scheme, or by prediscretizing numeric attributes into nominal ones. We will see how in Chapters 6 and 7, respectively. However, there are schemes that work most naturally with attributes that are numeric. We look at simple ones here, ones that form components of more complex learning methods which we will meet later.

Numeric prediction

When the outcome, or class, is numeric, and all the attributes are numeric, linear regression is a natural technique to consider. This is a staple method in statistics. The idea is to express the class as a linear combination of the attributes, with predetermined weights:

$$x = w_0 + w_1 a_1 + w_2 a_2 + \ldots + w_k a_k,$$

where x is the class, $a_1, a_2, \ldots, a_k$ are the attribute values, and $w_0, w_1, \ldots, w_k$ are weights.

The weights are calculated from the training data. Here the notation gets a little heavy, because we need a way of expressing the attribute values for each training instance. The first instance will have a class, say $x^{(1)}$, and attribute values, $a_1^{(1)}, a_2^{(1)}, \ldots, a_k^{(1)}$, where the superscript denotes that it is the first example. Moreover, it is notationally convenient to assume an extra attribute a_0 whose value is always 1.

The predicted value for the first instance's class can be written as

$$w_0 a_0^{(1)} + w_1 a_1^{(1)} + w_2 a_2^{(1)} + \ldots + w_k a_k^{(1)} = \sum_{j=0}^{k} w_j a_j^{(1)}.$$

This is the predicted, not the actual, value for the first instance's class. Of interest is the difference between the predicted and actual values. The method of linear regression is to choose the coefficients w_j—there are $k + 1$ of them—to minimize the sum of the squares of these differences over all the training instances. Suppose there are n training instances; denote the ith one with a superscript (i). Then the sum of the squares of the differences is

$$\sum_{i=1}^{n} \left(x^{(i)} - \sum_{j=0}^{k} w_j a_j^{(i)} \right)^2,$$

where the expression inside the parentheses is the difference between the ith instance's actual class and its predicted class. This sum of squares is what we have to minimize by choosing the coefficients appropriately.

This is all starting to look rather formidable. However, the minimization technique is straightforward if you have the appropriate math background. Suffice it to say that provided there are enough examples—roughly speaking, more examples than attributes—choosing weights to minimize the sum of the squared differences is really not difficult. It does involve a matrix inversion operation, but this is readily available as prepackaged software.

Once the math has been accomplished, the result is a set of numeric weights, based on the training data, that can be used to predict the class of new instances. We saw an example of this when looking at the CPU performance data, and the actual numeric weights are given in Figure 3.6a. This formula can be used to predict the CPU performance of new test instances.

Classification

Linear regression can easily be used for classification in domains with numeric attributes—in fact, *any* regression technique, whether linear or nonlinear, can easily be used for classification. The trick is to perform a regression for each class, setting the output equal to 1 for training instances that belong to the class and 0 for those that do not. The result is a linear expression for each class. Then, given a test example of unknown class, calculate the value of each linear expression and choose the one that is largest. This scheme is sometimes called *multi-response linear regression*.

One way of looking at multi-response linear regression is to imagine that it approximates a numeric *membership function* for each class. The membership function is 1 for instances that belong to that class and 0 for other instances. Given a new instance we calculate its membership for each class and select the biggest.

This is not the only way to transform regression into classification. Another way is to calculate a regression line for every *pair* of classes, using only the instances from these two classes, assigning one member of the pair an output of +1 and the other an output of –1. Being based on pairs, this is far more computation-intensive but is likely to give more accurate results. The output on an unknown test example can be based on which class receives the most "votes," or for a more conservative decision, a single unanimously chosen class can be sought, with a "don't know" result if there is no unanimous winner.

Discussion

Linear regression is an excellent, simple scheme for numeric prediction which has been widely used in statistical applications for decades. However, linear models suffer from the disadvantage of, well, linearity. If the data exhibits a non-linear dependency, the best-fitting straight line will be found, where "best" is interpreted in the least-mean-squared-difference sense. This line may not fit very well. However, linear models serve very well as building blocks for more complex learning schemes.

The use of linear functions for classification can easily be visualized in instance space. Focus for the moment on a particular pair of classes. With multi-response linear regression, each class receives a weight vector calculated from the training data. Suppose the weight vector for class 1 is

$$w_0^{(1)} + w_1^{(1)}a_1 + w_2^{(1)}a_2 + \ldots + w_k^{(1)}a_k$$

and that for class 2 it is the same, with appropriate superscripts. Then an instance will be assigned to class 1 rather than class 2 if

$$w_0^{(1)} + w_1^{(1)}a_1 + \ldots + w_k^{(1)}a_k > w_0^{(2)} + w_1^{(2)}a_1 + \ldots + w_k^{(2)}a_k,$$

in other words if

$$(w_0^{(1)} - w_0^{(2)}) + (w_1^{(1)} - w_1^{(2)})a_1 + \ldots + (w_k^{(1)} - w_k^{(2)})a_k > 0.$$

This is a linear equality in the attribute values, and so the boundary between each pair of classes is a linear plane, or *hyperplane*, in instance space. It is very easy to visualize sets of points that *cannot* be separated by a single linear plane, and these cannot be discriminated correctly by a multi-response linear regression learner. Neither can they be discriminated by the pairwise learner, because it also involves a linear boundary. The only difference is that the boundary between two classes is governed only by the training instances in those classes and is not influenced by the other classes.

4.7 Instance-based learning

In instance-based learning the training examples are stored verbatim, and a distance function is used to determine which member of the training set is closest to an unknown test instance. Once the nearest training instance has been located, its class is predicted for the test instance. The only remaining problem is defining the distance function, and that is not very difficult to do, particularly if the attributes are numeric.

The distance function

Although there are other possible choices, most instance-based learners use Euclidean distance. The distance between an instance with attribute values $a_1^{(1)}$, $a_2^{(1)}, \ldots, a_k^{(1)}$ (where k is the number of attributes) and one with values $a_1^{(2)}$, $a_2^{(2)}, \ldots, a_k^{(2)}$ is defined as

$$\sqrt{(a_1^{(1)} - a_1^{(2)})^2 + (a_2^{(1)} - a_2^{(2)})^2 + \ldots + (a_k^{(1)} - a_k^{(2)})^2}.$$

When comparing distances it is not necessary to perform the square root operation; the sums of squares can be compared directly. One alternative to the Euclidean distance is the Manhattan or city-block metric, where the difference between attribute values is not squared but just added up (after taking the absolute value). Others are obtained by taking powers higher than the square. Higher powers increase the influence of large differences at the expense of small differences: generally the Euclidean distance represents a good compromise. Other distance metrics may be more appropriate in special circumstances. The key is to think of actual instances and what it means for them to be separated by a certain distance—what would twice that distance mean, for example?

Different attributes are measured on different scales, so if the Euclidean distance formula is used directly, the effect of some attributes might be completely dwarfed by others that have larger scales of measurement. Consequently it is usual to normalize all attribute values to lie between 0 and 1, by calculating

$$a_i = \frac{v_i - \min v_i}{\max v_i - \min v_i},$$

where v_i is the actual value of attribute i, and the maximum and minimum are taken over all instances in the training set.

These formulae implicitly assume numeric attributes. Here the difference between two values is just the numerical difference between them, and it is this difference that is squared and added to yield the distance function. For nominal attributes that take on values that are symbolic rather than numeric, the difference between two values that are not the same is often taken to be 1, whereas if the values are the same the difference is 0. No scaling is required in this case because only the values 0 and 1 are used.

A common policy for handling missing values is as follows. For nominal attributes, assume that a missing feature is maximally different from any other feature value. Thus if either (or both) values are missing, or if the values are different, the difference between them is taken as 1; the difference is 0 only if they are not missing and both are the same. For numeric attributes, the difference between two missing values is also taken as 1. However, if just one value is missing, the difference is often taken as either the (normalized) size of the other value or one minus that size, whichever is larger. This means that if values are missing, the difference is as large as it can possibly be.

Discussion

Nearest-neighbor instance-based learning is simple and often works very well. In the scheme described above, each attribute has exactly the same influence on the decision, just as it does in the Naive Bayes method. Instance-based learning is time-consuming for datasets of realistic size because the entire training data must be scanned to classify each test instance. Improved procedures, described in Chapter 6, address both of these shortcomings.

Another problem with instance-based methods is that the database can easily become corrupted by noisy exemplars. One solution is to adopt the k-nearest neighbor strategy, where some fixed, small number k of nearest neighbors—say five—are located and used together to determine the class of the test instance via simple majority vote. (Note: We used k to denote the number of attributes above; this is a different, independent usage.) However, computation time inevitably increases. Another way of proofing the database against noise is to choose the exemplars that are added to it selectively and judiciously; again, we return to this in Chapter 6.

The nearest-neighbor method originated many decades ago, and statisticians analyzed k-nearest-neighbor schemes in the early 1950s. If the number of training instances is large, it makes intuitive sense to use more than one single nearest neighbor, but clearly this is dangerous if there are not many instances. It can be shown that when k and the number n of instances both become infinite in such a way that $k/n \rightarrow 0$, the probability of error approaches the theoretical minimum for the dataset. The nearest-neighbor method was adopted as a classification scheme in the early 1960s and has been widely used in the field of pattern recognition for over three decades.

4.8 Further reading

The 1R scheme was proposed and thoroughly investigated by Holte (1993). It was never really intended as a machine learning "method": the point was more to demonstrate that very simple structures underlay most of the practical datasets being used to evaluate machine learning schemes at the time, and that putting high-powered inductive inference schemes to work on simple datasets was like using a sledge-hammer to crack a nut. Why grapple with a complex decision tree when a simple rule will do?

Bayes was an eighteenth-century English philosopher who set out his theory of probability in an "Essay towards solving a problem in the doctrine of chances," published in the *Philosophical Transactions of the Royal Society of London* (Bayes 1763); the rule that bears his name has been a cornerstone of probability theory ever since. The difficulty with the application of Bayes rule in practice is the assignment of prior probabilities. Some statisticians, dubbed Bayesians, take the rule as gospel and insist that people make serious attempts to estimate prior probabilities accurately—though such estimates are often subjective. Others, non-Bayesians, prefer the kind of prior-free analysis that typically ends up generating statistical confidence intervals, which we meet in the next chapter. With a particular dataset, prior probabilities are usually reasonably easy to estimate, which encourages a Bayesian approach to learning. The independence assumption made by the Naive Bayes method is a great stumbling block, however, and some attempts are being made to apply Bayesian analysis without assuming independence. The resulting models are called Bayes Networks (Heckerman et al. 1995).

Bayesian techniques have long been used in the field of pattern recognition (Duda and Hart 1973), but only recently have they been taken seriously by machine learning researchers (e.g., Langley et al. 1992) and made to work on datasets with redundant attributes (Langley and Sage 1994) and numeric attributes (John and Langley 1995). The label "Naive Bayes" is unfortunate because it is hard to use this method without feeling simple-minded. However, there is nothing naive about its use in appropriate circumstances.

The classic paper on decision tree induction is Quinlan (1986), which describes the basic ID3 procedure developed in this chapter. A comprehensive description of the method, including the improvements that are embodied in C4.5, appears in a classic book by Quinlan (1993), which gives a listing of the complete C4.5 system, written in the C programming language. PRISM was developed by Cendrowska (1987), who also introduced the contact lens dataset.

Association rules are introduced and discussed in the database literature rather than in the machine learning literature. Here the emphasis is very much on dealing with huge amounts of data, rather than on sensitive ways of testing and evaluating algorithms on limited datasets. The algorithm introduced in this chapter is the APRIORI method developed by Agrawal and his associates (Agrawal et al. 1993a, 1993b; Agrawal and Srikant 1994). A survey of association-rule mining appears in Chen et al. (1996).

Linear regression is described in most standard statistical texts, and a particularly comprehensive treatment can be found in Lawson and Hanson (1995). The use of linear models for classification enjoyed a great deal of popularity in the 1960s; Nilsson (1965) is an excellent reference. He defines a *linear threshold unit* as a binary test of whether a linear function is greater or less than zero, as we suggested using for pairwise classification; and a *linear machine* as a set of linear functions, one for each class, whose value for an unknown example is compared and the largest chosen as its predicted class. In the distant past, linear classifiers fell out of favor on publication of an influential book which showed that they had fundamental limitations (Minsky and Papert 1969); however, more complex systems of linear functions have enjoyed a resurgence in recent years in the form of neural networks. Multi-response linear classifiers have found a new application recently for an operation called *stacking* that combines the output of other learning algorithms, described in Chapter 7 (see Breiman 1996a).

Fix and Hodges (1951) performed the first analysis of the nearest-neighbor scheme, and Johns (1961) pioneered its use in classification problems. Nearest-neighbor methods gained popularity in machine learning through the work of Aha (1992), who showed that instance-based learning can be combined with noisy exemplar pruning and attribute weighting, and the resulting schemes perform well in comparison with other learning methods. We take this up again in Chapter 6.

chapter five

Credibility: Evaluating what's been learned

Evaluation is the key to making real progress in data mining. There are lots of ways of inferring structure from data: we have encountered many already and will see further refinements, and some new methods, in the next chapter. But to determine which methods to use on a particular problem we need systematic ways to evaluate how different methods work and to compare one with another. And evaluation is not as simple as it might appear at first sight.

What's the problem? We have the training set; surely we can just look at how well different methods do on that. Well, no: as we will see very shortly, performance on the training set is definitely not a good indicator of performance on an independent test set. We need ways of predicting performance bounds in practice, based on experiments with whatever data can be obtained.

When a vast supply of data is available, this is no problem: just make a model based on a large training set, and try it out on another large test set. But although data mining sometimes involves "big data"—particularly in marketing, sales, and customer support applications—it is often the case that data, quality data, is scarce. Those oil slicks mentioned in Chapter 1 (page 22) had to be detected and marked manually—a skilled and labor-intensive process—before being used as training data. Even in the loan application (page 21) there turned out to be only a thousand training examples of the appropriate type. The electricity supply data (page 23) went back fifteen years, five thousand days—but only fifteen Christmas days and Thanksgivings, and just four February 29s and presidential elections. The electromechanical diagnosis application (page 24) was able to capitalize on twenty years of recorded experience, but this yielded only three hundred usable examples of faults. Marketing and sales applications (page 25) certainly involve big data, but many others do not: training data frequently relies on specialist human expertise—and that is always in short supply.

The question of predicting performance based on limited data is an interesting, and still controversial, one. We will encounter many different techniques, of which one—*repeated cross-validation*—is gaining ascendance and is probably the evaluation method of choice in most practical limited-data situations. Comparing the performance of different machine learning schemes on a given problem is another matter that is not so easy as it sounds: to be certain that apparent differences are not due to chance effects, statistical tests are needed. So far we have tacitly assumed that what is being predicted is the ability to classify test instances accurately; however, some situations involve predicting class probabilities rather than the classes themselves, while others involve predicting numeric rather than nominal values, and different methods are needed in each case. Then we look at the question of cost. In most practical data mining situations, the cost of a misclassification error depends on the type of error it is—whether, for example, a positive example was erroneously classified as negative or vice versa. When doing data mining, and evaluating its performance, it is often essential to take these costs into account. Fortunately there is a simple technique for adjusting the training set to make most learning schemes cost-sensitive without having to grapple with the internals of the algorithm. Finally, the whole notion of evaluation has fascinating philosophical connections. For two thousand years philosophers have debated the question of how to evaluate scientific theories, and the issues are brought into sharp focus by data mining because what is extracted is essentially a "theory" of the data.

5.1 Training and testing

For classification problems, it is natural to measure a classifier's performance in terms of the *error rate*. The classifier predicts the class of each instance: if it is correct, that is counted as a *success*; if not, it is an *error*. The error rate is just the proportion of errors made over a whole set of instances, and it measures the overall performance of the classifier.

Of course, what we are interested in is the likely future performance on new data, not the past performance on old data. We already know the classifications of each instance in the training set, which after all is why we can use it for training. We are not generally interested in learning about those classifications—although we might be if our purpose is data cleaning rather than prediction. So the question is, is the error rate on old data likely to be a good indicator of the error rate on new data? And the answer is a resounding *no*—not if the old data was used during the learning process to train the classifier.

This is a surprising fact, and a very important one. Error rate on the training set is *not* likely to be a good indicator of future performance. Why? Since the classifier has been learned from the very same training data, any estimate of performance based on that data will be optimistic, and may be hopelessly optimistic.

We have already seen an example of this in the labor relations dataset. Figure 1.3b was generated directly from the training data, and Figure 1.3a was obtained from it by a process of pruning. The former is more accurate on the data that was used to train the classifier, but will probably perform less well on independent test data because it is overfitted to the training data. The first tree will look good according to the error rate on the training data, better than the second tree. But this does not reflect how they will perform on independent test data.

The error rate on the training data is called the *resubstitution error,* because it is calculated by resubstituting the training instances into a classifier that was constructed from them. Although it is not a reliable predictor of the true error rate on new data, it is nevertheless often useful to know.

To predict the performance of a classifier on new data, we need to assess its error rate on a dataset that played no part in the formation of the classifier. This independent dataset is called the *test set.* We do make the assumption that both the training data and the test data are representative samples of the underlying problem.

In some cases the test data might be distinct in nature from the training data. Consider, for example, the credit risk problem from Chapter 1 (Section 1.3). Suppose the bank had training data from branches in New York City and Florida and wanted to know how well a classifier trained from one of these datasets would perform in a new branch in Nebraska. It should probably use the Florida data as test data for evaluating the New York–trained classifier, and the New York data to evaluate the Florida-trained classifier. If the data sets were amalgamated before training, performance on the test data would probably not be a good indicator of performance on future data in a completely different state.

It is important that the test data was not used *in any way* to create the classifier. For example, some learning schemes involve two stages, one to come up with a basic structure and the second to optimize parameters involved in that structure, and separate sets of data may be needed in the two stages. Or you might try out several learning schemes on the training data and then evaluate them—on a fresh dataset, of course—to see which one works best. But none of this data may be used to determine an estimate of the future error rate. In such situations people often talk about three datasets: the *training* data, the *validation* data, and the *test* data. The training data is used by one or more learning schemes to come up with classifiers. The validation data is used to optimize parameters of those classifiers, or to select a particular one. Then the test data is used to calculate the error rate of the final, optimized scheme. Each of the three sets must be chosen independently: the validation set must be different from the training set to get good performance in the optimization or selection stage, and the test set must be different from both to get a reliable estimate of the true error rate.

It may be that once the error rate has been determined, the test data is bundled back into the training data to produce a new classifier for actual use. There is nothing wrong with this: it is just a way of maximizing the amount of data used to generate the classifier that will actually be employed in practice. What is important is that error rates are not quoted based on any of this data. Also, once the validation data has been used—maybe to determine the best type of learning scheme to use—then it can be bundled back into the training data to retrain that learning scheme, maximizing the use of data.

If lots of data is available, there is no problem: we take a large sample and use it for training, then another independent large sample of different data and use it for testing. Provided both samples are representative, the error rate on the test set will give a true indication of future performance. Generally speaking, the larger the training sample the better the classifier, although the returns begin to diminish once a certain volume of training data is exceeded. And the larger the test sample, the more accurate the error estimate. The accuracy of the error estimate can be quantified statistically, as we shall see in the next section.

The real problem occurs when there is not a vast supply of data available. In many situations the training data must be classified manually—and so must the test data, of course, to obtain error estimates. This may limit the amount of data that can be used for training, validation, and testing, and the problem becomes how to make the most of a limited dataset. From this dataset, a certain amount is held over for testing—this is called the *holdout* procedure—and the remainder used for training (and, if necessary, part of that is set aside for validation). There's a dilemma here: to get a good classifier, we want to use as much of the data as possible for training; to get a good error estimate, we want to use as much of it as possible for testing. Sections 5.3 and 5.4 review widely used methods for dealing with this dilemma.

5.2 Predicting performance

Suppose we measure the error of a classifier on a test set and obtain a certain numerical error rate—say 25%. Actually, in this section we will talk about success rate rather than error rate, so this corresponds to a success rate of 75%. Now, this is only an estimate. What can you say about the *true* success rate on the target population? Sure, it's expected to be close to 75%. But how close?—within 5%? 10%? It must depend on the size of the test set. Naturally we would be more confident of the 75% figure if it was based on a test set of 10,000 instances than a test set of a 100 instances. But how much more confident?

To answer these questions, we need some statistical reasoning. In statistics, a succession of independent events that either succeed or fail is called a *Bernoulli process*. The classic example is coin tossing. Each toss is an independent event. Let's say we always predict heads; but rather than "heads" or tails," each toss is considered a "success" or a "failure." Let's say the coin is biased, but we don't know what the probability of heads is. Then if we actually toss the coin 100 times and 75 of them are heads, we have a situation very like the one described above for a classifier with an observed 75% success rate on a test set. What can we say about the true success probability? In other words, imagine that there is a Bernoulli process—a biased coin—whose true (but unknown) success rate is p. Suppose that out of N trials, S are successes: thus the observed success rate is $f = S/N$. The question is, what does this tell you about the true success rate p?

The answer to this question is usually expressed as a confidence interval, that is, p lies within a certain specified interval with a certain specified confidence. For example, if $S = 750$ successes are observed out of $N = 1000$ trials, this indicates that the true success rate must be around 75%. But how close to 75%? It turns out that with 80% confidence, the true success rate p lies between 73.3% and 76.8%. If $S = 75$ successes are observed out of $N = 100$ trials, this also indicates that the true success rate must be around 75%. But the experiment is smaller, and the 80% confidence interval for p is wider, stretching from 70% to 81%.

These figures are easy to relate to qualitatively, but how are they derived quantitatively? We reason as follows. The mean and variance of a single Bernoulli trial with success rate p are p and $p(1 - p)$, respectively. If N trials are taken from a Bernoulli process, the expected success rate $f = S/N$ is a random variable with the same mean p; the variance is reduced by a factor of N to $p(1 - p)/N$. For large N, the distribution of this random variable approaches the normal distribution. These are all facts of statistics: we will not go into how they are derived.

The probability that a random variable X, with 0 mean, lies within a certain confidence range of width $2z$ is

$\Pr[-z \le X \le z] = c.$

For a normal distribution, values of c and corresponding values of z are given in tables printed at the back of most statistical texts. However, the tabulations conventionally take a slightly different form: they give the confidence that X will lie outside the range, and they give it for the upper part of the range only:

$\Pr[X \ge z].$

This is called a *one-tailed* probability because it refers only to the upper "tail" of the distribution. Normal distributions are symmetric, so the probabilities for the lower tail

$\Pr[X \le z]$

are just the same.

Table 5.1 gives an example. Like other tables for the normal distribution, this assumes that the random variable X has a mean of 0 and a variance of 1. Alternatively, you might say that the z figures are measured in *standard deviations from the mean*. Thus the figure for $\Pr[X \ge z] = 5\%$ implies that there is a 5% chance that X lies more than 1.65 standard deviations above the mean. Because the distribution is symmetric, the chance that X lies more than 1.65 standard deviations from the mean (above or below) is 10%, or

$\Pr[-1.65 \le X \le 1.65] = 90\%.$

All we need to do now is reduce the random variable f to have 0 mean and unit variance. We do this by subtracting the mean p, and dividing by the standard deviation $\sqrt{p(1-p)/N}$. This leads to

$$\Pr\left[-z < \frac{f-p}{\sqrt{p(1-p)/N}} < z \right] = c.$$

Now here is the procedure for finding confidence limits. Given a particular confidence figure c, consult Table 5.1 for the corresponding z value. To use the table you will first have to subtract c from 1, and then halve the result, so that for $c = 90\%$ you use the table entry for 5%. Linear interpolation can be used for intermediate confidence levels. Then write the inequality in the above expression as an equality and invert it to find an expression for p.

The final step involves solving a quadratic equation. Although not hard to do, it leads to an unpleasantly formidable expression for the confidence limits:

$$p = \left(f + \frac{z^2}{2N} \pm z\sqrt{\frac{f}{N} - \frac{f^2}{N} + \frac{z^2}{4N^2}} \right) \Bigg/ \left(1 + \frac{z^2}{N} \right).$$

Table 5.1	Confidence limits for the normal distribution.

$Pr[X \geq z]$	z
0.1%	3.09
0.5%	2.58
1%	2.33
5%	1.65
10%	1.28
20%	0.84
40%	0.25

The ± in this expression gives two values for p that represent the upper and lower confidence boundaries. Although the formula looks complicated, it is not hard to work out in particular cases.

This result can be used to obtain the values in the numeric example above. Setting $f = 75\%$, $N = 1000$, and $c = 80\%$ (so that $z = 1.28$) leads to the interval [0.733, 0.768] for p, while $N = 100$ leads to [0.70, 0.81] for the same level of confidence. Note that the normal distribution assumption is only valid for large N (say $N > 100$). Thus $f = 75\%$ and $N = 10$ leads to confidence limits [0.65, 1.02]—but these should be taken with a grain of salt, particularly the upper one! Probabilities, of course, can never be greater than 1.

5.3 Cross-validation

Now consider what to do when the amount of data for training and testing is limited. The *holdout* method reserves a certain amount for testing and uses the remainder for training (and sets part of that aside for validation, if required). In practical terms, it is common to hold one-third of the data out for testing and use the remaining two-thirds for training.

Of course, you may be unlucky: the sample used for training (or testing) may not be representative. In general, you can't tell whether a sample is representative or not. But there is one simple check that might be worthwhile: each of the classes in the full dataset should be represented in about the right proportion in the training and testing sets. If, by bad luck, all examples with a certain class were missed out of the training set, you could hardly expect a classifier learned from that data to perform well on the examples of that class—and the situation would be exacerbated by the fact that the class would necessarily be overrepresented in the test set since none of its instances made it into the training set! Instead, you should ensure that the random sampling is done in such a way as to guarantee that each class is properly represented in both training and test sets. This procedure is called *stratification*, and we might speak of *stratified holdout*. While it is well worth doing, stratification provides only a primitive safeguard against uneven representation in training and test sets.

A more general way to mitigate any bias caused by the particular sample chosen for holdout is to repeat the whole process, training and testing, several times with different random samples. In each iteration a certain proportion—say two-thirds—of the data is randomly selected for training, possibly with stratification, and the remainder used for testing. The error rates on the different iterations are averaged to yield an overall error rate. This is the *repeated holdout* method of error rate estimation.

In a single holdout procedure, you might consider swapping the roles of the testing and training data—that is, train the system on the test data and test it on the training data—and average the two results, thus reducing the effect of uneven representation in training and test sets. Unfortunately, this is only really plausible with a 50:50 split between training and test data, which is generally not ideal—it is better to use more than half the data for training, even at the expense of test data. However, a simple variant forms the basis of an important statistical technique called *cross-validation*. In cross-validation, you decide on a fixed number of *folds*, or partitions of the data. Suppose we use three. Then the data is split into three approximately equal partitions, and each in turn is used for testing while the remainder is used for training. That is, use two-thirds for training and one-third for testing, and repeat the procedure three times so that in the end, every instance has been used exactly once for testing. This is called *threefold cross-validation*, and if stratification is adopted as well—which it often is—it is *stratified threefold cross-validation*.

The standard way of predicting the error rate of a learning technique given a single, fixed sample of data is to use stratified tenfold cross-validation. The data is divided randomly into ten parts, in each of which the class is represented in approximately the same proportions as in the full dataset. Each part is held out in turn and the learning scheme trained on the remaining nine-tenths; then its error rate is calculated on the holdout set. Thus the learning procedure is executed a total of ten times, on different training sets (each of which have a lot in common). Finally, the ten error estimates are averaged to yield an overall error estimate.

Why ten? Extensive tests on numerous different datasets, with different learning techniques, have shown that ten is about the right number of folds to get the best estimate of error, and there is also some theoretical evidence that backs this up. Although these arguments are by no means conclusive, and debate continues to rage in machine learning and data mining circles about what is the best scheme for evaluation, tenfold cross-validation has become the standard method in practical terms. Tests have also shown that the use of stratification improves results slightly. Thus the standard evaluation technique in situations where only limited data is available is stratified tenfold cross-validation. Note that neither the stratification nor the division into ten folds has to be exact: it is enough to divide the data into ten approximately equal sets, in each of which the various class values are represented in approximately the right proportion. Statistical evaluation is not an exact science. Moreover, there is nothing magic about the exact number ten: fivefold or twentyfold cross-validation is likely to be almost as good.

A single tenfold cross-validation might not be enough to get a reliable error estimate. Different tenfold cross-validation experiments with the same learning scheme and dataset often produce different results, because of the effect of random variation in choosing the folds themselves. Stratification reduces the variation, but it certainly does not eliminate it entirely. When going for an accurate error estimate, it is standard procedure to repeat the cross-validation process ten times—that is, ten tenfold cross-validations—and average the results. This involves invoking the learning algorithm one hundred times, on datasets that are all nine-tenths the size of the original one. Getting a good measure of performance is a computation-intensive undertaking.

5.4   Other estimates

Tenfold cross-validation is the standard way of measuring the error rate of a learning scheme on a particular dataset; for reliable results, ten times tenfold cross-validation. But many other methods are used instead. Two that are particularly prevalent are *leave-one-out* cross-validation, and the *bootstrap*.

Leave-one-out

Leave-one-out cross-validation is simply n-fold cross-validation, where n is the number of instances in the dataset. Each instance in turn is left out, and the learning scheme is trained on all the remaining instances. It is judged by its correctness on the remaining instance, 1 or 0 for success or failure. The results of all n judgments, one for each member of the dataset, are averaged, and that average represents the final error estimate.

This procedure is an attractive one for two reasons. First, the greatest possible amount of data is used for training in each case, which presumably increases the chance that the classifier is an accurate one. Second, the procedure is deterministic: no random sampling is involved. There is no point in repeating it ten times, or repeating it all: the same result will be obtained each time. Set against this is the high computational cost, for the entire learning procedure must be executed n times, and this is usually quite infeasible for large datasets. Nevertheless, leave-one-out seems to offer a chance of squeezing the maximum out of a small dataset and getting as accurate an estimate as can possibly be obtained.

But there is a disadvantage to leave-one-out cross-validation, apart from the computational expense. By its very nature, it cannot be stratified—worse than that, it *guarantees* a nonstratified sample. Stratification involves getting the correct proportion of examples in each class into the test set, and this is impossible when the test set contains only a single example. A dramatic, though highly artificial, illustration of the problems this might cause is to imagine a completely random dataset that contains the same number of each of two classes. The best that an inducer can do with random data is to predict the majority class, giving a true error rate of 50%. But in each fold of leave-one-out, the opposite class to the test instance is in the majority—and therefore the predictions will always be incorrect, leading to an estimated error rate of 100%!

The bootstrap

The second estimation method we describe, the bootstrap, is based on the statistical procedure of sampling *with replacement*. Previously, whenever a sample was taken from the dataset to form a training or test set, it was drawn without replacement. That is, the same instance, once selected, could not be selected again. It is like picking teams for football: you can't choose the same person twice. But dataset instances are not like people. Most learning schemes *can* use the same instance twice, and it makes a difference to the result of learning if it is present in the training set twice. (Mathematical sticklers will notice that we should not really be talking about "sets" at all if the same object can appear more than once.)

The idea of the bootstrap is to sample the dataset with replacement to form a training set. We will describe a particular variant, mysteriously (but for a reason that will soon become apparent) called the *0.632 bootstrap*. For this, a dataset of n instances is sampled n times, with replacement, to give another dataset of n instances. Since some elements in this second dataset will (almost certainly) be repeated, there must be some instances in the original dataset that have not been picked: we will use these as test instances.

What is the chance that a particular instance will not be picked for the training set? It has a $1/n$ probability of being picked each time, and so a $1-1/n$ probability of *not* being picked. Multiply this up according to the number of picking opportunities, which is n, and the result is a figure of

$$\left(1 - \frac{1}{n}\right)^n \approx e^{-1} = 0.368$$

(where *e* is the base of natural logarithms, 2.7183, not the error rate!) for the chance of a particular instance not being picked at all. Thus for a reasonably large dataset, the test set will contain about 36.8% of the instances, and the training set will contain about 63.2% of them (now you can see why it's called the *0.632 bootstrap*). Some instances will be repeated in the training set, bringing it up to a total size of *n*, the same as in the original dataset.

The figure obtained by training a learning system on the training set and calculating its error over the test set will be a pessimistic estimate of the true error rate, because the training set, although its size is *n*, nevertheless contains only 63% of the instances, which is not a great deal compared, for example, to the 90% used in tenfold cross-validation. To compensate for this, the test set error rate is combined with the resubstitution error on the instances in the training set. The resubstitution figure, as we warned earlier, gives a very optimistic estimate of the true error and should certainly not be used as an error figure on its own. But the bootstrap procedure combines it with the test error rate to give a final estimate *e* as follows

$$e = 0.632 \cdot e_{\text{test instances}} + 0.368 \cdot e_{\text{training instances}}$$

Then, the whole bootstrap procedure is repeated several times, with different replacement samples for the training set, and the results averaged.

The bootstrap procedure may be the best way of estimating error for very small datasets. However, like leave-one-out cross-validation, it has disadvantages that can be illustrated by considering a special, artificial situation. In fact, the very dataset we considered above will do: a completely random dataset with two classes. The true error rate is 50% for any prediction rule. But a scheme that memorized the training set would give a perfect resubstitution score of 100%, so that $e_{\text{training instances}} = 0$, and the 0.632 bootstrap will mix this in with a weight of 0.368 to give an overall error rate of only 31.6% ($0.632 \times 50\%$ + $0.368 \times 0\%$), which is misleadingly optimistic.

5.5 Comparing data mining schemes

Often we are interested in comparing two different learning schemes on the same problem to see which is the better one to use. The obvious way to do this is to determine the error rate for each scheme using, say, tenfold cross-validation, and choose the one that gives the smaller error. However, this is unreliable because there is substantial variance in an individual tenfold cross-validation. The variance can be reduced by averaging the results of several cross-validations—ten cross-validations were suggested above—but although this will certainly improve matters, it is still not clear whether the results it produces are reliable. The best way is to use a statistical test that gives the kind of confidence bounds that we discussed earlier when considering how to predict true performance from a given test-set error rate.

If there were unlimited data, we could simply use a large amount for training and evaluate performance on an independent test set, obtaining confidence bounds as described earlier. However, we assume a limited data situation. We have settled on tenfold cross-validation as the best indicator of the "true" performance of a learning scheme in such a situation: let us take that as given. But any particular cross-validation experiment yields only an approximation of the true cross-validation error figure. We can sample from the distribution of cross-validation experiments by using different random partitions of the given dataset, treating the error rates calculated in these cross-validation runs as different, independent samples from a probability distribution.

From this point of view, when comparing two learning schemes by comparing the average error rate over several cross-validations, we are effectively trying to determine whether the mean of a set of samples—samples of the cross-validation estimate, that is—is significantly greater than, or significantly less than, the mean of another. This is a job for a statistical device known as the *t-test*, or *Student's t-test*. Because the same cross-validation split can be used for both methods to obtain a matched pair of results, one for each scheme, giving a set of pairs for different cross-validation splits, a more sensitive version of the t-test known as a *paired t-test* can be used.

We need some notation. There is a set of samples $x_1, x_2, \ldots, x_k$ obtained by successive tenfold cross-validations using one learning scheme, and a second set of samples $y_1, y_2, \ldots, y_k$ obtained by successive tenfold cross-validations of the other. Each cross-validation is generated using a different tenfold partition of the data; k would be 10 if we were using ten tenfold cross-validations. We will get best results if exactly the same cross-validation partitions are used for both schemes, so that x_1 and y_1 are obtained using the same cross-validation split, as are x_2 and y_2, and so on. Denote the mean of the first set of samples by $\overline{x}$ and the mean of the second set by $\overline{y}$. We are trying to determine whether $\overline{x}$ is significantly different from $\overline{y}$.

If there are enough samples, the mean ($\overline{x}$) of a set of independent samples ($x_1, x_2, \ldots, x_k$) has a normal (that is, Gaussian) distribution, regardless of the distribution underlying the samples themselves. Call the true value of the mean μ. If we knew the variance of that normal distribution, so that it could be reduced to have 0 mean and unit variance, we could obtain confidence limits on μ, given the mean of the samples ($\overline{x}$). However, the variance is unknown, and the only way we can get at it is to estimate it from the set of samples.

That is not hard to do. The variance of $\overline{x}$ can be estimated by dividing the variance calculated from the samples $x_1, x_2, \ldots, x_k$—call it σ_x^2—by k. But the fact that we have to *estimate* the variance changes things somewhat. We can reduce the distribution of μ to have 0 mean and unit variance by using

$$\frac{\overline{x} - \mu}{\sqrt{\sigma_x^2/k}} \,.$$

Because the variance is only an estimate, this does *not* have a normal distribution (although it does become normal for large values of k). Instead, it has what is called a *Student's distribution with k–1 degrees of freedom*. What this means in practice is that we have to use a table of confidence intervals for Student's distribution, rather than the confidence table for the normal distribution given earlier. For 9 degrees of freedom (which is the correct number if we are using the average of ten cross-validations), the appropriate confidence limits are shown in Table 5.2. If you compare them with Table 5.1, you will see that the Student's figures are slightly more conservative—for a given degree of confidence, the interval is slightly wider—and this reflects the additional uncertainty caused by having to estimate the variance. Different tables are needed for different numbers of degrees of freedom, and if there are more than 100 degrees of freedom, the confidence limits are very close to those for the normal distribution. Like those in Table 5.1, the figures in Table 5.2 are for a "one-sided" confidence interval.

To decide whether the means $\overline{x}$ and $\overline{y}$, each an average of the same number k of samples, are the same or not, we consider the differences d_i between corresponding observations, $d_i = x_i - y_i$. This is legitimate because the observations are paired. The mean of this difference is just the difference between the two means, $\overline{d} = \overline{x} - \overline{y}$, and, like the means themselves, it has a Student's distribution with k–1 degrees of freedom. If the means are the same, the difference is 0 (this is called the *null hypothesis*); if they're significantly different, the difference will be significantly different from 0. So for a given confidence level, we will check whether the actual difference exceeds the confidence limit.

First reduce the difference to a 0-mean, unit-variance variable called the *t*-statistic:

$$t = \frac{\overline{d}}{\sqrt{\sigma_d^2/k}} \,,$$

where σ_d^2 is the variance of the difference samples. Then decide on a confidence level—generally, 5% or 1% is used in practice. From this the confidence limit z is determined using Table 5.2 if k is 10, or if not a confidence table of the Student distribution for the k value in question. A two-tailed test is appropriate because we do not know in advance whether the mean of the xs is likely to be greater

Table 5.2	Confidence limits for Student's distribution with 9 degrees of freedom.
$\Pr[X \geq z]$	z
0.1%	4.30
0.5%	3.25
1%	2.82
5%	1.83
10%	1.38
20%	0.88

than that of the ys or vice versa: thus for a 1% test we use the value corresponding to 0.5% in Table 5.2. If the value of t according to the formula above is greater than z, or less than $-z$, we reject the null hypothesis that the means are the same and conclude that there really is a significant difference between the two learning methods on that dataset.

Two observations are worth making on this procedure. The first is technical: what if the observations were not paired? That is, what if we were unable, for some reason, to assess the error of each learning scheme on the same cross-validation splits of the dataset? What if the number of cross-validations for each scheme were not even the same? These conditions could arise if someone else had evaluated one of the schemes and published several different cross-validation estimates on a dataset—or perhaps just their mean and variance—and we wished to compare this with a different learning scheme. Then it is necessary to use a regular, nonpaired t-test. If the means are normally distributed, as we are assuming, the difference between the means is also normally distributed. Instead of taking the mean of the difference, $\bar{d}$, we use the difference of the means, $\bar{x} - \bar{y}$. Of course, that's the same thing: the mean of the difference *is* the difference of the means. But the variance of the difference $\bar{d}$ is *not* the same. If the variance of the samples $x_1, x_2, \ldots, x_k$ is σ_x^2 and the variance of the samples $y_1, y_2, \ldots, y_\ell$ is σ_y^2, the best estimate of the variance of the difference of the means is

$$\frac{\sigma_x^2}{k} + \frac{\sigma_y^2}{\ell}.$$

It is this variance (or rather, its square root) that should be used as the denominator of the t-statistic given above. The degrees of freedom, necessary for consulting Student's confidence tables, should be taken conservatively to be the minimum of the degrees of freedom of the two samples. Essentially, knowing that the observations are paired allows the use of a better estimate for the variance, which will produce tighter confidence bounds.

The second observation concerns the use of tenfold cross-validation estimates from the same dataset. Given a single dataset, we have estimated the variance of tenfold cross-validation measures of the error rate by taking different partitions of the dataset and calculating the tenfold cross-validation estimates on each partition. This allows us to obtain a variance figure for the error rate. But these estimates are not actually independent because there is only a single dataset: the variance figure that should really be used is that for different tenfold cross-validation estimates of the error rate *using different samples for the dataset.* That is not possible in a practical situation, because only one dataset is available—if there was more data, we would already be using it! Thus we have only really tested whether our *estimates* are significantly different, not the "true" performance of the classifiers across different training datasets. However, numerous experiments have shown that repeated tenfold cross-validation is one of the most accurate estimators available. This is what we recommend in practice, repeating the entire cross-validation procedure perhaps ten times.

5.6   Predicting probabilities

Throughout this section we have tacitly assumed that the goal is to maximize the success rate of the predictions. The outcome for each test instance is either *correct*, if the prediction agrees with the actual value for that instance, or *incorrect*, if it does not. There are no grays: everything is black or white, correct or incorrect. In many situations, this is the most appropriate perspective. If the learning scheme, when it is actually applied, results in either a correct or an incorrect prediction, success is the right measure to use. This is sometimes called a *0–1 loss function*: the "loss" is either 0 if the prediction is correct, or 1 if it is not. The use of *loss* is conventional, though a more optimistic terminology might couch the outcome in terms of profit instead.

Other situations are softer-edged. Most learning schemes can associate a probability with each prediction (as the Naive Bayes scheme does). It might be more natural to take this probability into account when judging correctness. For example, a correct outcome predicted with a probability of 99% should perhaps weigh more heavily than one predicted with a probability of 51% and, in a two-class situation, perhaps the latter is not all that much better than an *incorrect* outcome predicted with probability 51%. Whether it is appropriate to take prediction probabilities into account depends on the application. If the ultimate application really is just a prediction of the outcome, and no prizes are awarded for a realistic assessment of the likelihood of the prediction, it does not seem appropriate to use probabilities. If the prediction is subject to further processing, however—perhaps involving assessment by a person, or a cost analysis, or maybe even serving as input to a second-level learning process—then it may well be appropriate to take prediction probabilities into account.

Quadratic loss function

Suppose for a single instance there are k possible outcomes, or classes, and for a given instance the learning scheme comes up with a probability vector p_1, $p_2, \ldots, p_k$ for the classes (where these probabilities sum to 1). The actual outcome for that instance will be one of the possible classes. However, it is convenient to express it as a vector $a_1, a_2, \ldots, a_k$ whose ith component, where i is the actual class, is 1, and all other components are 0. We can express the penalty associated with this situation as a loss function that depends on both the p vector and the a vector.

One criterion that is frequently used to evaluate probabilistic prediction is the *quadratic loss function,*

$$\Sigma_j (p_j - a_j)^2.$$

Note that this is for a single instance: the summation is over possible outputs, not over different instances. Just one of the as will be 1 and the rest 0, so the sum contains contributions of p_j^2 for the incorrect predictions and $(1 - p_i)^2$ for the correct one: consequently it can be written

$$1 - 2p_i + \Sigma_j p_j^2,$$

where i is the correct class. When the test set contains several instances, the loss function is summed over them all.

It is an interesting theoretical fact that if you seek to minimize the value of the quadratic loss function in a situation where the actual class is generated probabilistically, the best strategy is to choose for the p vector the actual probabilities of the different outcomes, that is, $p_i = \Pr[\text{class} = i]$. If the true probabilities are known, they will be the best values for p. If they are not, a system that strives to minimize the quadratic loss function will be encouraged to use its best estimate of $\Pr[\text{class} = i]$ as the value for p_i.

This is quite easy to see. Denote the true probabilities by $p_1^*, p_2^*, \ldots, p_k^*$, so that $p_i^* = \Pr[\text{class} = i]$. The expected value of the quadratic loss function over test instances can be rewritten as follows:

$$E\left[\Sigma_j (p_j - a_j)^2\right] = \Sigma_j (E[p_j^2] - 2E[p_j a_j] + E[a_j^2])$$
$$= \Sigma_j (p_j^2 - 2p_j p_j^* + p_j^*) = \Sigma_j ((p_j - p_j^*)^2 + p_j^*(1 - p_j^*)).$$

The first stage just involves bringing the expectation inside the sum and expanding the square. For the second, p_j is just a constant and the expected value of a_j is simply p_j^*; moreover, since a_j is either 0 or 1, $a_j^2 = a_j$ and its expected value is p_j^* too. The third stage is straightforward algebra. To minimize the resulting sum, it is clear that it is best to choose $p_j = p_j^*$ so that the squared term disappears and all that is left is a term that is just the variance of the true distribution governing the actual class.

Minimizing the squared error has a long history in prediction problems. In the present context, the quadratic loss function forces the predictor to be honest about choosing its best estimate of the probabilities—or, rather, it gives preference to predictors that are able to make the best guess at the true probabilities. Moreover, the quadratic loss function has some useful theoretical properties that we will not go into here. For all these reasons it is frequently used as the criterion of success in probabilistic prediction situations.

Informational loss function

Another popular criterion for the evaluation of probabilistic prediction is the *informational loss function*

$$-\log_2 p_i$$

where the ith prediction is the correct one. This represents the information (in bits) required to express the actual class i with respect to the probability distribution $p_1, p_2, \ldots, p_k$. In other words, if you were given the probability distribution and someone had to communicate to you which class was the one that actually occurred, this is the number of bits they would need to encode the information if they did it as effectively as possible. (Of course, it is always possible to use *more* bits.) Since probabilities are always less than 1, their logarithms are negative, and the minus sign makes the outcome positive. For example, in a two-class situation—heads or tails—with an equal probability of each class, the occurrence of a head would take one bit to transmit, because $-\log_2 1/2$ is 1.

The expected value of the informational loss function, if the true probabilities are $p_1^*, p_2^*, \ldots, p_k^*$, is

$$-p_1^* \log_2 p_1 - p_2^* \log_2 p_2 - \ldots - p_k^* \log_2 p_k.$$

Like the quadratic loss function, this expression is minimized by choosing $p_j = p_j^*$, in which case the expression becomes the entropy of the true distribution:

$$-p_1^* \log_2 p_1^* - p_2^* \log_2 p_2^* - \ldots - p_k^* \log_2 p_k^*.$$

Thus the informational loss function also rewards honesty in predictors that know the true probabilities and encourages predictors that do not to put forward their best guess.

The informational loss function also has a *gambling* interpretation, where you imagine gambling on the outcome, placing odds on each possible class and winning according to the class that comes up. Successive instances are like successive bets: you carry wins (or losses) over from one to the next. The logarithm of the total amount of money you win over the whole test set is the value of the informational loss function. In gambling, it pays to be able to predict the odds as accurately as possible and, in that sense, honesty pays too.

One problem with the informational loss function is that if you assign a probability of zero to an event that actually occurs, the function's value is minus infinity. This corresponds to losing your shirt when gambling. Prudent punters never bet *everything* on a particular event, no matter how certain it appears. Likewise, prudent predictors operating under the informational loss function do not assign zero probability to any outcome. This does lead to a problem when no information is available about that outcome on which to base a prediction: this is called the *zero-frequency problem,* and various plausible solutions have been proposed, such as the Laplace estimator discussed for Naive Bayes on page 85.

Discussion

If you are in the business of evaluating predictions of probabilities, which of the two loss functions should you use? That's a good question, and there is no universally agreed-upon answer—it's really a matter of taste. They both do the fundamental job expected of a loss function: they give maximum reward to predictors that are capable of predicting the true probabilities accurately. However, there are some objective differences between the two that may help you form an opinion.

The quadratic loss function takes account not only of the probability assigned to the event that actually occurred, but the other probabilities as well. For example, in a four-class situation, suppose you assigned 40% to the class that actually came up, and distributed the remainder among the other three classes. The quadratic loss will depend on how you distributed it, because of the sum of the p_j^2 that occurs in the expression given earlier for the quadratic loss function. The loss will be smallest if the 60% was distributed evenly among the three classes: an uneven distribution will increase the sum of the squares. The informational loss function, on the other hand, depends solely on the probability assigned to the class that actually occurred. If you're gambling on a particular event coming up, and it does, who cares how you distributed the remainder of your money among the other events?

If you assign a very small probability to the class that actually occurs, the information loss function will penalize you massively. The maximum penalty, for a zero probability, is infinite. The gambling world penalizes mistakes like this harshly too! The quadratic loss function, on the other hand, is milder, being bounded by

$$1 + \Sigma_j p_j^2,$$

which can never exceed 2.

Finally, proponents of the informational loss function point to a general theory of performance assessment in learning called the *minimum description length principle*. They argue that the size of the structures that a scheme learns can be measured in bits of information, and if the same units are used to measure the loss, the two can be combined in useful and powerful ways. We return to this in Section 5.9.

5.7 Counting the cost

The evaluations that have been discussed so far do not take into account the cost of making wrong decisions, wrong classifications. Optimizing classification rate without considering the cost of the errors often leads to strange results. In one case, machine learning was being used to determine the exact day when each cow in a dairy herd was in estrus, or "in heat." Cows were identified by electronic ear tags, and various attributes were used such as milk volume and chemical composition (recorded automatically by a high-tech milking machine), and milking order—for cows are regular beasts and generally arrive in the milking shed in the same order, except in unusual circumstances like estrus. In a modern dairy operation it's important to know when a cow is ready: animals are fertilized by artificial insemination, and missing a cycle will delay calving unnecessarily, causing complications further down the line. In early experiments, machine learning schemes stubbornly predicted that each cow was *never* in estrus. Like humans, cows have a menstrual cycle of approximately thirty days, so this "null" rule is correct about 97% of the time—an impressive degree of accuracy in any agricultural domain! What was wanted, of course, were rules that predicted the "in estrus" situation more accurately than the "not in estrus" one: the costs of the two kinds of error were different. Evaluation by classification accuracy tacitly assumes equal error costs.

Other examples where errors cost different amounts include loan decisions: the cost of lending to a defaulter is far greater than the lost-business cost of refusing a loan to a non-defaulter. And oil-slick detection: the cost of failing to detect an environment-threatening real slick is far greater than the cost of a false alarm. And load forecasting: the cost of gearing up electricity generators for a storm that doesn't hit is far less than the cost of being caught completely unprepared. And diagnosis: the cost of misidentifying problems with a machine that turns out to be fault-free is less than the cost of overlooking problems with one that is about to fail. And promotional mailing: the cost of sending junk mail to a household that doesn't respond is far less than the lost-business cost of not sending it to a household that would have responded. Why, these are all the examples of Chapter 1! And, in truth, you'd be hard pressed to find an application in which the costs of different kinds of error were the same.

If the costs are known, it is easy to take them into account in a financial analysis of the decision-making process. We restrict attention to the two-class case with classes yes and no, lend or not lend, mark a suspicious patch as an oil-slick or not, and so on. Then the four different possible outcomes of a single prediction are shown in Table 5.3. The *true positive* and *true negative* are correct classifications. A *false positive* is when the outcome is incorrectly predicted as yes (or *positive*), when it is in fact no (*negative*). A *false negative* is when the outcome is incorrectly predicted as negative when it is in fact positive. Note incidentally that in a multiclass prediction, the result on a test set is often displayed as a two-dimensional *confusion matrix* with a row and column for each class. Each matrix element shows the number of test examples for which the *actual* class is the row and the *predicted* class is the column; good results correspond to large numbers down the main diagonal and small, ideally zero, off-diagonal elements. Table 5.3 is a confusion matrix for the two-class case.

These two kinds of error, false positives and false negatives, will generally have different costs: likewise the two types of correct classification will have different benefits. The "success rate" that has been used up to now is just the number of true positives and true negatives divided by the total number of test instances. Taking costs into account allows this to be replaced by the average cost (or, thinking more positively, profit) per decision. Moreover, a financial analysis of the decision-making process will take into account the cost of using the machine-learning tool—including the cost of gathering the training data—and the cost of using the model, or decision structure, that it produces—that is, the cost of determining the attributes for the test instances. If all costs are

Table 5.3	Different outcomes of a two-class prediction.		
		predicted class	
		yes	no
actual class	yes	true positive	false negative
	no	false positive	true negative

known, and the projected number of the four different outcomes can be estimated—say, using cross-validation—it is straightforward to perform this kind
of financial analysis.

Lift charts

The problem is that, in practice, costs are rarely known with any degree of accuracy, and people will want to ponder various different scenarios. Imagine you're
in the direct mailing business and are contemplating a mass mailout of a promotional offer to a million households—most of whom won't respond, of course.
Let us say that, based on previous experience, the proportion who normally
respond is known to be 0.1% (1,000 respondents). Suppose a data mining tool is
available which, based on known information about the households, identifies a
subset of a 100,000 for which the response rate is 0.4% (400 respondents). It may
well pay off to restrict the mailout to these 100,000 households—that depends on
the mailing cost compared to the return gained for each response to the offer. In
marketing terminology, the increase in response rate, a factor of four in this case,
is known as the *lift* factor yielded by the learning tool. If you knew the costs, you
could determine the payoff implied by a particular lift factor.

But you probably want to evaluate other possibilities too. The same data mining scheme, with different parameter settings, may be able to identify 400,000
households for which the response rate will be 0.2% (800 respondents), corresponding to a lift factor of two. Again, whether this would be a more profitable
target for the mailout can be calculated from the costs involved. It may be necessary to factor in the cost of creating and using the model—including collecting
the information that is required to come up with the attribute values. After all, if
developing the model is very expensive, a mass mailing may be more cost-effec-
tive than a targeted one.

Given a learning scheme that outputs probabilities for the predicted class of
each member of the set of test instances (as Naive Bayes does), your job is to find
subsets of test instances that have a high proportion of positive instances, higher
than in the test set as a whole. To do this, the instances should be sorted in
descending order of predicted probability of yes. Then, to find a sample of a
given size with the greatest possible proportion of positive instances, just read
the requisite number of instances off the list, starting at the top. If each test
instance's class is known, you can calculate the lift factor by simply counting the
number of positive instances that the sample includes, dividing by the sample
size to get a success proportion, and dividing by the success proportion for the
complete test set to get a lift factor.

Table 5.4 shows an example, for a small dataset with 100 instances of which
20 are yes responses—an overall success proportion of 20%. The instances have
been sorted in descending probability order according to the predicted proba-

Table 5.4	Data for a lift chart.					
rank	predicted probability	actual class		rank	predicted probability	actual class
1	0.95	yes		11	0.77	no
2	0.93	yes		12	0.76	yes
3	0.93	no		13	0.73	yes
4	0.88	yes		14	0.65	no
5	0.86	yes		15	0.63	yes
6	0.85	yes		16	0.58	no
7	0.82	yes		17	0.56	yes
8	0.80	yes		18	0.49	no
9	0.80	no		19	0.48	yes
10	0.79	yes		…	…	…

bility of a yes response. The first instance is the one that the learning scheme thinks is most likely to be positive, the second is the next most likely, and so on. The numeric values of the probabilities are not of importance: rank is the only thing that matters. With each rank is given the actual class of the instance. Thus the learning scheme was right about items 1 and 2—they are indeed positives—but wrong about item 3—it turned out to be a negative. Now, if you were seeking the most promising sample of size 10, but only knew the predicted probabilities and not the actual classes, your best bet would be the top ten ranking instances. Eight of these are positive, so the success proportion for this sample is 80%, corresponding to a lift factor of four.

If you knew the different costs involved, you could work them out for each sample size and choose the most profitable. But a graphical depiction of the various possibilities will often be far more revealing than presenting a single "optimal" decision. Repeating the above operation for different sized samples allows you to plot a lift chart like that of Figure 5.1. The horizontal axis shows the sample size as a proportion of the total possible mailout. The vertical axis shows the number of responses obtained. The lower left and upper right points correspond to no mailout at all, with a response of 0, and a full mailout, with a response of 1,000. The diagonal line gives the expected result for differently sized random samples. But we do not choose random samples, we choose those instances which, according to the data mining tool, are most likely to generate a positive

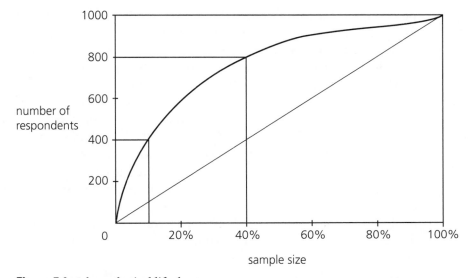

Figure 5.1 A hypothetical lift chart.

response. These correspond to the upper line, which is derived by summing the actual responses over the corresponding percentage of the instance list sorted in probability order. The two particular scenarios discussed above are marked: a 10% mailout that yields 400 respondents and a 40% one that yields 800.

Where you'd like to be in a lift chart is near the upper left-hand corner: at the very best, 1,000 responses from a mailout of just 1,000, where you send only to those households that will respond and are rewarded with a 100% success rate. Any selection procedure worthy of the name will keep you above the diagonal—otherwise you'd be seeing a response that was worse than for random sampling. So the operating part of the diagram is the upper triangle, and the farther to the northwest the better.

ROC curves

Lift charts are a valuable tool, widely used in marketing. They are closely related to a graphical technique for evaluating data mining schemes known as *ROC curves,* which are used in just the same situation as above, where the learner is trying to select samples of test instances that have a high proportion of positives. The acronym stands for "receiver operating characteristic," a term used in signal detection to characterize the tradeoff between hit rate and false alarm rate over a noisy channel. The ROC curve plots the number of positives included in the sample on the vertical axis, expressed as a percentage of the total number of positives, against the number of negatives included in the sample, expressed as a percentage of the total number of negatives, on the horizontal axis. The vertical axis is the same as the lift chart's, except that it is expressed as a percentage. The horizontal axis is slightly different—number of negatives rather than sample size. However, in direct marketing situations where the proportion of positives is very small anyway (like 0.1%), there is a negligible difference between the size of a sample and the number of negatives it contains, so the ROC curve and lift chart look very similar. As with lift charts, the northwest corner is the place to be.

Figure 5.2 shows an example ROC curve—the jagged line—for the sample of test data in Table 5.4. You can follow it along with the table. From the origin: go up two (two positives), along one (one negative), up five (five positives), along (negative), up, along, up twice, and so on. Each point corresponds to drawing a line at a certain position on the ranked list and counting the yeses and nos above it, plotting them vertically and horizontally respectively. As you go farther down the list, corresponding to a larger sample, the number of positives and negatives both increase.

The jagged ROC line in Figure 5.2 depends intimately on the details of the particular sample of test data. This sample dependence can be reduced by applying cross-validation: for each different number of nos—that is, each position along the horizontal axis—take just enough of the highest-ranked instances to include that number of nos, and count the number of yeses they contain; finally, average that number over different folds of the cross-validation. The result is the smooth curve in Figure 5.2. ROC curves depict the performance of a classifier without regard to class distribution or error costs.

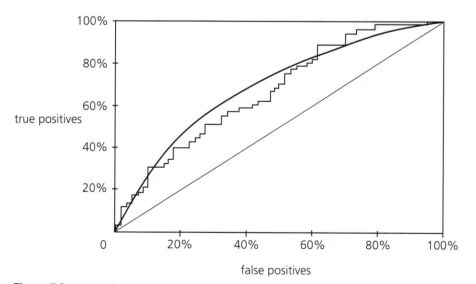

Figure 5.2 A sample ROC curve.

Let's look more closely at this method of generating a smoothed ROC curve. For each position on the horizontal axis, find the corresponding point on the vertical axis using tenfold cross-validation, where the quantity being calculated, and averaged over the ten folds, is the number of yes responses in a sample containing the appropriate number of nos. But there's no need to repeat the tenfold cross-validation again and again for every horizontal position: given the outcome of one fold of the cross-validation—a probability-ranked list of instances—you can read off the vertical position for every horizontal position just by recording the number of yeses in samples containing each possible number of nos. Averaging these figures over the ten folds is tantamount to plotting the number of yeses against the number of nos on a scatter diagram, drawing vertical bands corresponding to different numbers of nos, and averaging the points within each vertical band.

It is instructive to look at cross-validated ROC curves obtained using different learning schemes. For example, in Figure 5.3, method A excels if a small, focused sample is sought; that is, if you are working toward the left-hand side of the graph. Clearly, if you aim to cover just 40% of the true positives you should choose method A, which gives a false positive rate of around 5%, rather than B, which gives over 20% false positives. But method B excels if you are planning a large sample: if you are covering 80% of the true positives, B will give a false positive rate of 60% as compared with A's 80%. The shaded area is called the *convex hull* of the two curves, and you should always operate at a point that lies on the upper boundary of the convex hull.

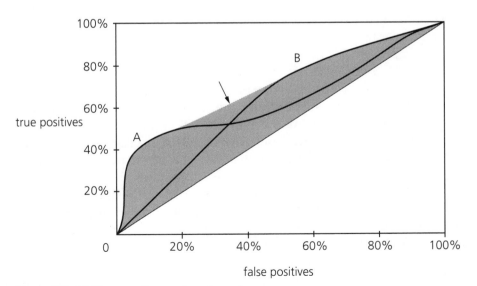

Figure 5.3 ROC curves for two learning schemes.

What about the region in the middle where neither method A nor B lies on the convex hull? It is a remarkable fact that you can get anywhere in the shaded region by combining methods A and B, using them at random with appropriate probabilities. To see this, choose a particular probability cutoff for method A that gives true and false positive rates of t_A and f_A respectively, and another cutoff for B that gives t_B and f_B. If you use these two schemes at random with probability p and q, where $p + q = 1$, then you will get true and false positive rates of $pt_A + qt_A$ and $pf_A + qf_A$. This represents a point lying on the straight line joining the points (t_A, f_A) and (t_B, f_B), and by varying p and q you can trace out the whole line between these two points. By this device, the entire shaded region can be reached. Only if a particular scheme generates a point that lies on the convex hull should it be used alone: otherwise it would always be better to use a combination of classifiers corresponding to a point that lies on the convex hull.

Cost-sensitive learning

So far we have assumed that the learning scheme is inherently cost-sensitive and outputs probabilities, like Naive Bayes. Most classifiers can easily be adapted to compute probabilities. In a decision tree, for example, the probability distribution is just the distribution of instances at the corresponding leaf. However, most learning schemes—including those that learn decision trees—are not really cost-sensitive: they generate the same classifier independent of the costs assigned to each class. Even though the same decision tree can be used to plot an entire ROC curve, the cost information is not being used during learning. Much better performance might be obtained if the classifier were adjusted to different cost situations by the learning algorithm. Fortunately, there is a simple and general way to make *any* learning scheme cost-sensitive, in a two-class situation.

The idea is to make the learner cost-sensitive by generating data samples with different proportions of yes and no instances. Suppose you artificially increase the number of no instances in a dataset by a factor of ten, and then use the dataset for training. If the learning scheme is striving to minimize the number of errors made, it will come up with a decision structure that is skewed toward the avoidance of errors on the no instances, since any such errors are effectively penalized tenfold. If data with the original proportion of no instances is used for testing, fewer errors will be made on no instances than on yes instances—that is, there will be fewer false positives than false negatives—because false positives have been weighted ten times more heavily than false negatives. This gives a general technique for building classification structures that are cost-sensitive, by varying the proportion of instances in the training set.

One way of varying the proportion of training instances is to duplicate instances in the dataset. However, many learning schemes allow instances to be weighted. As mentioned in Section 3.2, missing values can be accommodated when building decision trees by notionally splitting the instance into pieces, using a numeric weighting scheme, and sending part of it down each branch. Instance weights are normally initialized to 1. To build cost-sensitive decision trees, they can be initialized to the relative costs of the two kinds of error, false positives and false negatives.

Now the way to obtain ROC curves from learning schemes that are not cost-sensitive is clear. For each fold of a tenfold cross-validation, weight the instances for a selection of different cost ratios, train the scheme on each weighted set, count the true positives and false positives in the test set, and plot the resulting point on the ROC axes. (It doesn't matter whether the test set is weighted or not because the axes in the ROC diagram are expressed as the *percentage* of true and false positives.) Then average the points in each vertical band to make a smoothed curve. This yields a general technique for cost-sensitive learning that places no constraints on the underlying learning scheme. However, it is far more costly than the method described above for inherently cost-sensitive probabilistic classifiers like Naive Bayes, because it involves a separate tenfold cross-validation for every point on the curve.

Discussion

People have grappled with the fundamental tradeoff illustrated by lift charts and ROC curves in a wide variety of domains. Information retrieval is a good example. Given a query, a Web search engine produces a list of hits that represent documents supposedly relevant to the query. Compare one system that locates 100 documents, 40 of which are relevant, with another that locates 400 documents, 80 of which are relevant. Which is better? The answer should now be obvious: it depends on the relative cost of false positives—documents returned that aren't relevant—and false negatives—documents that are relevant that aren't returned. Information retrieval researchers define parameters called *recall* and *precision*:

$$\text{recall} = \frac{\text{number of documents retrieved that are relevant}}{\text{total number of documents that are relevant}}$$

$$\text{precision} = \frac{\text{number of documents retrieved that are relevant}}{\text{total number of documents that are retrieved}}.$$

For example, if the list of yeses and nos in Table 5.4 represented a ranked list of retrieved documents and whether they were relevant or not, and the entire collection contained a total of 40 relevant documents, then "recall at 10" would refer to recall for the top 10 documents, that is $8/40 = 20\%$; while "precision at 10" would be $8/10 = 80\%$. Information retrieval experts use *recall-precision*

Table 5.5		Different measures used to evaluate the false positive versus false negative tradeoff.		
	domain	plot	axes	explanation of axes
lift chart	marketing	TP vs. subset size	TP	number of true positives
			subset size	$\dfrac{TP + FP}{TP + FP + TN + FN} \times 100\%$
ROC curve	communications	TP rate vs. FP rate	TP rate	$\dfrac{TP}{TP + FN} \times 100\%$
			FP rate	$\dfrac{FP}{FP + TN} \times 100\%$
recall-precision curve	information retrieval	recall vs. precision	recall	same as TP rate above
			precision	$\dfrac{TP}{TP + FP} \times 100\%$

curves which plot one against the other, for different numbers of retrieved documents, in just the same way as ROC curves and lift charts—except that since the axes are different, the curves are hyperbolic in shape and the desired operating point is toward the upper right.

Table 5.5 summarizes the three different ways we have met of evaluating the same basic tradeoff; TP, FP, TN, and FN are the number of true positives, false positives, true negatives, and false negatives, respectively. You want to choose a set of instances with a high proportion of yes instances and a high coverage of the yes instances: you can increase the proportion by (conservatively) using a smaller coverage, or (liberally) increase the coverage at the expense of the proportion. Different techniques give different tradeoffs and can be plotted as two different lines on any of these graphical charts.

People also seek single measures that characterize performance. Two that are used in information retrieval are *three-point average recall,* which gives the average precision obtained at recall values of 20%, 50%, and 80%; and *eleven-point average recall,* which gives the average precision obtained at recall values of 0%, 10%, 20%, 30%, 40%, 50%, 60%, 70%, 80%, 90%, and 100%. Also used in information retrieval is the *F-measure,* which is

$$\frac{2 \times \text{recall} \times \text{precision}}{\text{recall} + \text{precision}} = \frac{2TP}{2TP + FP + FN}.$$

A rather different measure is the product

$$\text{TP rate} \times (1 - \text{FP rate}) = \frac{\text{TP} \times \text{TN}}{(\text{TP} + \text{FP}) \times (\text{FP} + \text{TN})};$$

while finally, of course, there is our old friend the success rate:

$$\frac{\text{TP} + \text{TN}}{\text{TP} + \text{FP} + \text{TN} + \text{FN}}.$$

Although such measures may be useful if costs and class distributions are unknown and one scheme must be chosen to handle all situations, no single number is able to capture the tradeoff. That can only be done by two-dimensional depictions like lift charts, ROC curves, and recall-precision diagrams.

5.8 Evaluating numeric prediction

All the evaluation measures we have discussed pertain to classification situations rather than numeric prediction situations. The basic principles—using an independent test set rather than the training set for performance evaluation, the holdout method, cross-validation—apply equally well to numeric prediction. But the basic quality measure offered by the error rate is no longer appropriate: errors are not simply present or absent, they come in different sizes.

Several alternative measures, summarized in Table 5.6, can be used to evaluate the success of numeric prediction. The predicted values on the test instances are $p_1, p_2, \ldots, p_n$; the actual values are $a_1, a_2, \ldots, a_n$. Notice that p_i means something very different here than it did in the last section: there it was the probability that a particular prediction was in the ith class; here it refers to the numerical value of the prediction for the ith test instance.

Mean-squared error is the principal and most commonly used measure; sometimes the square root is taken to give it the same dimensions as the predicted value itself. Many mathematical techniques (such as linear regression, discussed in Chapter 4) use the mean-squared error because it tends to be the easiest measure to manipulate mathematically: it is, as mathematicians say, "well-behaved." However, here we are considering it as a performance measure: all the performance measures are easy to calculate and so mean-squared error has no particular advantage. The question is, is it an appropriate measure for the task at hand?

Mean absolute error is an alternative: just average the magnitude of the individual errors without taking account of their sign. Mean-squared error tends to exaggerate the effect of outliers—instances whose prediction error is larger than the others—while absolute error does not have this effect: all sizes of error are treated evenly according to their magnitude.

Table 5.6	Performance measures for numeric prediction (p are predicted values and a are actual values).

mean-squared error	$\dfrac{(p_1 - a_1)^2 + \ldots + (p_n - a_n)^2}{n}$
root mean-squared error	$\sqrt{\dfrac{(p_1 - a_1)^2 + \ldots + (p_n - a_n)^2}{n}}$
mean absolute error	$\dfrac{|p_1 - a_1| + \ldots + |p_n - a_n|}{n}$
relative squared error	$\dfrac{(p_1 - a_1)^2 + \ldots + (p_n - a_n)^2}{(a_1 - \bar{a})^2 + \ldots + (a_n - \bar{a})^2}$, where $\bar{a} = \dfrac{1}{n}\sum_i a_i$
root relative squared error	$\sqrt{\dfrac{(p_1 - a_1)^2 + \ldots + (p_n - a_n)^2}{(a_1 - \bar{a})^2 + \ldots + (a_n - \bar{a})^2}}$
relative absolute error	$\dfrac{|p_1 - a_1| + \ldots + |p_n - a_n|}{|a_1 - \bar{a}| + \ldots + |a_n - \bar{a}|}$
correlation coefficient	$\dfrac{S_{PA}}{S_P S_A}$, where $S_{PA} = \dfrac{\sum_i (p_i - \bar{p})(a_i - \bar{a})}{n - 1}$
	$S_P = \dfrac{\sum_i (p_i - \bar{p})^2}{n - 1}$, $S_A = \dfrac{\sum_i (a_i - \bar{a})^2}{n - 1}$

Sometimes it is the *relative* rather than *absolute* error values that are of importance. For example, if a 10% error is equally important whether it is an error of 50 in a prediction of 500 or an error of 0.2 in a prediction of 2, then averages of absolute error will be meaningless: relative errors are appropriate. This effect would be taken into account by using the relative errors in the mean-squared error calculation, or the mean absolute error calculation.

Relative squared error in Table 5.6 refers to something quite different. The error is made relative to what it would have been if a simple predictor had been used. And the simple predictor in question is just the average of the actual values from the training data. Thus relative squared error takes the total squared error and normalizes it by dividing by the total squared error of the default predictor.

Root relative squared error just reduces relative squared error to the same dimensions as the quantity being predicted by taking the square root.

The next error measure goes by the glorious name of *relative absolute error* and is simply the total absolute error, with the same kind of normalization. In these three relative error measures, the errors are normalized by the error of the simple predictor that predicts average values.

The final measure in Table 5.6 is the *correlation coefficient*, which measures the statistical correlation between the *a*s and the *p*s. The correlation coefficient ranges from 1 for perfectly correlated results, through 0 when there is no correlation at all, to −1 when the results are perfectly correlated negatively. Of course, negative values should not occur for reasonable prediction methods. Correlation is slightly different from the other measures because it is scale-independent in that, if you take a particular set of predictions, the error is unchanged if all the predictions are multiplied by a constant factor while the actual values are left unchanged. This factor appears in every term of S_{PA} in the numerator, and in every term of S_p in the denominator, thus canceling out. (This is not true for the relative error figures, despite normalization: if you multiply all the predictions by a large constant, then the difference between the predicted and actual values will change dramatically, as will the percentage errors.) It is also different in that good performance leads to a large value of the correlation coefficient, whereas since the other methods measure error rate, good performance is indicated by small values.

Which of these measures is appropriate in any given situation is a matter that can only be determined by studying the application itself. What are we trying to minimize? What is the cost of different kinds of error? Often it is not easy to decide. The squared error measures and root squared error measures weigh large discrepancies much more heavily than small ones whereas the absolute error measures do not. Taking the square root (root mean-squared error, root relative squared error) reduces the figure to the same dimensionality as the quantity being predicted. The relative error figures try to compensate for the basic predictability or unpredictability of the output variable: if it tends to lie fairly close to its average value, then you expect prediction to be good and the relative figure will compensate for this. Otherwise, if the error figure in one situation is far greater than in another situation, it may be because the quantity in the first situation is inherently more variable and therefore harder to predict, not because the predictor is any worse.

Fortunately, it turns out that in most practical situations the best numerical prediction method is still the best no matter which error measure is used. For example, Table 5.7 shows the result of four different numeric prediction techniques on a given dataset, measured using cross-validation. Method D is the best according to all five metrics: it has the smallest value for each error measure

Table 5.7	Performance measures for four numeric prediction models.			
	A	B	C	D
root mean-squared error	67.8	91.7	63.3	57.4
mean absolute error	41.3	38.5	33.4	29.2
root relative squared error	42.2%	57.2%	39.4%	35.8%
relative absolute error	43.1%	40.1%	34.8%	30.4%
correlation coefficient	0.88	0.88	0.89	0.91

and the largest correlation coefficient. Method C is the second best by all five metrics. The performance of A and B is open to dispute: they have the same correlation coefficient; A is better than B according to both mean-squared and relative squared errors; and the reverse is true for both absolute and relative absolute error. It is likely that the extra emphasis that the squaring operation gives to outliers accounts for the differences in this case. In other situations, differences might be observed between the absolute and relative error measures.

When comparing two different learning schemes that involve numeric prediction, the methodology developed in Section 5.5 still applies. Whatever performance measure is chosen, it should be estimated using (say) tenfold cross-validation. The same partition of the dataset should be used for each learning scheme to provide a paired observation. The whole procedure should be repeated—say ten times—to give a set of paired observations. The difference of each pair will be normally distributed, and if there is no significant difference between the two schemes, the distribution will have zero mean. An estimate of the variance can be calculated directly from the set of difference observations. Because the variance is estimated, Student's distribution is appropriate: the t-statistic is calculated by normalizing the mean difference by the square root of the variance estimate. Student's tables for the appropriate number of degrees of freedom are consulted to find the confidence limit z that corresponds to the desired confidence level (ensuring that the figures obtained are for a two-sided rather than a one-sided test). The difference between the two schemes is deemed significant, on the chosen performance measure, if the t-statistic exceeds the confidence limit z.

5.9 The minimum description length principle

What is learned by a machine learning scheme is a kind of "theory" of the domain from which the examples are drawn, a theory that is predictive in that it is capable of generating new facts about the domain—in other words, the class of unseen instances. Theory is rather a grandiose term: we are using it here only in the sense of a predictive model. Thus theories might comprise decision trees, or sets of rules—they don't have to be any more "theoretical" than that.

There is a longstanding tradition in science that, other things being equal, simple theories are preferable to complex ones. This is known as *Occam's Razor* after the medieval philosopher William of Occam (or Ockham). Occam's Razor shaves philosophical hairs off a theory. The idea is that the best scientific theory is the smallest one that explains all the facts. As Einstein is reputed to have said, "Everything should be made as simple as possible, but no simpler." Of course, quite a lot is hidden in the phrase "other things being equal," and it can be hard to assess objectively whether a particular theory really does "explain" all the facts on which it is based—that's what controversy in science is all about.

In our case, in machine learning, most theories make errors. And if what is learned is a theory, then the errors it makes are like *exceptions* to the theory. One way to ensure that other things *are* equal is to insist that the information embodied in the exceptions is included as part of the theory when its "simplicity" is judged.

Imagine an imperfect theory, for which there are a few exceptions. Not all the data is explained by the theory, but most is. What we do is simply adjoin the exceptions to the theory, specifying them explicitly as exceptions. This new theory is larger: that is a price that, quite justifiably, has to be paid for its inability to explain all the data. However, it may be that the simplicity—is it too much to call it *elegance*?—of the original theory is sufficient to outweigh the fact that it does not quite explain everything, compared to a large, baroque theory that is more comprehensive and accurate.

For example, if Kepler's three laws of planetary motion did not at the time account for the known data quite so well as Copernicus's latest refinement of the Ptolemaic theory of epicycles, they had the advantage of being far less complex, and that would have justified any slight apparent inaccuracy. Kepler was well aware of the benefits of having a theory that was compact, despite the fact that his theory violated his own aesthetic sense because it depended on "ovals" rather than pure circular motion. He expressed this in a forceful metaphor: "I have cleared the Augean stables of astronomy of cycles and spirals, and left behind me only a single cartload of dung."

The *minimum description length* or MDL principle takes the stance that the best theory for a body of data is one that minimizes the size of the theory plus the amount of information necessary to specify the exceptions relative to the theory—the smallest cartload of dung. In statistical estimation theory, this has been applied successfully to various parameter-fitting problems. It applies to machine learning as follows. Given a set of instances, a learning scheme infers a theory—be it ever so simple; unworthy, perhaps, to be called a "theory"—from them. Using a metaphor of communication, imagine that the instances are to be transmitted through a noiseless channel. Any similarity that is detected among them can be exploited to give a more compact coding. According to the MDL principle, the best generalization is the one that minimizes the number of bits required to communicate the generalization, along with the examples from which it was made.

Now the connection with the informational loss function introduced in Section 5.6 should be starting to emerge. That function measures the error in terms of the number of bits required to transmit the instances, given the probabilistic predictions made by the theory. According to MDL we need to add to this the "size" of the theory in bits, suitably encoded, to get an overall figure for complexity. However, the MDL principle refers to the information required to transmit the examples from which the theory was formed, that is, the *training* instances—not a test set. The overfitting problem is avoided because a complex theory that overfits will be penalized relative to a simple one by virtue of the fact that it takes more bits to encode. At one extreme is a very complex, highly overfitted theory that makes no errors on the training set. At the other is a very simple theory—the null theory—which does not help at all when transmitting the training set. And in between are theories of intermediate complexity which make probabilistic predictions that are imperfect and need to be corrected by transmitting some information about the training set. The MDL principle provides a means of comparing all these possibilities on an equal footing to see which is the best. We have found the holy grail: an evaluation scheme that works on the training set alone and does not need a separate test set. But the devil is in the details, as we shall see.

Suppose a learning scheme comes up with a theory T, based on a training set E of examples, that requires a certain number of bits $L[T]$ to encode (L for "length"). Given the theory, the training set itself can be encoded in a certain number of bits, $L[E|T]$. $L[E|T]$ is in fact given by the informational loss function summed over all members of the training set. Then the total description length of theory plus training set is

$$L[T] + L[E|T]$$

and the MDL principle recommends choosing the theory T that minimizes this sum.

There is a remarkable connection between the MDL principle and basic probability theory. Given a training set E, we seek the "most likely" theory T, that is, the theory for which the a posteriori probability $\Pr[T|E]$—the probability after the examples have been seen—is maximized. Bayes's rule of conditional probability, the very same rule that we encountered in Section 4.2, dictates that

$$\Pr[T|E] = \frac{\Pr[E|T]\Pr[T]}{\Pr[E]}.$$

Taking negative logarithms,

$$-\log \Pr[T|E] = -\log \Pr[E|T] - \log \Pr[T] + \log \Pr[E].$$

Maximizing the probability is the same as minimizing its negative logarithm. Now (as we saw in Section 5.6) the number of bits required to code something is just the negative logarithm of its probability. Furthermore, the final term, $\log \Pr[E]$, depends solely on the training set and not on the learning scheme. Thus choosing the theory that maximizes the probability $\Pr[T|E]$ is tantamount to choosing the theory that minimizes

$$L[E|T] + L[T]$$

—in other words, the MDL principle!

This astonishing correspondence with the notion of maximizing the a posteriori probability of a theory after the training set has been taken into account gives credence to the minimum description length principle. But it also points out where the problems will sprout when MDL is applied in practice. The difficulty with applying Bayes's rule directly is in finding a suitable a priori probability distribution for the theories $\Pr[T]$. In the MDL formulation, that translates into finding how to code the theory T into bits in the most efficient way. There are many ways of coding things, and they all depend on presuppositions that must be shared by encoder and decoder. If you know in advance that the theory is going to take a certain form, you can use that information to encode it more efficiently. How are you going to actually encode T? The devil is in the details.

Encoding E with respect to T to obtain $L[E|T]$ seems a little more straightforward: we have already met the informational loss function. But actually, when you encode one member of the training set after another, you are encoding a *sequence* rather than a *set*. It is not necessary to transmit the training set in any particular order, and it ought be possible to use that fact to reduce the number of bits required. Often, this is simply approximated by subtracting $\log n!$ (where n is the number of elements in E), which is the number of bits needed to specify a particular permutation of the training set (and since this is the same for all theories, it doesn't actually affect the comparison between them). But one can imagine using the frequency of the individual errors to reduce the number of bits needed to code them. Of course, the more sophisticated the method that is used to code the errors, the less the need for a theory in the first place—so that whether a theory is justified or not depends to some extent on how the errors are coded. The details, the details.

We will not go into the details of different coding methods here. The whole question of using MDL to evaluate a learning scheme based solely on the training data is an area of active research and vocal disagreement among researchers.

We end this section as we began, on a philosophical note. It is important to appreciate that Occam's Razor, the preference of simple theories over complex ones, has the status of a philosophical position or "axiom" rather than something that can be proven from first principles. While it may seem self-evident to us, this is a function of our education and the times we live in. A preference for simplicity is—or may be—culture-specific rather than absolute.

For example, the Greek philosopher Epicurus (who enjoyed good food and wine and supposedly advocated sensual pleasure—in moderation—as the highest good) expressed almost the opposite sentiment. His *principle of multiple explanations* advises "if more than one theory is consistent with the data, keep them all" on the basis that if several explanations are equally in agreement, it may be possible to achieve a higher degree of precision by using them together—and anyway, it would be unscientific to discard some arbitrarily. This brings to mind instance-based learning, where all the evidence is retained to provide robust predictions, and resonates strongly with decision-combination methods like bagging and boosting (discussed in Chapter 7) that actually do gain predictive power by using multiple explanations together.

5.10 Applying MDL to clustering

One of the nice things about the minimum description length principle is that unlike other evaluation criteria, it can be applied under widely different circumstances. Although in some sense equivalent to Bayes's rule in that, as we saw above, devising a coding scheme for theories is tantamount to assigning them a prior probability distribution, schemes for coding are somehow far more tangible and easier to think about in concrete terms than intuitive prior probabilities. To illustrate this we will briefly describe—without entering into coding details—how you might go about applying MDL to clustering.

Clustering seems intrinsically difficult to evaluate. Whereas classification or association learning has an objective criterion of success—predictions made on test cases are either right or wrong—this is not so with clustering. It seems that the only realistic evaluation is whether the result of learning—the clustering—proves useful in the application context. (It is worth pointing out that really this is the case for all types of learning, not just clustering.)

Despite this, clustering can be evaluated from a description length perspective. Suppose a clustering learning technique divides the training set E into k clusters. If these clusters are natural ones, it should be possible to use them to encode E more efficiently. The very best clustering will support the most efficient encoding.

One way of encoding the instances in E with respect to a given clustering is to start by encoding the cluster centers—the average value of each attribute over all instances in the cluster. Then, for each instance in E, transmit which cluster it belongs to (in $\log_2 k$ bits), followed by its attribute values with respect to the cluster center, perhaps as the numeric difference of each attribute value from the center. Couched as it is in terms of averages and differences, this description presupposes numeric attributes and raises thorny questions of how to code numbers efficiently. Nominal attributes can be handled in a similar manner: for each cluster there is a probability distribution for the attribute values, and the distributions are different for different clusters. The coding issue becomes more straightforward: attribute values are coded with respect to the relevant probability distribution, a standard operation in data compression.

If the data exhibits extremely strong clustering, this technique will result in a smaller description length than simply transmitting the elements of E without any clusters. However, if the clustering effect is not so strong, it will likely increase rather than decrease the description length. The overhead of transmitting cluster-specific distributions for attribute values will more than offset the advantage gained by encoding each training instance relative to the cluster it lies in. This is where more sophisticated coding techniques come in. Once the cluster centers have been communicated, it is possible to transmit cluster-specific probability distributions adaptively, in tandem with the relevant instances: the instances themselves help to define the probability distributions, and the probability distributions help to define the instances. We will not venture further into coding techniques here. The point is that the MDL formulation, properly applied, may be flexible enough to support the evaluation of clustering. But actually doing it satisfactorily in practice is not easy.

5.11   Further reading

The statistical basis of confidence tests is well covered in most statistics texts, which also give tables of the normal distribution and Student's distribution. (We use an excellent course text by Wild and Seber [1995], which we recommend very strongly if you can get hold of it). Cross-validation is a standard statistical technique, and its application in machine learning has been extensively investigated and compared with the bootstrap by Kohavi (1995). The bootstrap technique itself is thoroughly covered by Efron and Tibshirani (1993).

Lift charts are described by Berry and Linoff (1997). The use of ROC analysis in signal detection theory is covered by Egan (1975); this work has been extended for visualizing and analyzing the behavior of diagnostic systems (Swets 1988) and is also used in medicine (Beck and Schultz 1986). Provost and Fawcett (1997) brought the idea of ROC analysis to the attention of the machine learning and data mining community. Witten et al. (1999) explain the use of recall and precision in information retrieval systems; the F-measure is described by van Rijsbergen (1979).

The minimum description length principle was formulated by Rissanen (1985). Kepler's discovery of his economical three laws of planetary motion, and his doubts about them, are recounted by Koestler (1964).

Epicurus's principle of multiple explanations is mentioned by Li and Vitanyi (1992), quoting from Asmis (1984).

chapter six

Implementations: Real machine learning schemes

We have seen the basic ideas of several machine learning methods and studied in detail how to assess their performance on practical data mining problems. Now we are well prepared to look at real, industrial-strength machine learning algorithms. Our aim is to explain these algorithms both at a conceptual level and with a fair amount of technical detail, so that you can understand them fully and appreciate the key implementation issues that arise.

In truth, there is a world of difference between the simplistic methods described in Chapter 4 and the actual algorithms that are widely used in practice. The principles are the same. So are the inputs and outputs—methods of knowledge representation. But the algorithms are far more complex, principally because they have to deal robustly and sensibly with real-world problems like numeric attributes, missing values, and—most challenging of all—noisy data. In order to understand how the various schemes cope with noise, we will have to draw on some of the statistical knowledge that we learned in Chapter 5.

Because of the nature of the material it contains, this chapter differs from the others in the book. It is more encyclopedic than tutorial in nature, covering small, perhaps even tedious, details of a wide variety of different methods. Many readers will probably not want to work in detail through the whole range of schemes here—after all, the principles have already been explained in Chapter 4. Consequently each section of this chapter is self-contained, including the references to further reading, which are gathered together in a *Discussion* subsection at the end of each section. You can choose to read whichever ones you are interested in—or none at all, if there are no individual machine learning schemes that you're particularly interested in. If you'd like to read some details but aren't sure where to begin, try the next section, which describes decision trees—probably the single most widely used machine learning technique used in practical data mining—and then decide if you want to go further and learn about the other methods. We return to a more tutorial, less exhaustive style in Chapter 7 when we look at some more advanced topics in the application of machine learning techniques.

Chapter 4 began with rudimentary rule induction and went on to look at statistical modeling and decision trees. Then we returned to rule induction, and continued with association rules, linear models, and the simple nearest-neighbor method of instance-based learning. The present chapter develops all these topics except two, statistical modeling and association rules, which have both already been covered in adequate detail.

We begin with decision tree induction and work up to describe the C4.5 system, a landmark decision tree program that is the machine learning method most widely used in practice to date. Next we discuss systems for decision rule induction. Despite the simplicity of the idea, inducing decision rules that perform comparably with state-of-the-art decision trees turns out to be quite difficult in practice. Most high-performance rule inducers find an initial rule set and then refine it using a rather complex optimization stage that discards or adjusts individual rules to make them work better together. We describe the ideas that underlie rule learning in the presence of noise, and then go on to cover a recently developed scheme that operates by forming partial decision trees, an approach that has been demonstrated to perform as well as other state-of-the-art rule learners while avoiding their complex and ad hoc heuristics. Following this, we take a brief look at how to generate rules with exceptions, which were described in Section 3.5.

There has been resurgence of interest in linear models with the introduction of *support vector machines,* a kind of blend of linear modeling and instance-based learning. Support vector machines select a small number of critical boundary instances called *support vectors* from each class and build a linear discriminant function that separates them as widely as possible. These systems transcend the limitations of linear boundaries by making it practical to include extra, nonlinear terms in the calculation, making it possible to form quadratic, cubic, higher-order decision boundaries. We describe the idea of support vector machines next, although we shrink from covering implementation details because of the extensive mathematical background that would be required. Then we go on to instance-based learners, developing the simple nearest-neighbor method introduced in Section 4.7.

Two topics that were not treated in Chapter 4 are methods for numeric prediction, for which a tree representation was introduced in Section 3.7, and methods for producing clusters. The last two sections of this chapter rectify this. We detail a scheme for producing decision trees that predict a numeric "class" value, and go on to discuss locally weighted regression, an instance-based strategy for numeric prediction. Finally we review the dominant methods for generating clusters from datasets in which there is no class value.

6.1 Decision trees

The first machine learning scheme that we will develop in detail derives from the simple divide-and-conquer algorithm for producing decision trees that was described in Section 4.3. It needs to be extended in several ways before it is ready to be used on real-world problems. First we will consider how to deal with numeric attributes and, after that, missing values. Then we look at the all-important problem of pruning decision trees, for although trees constructed by the divide-and-conquer algorithm as described perform well on the training set, they are usually overfitted to the training data and do not generalize well to independent test sets. Next we consider how to convert decision trees to classification rules. In all these aspects we are guided by the popular decision tree algorithm C4.5 which, with its commercial successor C5.0, has emerged as the industry workhorse for off-the-shelf machine learning. Finally we look at the options provided by C4.5 and C5.0 themselves.

Numeric attributes

The method we have described only works when all of the attributes are nominal, whereas, as we have seen, most real datasets contain some numeric attributes. It is not too difficult to extend the algorithm to deal with these. For a numeric attribute we will restrict the possibilities to a two-way, or binary, split. Suppose we use the version of the weather data that has some numeric features

(Table 1.3). Then, when temperature is being considered for the first split, the temperature values involved are

64	65	68	69	70	71	72	75	80	81	83	85
yes	no	yes	yes	yes	no	no yes	yes yes	no	yes	yes	no

(repeated values have been collapsed together), and there are only eleven possible positions for the breakpoint—eight if the breakpoint is not allowed to separate items of the same class. The information gain for each can be calculated in the usual way. For example, the test temperature < 71.5 produces 4 yeses and 2 nos, whereas temperature > 71.5 produces 5 yeses and 3 nos, and so the information value of this test is

$$\text{info}([4, 2], [5, 3]) = (6/14) \times \text{info}([4, 2]) + (8/14) \times \text{info}([5, 3]) = 0.939 \text{ bits.}$$

It is common to place numeric thresholds halfway between the values that delimit the boundaries of a concept, although something might be gained by adopting a more sophisticated policy. For example, we will see below that although the simplest form of instance-based learning puts the dividing line between concepts in the middle of the space between them, other methods that involve more than just the two nearest examples have been suggested.

When creating decision trees using the divide-and-conquer method, once the first attribute to split on has been selected, a top-level tree node is created that splits on that attribute, and the algorithm proceeds recursively on each of the child nodes. For each numeric attribute, it appears that the subset of instances at each child node must be resorted according to that attribute's values—and indeed this is how programs for inducing decision trees are usually written. However, it is not actually necessary to resort, because the sort order at a parent node can be used to derive the sort order for each child, leading to a speedier implementation. Consider the temperature attribute in the weather data, whose sort order (this time including duplicates), is

64	65	68	69	70	71	72	72	75	75	80	81	83	85
7	*6*	*5*	*9*	*4*	*14*	*8*	*12*	*10*	*11*	*2*	*13*	*3*	*1*

The italicized number below each temperature value represents the number of the instance that has that value: thus instance number 7 has temperature value 64, instance 6 has temperature 65, and so on. Suppose we decide to split at the top level on the attribute outlook. Consider the child node for which outlook = sunny—in fact, the examples with this value of outlook are numbers 1, 2, 8, 9, and 11. If the italicized sequence is stored with the example set (and a different sequence must be stored for each numeric attribute)—that is, instance 7 contains a pointer to instance 6, instance 6 points to instance 5, 5 points to 9, and so on—then it is a simple matter to read off in order the examples for which `out-look = sunny`. All that is necessary is to scan through the instances in the indicated order, checking the `outlook` attribute for each and writing down the ones with the appropriate value:

9   8   11   2   1

Thus repeated sorting can be avoided by storing with each subset of instances the sort order for that subset according to each numeric attribute. The sort order must be determined for each numeric attribute at the beginning; no further sorting is necessary thereafter.

When a decision tree tests a nominal attribute as described in Chapter 4 (Section 4.3), a branch is made for each possible value of the attribute. However, we have restricted splits on numeric attributes to be binary. This creates an important difference between numeric attributes and nominal ones: once you have branched on a nominal attribute, you have used all the information that it offers, whereas successive splits on a numeric attribute may continue to yield new information. Whereas a nominal attribute can only be tested once on any path from the root of a tree to the leaf, a numeric one can be tested many times. This can yield trees that are messy and difficult to understand because the tests on any single numeric attribute are not located together but can be scattered along the path. An alternative, which is harder to accomplish but produces a more readable tree, is to allow a multiway test on a numeric attribute, testing against several different constants at a single node of the tree. A simpler but less powerful solution is to prediscretize the attribute as discussed in Section 7.2.

Missing values

The next enhancement to the decision-tree-building algorithm deals with the problems of missing values. Missing values are endemic in real-world datasets. As explained in Chapter 2 (page 52), one way of handling missing values is to treat them as simply another possible value of the attribute; this is appropriate if the fact that the attribute is missing is significant in some way. In this case, no further action need be taken. But if there is no particular significance in the fact that a certain instance has a missing attribute value, a more subtle solution is needed. It is tempting to simply ignore all instances in which some of the values are missing, but this solution is often too draconian to be viable. Instances with missing values often provide a good deal of information. Sometimes the attributes whose values are missing play no part in the decision, in which case these instances are as good as any other.

One question is how to apply a given decision tree to an instance in which some of the attributes to be tested have missing values. We outlined a solution in Section 3.1 that involves notionally splitting the instance into pieces, using a numeric weighting scheme, and sending part of it down each branch in proportion to the number of training instances going down that branch. Eventually the various parts of the instance will each reach a leaf node, and the decisions at these leaf nodes must be recombined using the weights that have percolated to the leaves. The information gain and gain ratio calculations described in Section 4.3 can also be applied to partial instances. Instead of having integer counts, the weights are used when computing both gain figures.

Another question is how to partition the training set once a splitting attribute has been chosen, to allow recursive application of the decision-tree formation procedure on each of the daughter nodes. The same weighting procedure is used. Instances for which the relevant attribute value is missing are notionally split into pieces, one piece for each branch, in the same proportion as the known instances go down the various branches. Pieces of the instance contribute to decisions at lower nodes in the usual way via the information gain calculation, except that they are weighted accordingly. They may be further split at lower nodes, of course, if the values of other attributes are unknown as well.

Pruning

When we looked at the labor negotiations problem in Chapter 1, we found that the simple decision tree in Figure 1.3a actually performs better than the more complex one in Figure 1.3b—and it makes more sense, too. Now it is time to learn how to prune decision trees.

By building the complete tree and pruning it afterward, we are adopting a strategy of *postpruning* (sometimes called *backward* pruning) rather than *prepruning* (or *forward* pruning). Prepruning would involve trying to decide during the tree-building process when to stop developing subtrees—quite an attractive prospect because that would avoid all the work of developing subtrees only to throw them away afterward. However, postpruning does seem to offer some advantages. For example, situations occur in which two attributes individually seem to have nothing to contribute, but are powerful predictors when combined—a sort of combination-lock effect where the correct combination of the two attribute values is very informative whereas the attributes taken individually are not. Most decision tree builders postprune; it is an open question whether prepruning strategies can be developed that perform as well.

Two rather different operations have been considered for postpruning: *subtree replacement* and *subtree raising*. At each node, a learning scheme might decide whether it should perform subtree replacement, subtree raising, or leave the subtree as it is, unpruned. Subtree replacement is the primary pruning operation and we look at it first. The idea is to select some subtrees and replace them by single leaves. For example, the whole subtree in Figure 1.3a, involving two internal nodes and four leaf nodes, has been replaced by the single leaf bad. This will certainly cause the accuracy on the training set to decrease if the original tree was produced by the decision tree algorithm described above, because that continued to build the tree until all leaf nodes were pure (or until all attributes had been tested). However, it may increase the accuracy on an independently chosen test set.

When subtree replacement is implemented, it proceeds from the leaves and works back up toward the root. In the Figure 1.3 example, the whole subtree in (a) would not be replaced at once. First, consideration would be given to replacing the three daughter nodes in the `health plan contribution` subtree by a single leaf node. Assume that a decision is made to perform this replacement—we will discuss how this decision is made shortly. Then, continuing to work back from the leaves, consideration would be given to replacing the `working hours per week` subtree, which now has just two daughter nodes, by a single leaf node. In the Figure 1.3 example this replacement was indeed made, which accounts for the entire subtree in (a) being replaced by a single leaf marked `bad`. Finally, consideration would be given to replacing the two daughter nodes in the `wage increase 1st year` subtree by a single leaf node. In this case that decision was not made, so the tree remains as shown on Figure 1.3a. Again, we will examine how these decisions are actually made below.

The second pruning operation, subtree raising, is more complex, and it is not clear that it is always worthwhile. However, because it is used in the influential decision tree building system C4.5, we describe it here. Subtree raising does not occur in the Figure 1.3 example, so we will use the artificial example of Figure 6.1 for illustration. Here, consideration is given to pruning the tree in (a), and

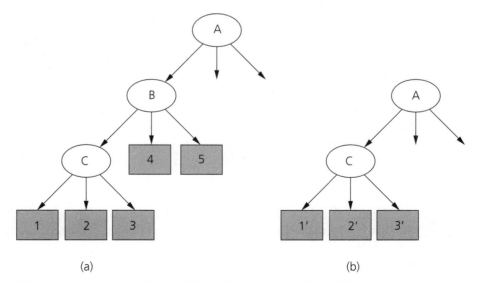

(a)   (b)

Figure 6.1 Example of subtree raising, where node C is "raised" to subsume node B.

the result is shown in (b). The entire subtree from c downward has been "raised" to replace the B subtree. Note that although the daughters of B and c are shown as leaves, they can be entire subtrees. Of course, if we perform this raising operation, it is necessary to reclassify the examples at the nodes marked 4 and 5 into the new subtree headed by c. This is why the daughters of that node are marked with primes: 1′, 2′, and 3′—to indicate that they are not the same as the original daughters 1, 2, 3, but differ by the inclusion of the examples originally covered by 4 and 5.

Subtree raising is a potentially time-consuming operation. In actual implementations it is generally restricted to raising the subtree of the most popular branch. That is, we consider doing the raising illustrated in Figure 6.1 provided that the branch from B to c has more training examples than the branches from B to 4 or from B to 5. Otherwise, if (for example) 4 were the majority daughter of B, we would consider raising the node 4 to replace B and reclassifying all examples under c, as well as the examples from 5, into the new node.

Estimating error rates

So much for the two pruning operations. Now we must address the question of how to decide whether to replace an internal node by a leaf (for subtree replacement), or whether to replace an internal node by one of the nodes below (for subtree raising). To make this decision rationally, it is necessary to estimate the error rate that would be expected at a particular node given an independently chosen test set. We need to estimate the error at internal nodes as well as at leaf nodes. If we had such an estimate, it would be clear whether to replace, or raise, a particular subtree simply by comparing the estimated error of the subtree with that of its proposed replacement. Before estimating the error for a subtree proposed for raising, examples that lie under siblings of the current node—the examples at 4 and 5 of Figure 6.1—would have to be temporarily reclassified into the raised tree.

It is no use taking the training set error as the error estimate: that would not lead to any pruning because the tree has been constructed expressly for that particular training set. One way of coming up with an error estimate is the standard verification technique: hold back some of the data originally given and use it as an independent test set to estimate the error at each node. This is called *reduced-error* pruning. It suffers from the disadvantage that the actual tree is based on less data.

The alternative is to try to make some estimate of error based on the training data itself. That is what C4.5 does, and we will describe its method here. It is a heuristic based on some statistical reasoning, but the statistical underpinning is rather weak and ad hoc. However, it seems to work well in practice. The idea is to consider the set of instances that reach each node and imagine that the majority class is chosen to represent that node. That gives us a certain number of "errors," E, out of the total number of instances, N. Now imagine that the true probability of error at the node is q, and that the N instances are generated by a Bernoulli process with parameter q, of which E turn out to be errors.

This is almost the same situation as we considered when looking at the hold-out method in Section 5.2, where we calculated confidence intervals on the true success probability p, given a certain observed success rate. There are two differences. One is trivial: here we are looking at the error rate q rather than the success rate p; these are simply related by $p + q = 1$. The second is more serious: here the figures E and N are measured from the training data, whereas in Section 5.2 we were considering independent test data instead. Because of this difference we make a pessimistic estimate of the error rate by using the upper confidence limit, rather than stating the estimate as a confidence range.

The mathematics involved is just the same as before. Given a particular confidence c (the default figure used by C4.5 is $c = 25\%$), we find confidence limits z such that

$$\Pr\left[\frac{f-q}{\sqrt{q(1-q)/N}} > z\right] = c,$$

where N is the number of samples, $f = E/N$ is the observed error rate, and q is the true error rate. As before, this leads to an upper confidence limit for q. Now we use that upper confidence limit as a (pessimistic) estimate for the error rate e at the node:

$$e = \frac{f + \frac{z^2}{2N} + z\sqrt{\frac{f}{N} - \frac{f^2}{N} + \frac{z^2}{4N^2}}}{1 + \frac{z^2}{N}}.$$

Note the use of the + sign before the square root in the numerator, to obtain the upper confidence limit. Here, z is the number of standard deviations corresponding to the confidence c, which for $c = 25\%$ is $z = 0.69$.

To see how all this works in practice, let's look again at the labor negotiations decision tree of Figure 1.3, salient parts of which are reproduced in Figure 6.2 with the number of training examples that reach the leaves added. We use the above formula with a 25% confidence figure, that is with $z = 0.69$. Consider the lower left leaf, for which $E = 2$, $N = 6$, and so $f = 0.33$. Plugging these figures into the formula, the upper confidence limit is calculated as $e = 0.47$. That means that instead of using the training set error rate for this leaf, which is 33%, we will use the pessimistic estimate of 47%. This is pessimistic indeed, considering that the error rate could not possibly exceed 50% for a two-class problem. But things are worse for the neighboring leaf, where $E = 1$ and $N = 2$, because

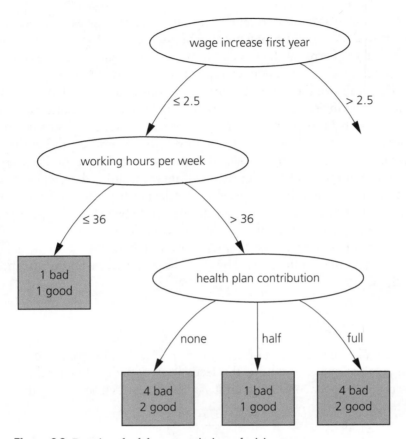

Figure 6.2 Pruning the labor negotiations decision tree.

the upper confidence becomes $e = 0.72$. The third leaf has the same value of e as the first. The next step is to combine the error estimates for these three leaves in the ratio of the number of examples they cover, 6:2:6, which leads to a combined error estimate of 0.51. Now we consider the error estimate for the parent node, health plan contribution. This covers nine bad examples and five good ones, so the training set error rate is $f = 5/14$. For these values, the above formula yields a pessimistic error estimate of $e = 0.46$. Since this is less than the combined error estimate of the three children, they are pruned away.

The next step is to consider the working hours per week node, which now has two children that are both leaves. The error estimate for the first, with $E = 1$ and $N = 2$, is $e = 0.72$, while for the second it is $e = 0.46$ as we have just seen. Combining these in the appropriate ratio of 2:14 leads to a value that is higher than the error estimate for the working-hours node, so the subtree is pruned away and replaced by a leaf node.

The estimated error figures obtained in these examples, which frequently exceed the maximum possible value of 0.5, underscore the fact that the estimate is only a heuristic one and is based on a number of shaky assumptions: the use of the upper confidence limit; the assumption of a normal distribution; and the fact that statistics from the training set are used. However, the qualitative behavior of the error formula is correct, and the method seems to work reasonably well in practice. If necessary, the underlying confidence level, which we have taken to be 25%, can be tweaked to produce more satisfactory results.

Complexity of decision tree induction

Now that we have learned how to accomplish the pruning operations, we have finally covered all the central aspects of decision tree induction. Let's take stock and consider the computational complexity of inducing decision trees. We will use the standard order notation: $O(n)$ stands for a quantity that grows at most linearly with n, $O(n^2)$ grows at most quadratically with n, and so on.

Suppose the training data contains n instances and m attributes. We need to make some assumption about the size of the tree, and we will assume that its depth is on the order of $\log n$, that is $O(\log n)$. This is the standard rate of growth of a tree with n leaves, provided that it remains "bushy" and doesn't degenerate into a few very long stringy branches. Note that we are tacitly assuming that most of the instances are different from each other, and—this is almost the same thing—that the m attributes provide enough tests to allow the instances to be differentiated. For example, if there were only a few binary attributes, they would allow only so many instances to be differentiated and the tree could not grow past a certain point, rendering an "in the limit" analysis meaningless.

The computational cost of building the tree in the first place is

$$O(mn \log n).$$

Consider the amount of work done for one attribute over all nodes of the tree. Not all the examples need to be considered at each node, of course. But at each possible tree depth, the entire set of n instances must be considered. And since there are $\log n$ different depths in the tree, the amount of work for this one attribute is $O(n \log n)$. At each node all attributes are considered, so the total amount of work is $O(mn \log n)$.

This reasoning makes some assumptions. If some attributes are numeric, they must be sorted, but once the initial sort has been done there is no need to re-sort at each tree depth if the appropriate algorithm is used (described on pages 160–161). And the initial sort takes $O(n \log n)$ operations for each of up to m attributes: thus the above complexity figure is unchanged. If the attributes are nominal, all attributes do *not* have to be considered at each tree node—

because attributes that are used further up the tree cannot be reused. However, if attributes are numeric, they can be reused and so they have to be considered at every tree level.

Next, consider pruning by subtree replacement. First an error estimate must be made for every tree node. Provided counts are maintained appropriately, this is linear in the number of nodes in the tree. Then each node needs to be considered for replacement. The tree has at most n leaves, one for each instance. If it were a binary tree, each attribute being numeric or two-valued, that would give it $2n-1$ nodes; multiway branches would only serve to decrease the number of internal nodes. Thus the complexity of subtree replacement is

$$O(n).$$

Finally, subtree lifting has a basic complexity equal to subtree replacement. But there is an added cost because instances need to be reclassified during the lifting operation. During the whole process, each instance may have to be reclassified at every node between its leaf and the root, that is, as many as $O(\log n)$ times. That makes the total number of reclassifications $O(n \log n)$. And reclassification is not a single operation: one that occurs near the root will take $O(\log n)$ operations, and one of average depth will take half this. Thus the total complexity of subtree lifting is

$$O(n (\log n)^2).$$

Thus, taking into account all these operations, the full complexity of decision tree induction is

$$O(mn \log n) + O(n (\log n)^2).$$

From trees to rules

It is possible to read a set of rules directly off a decision tree, as noted in Section 3.3, by generating a rule for each leaf and making a conjunction of all the tests encountered on the path from the root to that leaf. This produces rules that are unambiguous in that it doesn't matter in what order they are executed. However, the rules are more complex than necessary.

The estimated error rate described above provides exactly the mechanism necessary to prune the rules. Given a particular rule, each condition in it is considered for deletion by tentatively removing it, working out which of the training examples are now covered by the rule, calculating from this a pessimistic estimate of the error rate of the new rule, and comparing this with the pessimistic estimate for the original rule. If the new rule is better, delete that condition and carry on, looking for other conditions to delete. Leave the rule when there are no conditions left that will improve it if they are removed. Once all rules have been pruned in this way, it is necessary to see if there are any duplicates and remove them from the rule set.

This is a greedy approach to detecting redundant conditions in a rule, and there is no guarantee that the best set of conditions will be removed. An improvement would be to consider all subsets of conditions, but this is usually prohibitively expensive. Another solution might be to use an optimization technique like simulated annealing or a genetic algorithm to select the best version of this rule. However, the simple greedy solution seems to produce quite good rule sets.

The problem, even with the greedy method, is computational cost. For every condition that is a candidate for deletion, the effect of the rule must be reevaluated on all the training instances. This means that rule generation from trees tends to be very slow, and there are much faster methods that generate classification rules directly without forming a decision tree first.

C4.5: Choices and options

We finish our study of decision trees by making a few remarks about practical use of the landmark decision tree program C4.5 and its successor C5.0. These were devised by Ross Quinlan over a twenty-year period beginning in the late 1970s. A complete description of C4.5, the early 1990s version, appears as an excellent and readable book (Quinlan 1993), along with the full source code. The more recent version, C5.0, is now available commercially. Its decision tree induction seems to be essentially the same as in C4.5, and tests show some differences but negligible improvements. However, its rule generation is greatly speeded up and clearly uses a different technique, although this has not been described in the open literature.

C4.5 works essentially as described in the above sections. The default confidence value is set as 25% and works reasonably well in most cases; possibly it should be altered to a lower value, which causes more drastic pruning, if the actual error rate of pruned trees on test sets is found to be much higher than the estimated error rate. There is one other important parameter, whose effect is to eliminate tests for which almost all of the training examples have the same outcome. Such tests are often of little use. Consequently tests are not incorporated into the decision tree unless they have at least two outcomes which have at least a minimum number of instances. The default value for this minimum is two, but it is controllable and should perhaps be increased for tasks where there is a lot of noisy data.

Discussion

Top-down induction of decision trees is probably the most extensively studied method of machine learning used in data mining. Researchers have investigated a panoply of variations for almost every conceivable aspect of the learning process—for example, different criteria for attribute selection, or modified pruning methods. However, they are rarely rewarded by substantial improvements in accuracy over a spectrum of diverse datasets. Sometimes the size of the induced trees is significantly reduced when a different pruning strategy is adopted, but often the same effect can be achieved by setting C4.5's pruning parameter to a smaller value.

In our discussion of decision trees, we have assumed that only one attribute is used to split the data into subsets at each node of the tree. However, it is possible to allow tests that involve several attributes at a time. For example, with numeric attributes each test can be on a linear combination of attribute values. Then the final tree consists of a hierarchy of linear models of the kind we have discussed in Chapter 4 (Section 4.6), and the splits are no longer restricted to being axis-parallel. Trees with tests involving more than one attribute are called *multivariate* decision trees, in contrast to the simple *univariate* trees that we normally use. Multivariate tests were introduced with the CART system for learning decision trees (Breiman et al. 1984). They are often more accurate and smaller than univariate trees but take much longer to generate and are also more difficult to interpret.

6.2 Classification rules

We call the basic covering algorithm for generating rules that was described in Section 4.4 a *separate-and-conquer* technique because it identifies a rule that covers instances in the class (and excludes ones not in the class), separates them out, and continues on those that are left. Such algorithms have been used as the basis of many systems that generate rules. There we described a simple correctness-based measure for choosing what test to add to the rule at each stage. However, there are many other possibilities, and the particular criterion that is used has a significant effect on the rules produced. We examine different criteria for choosing tests below. Following that we will see how a simple change in the covering algorithm can produce rules in quite a different form, and then we look at how the basic rule-generation algorithm can be extended to more practical situations by accommodating missing values and numeric attributes.

But the real problem with all these rule-generation schemes is that they tend to overfit the training data and do not generalize well to independent test sets, particularly on noisy data. We tackle this problem next. In order to be able to generate good rule sets for noisy data, it is necessary to have some way of measuring the worth, or significance, of individual rules. We begin by looking at a few examples of possible rules—some good and some bad—for the contact lens problem, and introduce a way of measuring their quality. Then we show how this quality measure can be used to avoid overfitting. We also discuss how to generate rules that are to be interpreted sequentially. Then we show one way of calculating the quality measure, based on notions from probability theory. A completely different approach to assessing the worth of rules is to evaluate their error rate on an independent set of instances, held back from the training set, and we discuss this next. After that, we present a new rule-learning algorithm that works by repeatedly building partial decision trees and extracting rules from them. Finally we consider how to generate rules with exceptions, and exceptions to the exceptions.

Criteria for choosing tests

When we introduced the basic covering algorithm for rule learning in Section 4.4, we had to figure out a way of deciding which of many possible tests to add to a rule to prevent it from covering any negative examples. For this we used the test that maximizes the ratio

p/t

where t is the total number of instances that the new rule will cover, and p is the number of these that are positive—that is, belong to the class in question. This attempts to maximize the "correctness" of the rule, on the basis that the higher the proportion of positive examples it covers, the more correct a rule is. One alternative is to calculate an information gain

$$p\left[\log\frac{p}{t} \ - \ \log\frac{P}{T} \right],$$

where p and t are the number of positive instances and the total number of instances covered by the new rule, as before, and P and T are the corresponding number of instances that satisfied the rule *before* the new test was added. The rationale for this is that it represents the total information gained regarding the current positive examples, which is given by the number of them that satisfy the new test, multiplied by the information gained regarding each one of them.

The basic criterion for choosing a test to add to a rule is to find one that covers as many positive examples as possible, while covering as few negative examples as possible. The original correctness-based heuristic, which is just the percentage of positive examples among all examples covered by the rule, attains a maximum when no negative examples are covered regardless of the number of positive examples covered by the rule. Thus a test that makes the rule exact will be preferred to one that makes it inexact no matter how few positive examples the former rule covers, nor how many positive examples the latter covers. For example, if we can choose between a test that covers one example, which is positive, this criterion will prefer it over a test that covers one thousand positive examples along with one negative one.

The information-based heuristic, on the other hand, places far more emphasis on covering a large number of positive examples regardless of whether the rule so created is exact. Of course, both algorithms continue adding tests until the final rule produced is exact, which means that the rule will be finished earlier using the correctness measure, whereas more terms will have to be added if the information-based measure is used. Thus the correctness-based measure might find special cases and eliminate them completely, saving the larger picture for later (when the more general rule might be simpler because awkward special cases have already been dealt with), whereas the information-based measure will try to generate high-coverage rules first and leave the special cases until later. It is by no means obvious that either strategy is superior to the other at producing an exact rule set. Moreover, the whole situation is complicated by the fact that, as described below, rules may be pruned and inexact ones tolerated.

Missing values, numeric attributes

As with divide-and-conquer decision tree algorithms, the nasty practical considerations of missing values and numeric attributes need to be addressed. In fact, there is not much more to say. Now that we know how these problems can be solved for decision tree induction, appropriate solutions for rule induction are easily given.

When producing rules using covering algorithms, missing values can best be treated as though they don't match any of the tests. This is particularly suitable when a decision list is being produced, for it encourages the learning algorithm to separate out positive instances using tests that are known to succeed. It has the effect that either instances with missing values are dealt with by rules involving other attributes that are not missing, or any decisions about them are deferred until most of the other instances have been taken care of, at which time tests will probably emerge that involve other attributes. Covering algorithms for decision lists have a decided advantage over decision tree algorithms in this respect: tricky examples can be left until late in the process, at which time they will appear less tricky because most of the other examples have already been classified and removed from the instance set.

Numeric attributes can be dealt with in exactly the same way as they are for trees. For each numeric attribute, instances are sorted according to the attribute's value and, for each possible threshold, a binary less-than/greater-than test is considered and evaluated in exactly the same way that a binary attribute would be.

Good rules and bad rules

Suppose you don't want to generate perfect rules that guarantee to give the correct classification on all instances in the training set, but would rather generate "sensible" ones that avoid overfitting the training set and thereby stand a better chance of performing well on new test instances. How do you decide which rules are worthwhile? How do you tell when it becomes counterproductive to continue adding terms to a rule to exclude a few pesky instances of the wrong type, all the while excluding more and more instances of the right type, too?

Let's look at a few examples of possible rules—some good and some bad—for the contact lens problem in Table 1.1. Consider first the rule

```
If astigmatism = yes and tear production rate = normal
   then recommendation = hard
```

This gives a correct result for 4 out of the 6 cases that it covers; thus its success fraction is 4/6. This contrasts with the default or "no-information" rule for the same outcome, which is always to recommend hard lenses whatever the situation. That gives a correct result for 4 out of the total of 24 cases. Thus the rule improves accuracy from 4/24 to 4/6—a very considerable improvement.

One way to quantify the value of a rule is to consider the probability of a completely random rule giving an equally good, or better, improvement in accuracy. This figure can be calculated based on the accuracy improvement; we will discuss the details below. In this case, improvement from 4/24 to 4/6 has a probability of $p = 0.0014$, or 0.14%, of occurring by chance. The fact that this is so small indicates that the rule is a good one.

Let's examine the corresponding figure for different rules. Each of the simpler rules

```
If astigmatism = yes then recommendation = hard
If tear production rate = normal then recommendation = hard
```

improves accuracy from 4/24 to 4/12, which corresponds to a 4.7% probability of the rule occurring by chance. This much higher probability is a reflection of the relatively low quality of the rule.

Suppose we add a further term to the earlier rule to make it a "perfect" one:

```
If astigmatism = yes and tear production rate = normal
   and age = young then recommendation = hard
```

This improves accuracy from the default of 4/24 to 2/2. This does not seem as impressive as the original improvement to 4/6, and this is reflected in a probability of 2.2% that the new rule (giving 2/2) occurs by chance, as opposed to the 0.14% probability yielded by the original one (giving 4/6). Thus we conclude that adding the third term to the rule is, on balance, counterproductive: it's true that it makes it error-free and hence "perfect," but it also makes it very restrictive.

Here's a really bad rule:

```
If astigmatism = yes and tear production rate = normal
    then recommendation = none
```

It has the same left-hand side as the first rule we examined, but the recommendation is none rather than hard. This rule is not a good rule, but it does get some instances correct, with accuracy 2/6. But the default for this outcome is 15/24, because 15 of the total set of 24 cases have the recommendation none. And because of this high default accuracy, the probability of a rule doing better by chance alone is 98.5%! That makes it a very bad rule.

Of all the rules you could form for the contact lens data, the best, as measured by our probability figure, is

```
If astigmatism = no and tear production rate = normal
    then recommendation = soft
```

This rule covers every one of the five soft cases, along with just one other instance, giving an accuracy of 5/6. The default accuracy for this outcome is 5/24, working out to a probability of only 0.01% that the rule would have arisen by chance alone.

Contrast this with the most *accurate* rule:

```
If tear production rate = reduced then recommendation = none
```

This gives massive, error-free accuracy of 12/12, but the default accuracy for this outcome is 15/24. This works out to a probability of 0.17% that the rule would have arisen by chance alone—impressively small, certainly, but not nearly as good as the best rule mentioned above.

Generating good rules

We will return to the question of how to calculate these probabilities shortly. But first consider how to use the rule evaluation measure to prune rules to avoid overfitting. Note that if the rules are intended as a summary of a dataset which is known to be complete—as the contact lens data is—and accurate, pruning should not be considered. This is very much the exceptional case, however. Practical datasets are never complete, and rarely completely accurate. Despite the fact that its completeness makes it a rather dubious candidate for pruning, we will continue to use the contact lens data for illustration: its special nature does not in any way affect the evaluations that will be performed.

First a perfect rule is generated by adding term after term until the rule gives no errors on the training set. This rule may be overspecialized, as indicated by a relatively large probability measure. So it is pruned by removing the last term that was added. If the new rule is better—that is, its probability measure is smaller—then we continue by removing its last term to see whether the improvement continues. We stop the process only when removing the last term makes the rule *worse*.

As an example, we apply this pruning process to the "perfect," but overspecialized, rule discussed earlier,

```
If astigmatism = yes and tear production rate = normal
    and age = young then recommendation = hard
```

which has accuracy 2/2 and probability measure 2.2%. Cutting off the last term (age = young) changes the accuracy to 4/6 and improves the measure to 0.14%. Cutting off the now-last term (tear production rate = normal) changes the accuracy to 4/12, which corresponds to a probability of 4.7%. So we stop at the best rule, which is

```
If astigmatism = yes and tear production rate = normal
    then recommendation = hard
```

Why not do the pruning as we build the rule up, rather than building up the whole thing and then throwing parts away? That is, why not preprune rather than postprune? Just as with pruning decision trees, when it is often best to grow the tree to its maximum size and then prune back, so with rules it is often best to make a perfect rule and then prune it. Who knows?—adding that last term may make a really good rule, a situation that we might never have noticed had we adopted an aggressive prepruning strategy.

Generating good decision lists

Now consider how to come up with a good decision list of rules that are to be interpreted sequentially. It's easy. First produce an approximation to the best possible rule—the one with the lowest probability measure. Do this by generating the best rule for each outcome (that is, for recommendation hard, soft, and none in the contact lens case). We have already mentioned that in our example this is the rule

```
If astigmatism = no and tear production rate = normal
    then recommendation = soft
```

with accuracy of 5/6 and probability measure 0.01%. This will be the first rule. Now remove the instances it covers from the instance set; in this case, there are six. After all, if one of these instances were encountered when evaluating the rules, the first rule would fire and the other rules would not even be considered. Now repeat the process on the reduced instance set, and continue until no

```
Initialize E to the instance set
Until E is empty do
  For each class C for which E contains an instance
    Use the basic covering algorithm to create the best perfect
        rule for class C
    Calculate the probability measure m(R) for the rule, and for
        the rule with the final condition omitted m(R-)
    While m(R-) < m(R), remove the final condition from the rule
        and repeat the previous step
  From the rules generated, select the one with the smallest
        m(R)
  Print the rule
  Remove the instances covered by the rule from E
Continue
```

Figure 6.3 Generating rules using a probability measure.

instances remain. This generates an ordered sequence of rules that are, in general, simpler and less numerous than if the rules were generated for each class at a time as we described in previous covering algorithms for rule generation.

Figure 6.3 summarizes the algorithm we have developed. This method differs from the previous rule-generation schemes we have described in that the classes are not considered one by one; rather, a rule is generated for every class and the best rule is chosen at each stage according to the probability measure that will be described in the next section. The basic covering algorithm for rule generation (Figure 4.8) is used to generate a good rule for each class, choosing conditions to add to the rule using the accuracy measure p/t that we discussed earlier. Then the probability measure is used to prune the rule by removing tests, the last-added one first, so long as the probability measure continues to decrease. Thus the method uses a combination of the accuracy measure (for growing rules) and the probability measure (for pruning them).

This algorithm will not necessarily generate the best possible rule, for several reasons. First, the basic covering algorithm adds tests according to their accuracy and coverage: this will not necessarily produce the best candidate rule for pruning. Second, the pruning starts from the last test added and works backward along the rule: this will not necessarily choose the best tests to prune. Third, pruning ceases as soon as the probability measure rises: it may be that continuing past this point will generate an even better pruned rule. The only way to find the *best* rule is to evaluate all possible rules exhaustively, and this is generally far too time-consuming to consider. Generally the method described does a good job at far lower cost.

There are several possible variants on this scheme for generating good decision lists that use the same basic probability measure. For example, a prepruning policy could be used that simply stops growing a rule at the point where adding another condition reduces the value of the probability measure. As we explained with regard to decision tree pruning, it is an open question whether prepruning strategies can be made to perform as well as postpruning.

Probability measure for rule evaluation

The final question is how to come up with the probability measure that assesses the worth of a rule. We have to calculate the probability of a completely random rule giving an equally good, or better, improvement in accuracy as the rule under consideration. The details are a little technical and this section can safely be skipped.

We have been talking about rules with an accuracy of, for example, 4/6, compared with a default accuracy of, for example, 4/24. Consider a general rule R for a particular class. We will denote its accuracy by p/t, as compared with a default accuracy of P/T. In this example the rule's accuracy is $p/t = 4/6$, and the default accuracy is $P/T = 4/24$. These quantities are depicted in Figure 6.4.

What is the probability that a randomly selected rule with the same coverage as rule R would perform at least as well as R does? R selects t cases, and some—hopefully many—of these are in the desired class, call it c. Mathematically, the random-rule probability is

$$\Pr[\text{of } t \text{ cases selected at random, exactly } i \text{ are in class } c] = \frac{\binom{P}{i}\binom{T-P}{t-i}}{\binom{T}{t}}$$

(where the parentheses indicate the combinatorial "choose" function). This is because i of the instances are chosen from class c, which contains P members,

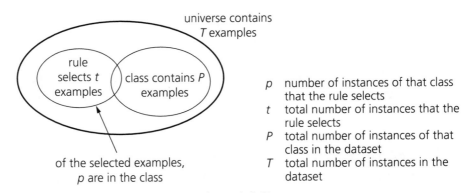

p	number of instances of that class that the rule selects
t	total number of instances that the rule selects
P	total number of instances of that class in the dataset
T	total number of instances in the dataset

Figure 6.4 Definitions for deriving the probability measure.

and $t - i$ instances are chosen from the rest of the instance set, which contains $T - P$ members. In statistics, this probability distribution is called *hypergeometric*. Notice that we are assuming that the selection is done "without replacement," which seems the most reasonable assumption to make when talking about a particular dataset.

Of the t cases that are selected by the rule R that we are considering, p are actually in class c. Thus the probability that a randomly chosen rule will do as well as or better than R is

$$m(\text{R}) = \sum_{i=p}^{\min(t,P)} \Pr[\text{of } t \text{ cases selected at random, exactly } i \text{ are in class } c].$$

This is a measure of the quality of rule R. Small values mean good rules because the value measures the probability that this good a rule would have arisen by chance. Unfortunately, this probability is quite time-consuming to calculate.

If the total number of instances T is large, a good approximation to the probability that exactly i of the selected t instances are in class c is obtained by sampling "with replacement":

$$\Pr[\text{of } t \text{ cases selected at random, exactly } i \text{ are in class } c] = \binom{t}{i}\left(\frac{P}{T}\right)^i\left(1-\frac{P}{T}\right)^{t-i}.$$

This corresponds to selection with replacement, giving a constant probability P/T that a selected instance will be in class c. In statistics, this probability distribution is called *binomial*. Using it in the expression for $m(\text{R})$ above leads to an approximate expression for the probability that a randomly chosen rule will do as well as or better than R.

A further approximation is to note that the coverage t of any particular rule is likely to be smaller than the total number of occurrences P of any class, and that the cumulative binomial probability is related to the incomplete beta function $I_x(a,b)$ as follows:

$$\sum_{i=p}^{t}\binom{t}{i}\left(\frac{P}{T}\right)^i\left(1-\frac{P}{T}\right)^{t-i} = I_{\frac{P}{T}}(p, t - p + 1).$$

For values of t greater than a dozen or so, a numerical evaluation of the incomplete beta function is a better way to evaluate this sum than explicit calculation of the binomial coefficients. This, finally, is the formula that we use to calculate the "value" of a rule.

Evaluating rules using a test set

The probability measure just described was introduced as a way of finding the best pruned version of a rule, and as a way of comparing two rules. But in order for this, or indeed any other, measure to be valid in a statistical sense, it must be evaluated on data that has not been used for building the rule.

Suppose we split the training data into two parts that we will call a *growing set* and a *pruning set*. The growing set is used to form a rule using the basic covering algorithm. Then a test is deleted from the rule, and the effect is evaluated by trying out the truncated rule on the pruning set and seeing whether it performs better than the original rule. This pruning process repeats until the rule cannot be improved by deleting any further tests. The whole procedure is repeated for each class, obtaining one best rule for each class, and the overall best rule is established by evaluating the rules on the pruning set. This rule is then added to the rule set, the instances it covers removed from the training data—from both growing and pruning sets—and the process is repeated.

It is essential that the growing and pruning sets are separate, because it is misleading to evaluate a rule on the very data that was used to form it: that would lead to serious errors by preferring rules that were overfitted. Usually the training set is split so that two-thirds of instances are used for growing and one-third for pruning. A disadvantage, of course, is that learning occurs from instances in the growing set only, and so the algorithm might miss important rules because some key instances had been assigned to the pruning set. Moreover, the wrong rule might be preferred because the pruning set contains only one-third of the data and may not be completely representative. These effects can be ameliorated by resplitting the training data into growing and pruning sets at each cycle of the algorithm, that is, after each rule is finally chosen.

The idea of using a separate pruning set for evaluating individual rules is called *reduced-error pruning*. Of course, there are many different ways to assess the worth of a rule. The probability measure derived in the previous section is one possibility, though implementers of reduced-error pruning have tended toward simpler measures. A very simple measure is to consider how well the rule would do at discriminating the predicted class from other classes if it were the only rule in the theory, operating under the closed-world assumption. If it gets p instances right out of t instances that it covers, and there are P instances of this class out of a total T of instances altogether, then it gets p positive instances right. The instances that it does not cover include $N-n$ negative ones, where $n = t - p$ is the number of negative instances that the rule covers and $N = T - P$ is the total number of negative instances. Thus the rule has an overall success ratio of

$$[p + (N - n)]/T,$$

and this quantity, evaluated on the test set, has been used to evaluate the success of a rule when using reduced-error pruning.

This measure is open to criticism because it treats noncoverage of negative examples as equally important as coverage of positive ones, which is unrealistic in a situation where what is being evaluated is one rule that will eventually serve alongside many others. For example, a rule that gets $p = 2000$ instances right out of a total coverage of 3000 (that is, it gets $n = 1000$ wrong) is judged as more successful than one that gets $p = 1000$ out of a total coverage of 1001 (that is, $n = 1$ wrong), because $[p + (N-n)]/T$ is $[1000 + N]/T$ in the first case but only $[999 + N]/T$ in the second. This is counterintuitive: the first rule is clearly less predictive than the second, for it has 33% as opposed to only 0.1% chance of being incorrect.

Using the success rate p/t as a measure, as was done in the original formulation of the covering algorithm (Figure 4.8), is not a good solution either, for it would prefer a rule that got a single instance right ($p = 1$) out of a total coverage of 1 (so $n = 0$) to the far more useful rule that got 1000 right out of 1001. Another heuristic that has been used is $(p-n)/t$, but that suffers from exactly the same problem because $(p-n)/t = 2p/t - 1$ and so the result, when comparing one rule with another, is just the same as with the success rate. It seems hard to find a simple measure of the worth of a rule that corresponds with intuition in all cases: perhaps the probability-based measure described above is the best choice despite its complexity.

Whatever heuristic is used to measure the worth of a rule, the reduced-error pruning algorithm is the same. It is usually implemented in a form called *incremental* reduced-error pruning which produces rules incrementally, removing the instances that they cover from the training set as it does so. The algorithm is given in Figure 6.5.

```
Initialize E to the instance set
Split E into Grow and Prune in the ratio 2:1
  For each class C for which Grow and Prune both contain an
      instance
    Use the basic covering algorithm to create the best perfect
        rule for class C
    Calculate the worth w(R) for the rule on Prune, and of the
        rule with the final condition omitted w(R-)
    While w(R-) > w(R), remove the final condition from the rule
        and repeat the previous step
  From the rules generated, select the one with the largest w(R)
  Print the rule
  Remove the instances covered by the rule from E
Continue
```

Figure 6.5 Algorithm for forming rules by incremental reduced error pruning.

This method has been used to produce rule induction schemes that can process vast amounts of data and operate very quickly. It can be accelerated by generating rules for the classes in order rather than generating a rule for each class at every stage and choosing the best: a suitable ordering is the increasing order in which they occur in the training set, so that the rarest class is processed first and the most common ones later. Another significant speedup is obtained by stopping the whole process when a rule of sufficiently low accuracy is generated, so as not to spend time generating a lot of rules at the end with very small coverage. However, very simple terminating conditions (such as stopping when the accuracy of a rule is lower than the default accuracy for the class it predicts) do not give the best performance, and the only conditions that have been found that seem to perform well are rather complicated ones based on the minimum description length principle.

In general, rules generated using incremental reduced-error pruning in this manner seem to perform quite well, particularly on large datasets. However, it has been found that a worthwhile performance advantage can be obtained by performing a global optimization step on the set of rules that is induced. The motivation is to increase the accuracy of the rule set by revising or replacing individual rules. Experiments show that both the size and the performance of rule sets are significantly improved by postinduction optimization. On the other hand, the process itself is rather complex and heuristic.

Obtaining rules from partial decision trees

There is an alternative approach to rule induction that avoids global optimization but nevertheless produces accurate, compact rule sets. The method combines the divide-and-conquer strategy for decision tree learning with the separate-and-conquer one for rule learning. It adopts the separate-and-conquer strategy in that it builds a rule, removes the instances it covers, and continues creating rules recursively for the remaining instances until none are left. However, it differs from the standard approach in the way that each rule is created. In essence, to make a single rule, a pruned decision tree is built for the current set of instances, the leaf with the largest coverage is made into a rule, and the tree is discarded.

The prospect of repeatedly building decision trees only to discard most of them is not as bizarre as it first seems. Using a pruned tree to obtain a rule instead of building it incrementally by adding conjunctions one at a time avoids a tendency to overprune that is a characteristic problem of the basic separate-and-conquer rule learner. Using the separate-and-conquer methodology in conjunction with decision trees adds flexibility and speed. It is indeed wasteful to build a full decision tree just to obtain a single rule, but the process can be accelerated significantly without sacrificing the above advantages.

```
Expand-subset (S):
  Choose a test T and use it to split the set of examples into
      subsets
  Sort subsets into increasing order of average entropy
  while (there is a subset X that has not yet been expanded
          AND all subsets expanded so far are leaves)
    expand-subset(X)
  if (all the subsets expanded are leaves
      AND estimated error for subtree >= estimated error for
          node)
    undo expansion into subsets and make node a leaf
```

Figure 6.6 Algorithm for expanding examples into a partial tree.

The key idea is to build a partial decision tree instead of a fully explored one. A partial decision tree is an ordinary decision tree that contains branches to undefined subtrees. To generate such a tree, the construction and pruning operations are integrated in order to find a "stable" subtree that can be simplified no further. Once this subtree has been found, tree-building ceases and a single rule is read off.

The tree-building algorithm is summarized in Figure 6.6: it splits a set of instances recursively into a partial tree. The first step chooses a test and divides the instances into subsets accordingly. The choice is made using the same information-gain heuristic that is normally used for building decision trees (Section 4.3). Then the subsets are expanded in increasing order of their average entropy. The reason for this is that the later subsets will most likely not end up being expanded, and a subset with low average entropy is more likely to result in a small subtree and therefore produce a more general rule. This proceeds recursively until a subset is expanded into a leaf, and then continues further by backtracking. But as soon as an internal node appears which has all its children expanded into leaves, the algorithm checks whether that node is better replaced by a single leaf. This is just the standard "subtree replacement" operation of decision tree pruning (Section 6.1). If replacement is performed, the algorithm backtracks in the standard way, exploring siblings of the newly replaced node. However, if during backtracking a node is encountered all of whose children are not leaves—and this will happen as soon as a potential subtree replacement is *not* performed—then the remaining subsets are left unexplored and the corresponding subtrees are left undefined. Owing to the recursive structure of the algorithm, this event automatically terminates tree generation.

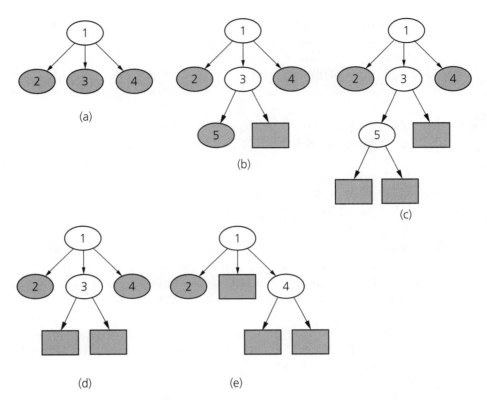

Figure 6.7 Example of building a partial tree.

Figure 6.7 shows a step-by-step example. During stages (a) through (c), tree-building continues recursively in the normal way, except that at each point the lowest-entropy sibling is chosen for expansion: node 3 between stages (a) and (b). Gray elliptical nodes are as yet unexpanded; rectangular ones are leaves. Between stages (b) and (c), the rectangular node will have lower entropy than its sibling, node 5, but cannot be expanded further because it is a leaf. Backtracking occurs and node 5 is chosen for expansion. Once stage (c) is reached, there is a node—node 5—that has all of its children expanded into leaves, and this triggers pruning. Subtree replacement for node 5 is considered, and accepted, leading to stage (d). Now node 3 is considered for subtree replacement, and this operation is again accepted. Backtracking continues, and node 4, having lower entropy than node 2, is expanded into two leaves. Now subtree replacement is considered for node 4: let us suppose that node 4 is not replaced. At this point, the process terminates with the three-leaf partial tree of stage (e).

If the data is noise-free and contains enough instances to prevent the algorithm from doing any pruning, just one path of the full decision tree has to be explored. This achieves the greatest possible performance gain over the naive method that builds a full decision tree each time. The gain decreases as more pruning takes place. For datasets with numeric attributes, the asymptotic time complexity of the algorithm is the same as building the full decision tree, because in this case the complexity is dominated by the time required to sort the attribute values in the first place.

Once a partial tree has been built, a single rule is extracted from it. Each leaf corresponds to a possible rule, and we seek the "best" leaf of those subtrees (typically a small minority) that have been expanded into leaves. Experiments show that it is best to aim at the most general rule by choosing the leaf that covers the greatest number of instances.

When a dataset contains missing values, these can be dealt with exactly as they are when building decision trees. If an instance cannot be assigned to any given branch because of a missing attribute value, it is assigned to each of the branches with a weight proportional to the number of training instances going down that branch, normalized by the total number of training instances with known values at the node. During testing, the same procedure is applied separately to each rule, thus associating a weight with the application of each rule to the test instance. That weight is deducted from the instance's total weight before it is passed to the next rule in the list. Once the weight has reduced to zero, the predicted class probabilities are combined into a final classification according to the weights.

This yields a simple but surprisingly effective method for learning decision lists for noisy data. Its main advantage over other comprehensive rule-generating schemes is simplicity, for other methods require a complex global optimization stage to achieve the same level of performance.

Rules with exceptions

In Section 3.5 we learned that a natural extension of rules is to allow them to have exceptions, and exceptions to the exceptions, and so on—indeed the whole rule set can be considered as exceptions to a default classification rule that is used when no other rules apply. The method of generating a "good" rule, using one of the measures discussed in the previous section, provides exactly the mechanism needed to generate rules with exceptions.

First, a default class is selected for the top-level rule: it is natural to use the class that occurs most frequently in the training data. Then, a rule is found pertaining to any class other than the default one. Of all such rules it is natural to seek the one with the most discriminatory power, for example, the one with the best evaluation on a test set. Suppose this rule has the form

```
if <condition> then class = <new class>
```

It is used to split the training data into two subsets: one containing all instances for which the rule's condition is `true`, and the other containing those for which it is `false`. If either of these subsets contains instances of more than one class, the algorithm is invoked recursively on that subset. For the subset for which the condition is `true`, the "default class" is the new class as specified by the rule; for the subset where the condition is `false`, the default class remains as it was before.

Let's examine how this algorithm would work for the rules with exceptions that were given in Section 3.5 for the Iris data of Table 1.4. We will represent the rules in the graphical form shown in Figure 6.8, which is in fact equivalent to the textual rules that we gave before in Figure 3.4. The default of `Iris setosa` is the entry node at the top left. Horizontal, dotted paths show exceptions, so the next box, which contains a rule that concludes `Iris versicolor`, is an exception to the default. Below this is an alternative, a second exception—alternatives are shown by vertical, solid lines—leading to the conclusion `Iris virginica`. Following the upper path along horizontally leads to an exception to the `Iris versicolor` rule that overrides it whenever the condition in the top right box holds, with the conclusion `Iris virginica`. Below this is an alternative, leading (as it happens) to the same conclusion. Returning to the box at bottom center, this has its own exception, the lower right box, which gives the conclusion `Iris versicolor`. The numbers at the lower right of each box give the "coverage" of the rule, expressed as the number of examples that satisfy it divided by the number that satisfy its condition but not its conclusion. For example, the condition in the top center box applies to 52 of the examples, and 49 of them are `Iris versicolor`. The strength of this representation is that you can get a very good feeling for the effect of the rules from the boxes toward the left-hand side; the boxes at the right cover just a few exceptional cases.

In order to create these rules, the default is first set to `Iris setosa` by taking the most frequently occurring class in the dataset. This is an arbitrary choice because for this dataset all classes occur exactly 50 times; as shown in Figure 6.8 this default "rule" is correct in 50 out of 150 cases. Then the best rule that predicts another class is sought: in this case it is

```
if petal-length ≥ 2.45 and petal-length < 5.355
    and petal-width < 1.75 then Iris-versicolor
```

This rule covers 52 instances, of which 49 are `Iris versicolor`. It divides the dataset into two subsets: the 52 instances that *do* satisfy the condition of the rule and the remaining 98, which do not. We work on the former subset first. The default class for these instances is `Iris versicolor`: there are only three exceptions, all of which happen to be `Iris virginica`. The best rule for this subset which does not predict `Iris versicolor` is identified next: it is

```
if petal-length ≥ 4.95 and petal-width < 1.55 then Iris-virginica
```

It covers two of the three Iris virginicas, and nothing else. Again it divides the subset into two: those instances that satisfy its condition and those that do not. Fortunately, in this case, all those instances that satisfy the condition do indeed have class Iris virginica, so there is no need for a further exception. However, the remaining instances still include the third Iris virginica, along with 49 Iris versicolors, which are the default at this point. Again the "best" rule is sought: it is

```
if sepal-length < 4.95 and sepal-width ≥ 2.45 then Iris-virginica
```

This rule covers the remaining Iris virginica and nothing else, so it also has no exceptions. Furthermore, all remaining instances in the subset that do not satisfy its condition have class Iris versicolor, which is the default, so no more needs to be done.

Return now to the second subset created by the initial rule, the instances that do not satisfy the condition

```
petal-length ≥ 2.45 and petal-length < 5.355 and petal-width < 1.75
```

Of the rules for these instances that do not predict the default class Iris setosa, the best is

```
if petal-length ≥ 3.35 then Iris-virginica
```

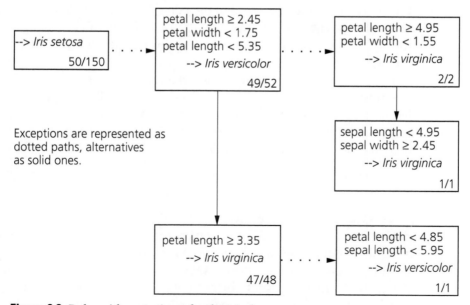

Figure 6.8 Rules with exceptions, for the Iris data.

It covers all 47 Iris virginicas that are in the example set (3 were removed by the first rule, as discussed above). It also covers one Iris versicolor. This needs to be taken care of as an exception, by the final rule,

```
if petal-length < 4.85 and sepal-length < 5.95 then Iris-versicolor
```

Fortunately, the set of instances that do *not* satisfy its condition are all the default, Iris setosa. Thus the procedure is finished.

The rules produced have the property that most of the examples are covered by the high-level rules, and the lower-level ones really do represent exceptions. For example, the last exception clause in the rules above, and the deeply nested *else* clause, both cover a solitary example, and removing them would have little effect. Even the remaining nested exception rule covers only two examples. Thus one can get an excellent feeling for what the rules do by ignoring all the deeper structure and looking only at the first level or two. That is the attraction of rules with exceptions.

Discussion

All algorithms for producing classification rules that we have discussed use the basic covering or separate-and-conquer approach. For the simple, noise-free case this produces PRISM (Cendrowska 1987), an algorithm that is straightforward and easy to understand. When applied to two-class problems with the closed-world assumption, it is only necessary to produce rules for one class: then the rules are in disjunctive normal form and can be executed on test instances without any ambiguity arising. When applied to multiclass problems, a separate rule set is produced for each class: thus a test instance may be assigned to more than one class, or to no class, and further heuristics are necessary if a unique prediction is sought.

To reduce overfitting in noisy situations, it is necessary to produce rules that are not "perfect" even on the training set. To do this requires a measure for the "goodness," or worth, of a rule. With such a measure, it is possible to abandon the class-by-class approach of the basic covering algorithm and start by generating the very best rule, regardless of which class it predicts, and then remove all examples covered by this rule and continue the process. This yields a method for producing a decision list rather than a set of independent classification rules, and decision lists have the important advantage that they do not generate ambiguities when interpreted.

To measure the worth of a rule based on its performance on the training set, a statistical measure is needed. The measure based on the binomial distribution was introduced in a system called INDUCT, a development of PRISM to produce approximate rules in noisy situations, developed by Gaines and Compton (1995). To avoid the risk of overfitting to the training set, one option is to withhold some of the training examples as a test set and measure the performance of the rule on that. This idea is called *reduced-error pruning* (Fürnkrantz and Widmer 1994), and it forms the basis for fast and effective rule induction (Cohen 1995).

The whole question of measuring the value of a rule has not yet been satisfactorily resolved. Many different measures have been proposed, some blatantly heuristic and others based on information-theoretic or probabilistic grounds. However, there seems to be no consensus on which is the best measure to use.

The rule-learning scheme based on partial decision trees was developed by Frank and Witten (1998). It produces rule sets that are as accurate as those generated by C4.5 and more accurate than other fast rule induction methods. However, its main advantage over other schemes is not performance but simplicity: by combining the top-down decision tree induction method with separate-and-conquer rule learning, it produces good rule sets without any need for global optimization.

The procedure for generating rules with exceptions was developed as an option in the INDUCT system by Gaines and Compton (1995), who called them *ripple-down* rules. In an experiment with a large medical dataset (22,000 instances, 32 attributes, 60 classes), they found that people can understand large systems of rules with exceptions more readily than equivalent systems of regular rules because that is the way they think about the complex medical diagnoses involved. Richards and Compton (1998) discuss their role as an alternative to classic knowledge engineering.

6.3 Extending linear classification: Support vector machines

Chapter 4 (Section 4.6) described how simple linear models can be used for classification in situations where all attributes are numeric. Their biggest disadvantage is that they can only represent linear boundaries between classes, which makes them too simple for many practical applications. Support vector machines use linear models to implement nonlinear class boundaries. (While it is a widely used term, *support vector machines* is something of a misnomer: these are algorithms, not machines.) How can this be possible? The trick is easy: transform the input using a nonlinear mapping, in other words, transform the instance space into a new space. With a nonlinear mapping, a straight line in the new space doesn't look straight in the original instance space. A linear model constructed in the new space can represent a nonlinear decision boundary in the original space.

Imagine applying this idea directly to the ordinary linear models in Section 4.6. For example, the original set of attributes could be replaced by one giving all products of n factors that can be constructed from these attributes. An example for two attributes, including all products with three factors, is

$$x = w_1 a_1^3 + w_2 a_1^2 a_2 + w_3 a_1 a_2^2 + w_4 a_2^3.$$

Here, x is the outcome, a_1 and a_2 are the two attribute values, and there are four weights w_i to be learned. As described in Section 4.6, the result can be used for classification by training one linear system for each class and assigning an unknown instance to the class that gives the greatest output x—the standard technique of multi-response linear regression. Then, a_1 and a_2 will be the attribute values for the test instance. In order to generate a linear model in the space spanned by these products, each training instance is mapped into the new space by computing all possible three-factor products of its two attribute values. The learning algorithm is then applied to the transformed instances. In order to classify an instance, it is processed by the same transformation prior to classification. There is nothing to stop us from adding in more synthetic attributes. For example, including a constant term, the original attributes themselves and all two-factor products of them would yield a total of eight weights to be learned. (Alternatively, adding an additional attribute whose value was always a constant would have the same effect.) Indeed, polynomials of sufficiently high degree can approximate arbitrary decision boundaries to any required accuracy.

It seems too good to be true—and it is. As you will probably have guessed, problems arise with this procedure due to the large number of coefficients introduced by the transformation in any realistic setting. The first snag is computational complexity. With ten attributes in the original dataset, suppose we want to include all products with five factors: then the learning algorithm will have to determine more than 2000 coefficients. If its run time is cubic in the number of attributes, as it is for linear regression, training will be infeasible. That is a problem of practicality. The second problem is one of principle: overfitting. If the number of coefficients is large relative to the number of training instances, the resulting model will be "too nonlinear"—it will overfit the training data. There are just too many parameters in the model.

The maximum margin hyperplane

Support vector machines solve both problems. They are based on an algorithm that finds a special kind of linear model, the *maximum margin hyperplane*. We already know what a hyperplane is—it's just another word for a linear model. To visualize a maximum margin hyperplane, imagine a two-class dataset whose classes are linearly separable; that is, there is a hyperplane in instance space that classifies all training instances correctly. The maximum margin hyperplane is the one that gives the greatest separation between the classes—it comes no closer to either than it has to. An example is shown in Figure 6.9, where the

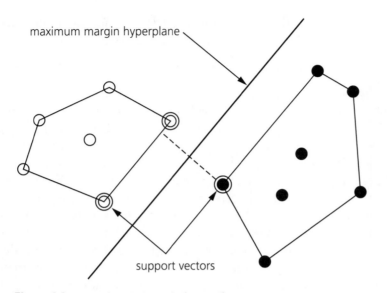

Figure 6.9 A maximum margin hyperplane.

classes are represented by open and filled circles respectively. Technically speaking, the "convex hull" of a set of points is the tightest enclosing convex polygon: its outline emerges when you connect every point of the set to every other point. Since we have supposed that the two classes are linearly separable, their convex hulls can't overlap. Among all hyperplanes that separate the classes, the maximum margin hyperplane is the one that is as far away as possible from both convex hulls—it is orthogonal to the shortest line connecting the hulls (shown dashed in the figure), intersecting it halfway.

The instances that are closest to the maximum margin hyperplane—the ones with minimum distance to it—are called *support vectors*. There is always at least one support vector for each class, often more. The important thing is that the set of support vectors uniquely defines the maximum margin hyperplane for the learning problem. Given the support vectors for the two classes, we can easily construct the maximum margin hyperplane. All other training instances are irrelevant—they can be deleted without changing the position and orientation of the hyperplane.

A hyperplane separating the two classes might be written

$$x = w_0 + w_1 a_1 + w_2 a_2$$

in the two-attribute case, where a_1 and a_2 are the attribute values, and there are three weights w_i to be learned. However, the equation defining the maximum margin hyperplane can be written in another form, in terms of the support vectors. Write the class value y of a training instance as either 1 (for yes, it is in this class) or -1 (for no, it is not). Then the maximum margin hyperplane is

$$x = b + \sum_{i \text{ is support vector}} \alpha_i y_i \mathbf{a}(i) \cdot \mathbf{a}.$$

Here, y_i is the class value of training instance $\mathbf{a}(i)$; while b and α_i are numeric parameters that have to be determined by the learning algorithm. Note that $\mathbf{a}(i)$ and $\mathbf{a}$ are vectors. The vector $\mathbf{a}$ represents a test instance—just as the vector $[a_1, a_2]$ represented a test instance in the earlier formulation. The vectors $\mathbf{a}(i)$ are the support vectors, those circled in Figure 6.9; they are selected members of the training set. The term $\mathbf{a}(i) \cdot \mathbf{a}$ represents the dot product of the test instance with one of the support vectors. If you are not familiar with dot product notation, you should still be able to understand the gist of what follows: just think of $\mathbf{a}(i)$ as the whole set of attribute values for the ith support vector. Finally, b and α_i are parameters that determine the hyperplane, just as the weights w_0, w_1, and w_2 are parameters that determine the hyperplane in the earlier formulation.

It turns out that finding the support vectors for the instance sets and determining the parameters b and α_i belongs to a standard class of optimization problems known as *constrained quadratic optimization*. There are off-the-shelf software packages for solving these problems (see Fletcher 1987, for a comprehensive and practical account of solution methods). However, the computational complexity can be reduced, and learning accelerated, if special-purpose algorithms for training support vector machines are applied—but the details of these algorithms lie beyond the scope of this book (Platt 1998).

Nonlinear class boundaries

We originally introduced support vector machines by claiming that they can be used to model nonlinear class boundaries. However, so far we have only described the linear case. Consider what happens when an attribute transformation, as described above, is applied to the training data before determining the maximum margin hyperplane. Recall that there are two problems with the straightforward application of such transformations to linear models: infeasible computational complexity on the one hand and overfitting on the other.

With support vectors, overfitting is unlikely to occur. The reason is that overfitting is inevitably associated with instability: changing one or two instance vectors will make sweeping changes to large sections of the decision boundary. But the maximum margin hyperplane is relatively stable: it only moves if training instances that are support vectors are added or deleted—and this is true even in the high-dimensional space spanned by the nonlinear transformation. Overfitting is caused by too much flexibility in the decision boundary. The support vectors are global representatives of the whole set of training points, and there are usually few of them, which gives little flexibility. Thus overfitting is unlikely to occur.

What about computational complexity? This is still a problem. Suppose that the transformed space is a high-dimensional one, so that the transformed support vectors and test instance have many components. According to the above equation, every time an instance is classified its dot product with all support vectors must be calculated. In the high-dimensional space produced by the nonlinear mapping, this is rather expensive. Obtaining the dot product involves one multiplication and one addition for each attribute, and the number of attributes in the new space can be huge. This problem occurs not only during classification but also during training, because the optimization algorithms have to calculate the same dot products very frequently.

Fortunately, it turns out that it is possible to calculate the dot product *before* the nonlinear mapping is performed, on the original attribute set. A high-dimensional version of the above equation is simply

$$x = b + \sum_i \alpha_i y_i (\mathbf{a}(i) \cdot \mathbf{a})^n,$$

where n is chosen as the number of factors in the transformation (3 in the example we used earlier). If you expand the term $(\mathbf{a}(i) \cdot \mathbf{a})^n$, you will find that it contains all the high-dimensional terms that would have been involved if the test and training vectors were first transformed by including all products of n factors, and the dot product was taken of the result. (If you actually do the calculation, you will notice that some constant factors—binomial coefficients—are introduced. However, these do not matter: it is the dimensionality of the space that concerns us; the constants merely scale the axes.) Because of this mathematical equivalence, the dot products can be computed in the original low-dimensional space, and the problem becomes feasible. In implementation terms, you take a software package for constrained quadratic optimization and every time $\mathbf{a}(i) \cdot \mathbf{a}$ is evaluated, you evaluate $(\mathbf{a}(i) \cdot \mathbf{a})^n$ instead. It's as simple as that, because in both the optimization and the classification algorithms, these vectors are only ever used in this dot product form. The training vectors, including the support vectors, and the test instance all remain in the original low-dimensional space throughout the calculations.

Throughout this section, we have assumed that the training data is linearly separable—either in the instance space or in the new space spanned by the nonlinear mapping. It turns out that support vector machines can be generalized to the case where the training data is not separable. This is accomplished by placing an upper bound on the coefficients α_i above. Unfortunately this parameter must be chosen by the user, and the best setting can only be determined by experimentation. Also, in all but trivial cases, it is not possible to determine a priori whether the data is linearly separable or not.

Finally, we should mention that compared with other methods like decision tree learners, even the fastest training algorithms for support vector machines are slow when applied in the nonlinear setting. On the other hand, they often produce very accurate classifiers because subtle and complex decision boundaries can be obtained.

Discussion

The function $(\mathbf{x} \cdot \mathbf{y})^n$, which computes the dot product of two vectors $\mathbf{x}$ and $\mathbf{y}$ and raises the result to the power n, is called a *polynomial kernel*. A good way of choosing the value of n is to start with 1 (a linear model) and increment it until the estimated error ceases to improve. Usually, quite small values suffice.

Other kernel functions can be used instead, to implement different nonlinear mappings. Two that are often suggested are called the *radial basis function kernel* and the *sigmoid kernel*. Which one produces the best results depends on the application, although the differences are rarely large in practice. It is interesting to note that a support vector machine with the radial basis function kernel is simply a type of neural network called a *radial basis function network,* and one with the sigmoid kernel implements a multilayer perceptron with no hidden layers, another type of neural network.

Support vector machines originated from research in statistical learning theory (Vapnik 1995), and a good starting point for exploration is a tutorial by Burges (1998). A general description, including generalization to the case where the data is not linearly separable, has been published by Cortes and Vapnik (1995). One of the fastest algorithms for learning support vector machines is that developed by Platt (1998). Also, there is an algorithm, based on similar ideas, that is almost as accurate as the standard support vector machine but much faster and easier to implement (Freund and Schapire 1998). Support vector machines can also be applied to numeric prediction (Schölkopf et al. 1999).

6.4 Instance-based learning

In Section 4.7 we saw how the nearest-neighbor rule can be used to implement a basic form of instance-based learning. There are several practical problems with this simple scheme. First, it tends to be slow for large training sets, because the entire set must be searched for each test instance. Second, it performs badly with noisy data, because the class of a test instance is determined by its single nearest neighbor without any "averaging" to help eliminate noise. Third, it performs badly when different attributes affect the outcome to different extents—in the extreme case, when some attributes are completely irrelevant—because all attributes contribute equally to the distance formula. Fourth, it does not perform explicit generalization, although we intimated in Section 3.8 (and illustrated in Figure 3.7) that some instance-based learning systems do indeed perform explicit generalization.

Reducing the number of exemplars

The plain nearest-neighbor rule stores a lot of redundant exemplars: it is almost always completely unnecessary to save all the examples seen so far. A simple variant is to classify each example with respect to the examples already seen, and to save only ones that are misclassified. We use the term *exemplars* to refer to the already-seen instances that are used for classification. Discarding correctly classified instances reduces the number of exemplars and proves to be an effective way to prune the exemplar database. Ideally, only a single exemplar is stored for each important region of the instance space. However, early in the learning process examples may be discarded that later turn out to be important, possibly leading to some decrease in predictive accuracy. As the number of stored instances increases, the accuracy of the model improves, and so the system makes fewer mistakes.

Unfortunately, the strategy of only storing misclassified instances does not work well in the face of noise. Noisy examples are very likely to be misclassified, and so the set of stored exemplars tends to accumulate those that are least useful. This effect is easily observed experimentally. Thus this strategy is only a stepping-stone on the way toward more effective instance-based learners.

Pruning noisy exemplars

Noisy exemplars inevitably lower the performance of any nearest-neighbor scheme that does not suppress them, because they have the effect of repeatedly misclassifying new instances. There are two ways of dealing with this. One is to locate, instead of the single nearest neighbor, the k nearest neighbors for some predetermined constant k, and assign the majority class to the unknown instance. The only problem here is determining a suitable value of k. Plain nearest-neighbor learning corresponds to $k = 1$. The more noise, the greater the optimal value of k. One way to proceed is to perform cross-validation tests with several different values and choose the best. Although this is expensive in computation time, it often yields excellent predictive performance.

A second solution is to monitor the performance of each exemplar that is stored and discard ones that do not perform well. This can be done by keeping a record of the number of correct and incorrect classification decisions that each exemplar makes. Two predetermined thresholds are set on the success ratio. When an exemplar's performance drops below the lower one, it is deleted from the exemplar set. If its performance exceeds the upper threshold, it is used for predicting the class of new instances. If its performance lies between the two, it is not used for prediction but whenever it is the closest exemplar to the new instance (and thus would have been used for prediction if its performance record had been good enough), its success statistics are updated as though it had been used to classify that new instance.

In order to accomplish this, we utilize the confidence limits on the success probability of a Bernoulli process that we derived in Section 5.2. Recall that we took a certain number of successes S out of a total number of trials N as evidence on which to base confidence limits on the true underlying success rate p. Given a certain confidence level of, say, 5%, we can calculate upper and lower bounds and be 95% sure that p lies between them.

To apply this to the problem of deciding when to accept a particular exemplar, suppose it has been used n times to classify other instances, and s of these have been successes. That allows us to estimate bounds, at a particular confidence level, on the true success rate of this exemplar. Now suppose that the exemplar's class has occurred c times out of a total number N of training instances. This allow us to estimate bounds on the default success rate, that is, the probability of successfully classifying an instance of this class without any information about other instances. We insist that the *lower* confidence bound on its success rate exceeds the *upper* confidence bound on the default success rate. We use the same method to devise a criterion for rejecting a poorly performing exemplar, requiring that the *upper* confidence bound on its success rate lies below the *lower* confidence bound on the default success rate.

With suitable choice of thresholds, this scheme works well. In a particular implementation, called IB3 for "Instance-Based learner version 3," a confidence level of 5% is used to determine acceptance, whereas a level of 12.5% is used for rejection. The lower percentage figure produces a wider confidence interval, which makes for a more stringent criterion because it is harder for the lower bound of one interval to lie above the upper bound of the other. The criterion for acceptance is more stringent than for rejection, making it more difficult for an instance to be accepted. The reason for a less stringent rejection criterion is that there is little to be lost by dropping instances with only moderately poor classification accuracies: they will probably be replaced by a similar instance later on. Using these thresholds the scheme has been found to improve the performance of instance-based learning and, at the same time, dramatically reduce the number of exemplars—particularly noisy exemplars—that are stored.

Weighting attributes

The Euclidean distance function, modified to scale all attribute values to between 0 and 1, works well in domains in which the attributes are equally relevant to the outcome. Such domains, however, are the exception rather than the rule. In most domains some attributes are irrelevant, and some relevant ones are less important than others. The next improvement in instance-based learning is to learn the relevance of each attribute incrementally by dynamically updating feature weights.

In some schemes, the weights are class-specific in that an attribute may be more important to one class than to another. To cater for this, a description is produced for each class that distinguishes its members from members of all other classes. This leads to the problem that an unknown test instance may be assigned several different classes, or no classes at all—a problem that is all too familiar from our discussion of rule induction. Heuristic solutions are applied to resolve these situations.

The distance metric incorporates the feature weights $w_1, w_2, \ldots, w_n$ on each dimension:

$$\sqrt{w_1^2(x_1 - y_1)^2 + w_2^2(x_2 - y_2)^2 + \ldots + w_n^2(x_n - y_n)^2}.$$

In the case of class-specific feature weights, there will be a separate set of weights for each class.

All attribute weights are updated after each training instance is classified, and the most similar exemplar (or the most similar exemplar of each class) is used as the basis for updating. Call the training instance x and the most similar exemplar y. For each attribute i, the difference $|x_i - y_i|$ is a measure of the contribution of that attribute to the decision. If this difference is small, the attribute contributes positively, whereas if it is large it may contribute negatively. The idea is to update the ith weight on the basis of the size of this difference and whether the classification was indeed correct. If the classification is correct the associated weight is increased; if it is incorrect it is decreased, the amount of increase or decrease being governed by the size of the difference, large if the difference is small and vice versa. The weight change is generally followed by a renormalization step. A simpler strategy, which may be equally effective, is to leave the weights alone if the decision is correct, and if it is incorrect increase the weights for those attributes that differ most greatly, accentuating the difference. Details of these weight adaptation algorithms are described by Aha (1992).

A good test of whether an attribute weighting scheme works is to add irrelevant attributes to all examples in a dataset. Ideally, the introduction of irrelevant attributes should have no effect on either the quality of predictions or the number of exemplars stored.

Generalizing exemplars

Generalized exemplars are rectangular regions of instance space, called *hyperrectangles* because they are high-dimensional. When classifying new instances, it is necessary to modify the distance function as described below to allow the distance to a hyper-rectangle to be computed. When a new exemplar is classified correctly, it is generalized by simply merging it with the nearest exemplar of the same class. The nearest exemplar may be either a single instance or a hyper-rectangle. In the former case a new hyper-rectangle is created that covers the old and the new instances. In the latter the hyper-rectangle is enlarged to encompass the new instance. Finally, if the prediction is incorrect and it was a hyper-rectangle that was responsible for the incorrect prediction, the hyper-rectangle's boundaries are altered so that it shrinks away from the new instance.

It is necessary to decide at the outset whether overgeneralization caused by nesting or overlapping hyper-rectangles is to be permitted or not. If it is to be avoided, a check is made before generalizing a new example to see whether any regions of feature space conflict with the proposed new hyper-rectangle. If they do, the generalization is aborted and the example is stored verbatim. Note that overlapping hyper-rectangles are precisely analogous to situations where the same example is covered by two or more rules in a rule set.

In some schemes generalized exemplars can be nested in that they may be completely contained within one another, in the same way that, in some representations, rules may have exceptions. To do this, whenever an example is incorrectly classified, a fallback heuristic is tried using the second nearest neighbor if it would have produced a correct prediction, in a further attempt to perform generalization. This second-chance mechanism promotes nesting of hyper-rectangles. If an example falls within a rectangle of the wrong class that already contains an exemplar of the same class, the two are generalized into a new "exception" hyper-rectangle nested within the original one. For nested generalized exemplars, the learning process frequently begins with a small number of seed instances in order to prevent all examples of the same class from being generalized into a single rectangle that covers most of the problem space.

Distance functions for generalized exemplars

With generalized exemplars it is necessary to generalize the distance function to compute the distance from an instance to a generalized exemplar, as well as to another instance. The distance from an instance to a hyper-rectangle is defined to be zero if the point lies within the hyper-rectangle. The simplest way to generalize the distance function to compute the distance from an exterior point to a hyper-rectangle is to choose the closest instance within it and measure the distance to that. However, this reduces the benefit of generalization because it reintroduces dependence on a particular single example. More precisely, whereas new instances that happen to lie within a hyper-rectangle continue to benefit from generalizations, ones that lie outside do not. It might be better to use the distance from the nearest part of the hyper-rectangle instead.

Figure 6.10 shows the implicit boundaries formed between two rectangular classes if the distance metric is adjusted to measure distance to the nearest point

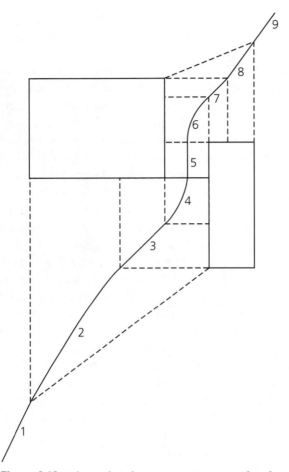

Figure 6.10 A boundary between two rectangular classes.

of a rectangle. Even in two dimensions the boundary contains a total of nine regions (they are numbered for easy identification); the situation will be more complex for higher-dimensional hyper-rectangles.

Proceeding from the lower left, the first region, in which the boundary is linear, lies outside the extent of both rectangles—to the left of both borders of the larger one and below both borders of the smaller one. The second is within the extent of one rectangle—to the right of the leftmost border of the larger rectangle—but outside that of the other—below both borders of the smaller one. In this region the boundary is parabolic, because the locus of a point that is the same distance from a given line as from a given point is a parabola. The third region is where the boundary meets the lower border of the larger rectangle when projected upward, and the left border of the smaller one when projected to the right. The boundary is linear in this region, because it is equidistant from these two borders. The fourth is where the boundary lies to the right of the larger rectangle but below the bottom of that rectangle. In this case the boundary is parabolic because it is the locus of points equidistant from the lower right corner of the larger rectangle and the left side of the smaller one. The fifth region lies between the two rectangles: here the boundary is vertical. The pattern is repeated in the upper right part of the diagram: first parabolic, then linear, then parabolic (although this particular parabola is almost indistinguishable from a straight line), and finally linear as the boundary finally escapes from the scope of both rectangles.

This simple situation certainly defines a complex boundary! Of course it is not necessary to represent the boundary explicitly, it is generated implicitly by the nearest-neighbor calculation. Nevertheless, the solution is still not a very good one. Whereas taking the distance from the nearest instance within a hyper-rectangle is overly dependent on the position of that particular instance, taking the distance to the nearest point of the hyper-rectangle is overly dependent on that corner of the rectangle—the nearest example might be a long way from the corner.

A final problem concerns measuring the distance to hyper-rectangles that overlap or are nested. This complicates the situation because an instance may fall within more than one hyper-rectangle. A suitable heuristic to use in this case is to choose the class of the most specific hyper-rectangle containing the instance, that is, the one covering the smallest area of instance space.

Whether or not overlap or nesting is permitted, the distance function should be modified to take account of both the observed prediction accuracy of exemplars, and the relative importance of different features, as described in the sections above on pruning noisy exemplars and attribute weighting.

Generalized distance functions

There are many different ways of defining a distance function, and it is hard to find rational grounds for choosing any one in particular. A novel possibility proposed recently is to consider one instance being transformed into another through a sequence of predefined elementary operations, and to calculate the probability of such a sequence occurring if operations were chosen at random. Robustness is improved if all possible transformation paths are considered, weighted by their probabilities, and the scheme generalizes naturally to the problem of calculating the distance between an instance and a set of other instances, by considering transformations to all instances in the set. Through such a technique it is possible to consider each instance as exerting a "sphere of influence," but a sphere with soft boundaries rather than the hard-edged cutoff implied by the k-nearest-neighbor rule, where any particular example is either "in" or "out" of the decision.

With such a measure, given a test instance whose class is unknown, its distance to the set of all training instances in each class in turn is calculated, and the "closest" class is chosen. It turns out that nominal and numeric attributes can be treated in a uniform manner within this transformation-based approach by defining different transformation sets, and it is even possible to take account of unusual attribute types—such as degrees of arc, or days of the week, which are measured on a circular scale.

Discussion

Nearest-neighbor methods gained popularity in machine learning through the work of Aha (1992), who showed that, when combined with noisy exemplar pruning and attribute weighting, instance-based learning performs well in comparison with other methods. It is worth noting that although we have discussed instance-based learning solely in the context of classification rather than numeric prediction problems, it applies to numeric prediction problems equally well: predictions can be obtained by combining the predicted values of the k nearest neighbors, weighting them by distance.

Viewed in instance space, the standard rule- and tree-based representations are only capable of representing class boundaries that are parallel to the axes defined by the attributes. This is not a handicap for nominal attributes, but it is for numeric ones. Non-axis-parallel class boundaries can only be approximated by covering the region above or below the boundary with several axis-parallel rectangles, the number of rectangles determining the degree of approximation. In contrast, the instance-based method can easily represent arbitrary linear boundaries. Even with just one example of each of two classes, the boundary implied by the nearest-neighbor rule is a straight line of arbitrary orientation, namely the perpendicular bisector of the line joining the examples.

Plain instance-based learning does not produce explicit knowledge representations except by selecting representative exemplars. However, when combined with exemplar generalization, a useful set of rules can be obtained that may be compared with those produced by other machine learning schemes. The rules tend to be more conservative because the distance metric, modified to incorporate generalized exemplars, can be used to process examples that do not fall within the rules. This reduces the pressure to produce rules that cover the whole example space, or even all of the training examples. On the other hand, the incremental nature of most instance-based learning schemes means that rules are formed eagerly, after only part of the training set has been seen; and this inevitably reduces their quality.

We have not given precise algorithms for variants of instance-based learning that involve generalization because it is not clear what the best way to do generalization is. Salzberg (1991) suggested that generalization with nested exemplars can achieve a high degree of classification of accuracy on a variety of different problems, a conclusion disputed by Wettschereck and Dietterich (1995) who argued that these results were fortuitous and do not hold in other domains. Martin (1995) explored the idea that poor performance is not caused by generalization but by the overgeneralization that occurs when hyper-rectangles nest or overlap. He demonstrated that if nesting and overlapping are avoided, excellent results are achieved in a large number of domains. The generalized distance function based on transformations is described by Cleary and Trigg (1995).

Exemplar generalization is a rare example of a learning strategy in which the search proceeds from specific to general rather than from general to specific as in the case of tree or rule induction. There is no particular reason why specific-to-general searching should necessarily be handicapped by forcing the examples to be considered in a strictly incremental fashion, and batch-oriented approaches exist that generate rules using a basic instance-based approach. Moreover, it seems that the idea of producing conservative generalizations and coping with instances that are not covered by choosing the "closest" generalization is an excellent one that will eventually be extended to ordinary tree- and rule-inducers.

6.5   Numeric prediction

Trees used for numeric prediction are just like ordinary decision trees except that at each leaf they store either a class value that represents the average value of instances that reach the leaf, in which case the tree is called a *regression tree*, or a linear regression model that predicts the class value of instances that reach the leaf, in which case it is called a *model tree*. In what follows we will talk about model trees because regression trees are really a special case.

Regression and model trees are constructed by first using a decision tree induction algorithm to build an initial tree. However, whereas most decision tree algorithms choose the splitting attribute to maximize the information gain, it is appropriate for numeric prediction to instead minimize the intrasubset variation in the class values down each branch. Once the basic tree has been formed, consideration is given to pruning the tree back from each leaf, just as with ordinary decision trees. The only difference between regression- and model-tree induction is that for the latter, each node is replaced by a regression plane instead of a constant value. And the attributes that serve to define that regression are precisely those that participate in decisions in the subtree that will be pruned, that is, in nodes underneath the current one.

Following an extensive discussion of model trees, we end this section with a brief discussion of another approach to numeric prediction, locally weighted linear regression. Whereas model trees derive from the basic divide-and-conquer decision tree methodology, locally weighted regression is inspired by the instance-based methods for classification that we discussed in the previous section. Like instance-based learning, it performs all "learning" at prediction time. Although locally weighted regression resembles model trees in that it uses linear regression to fit models locally to particular areas of instance space, it does so in quite a different way.

Model trees

When a model tree is used to predict the value for a test instance, the tree is followed down to a leaf in the normal way, using the instance's attribute values to make routing decisions at each node. The leaf will contain a linear model based on some of the attribute values, and this is evaluated for the test instance to yield a raw predicted value.

Instead of using this raw value directly, however, it turns out to be beneficial to use a smoothing process to compensate for the sharp discontinuities that will inevitably occur between adjacent linear models at the leaves of the pruned tree. This is a particular problem for models constructed from a small number of training instances. Smoothing can be accomplished by producing linear models for each internal node, as well as for the leaves, at the time the tree is built. Then, once the leaf model has been used to obtain the raw predicted value for a test instance, that value is filtered along the path back to the root, smoothing it at each node by combining it with the value predicted by the linear model for that node.

An appropriate smoothing calculation is

$$p' = \frac{np + kq}{n + k},$$

where p' is the prediction passed up to the next higher node, p is the prediction passed to this node from below, q is the value predicted by the model at this node, n is the number of training instances that reach the node below, and k is a smoothing constant. Experiments show that smoothing substantially increases the accuracy of predictions.

Exactly the same smoothing process can be accomplished by incorporating the interior models into each leaf model after the tree has been built. Then, during the classification process, only the leaf models are used. The disadvantage is that the leaf models tend to be larger and more difficult to comprehend, because many coefficients that were previously zero become nonzero when the interior nodes' models are incorporated.

Building the tree

The splitting criterion is used to determine which attribute is the best to split that portion T of the training data that reaches a particular node. It is based on treating the standard deviation of the class values in *T* as a measure of the error at that node, and calculating the expected reduction in error as a result of testing each attribute at that node. The attribute which maximizes the expected error reduction is chosen for splitting at the node.

The expected error reduction, which we call SDR for *standard deviation reduction,* is calculated by

$$\text{SDR} = sd(T) - \sum_i \frac{|T_i|}{|T|} \times sd(T_i)$$

where $T_1, T_2, \ldots$ are the sets that result from splitting the node according to the chosen attribute.

The splitting process terminates when the class values of the instances that reach a node vary only slightly, that is, when their standard deviation is just a small fraction (say, less than 5%) of the standard deviation of the original instance set. Splitting also terminates when just a few instances remain, say, four or fewer. Experiments show that the results obtained are not very sensitive to the exact choice of these thresholds.

Pruning the tree

As noted above, a linear model is needed for each interior node of the tree, not just at the leaves, for use in the smoothing process. Prior to pruning, a model is calculated for each node of the unpruned tree. The model takes the form

$$w_0 + w_1 a_1 + w_2 a_2 + \ldots + w_k a_k,$$

where $a_1, a_2, \ldots, a_k$ are attribute values. The weights $w_1, w_2, \ldots, w_k$ are calculated using standard regression. However, only the attributes that are tested in the subtree below this node are used in the regression, because the other attributes that affect the predicted value have been taken into account in the tests that lead to the node. Note that we have tacitly assumed that attributes are numeric: we discuss the handling of nominal attributes in the next subsection.

The pruning procedure makes use of an estimate, at each node, of the expected error for test data. First, the absolute difference between the predicted value and the actual class value is averaged over each of the training instances that reach that node. Because the tree has been built expressly for this dataset, this average will underestimate the expected error for unseen cases. To compensate, it is multiplied by the factor $(n+v)/(n-v)$, where n is the number of training instances that reach the node and v is the number of parameters in the linear model that gives the class value at that node.

The expected error for test data at a node is calculated as described above, using the linear model for prediction. Because of the compensation factor $(n+v)/(n-v)$, it may be that the linear model can be further simplified by dropping terms to minimize the estimated error. Dropping a term decreases the multiplication factor, which may be enough to offset the inevitable increase in average error over the training instances. Terms are dropped one by one, greedily, so long as the error estimate decreases.

Finally, once a linear model is in place for each interior node, the tree is pruned back from the leaves, so long as the expected estimated error decreases. The expected error for the linear model at that node is compared with the expected error from the subtree below. To calculate the latter, the error from each branch is combined into a single overall value for the node by weighting the branch by the proportion of the training instances that go down it, and combining the error estimates linearly using those weights.

Nominal attributes

Before constructing a model tree, all nominal attributes are transformed into binary variables which are then treated as numeric. For each nominal attribute, the average class value corresponding to each possible value in the enumeration is calculated from the training instances, and the values in the enumeration are sorted according to these averages. Then, if the nominal attribute has k possible values, it is replaced by $k-1$ synthetic binary attributes, the ith being 0 if the value is one of the first i in the ordering, and 1 otherwise. Thus all splits are binary: they involve either a numeric attribute or a synthetic binary one, treated as a numeric attribute.

It is possible to prove analytically that the best split at a node for a nominal variable with k values is one of the $k-1$ positions obtained by ordering the average class values for each value of the attribute. This sorting operation should really be repeated at each node; however, there is an inevitable increase in noise due to small numbers of instances at lower nodes in the tree (and in some cases nodes may not represent all values for some attributes), and not much is lost by performing the sorting just once, before starting to build a model tree.

Missing values

To take account of missing values, a modification is made to the standard deviation reduction formula. The final formula, including the missing value compensation, is

$$ \text{SDR} = \frac{m}{|T|} \times \left[sd(T) - \sum_{j \in \{L,R\}} \frac{|T_j|}{|T|} \times sd(T_j) \right], $$

where m is the number of instances without missing values for that attribute, and T is the set of instances that reach this node. T_L and T_R are sets that result from splitting on this attribute—for all tests on attributes are now binary.

When processing both training and test instances, once an attribute is selected for splitting it is necessary to divide the instances into subsets according to their value for this attribute. An obvious problem arises when the value is missing. An interesting technique called *surrogate splitting* has been developed to handle this situation. It involves finding another attribute to split on in place of the original one and using it instead. The attribute is chosen as the one most highly correlated with the original attribute. However, this technique is both complex to implement and time-consuming to execute.

A simpler heuristic is to use the class value as the surrogate attribute, in the belief that, a priori, this is the attribute most likely to be correlated with the one being used for splitting. Of course, this is only possible when processing the training set, because for test examples the class is not known. A simple solution for test examples is simply to replace the unknown attribute value by the average value of that attribute for the training examples that reach the node—which has the effect, for a binary attribute, of choosing the most populous subnode. This simple approach seems to work well in practice.

Let's consider in more detail how to use the class value as a surrogate attribute during the training process. We first deal with all instances for which the value of the splitting attribute is known. We determine a threshold for splitting in the usual way, by sorting the instances according to the value of their splitting attribute and, for each possible split point, calculating the SDR according to the above formula, choosing the split point that yields the greatest reduction in error. Only the instances for which the value of the splitting attribute is known are used to determine the split point.

Then we divide these instances into the two sets L and R according to the test. We determine whether the instances in L or R have the greater average class value, and we calculate the average of these two averages. Then, an instance for which this attribute value is unknown is placed into L or R according to whether its class value exceeds this overall average or not. If it does, it goes into whichever of L and R has the greater average class value, otherwise it goes into the one with the smaller average class value. When the splitting stops, all the missing values will be replaced by the average values of the corresponding attributes of the training instances reaching the leaves.

Pseudo-code for model tree induction

Figure 6.11 presents pseudo-code for the model tree algorithm we have described. The two main parts create a tree by successively splitting nodes, performed by split, and pruning it from the leaves upward, performed by prune. The node data structure contains a type flag indicating whether it is an internal node or a leaf, pointers to the left and right child, the set of instances that reach that node, the attribute that is used for splitting at that node, and a structure representing the linear model for the node.

```
MakeModelTree (instances)
{
  SD = sd(instances)
  for each k-valued nominal attribute
    convert into k-1 synthetic binary attributes
  root = newNode
  root.instances = instances
  split(root)
  prune(root)
  printTree(root)
}
split(node)
{
  if sizeof(node.instances) < 4 or sd(node.instances) < 0.05*SD
    node.type = LEAF
  else
    node.type = INTERIOR
    for each attribute
      for all possible split positions of the attribute
        calculate the attribute's SDR
    node.attribute = attribute with maximum SDR
    split(node.left)
    split(node.right)
}
prune(node)
{
  if node = INTERIOR then
    prune(node.leftChild)
    prune(node.rightChild)
    node.model = linearRegression(node)
    if subtreeError(node) > error(node) then
      node.type = LEAF
}
subtreeError(node)
{
  l = node.left; r = node.right
  if node = INTERIOR then
    return (sizeof(l.instances)*subtreeError(l)
          + sizeof(r.instances)*subtreeEerror(r))/sizeof(node.instances)
  else return error(node)
}
```

Figure 6.11 Pseudo-code for model tree induction.

The sd function called at the beginning of the main program and again at the beginning of split calculates the standard deviation of the class values of a set of instances. Then follows the procedure for obtaining synthetic binary attributes that was discussed above. Standard procedures for creating new nodes and printing the final tree are not shown. In split, sizeof returns the number of elements in a set. Missing attribute values are dealt with as described earlier. The SDR is calculated according to the equation at the beginning of the previous subsection. Although not shown in the code, it is set to infinity if splitting on the attribute would create a leaf with less than two instances. In prune, the linear-Regression routine recursively descends the subtree collecting attributes, performs a linear regression on the instances at that node as a function of those attributes, and then greedily drops terms if doing so improves the error estimate, as described earlier. Finally, the error function returns

$$\frac{n + v}{n - v} \times \frac{\sum instances \,|\text{deviation from predicted class value}|}{n}$$

where n is the number of instances at the node and v the number of parameters in the node's linear model.

Figure 6.12 gives an example of a model tree formed by this algorithm for a problem with two numeric and two nominal attributes. What is to be predicted is the rise time of a simulated servo system involving a servo amplifier, motor, lead screw, and sliding carriage. The nominal attributes play important roles. Four synthetic binary attributes have been created for each of the five-valued

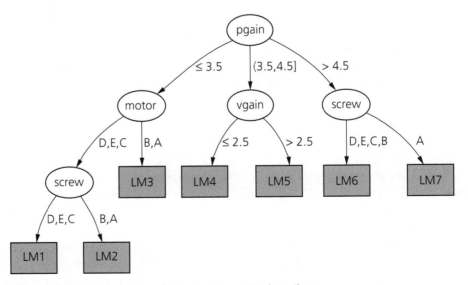

Figure 6.12 Model tree for a dataset with nominal attributes.

Table 6.1	Linear models in the model tree.							
model		LM1	LM2	LM3	LM4	LM5	LM6	LM7
constant term		−0.44	2.60	3.50	0.18	0.52	0.36	0.23
pgain								
vgain		0.82		0.42				0.06
motor = D	*vs* E, C, B, A		3.30		0.24	0.42		
motor = D, E	*vs* C, B, A	1.80			−0.16		0.15	0.22
motor = D, E, C	*vs* B, A				0.10	0.09		0.07
motor = D, E, C, B	*vs* A				0.18			
screw = D	*vs* E, C, B, A							
screw = D, E	*vs* C, B, A	0.47						
screw = D, E, C	*vs* B, A	0.63		0.28	0.34			
screw = D, E, C, B	*vs* A			0.90	0.16	0.14		

nominal attributes motor and screw, and are shown in Table 6.1 in terms of the two sets of values to which they correspond. The ordering of these values—D, E, C, B, A for motor, and coincidentally D, E, C, B, A for screw also—is determined from the training data: the rise time averaged over all examples for which motor = D is less than that averaged over examples for which motor = E, which is less than when motor = C, and so on. It is apparent from the magnitude of the coefficients in Table 6.1 that motor = D versus E, C, B, A plays a leading role in the LM2 model, and motor = D, E versus C, B, A plays a leading role in LM1. Both motor and screw also play a minor role in several of the models. The decision tree shows a three-way split on a numeric attribute. First a binary-splitting tree was generated in the usual way. It turned out that the root and one of its descendants tested the same attribute, pgain, and a simple algorithm was used to conflate these two nodes into the slightly more comprehensible tree that is shown.

Locally weighted linear regression

An alternative approach to numeric prediction is the method of locally weighted linear regression. With model trees, the tree structure divides the instance space into regions, and a linear model is found for each of them. In effect, the training data determines how the instance space is partitioned. Locally weighted regression, on the other hand, generates local models at prediction time by giving higher weight to instances in the neighborhood of the particular test instance. More specifically, it weights the training instances according to their distance to the test instance and performs a linear regression on the weighted data. Training instances close to the test instance receive a high weight, and those far away a low one. In other words, a linear model is tailor-made for the particular test instance at hand and used to predict the instance's class value.

In order to use locally weighted regression, you need to decide on a distance-based weighting scheme for the training instances. A common choice is to weight the instances according to the inverse of their Euclidean distance from the test instance. Another possibility is to use the Euclidean distance in conjunction with a Gaussian kernel function. However, there is no clear evidence that the choice of weighting function is critical. More important is the selection of a "smoothing parameter" that is used to scale the distance function—the distance is multiplied by the inverse of this parameter. If it is set to a small value, only instances very close to the test instance will receive significant weight; if it is large, more distant instances will also have a significant impact on the model. One way of choosing the smoothing parameter is to set it to the distance of the kth nearest training instance, so that its value becomes smaller as the volume of training data increases. The best choice of k depends on the amount of noise in the data. The more noise there is, the more neighbors should be included in the linear model. Generally, an appropriate smoothing parameter is found using cross-validation.

Like model trees, locally weighted linear regression is able to approximate nonlinear functions. One of its main advantages is that it is ideally suited for incremental learning: all training is done at prediction time, so new instances can be added to the training data at any time. However, like all instance-based methods, it is slow at deriving a prediction for a test instance. First, the training instances must be scanned to compute their weights; then a weighted linear regression is performed on these instances. Also, like other instance-based methods, locally weighted regression provides little information about the global structure of the training dataset.

Discussion

Regression trees were introduced in the CART system of Breiman et al. (1984). CART, for "classification and regression trees," incorporated a decision tree inducer for discrete classes very like that of C4.5, which was developed independently, as well as a scheme for inducing regression trees. Many of the techniques described above, such as the method of handling nominal attributes and the surrogate device for dealing with missing values, were included in CART. However, model trees did not appear until much more recently, being first described by Quinlan (1992).

Model tree induction is not so commonly used as decision tree induction, partly because comprehensive descriptions (and implementations) of the technique have become available only recently (Wang and Witten 1997). Neural nets are more commonly used for predicting numeric quantities, although they suffer from the disadvantage that the structures they produce are opaque and cannot be used to help understand the nature of the solution. Although there are techniques for producing understandable insights from the structure of neural networks, the arbitrary nature of the internal representation means that there may be dramatic variations between networks of identical architecture trained on the same data. By dividing the function being induced into linear patches, model trees provide a representation that is reproducible and at least somewhat comprehensible.

There are many variations of locally weighted regression. For example, nonlinear local models can be used instead of linear ones, and more sophisticated distance and weighting functions can be employed. Atkeson et al. (1997) have written an excellent survey on locally weighted learning.

6.6 Clustering

Clustering techniques apply when there is no class to be predicted but rather when the instances are to be divided into natural groups. These clusters presumably reflect some mechanism at work in the domain from which instances are drawn, a mechanism that causes some instances to bear a stronger resemblance to one another than they do to the remaining instances. Clustering naturally requires different techniques to the classification and association learning methods that we have considered so far.

As we saw in Section 3.9, there are different ways in which the result of clustering can be expressed. The groups that are identified may be exclusive, so that any instance belongs in only one group. Or they may be overlapping, so that an instance may fall into several groups. Or they may be probabilistic, whereby an instance belongs to each group with a certain probability. Or they may be hierarchical, such that there is a crude division of instances into groups at the top level, and each of these groups is refined further—perhaps all the way down to individual instances. Really, the choice between these possibilities should be dictated by the nature of the mechanisms that are thought to underlie the particular clustering phenomenon. However, because these mechanisms are rarely known—the very existence of clusters is, after all, something that we're trying to discover—and for pragmatic reasons too, the choice is usually dictated by the clustering tools that are available.

We will look here at three basically different clustering methods. The first is the classic k-means algorithm, which forms clusters in numeric domains, partitioning instances into disjoint clusters. Like the basic nearest-neighbor scheme of instance-based learning, it is a simple and straightforward technique that has been used for several decades. The second is an incremental clustering technique that was developed in the late 1980s and is embodied in a pair of systems called COBWEB (for nominal attributes) and CLASSIT (for numeric attributes). These methods come up with a hierarchical grouping of instances; we will examine them in some detail. They rely on a measure of cluster "quality" called *category utility*. The third is a statistical clustering method based on a *mixture model* of different probability distributions, one for each cluster, which—unlike the other two methods—assigns instances to classes probabilistically, not deterministically. We explain the basic technique and then sketch the working of a comprehensive clustering scheme called AUTOCLASS, based on the mixture model.

Iterative distance-based clustering

The *k*-means method is very simple. First, you specify in advance how many clusters are being sought: this is the parameter *k*. Then *k* points are chosen at random as cluster centers. Instances are assigned to their closest cluster center according to the ordinary Euclidean distance function. Next the centroid, or mean, of all instances in each cluster is calculated—this is the "means" part. These centroids are taken to be new center values for their respective clusters. Finally, the whole process is repeated with the new cluster centers. Iteration continues until the same points are assigned to each cluster in consecutive rounds, at which point the cluster centers have stabilized and will remain the same thereafter.

This clustering method is simple and reasonably effective. As with all practical clustering techniques, the final cluster centers do not represent a global minimum but only a local one, and completely different final clusters can arise from differences in the initial randomly chosen cluster centers. It is easy to imagine situations in which the algorithm will fail to find a reasonable clustering. For example, consider four instances arranged at the vertices of a rectangle in two-dimensional space. There are two natural clusters, formed by grouping together the two vertices at either end of a short side. But suppose the two initial cluster centers happen to fall at the midpoints of the *long* sides. This will form a stable configuration, the two clusters each containing the two instances at either end of a long side—no matter how great the difference between the long and short sides. To increase the chance of finding a global minimum, it is a simple matter to repeat the whole algorithm several times with different starting points and choose the best.

A large number of variants of the basic *k*-means procedure have been developed. Some produce a hierarchical clustering by applying the algorithm with *k* = 2 to the overall dataset and then repeating, recursively, within each cluster. Others concentrate instead on speeding up clustering. The basic algorithm can be rather time-consuming because a substantial number of iterations may be necessary, each involving finding the distance of the k cluster centers from every instance to determine the closest. There are simple approximations that will speed it up considerably, for example by dealing with projections of the dataset and making cuts along selected axes instead of the arbitrary hyperplane divisions implied by choosing the nearest cluster center, but they inevitably compromise the quality of the resulting clusters.

Incremental clustering

Whereas the k-means algorithm iterates over the whole dataset until convergence is reached, the next clustering method we examine works incrementally, instance by instance. At any stage the clustering forms a tree with instances at the leaves and a root node that represents the entire dataset. In the beginning the tree consists of the root alone. Instances are added one by one, and the tree is updated appropriately at each stage. Updating may merely be a case of finding the right place to put a leaf representing the new instance, or it may involve a radical restructuring of the part of the tree that is affected by the new instance. The key to deciding how and where to update is a quantity called *category utility* which measures the overall quality of a partition of instances into clusters. We defer detailed consideration of how this is defined until the next subsection and look first at how the clustering algorithm works.

The procedure is best illustrated by an example. We will use the familiar weather data again, but without the play attribute. To track progress the fourteen instances are labeled a, b, c, . . . , n (as in Table 4.6) and for interest we include the class yes or no in the label—although it should be emphasized that for this artificial dataset there is little reason to suppose that the two classes of instance should fall into separate categories. Figure 6.13 shows the situation at salient points throughout the clustering procedure.

At the beginning, when new instances are absorbed into the structure, they each form their own subcluster under the overall top-level cluster. Each new instance is processed by tentatively placing it into each of the existing leaves and evaluating the category utility of the resulting set of the top-level node's children to see if the leaf is a good "host" for the new instance. For each of the first five instances, there is no such host: it is better, in terms of category utility, to form a new leaf for each instance. With the sixth it finally becomes beneficial to form a cluster, joining the new instance f with the old one—the host—e. If you look back at Table 4.6 you will see that the fifth and sixth instances are indeed very similar, differing only in the windy attribute (and play, which is being ignored here). The next example, g, is placed in the same cluster (it differs from e only in outlook). This involves another call to the clustering procedure. First, g is evaluated to see which of the five children of the root makes the best host; it turns out to be the rightmost, the one that is already a cluster. Then the clustering algo-

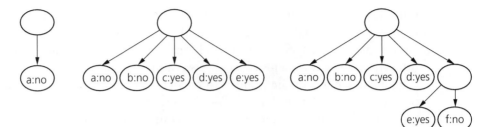

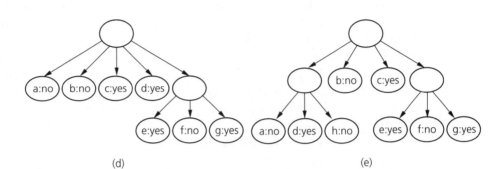

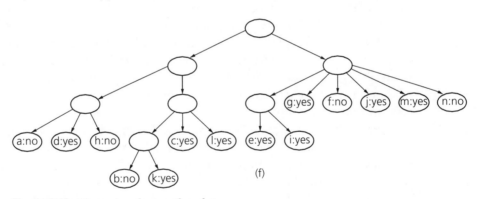

Figure 6.13 Clustering the weather data.

rithm is invoked with this as the root, and its two children are evaluated to see which would make the better host. In this case it proves best, according to the category utility measure, to add the new instance as a subcluster in its own right.

If we were to continue in this vein, there would be no possibility of any radical restructuring of the tree, and the final clustering would be excessively dependent on the ordering of examples. To avoid this, there is provision for restructuring, and you can see it come into play when instance h is added in the next step shown in Figure 6.13. In this case two existing nodes are *merged* into a single cluster: nodes a and d are merged before the new instance h is added.

One way of accomplishing this would be to consider all pairs of nodes for merging, and evaluate the category utility of each pair. However, that would be computationally expensive and would involve a lot of repeated work if it were undertaken whenever a new instance was added.

Instead, whenever the nodes at a particular level are scanned for a suitable host, both the best-matching node—the one that produces the greatest category utility for the split at that level—and the runner-up are noted. The best one will form the host for the new instance (unless that new instance is better off in a cluster of its own). However, before setting to work on putting the new instance in with the host, consideration is given to merging the host and the runner-up. In this case, a is the preferred host and d the runner-up. When a merge of a and d is evaluated, it turns out that it would improve the category utility measure. Consequently these two nodes are merged, yielding a version of the fifth hierarchy before h is added. Then, consideration is given to the placement of h in the new, merged node; and it turns out to be best to make it a subcluster in its own right, as shown.

An operation converse to merging is also implemented, called *splitting*, although it does not take place in this particular example. Whenever the best host is identified, and merging has not proven beneficial, consideration is given to splitting the host node. Splitting has exactly the opposite effect of merging, taking a node and replacing it by its children. For example, splitting the right-most node in Figure 6.13d would raise the e, f and g leaves up a level, making them siblings of a, b, c, and d. Merging and splitting provide an incremental way of restructuring the tree to compensate for incorrect choices caused by infelicitous ordering of examples.

The final hierarchy for all 14 examples is shown in Figure 6.13f. There are two major clusters, each of which subdivides further into its own subclusters. If the play/don't play distinction really represented an inherent feature of the data, a single cluster would be expected for each outcome. No such clean structure is observed, although a (very) generous eye might discern a slight tendency at lower levels for yes instances to group together, and likewise with no instances. Careful analysis of the clustering reveals some anomalies. (Table 4.6 will help if you want to follow this analysis in detail.) For example, instances a and b are actually very similar to each other, yet they end up in completely different parts of the tree. Instance b ends up with k, which is a worse match to it than a. Instance a ends up with d and h, even though it is certainly not as similar to d as it is to b. The reason why a and b become separated is that a and d get merged, as described above, because they form the best and second-best hosts for h. It was unlucky that a and b were the first two examples: if either had occurred later, it may well have ended up with the other. Subsequent splitting and remerging may be able to rectify this anomaly, but in this case they didn't.

Exactly the same scheme works for numeric attributes. Category utility is defined for these as well, based on an estimate of the mean and standard deviation of the value of that attribute. Details are deferred to the next subsection. However, there is one problem we must attend to here: when estimating the standard deviation of an attribute for a particular node, the result will be zero if the node contains only one instance, as it does more often than not. Unfortunately zero variances produce infinite values in the category utility formula. A simple heuristic solution is to impose a minimum variance on each attribute. It can be argued that since no measurement is completely precise, it is reasonable to impose such a minimum: it represents the measurement error in a single sample. This parameter is called *acuity.*

Figure 6.14a shows a hierarchical clustering produced by the incremental algorithm for part of the Iris dataset (30 instances, 10 from each class). At the top level there are two clusters (that is, subclusters of the single node representing the whole dataset). The first contains both Iris virginicas and Iris versicolors, and the second contains only Iris setosas. The Iris setosas themselves split into two subclusters, one with four cultivars and the other with six. The other top-level cluster splits into three subclusters, each with a fairly complex structure. Both the first and second contain only Iris versicolors, with one exception, a stray Iris virginica, in each case; the third contains only Iris virginicas. This represents a fairly satisfactory clustering of the Iris data: it shows that the three genera are not artificial at all but reflect genuine differences in the data. This is, however a slightly overoptimistic conclusion, because quite a bit of experimentation with the acuity parameter was necessary to obtain such a nice division.

The clusterings produced by this scheme contain one leaf for every instance. This produces an overwhelmingly large hierarchy for datasets of any reasonable size, corresponding, in a sense, to overfitting the particular dataset. Consequently a second numerical parameter called *cutoff* is used to suppress growth. Some instances are deemed sufficiently similar to others not to warrant formation of their own child node, and this parameter governs the similarity threshold. Cutoff is specified in terms of category utility: when the increase in category utility from adding a new node is sufficiently small, that node is cut off.

Figure 6.14b shows the same Iris data, clustered with cutoff in force. Many leaf nodes contain several instances: these are children of the parent node that have been cut off. The division into the three types of iris is a little easier to see from this hierarchy because some of the detail is suppressed. Again, however, some experimentation with the cutoff parameter was necessary to get this result, and in fact a sharper cutoff leads to much less satisfactory clusters.

Similar clusterings are obtained if the full Iris dataset of 150 instances is used. However, the results depend on the ordering of examples: Figure 6.14 was

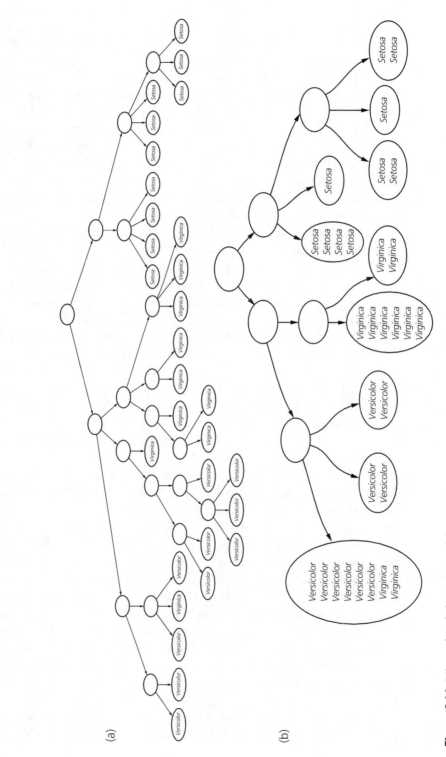

Figure 6.14 Hierarchical clusterings of the Iris data.

obtained by alternating the three varieties of iris in the input file. If all Iris setosas are presented first, followed by all Iris versicolors and then all Iris virginicas, the resulting clusters are quite unsatisfactory.

Category utility

Now we look at how the category utility, which measures the overall quality of a partition of instances into clusters, is calculated. In Section 5.9 we learned how the minimum description length measure could, in principle, be used to evaluate the quality of clustering. Category utility is not MDL-based but rather resembles a kind of quadratic loss function defined on conditional probabilities.

The definition of category utility is rather formidable:

$$CU(C_1, C_2, \ldots, C_k) = \frac{\sum_\ell \Pr[C_\ell] \sum_i \sum_j (\Pr[a_i = v_{ij} | C_\ell]^2 - \Pr[a_i = v_{ij}]^2)}{k},$$

where $C_1, C_2, \ldots, C_k$ are the k clusters; the outer summation is over these clusters; the next inner one sums over the attributes; a_i is the ith attribute, and it takes on values $v_{i1}, v_{i2}, \ldots$ which are dealt with by the sum over j. Note that the probabilities themselves are obtained by summing over all instances: thus there is a further implied level of summation.

This expression makes a great deal of sense if you take the time to examine it. The point of having a cluster is that it will give some advantage in predicting the values of attributes of instances in that cluster, that is, $\Pr[a_i = v_{ij} | C_\ell]$ is a better estimate of the probability that attribute a_i has value v_{ij}, for an instance in cluster C_ℓ, than $\Pr[a_i = v_{ij}]$, because it takes account of what cluster the instance is in. If that information doesn't help, the clusters aren't doing much good! So what the above measure calculates, inside the multiple summation, is the amount by which that information *does* help, in terms of the differences between squares of probabilities. This is not quite the standard squared-difference metric, because that sums the squares of the differences (which produces a symmetric result), and the present measure sums the difference of the squares (which, appropriately, does not). The differences between squares of probabilities is summed over all attributes and all their possible values, in the inner double summation. Then it is summed over all clusters, weighted by their probabilities, in the outer summation.

The overall division by k is a little hard to justify because the squared differences have already been summed over the categories. It essentially provides a "per cluster" figure for the category utility which discourages overfitting. Otherwise, since the probabilities are derived by summing over the appropriate instances, the very best category utility would be obtained by placing each instance in its own cluster. Then, $\Pr[a_i = v_{ij} | C_\ell]$ would be 1 for the value that attribute a_i actually has for the single instance in category C_ℓ and 0 for all other values; and the numerator of the category utility formula will end up as

$$n - \sum_i \sum_j (\Pr[a_i = v_{ij}])^2,$$

where n is the total number of values that the set of attributes can assume. This is the greatest value that the numerator can have, and so if it were not for the additional division by k in the category utility formula, there would never be any incentive to form clusters containing more than one member. This extra factor is best viewed as a rudimentary overfitting-avoidance heuristic.

This category utility formula applies only to nominal attributes. However, it can easily be extended to numeric attributes by assuming that their distribution is normal, with a given (observed) mean μ and standard deviation σ. The probability density function for an attribute a is

$$f(a) = \frac{1}{\sqrt{2\pi}\sigma} \exp\left(\frac{(a - \mu)^2}{2\sigma^2}\right).$$

The analog of summing the squares of attribute-value probabilities is

$$\sum_j \Pr[a_i = v_{ij}]^2 \Leftrightarrow \int f(a_i)^2 da_i = \frac{1}{2\sqrt{\pi}\sigma_i},$$

where σ_i is the standard deviation of the attribute a_i. Thus for a numeric attribute, we estimate the standard deviation from the data, both within the cluster and for the data over all clusters, and use these in the category utility formula:

$$CU(C_1, C_2, \ldots, C_k) = \frac{1}{k}\sum_\ell \Pr[C_\ell] \frac{1}{2\sqrt{\pi}} \sum_i \left(\frac{1}{\sigma_{i\ell}} - \frac{1}{\sigma_i}\right).$$

Now the problem mentioned above that occurs when the standard deviation estimate is zero becomes apparent: a zero standard deviation produces an infinite value of the category utility formula. Imposing a prespecified minimum variance on each attribute, the acuity, is a rough-and-ready solution to the problem.

Probability-based clustering

Some of the shortcomings of the heuristic clustering described above have already become apparent: the arbitrary division by k in the category utility formula which is necessary to prevent overfitting, the need to supply an artificial minimum value for the standard deviation of clusters, the ad hoc cutoff value to prevent every single instance from becoming a cluster in its own right. On top of this is the uncertainty inherent in incremental algorithms: To what extent is the result dependent on the order of examples? Are the local restructuring operations of merging and splitting really enough to reverse the effect of bad initial decisions caused by unlucky ordering? Does the final result represent even a *local* minimum of category utility? Add to these the problem that one never knows how far the final configuration is to a *global* minimum—and the standard trick of repeating the clustering procedure several times and choosing the best will destroy the incremental nature of the algorithm. Finally, doesn't the hierarchical nature of the result really beg the question of which are the *best* clusters? There are so many clusters in Figure 6.14 that it is hard to separate the wheat from the chaff.

A more principled statistical approach to the clustering problem can overcome some of these shortcomings. From a probabilistic perspective, the goal of clustering is to find the most likely set of clusters given the data (and, inevitably, prior expectations). Because no finite amount of evidence is enough to make a completely firm decision on the matter, instances—even training instances—should not be placed categorically in one cluster or the other: instead they have a certain probability of belonging to each cluster. This helps to eliminate the brittleness that is often associated with schemes that make hard and fast judgments.

The foundation for statistical clustering is a statistical model called *finite mixtures*. A *mixture* is a set of k probability distributions, representing k clusters, that govern the attribute values for members of that cluster. In other words, each distribution gives the probability that a particular instance would have a certain set of attribute values if it were *known* to be a member of that cluster. Each cluster has a different distribution. Any particular instance "really" belongs to one and only one of the clusters, but it is not known which one. Finally, the clusters are not equally likely: there is some probability distribution that reflects their relative populations.

The simplest finite mixture situation is when there is only one numeric attribute, which has a Gaussian or normal distribution for each cluster—but with different means and variances. The clustering problem is to take a set of instances—in this case each instance is just a number—and a prespecified number of clusters, and work out each cluster's mean and variance and the population distribution between the clusters. The mixture model combines several normal distributions, and its probability density function looks like a mountain range with a peak for each component.

Figure 6.15 shows a simple example. There are two clusters A and B, and each has a normal distribution with means and standard deviations μ_A and σ_A for A; μ_B and σ_B for B. Samples are taken from these distributions, using A with probability p_A and B with probability p_B (where $p_A + p_B = 1$), resulting in a dataset like that shown. Now, imagine being given the dataset without the classes—just data

A	51	B	62	B	64	A	48	A	39	A	51
A	43	A	47	A	51	B	64	B	62	A	48
B	62	A	52	A	52	A	51	B	64	B	64
B	64	B	64	B	62	B	63	A	52	A	42
A	45	A	51	A	49	A	43	B	63	A	48
A	42	B	65	A	48	B	65	B	64	A	41
A	46	A	48	B	62	B	66	A	48		
A	45	A	49	A	43	B	65	B	64		
A	45	A	46	A	40	A	46	A	48		

model

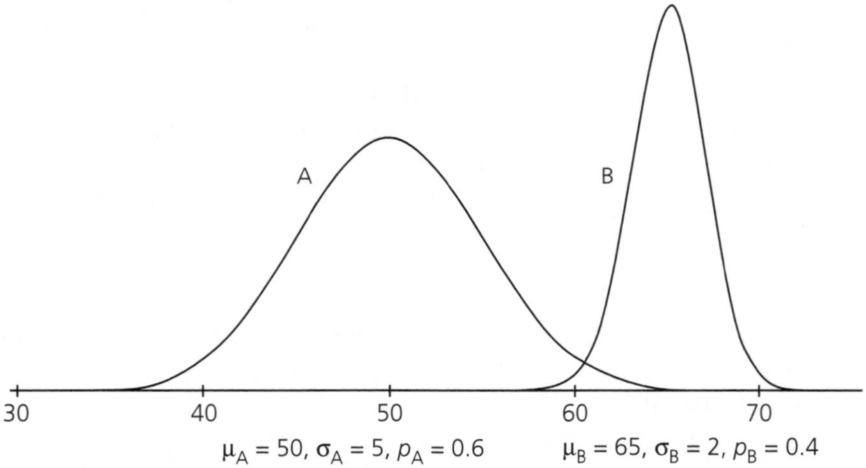

$\mu_A = 50, \sigma_A = 5, p_A = 0.6$ $\mu_B = 65, \sigma_B = 2, p_B = 0.4$

Figure 6.15 A two-class mixture model.

the numbers—and being asked to determine the five parameters that character-ize the model, μ_A, σ_A, μ_B, σ_B, and p_A (the parameter p_B can be calculated directly from p_A). That is the finite mixture problem.

If you knew which of the two distributions each instance came from, finding the five parameters would be easy—just estimate the mean and standard devia-tion for the A samples and the B samples separately, using the formulas

$$\mu = \frac{x_1 + x_2 + \ldots x_n}{n}$$

$$\sigma^2 = \frac{(x_1 - \mu)^2 + (x_2 - \mu)^2 + \ldots + (x_n - \mu)^2}{n - 1}.$$

(The use of $n-1$ rather than n as the denominator in the second formula is a technicality of sampling: it makes little difference in practice if n is used instead.) Here, $x_1, x_2, \ldots, x_n$ are the samples from the distribution A or B. To estimate the fifth parameter p_A, just take the proportion of the instances that are in the A cluster.

If you knew the five parameters, finding the probabilities that a given instance comes from each distribution would be easy. Given an instance x, the probability that it belongs to cluster A is

$$\Pr[A|x] = \frac{\Pr[x|A] \cdot \Pr[A]}{\Pr[x]} = \frac{f(x; \mu_A, \sigma_A)p_A}{\Pr[x]}$$

where $f(x; \mu_A, \sigma_A)$ is the normal distribution function for cluster A, that is,

$$f(x; \mu, \sigma) = \frac{1}{\sqrt{2\pi}\sigma} e^{-\frac{(x-\mu)^2}{2\sigma^2}}.$$

The denominator $\Pr[x]$ will disappear: we calculate the numerators for both $\Pr[A|x]$ and $\Pr[B|x]$ and normalize them by dividing by their sum. This whole procedure is just the same as the way numeric attributes are treated in the Naive Bayes learning scheme of Section 4.2. And the caveat discussed there applies here too: strictly speaking, $f(x; \mu_A, \sigma_A)$ is not the probability $\Pr[x|A]$, for the probability of x being any particular real number is zero; but the normalization process makes the final result correct. Note that the final outcome is not a particular cluster, but rather the *probabilities* with which x belongs to A and B.

The EM algorithm

The problem is that we know neither of these things: not the distribution that each training instance came from, nor the five parameters of the mixture model. So we adopt the procedure used for the k-means clustering algorithm, and iterate. Start with initial guesses for the five parameters, use them to calculate the cluster probabilities for each instance, use these probabilities to re-estimate the parameters, and repeat. (If you prefer, you can start with guesses for the classes of the instances instead.) This is called the *EM algorithm*, for "expectation–maximization." The first step, calculation of the cluster probabilities (which are the "expected" class values) is "expectation"; the second, calculation of the distribution parameters, is "maximization" of the likelihood of the distributions given the data.

A slight adjustment must be made to the parameter estimation equations to account for the fact that it is only cluster probabilities, not the clusters themselves, that are known for each instance. These probabilities just act like weights.

If w_i is the probability that instance i belongs to cluster A, the mean and standard deviation for A are

$$\mu_A = \frac{w_1 x_1 + w_2 x_2 + \dots + w_n x_n}{w_1 + w_2 + \dots + w_n}$$

$$\sigma_A^2 = \frac{w_1 (x_1 - \mu)^2 + w_2 (x_2 - \mu)^2 + \dots + w_n (x_n - \mu)^2}{w_1 + w_2 + \dots + w_n}$$

—where now the x_i are *all* the instances, not just those belonging to cluster A. (This differs in a small detail from the estimate for the standard deviation given on page 220: if all weights are equal, the denominator is n rather than $n-1$. Technically speaking, this is a "maximum likelihood" estimator for the variance, whereas the formula on page 220 is for an "unbiased" estimator. The difference is not important in practice.)

Now consider how to terminate the iteration. The k-means algorithm stops when the classes of the instances don't change from one iteration to the next—a "fixed point" has been reached. In the EM algorithm things are not quite so easy: the algorithm converges toward a fixed point but never actually gets there. But we can see how close it is by calculating the overall likelihood that the data came from this dataset, given the values for the five parameters. This overall likelihood is obtained by multiplying the probabilities of the individual instances i:

$$\prod_i (p_A \Pr[x_i | A] + p_B \Pr[x_i | B])$$

where the probabilities given the clusters A and B are determined from the normal distribution function $f(x; \mu, \sigma)$. This overall likelihood is a measure of the "goodness" of the clustering, and increases at each iteration of the EM algorithm. Again, there is a technical difficulty with equating the probability of a particular value of x with $f(x; \mu, \sigma)$, and in this case the effect does not disappear because no probability normalization operation is applied. The upshot is that the likelihood expression above is not a probability and does not necessarily lie between zero and one: nevertheless, its magnitude still reflects the quality of the clustering. In practical implementations its logarithm is calculated instead: this is done by summing the logs of the individual components, avoiding all the multiplications. But the overall conclusion still holds: you should iterate until the increase in log-likelihood becomes negligible. For example, a practical implementation might iterate until the difference between successive values of log-likelihood is less than 10^{-10} for ten successive iterations. Typically, the log-likelihood will increase very sharply over the first few iterations and then converge rather quickly to a point that is virtually stationary.

Although the EM algorithm is guaranteed to converge to a maximum, this is a *local* maximum and may not necessarily be the same as the global maximum. For a better chance of obtaining the global maximum, the whole procedure should be repeated several times, with different initial guesses for the parameter values. The overall log-likelihood figure can be used to compare the different final configurations obtained: just choose the largest of the local maxima.

Extending the mixture model

Now that we have seen the Gaussian mixture model for two distributions, let's consider how to extend it to more realistic situations. The basic method is just the same, but because the mathematical notation becomes formidable we will not develop it in full detail.

Changing the algorithm from two-class problems to multiclass problems is completely straightforward, so long as the number k of normal distributions is given in advance.

The model can be extended from a single numeric attribute per instance to multiple attributes, so long as independence between attributes is assumed. The probabilities for each attribute are multiplied together to obtain the joint probability for the instance, just as in the Naive Bayes method.

When the dataset is known in advance to contain correlated attributes, the independence assumption no longer holds. Instead, two attributes can be modeled jointly by a bivariate normal distribution, in which each has its own mean value but the two standard deviations are replaced by a "covariance matrix" with four numeric parameters. There are standard statistical techniques for estimating the class probabilities of instances, and for estimating the means and covariance matrix given the instances and their class probabilities. Several correlated attributes can be handled using a multivariate distribution. The number of parameters increases with the square of the number of jointly varying attributes. With n independent attributes, there are $2n$ parameters, a mean and standard deviation for each. With n covariant attributes there are $n + n(n + 1)/2$ parameters, a mean for each and an $n \times n$ covariance matrix which is symmetric and therefore involves $n(n + 1)/2$ different quantities. This escalation in the number of parameters has serious consequences for overfitting, as we will discuss below.

To cater for nominal attributes, the normal distribution must be abandoned. Instead, a nominal attribute with v possible values is characterized by v numbers representing the probability of each one. A different set of numbers is needed for every class; kv parameters in all. The situation is very similar to the Naive Bayes method. The two steps of expectation and maximization correspond exactly to operations we have studied before. Expectation—estimating the cluster to which each instance belongs, given the distribution parameters—is just like determining the class of an unknown instance. Maximization—estimating the parameters from the classified instances—is just like determining the attribute-value probabilities from the training instances, with the small difference that in the EM algorithm, instances are assigned to classes probabilistically rather than categorically. In Section 4.2 we encountered the problem that probability estimates can turn out to be zero, and the same problem occurs here too. Fortunately the solution is just as simple—use the Laplace estimator.

Naive Bayes assumes that attributes are independent—that is why it is called "naive." A pair of correlated nominal attributes with v_1 and v_2 possible values respectively can be replaced by a single covariant attribute with $v_1 v_2$ possible values. Again, the number of parameters escalates as the number of dependent attributes increases, and this has implications for probability estimates and overfitting which we will come to shortly.

The presence of both numeric and nominal attributes in the data to be clustered presents no particular problem. Covariant numeric and nominal attributes are more difficult to handle, and we will not discuss them here.

Missing values can be accommodated in various different ways. Missing values of nominal attributes can simply be left out of the probability calculations, as described in Section 4.2; alternatively they can be treated as an additional value of the attribute, to be modeled as any other value. Which is more appropriate depends on what it means for a value to be "missing." Exactly the same possibilities exist for numeric attributes.

With all these enhancements, probabilistic clustering becomes quite sophisticated. The EM algorithm is used throughout to do the basic work. The user must specify the number of clusters to be sought, the type of each attribute (numeric or nominal), which attributes are to modeled as covarying, and what to do about missing values. Moreover, different distributions than the ones described above can be used. Although the normal distribution is usually a good choice for numeric attributes, it is not suitable for attributes (such as weight) that have a predetermined minimum (zero, in the case of weight) but no upper bound, and in this case a "log-normal" distribution is more appropriate. Numeric attributes that are bounded above and below can be modeled by a "log-odds" distribution. Attributes that are integer counts rather than real values are best modeled by the "Poisson" distribution. A comprehensive system might allow these distributions to be specified individually for each attribute. In each case, the distribution involves numeric parameters—probabilities of all possible values for discrete attributes, mean and standard deviation for continuous ones.

In this section we have been talking about clustering. But you may be thinking that these enhancements could be applied just as well to the Naive Bayes algorithm too—and you'd be right. A comprehensive probabilistic modeler could accommodate both clustering and classification learning, nominal and numeric attributes with a variety of distributions, various possibilities of covariation, and different ways of dealing with missing values. The user would specify, as part of the domain knowledge, which distributions to use for which attributes.

Bayesian clustering

However, there is a snag: overfitting. You might say that if we are not sure which attributes are dependent on each other, why not be on the safe side and specify that *all* the attributes are covariant? The answer is that the more parameters there are, the greater the chance that the resulting structure is overfitted to the training data—and covariance increases the number of parameters dramatically. The problem of overfitting occurs throughout machine learning, and probabilistic clustering is no exception. There are two ways that it can occur: through specifying too large a number of clusters, and through specifying distributions with too many parameters.

The extreme case of too many clusters occurs when there is one cluster for every data point: clearly that will be overfitted to the training data. In fact, in the mixture model, problems will occur whenever any of the normal distributions becomes so narrow that it is centered on just one data point: consequently implementations generally insist that clusters contain at least two different data values.

Whenever there are a large number of parameters, the problem of overfitting arises. If you are unsure of which attributes are covariant, you might try out different possibilities and choose the one that maximizes the overall probability of the data given the clustering that was found. Unfortunately, the more parameters there are, the larger the overall data probability will tend to be—not necessarily due to better clustering, but to overfitting. The more parameters there are to play with, the easier it is to find a clustering that seems good.

It would be nice if somehow you could penalize the model for introducing new parameters. And one principled way of doing this is to adopt a fully Bayesian approach, where every parameter has a prior probability distribution. Then, whenever a new parameter is introduced, its prior probability must be incorporated into the overall likelihood figure. Since this will involve multiplying the overall likelihood by a number less than one—the prior probability—it will automatically penalize the addition of new parameters. In order to improve the overall likelihood, the new parameters will have to yield a benefit that outweighs the penalty.

In a sense, the Laplace estimator that we met in Section 4.2, and whose use we advocated above to counter the problem of zero probability estimates for nominal values, is just such a device. Whenever observed probabilities are small, the Laplace estimator exacts a penalty because it makes probabilities that are zero, or close to zero, greater, and this will decrease the overall likelihood of the data.

Making two nominal attributes covariant will exacerbate the problem. Instead of $v_1 + v_2$ parameters, where v_1 and v_2 are the number of possible values, there are now $v_1 v_2$, greatly increasing the chance of a large number of small estimated probabilities. In fact, the Laplace estimator is tantamount to using a particular prior distribution for the introduction of new parameters.

The same technique can be used to penalize the introduction of large numbers of clusters, just by using a prespecified prior distribution that decays sharply as the number of clusters increases.

AUTOCLASS is a comprehensive Bayesian clustering scheme that uses the finite mixture model, with prior distributions on all the parameters. It allows both numeric and nominal attributes and uses the EM algorithm to estimate the parameters of the probability distributions to best fit the data. Because there is no guarantee that the EM algorithm converges to the global optimum, the procedure is repeated for several different sets of initial values. But that is not all. AUTOCLASS considers different numbers of clusters, and can consider different amounts of covariance, and different underlying probability distribution types for the numeric attributes. This involves an additional, outer level of search. For example, it initially evaluates the log-likelihood for 2, 3, 5, 7, 10, 15, and 25 clusters: after that it fits a log-normal distribution to the resulting data and randomly selects from it more values to try. As you might imagine, the overall algorithm is extremely computation-intensive. In fact, the actual implementation starts with a prespecified time bound and continues to iterate as long as time allows. Give it longer and the results may be better!

Discussion

The three clustering methods that have been described produce quite different kinds of output. All are capable of taking new data in the form of a test set and classifying it according to clusters that were discovered by analyzing a training set. However, the incremental clustering method is the only one that generates an explicit knowledge structure that describes the clustering in a way that can be visualized and reasoned about. The other algorithms produce clusters that could be visualized in instance space if the dimensionality were not too high.

If a clustering method were used to label the instances of the training set with cluster numbers, that labeled set could then be used to train a rule or decision tree learner. The resulting rules or tree would form an explicit description of the classes. A probabilistic clustering scheme could be used for the same purpose, except that each instance would have multiple weighted labels and the rule or decision tree learner would have to be able to cope with weighted instances—as many can.

Another application of clustering is to fill in any values of the attributes that may be missing. For example, it is possible to make a statistical estimate of the value of unknown attributes of a particular instance, based on the class distribution for the instance itself and the values of the unknown attributes for other examples.

All the clustering methods we have examined make a basic assumption of independence between the attributes. AUTOCLASS does allow the user to specify in advance that two or more attributes are dependent and should be modeled with a joint probability distribution. (There are restrictions, however: nominal attributes may vary jointly, as may numeric attributes, but not both together. Moreover, missing values for jointly varying attributes are not catered for.) It may be advantageous to preprocess a dataset to make the attributes more independent, using a statistical technique such as the principal components transform. Note that joint variation that is specific to particular classes will not be removed by such techniques, only overall joint variation that runs across all classes.

The k-means algorithm is a classic technique, and many descriptions and variations are available (e.g., Hartigan 1975). The incremental clustering procedure, based on the merging and splitting operations, was introduced in systems called COBWEB for nominal attributes (Fisher 1987) and CLASSIT for numeric attributes (Gennari et al. 1990). Both are based on a measure of category utility that had been defined previously (Gluck and Corter 1985). The AUTOCLASS program is described by Cheeseman and Stutz (1995). Two implementations are available: the original research implementation, written in LISP, and a follow-up public implementation in C that is about ten or twenty times faster, but somewhat more restricted—for example, only the normal-distribution model is implemented for numeric attributes.

Moving on: Engineering the input and output

I n the last chapter we examined a vast array of machine learning methods: decision trees, decision rules, linear models, instance-based schemes, numeric prediction techniques, and clustering algorithms. All are sound, robust techniques that are eminently applicable to practical data mining problems.

But successful data mining involves far more than selecting a learning algorithm and running it over your data. For one thing, many learning schemes have various parameters, and suitable values must be chosen for these. In most cases, results can be improved markedly by a suitable choice of parameter values, and the appropriate choice depends on the data at hand. For example, decision trees can be pruned or unpruned and, in the former case, a pruning parameter may have to be chosen. In the k-nearest-neighbor method of instance-based learning, a value for k will have to be chosen. More generally, the learning scheme itself will have to be chosen from the range of available schemes. In all cases, the right choices depend on the data itself.

It is tempting to try out several learning schemes, and several parameter values, on your data to see which works best. But be careful! The best choice is not necessarily the one that performs best on the training data. We have repeatedly cautioned about the problem of overfitting, where a learned model is too closely tied to the particular training data from which it was built. It is dangerous to assume that performance on the training data faithfully represents the level of performance that can be expected on the fresh data to which the learned model will be applied in practice.

Fortunately we have already encountered the solution to this problem in Chapter 5. There are two good methods for estimating the expected true performance of a learning scheme: the use of a large dataset that is quite separate from the training data, in the case of plentiful data, and cross-validation (Section 5.3) if data is scarce. In the latter case, a single tenfold cross-validation is typically used in practice, although in particularly critical situations the entire procedure may be repeated ten times. Once suitable parameters have been chosen for the learning scheme, use the whole training set—all the available training instances—to produce the final learned model that is to be applied to fresh data.

Note that the performance obtained with the chosen parameter value during the tuning process is *not* a reliable estimate of the final model's performance, because the final model potentially overfits the data that was used for tuning. To ascertain how well it will perform, you need yet another large dataset that is quite separate from any data used during learning and tuning. The same is true for cross-validation: you need an "inner" cross-validation for parameter tuning, and an "outer" cross-validation for error estimation. With tenfold cross-validation, this involves running the learning scheme a hundred times. To summarize: When assessing the performance of a learning scheme, any parameter tuning that goes on should be treated as though it were an integral part of the training process.

There are other important processes that can materially improve success when applying machine learning techniques to practical data mining problems, and these are the subject of this chapter. They constitute a kind of data engineering: engineering the input data into a form suitable for the learning scheme chosen, and engineering the output model to make it more effective. You can look on them as a bag of tricks that you can apply to practical data mining problems to enhance the chance of success. Sometimes they work, other times they don't—and, at the present state of the art, it's hard to say in advance whether they will or not. In an area like this where trial and error is the most reliable guide, it is particularly important to be resourceful and have an understanding of what the tricks are.

We look at three different ways in which the input can be massaged to make it more amenable for learning schemes: attribute selection, attribute discretization, and data cleansing. A fourth way, which has been mentioned before in this book (when discussing relational data in Chapter 2, and support vector machines in Chapter 6), is to add new, synthetic attributes, whose purpose is to present existing information in a form that is suitable for the machine learning scheme to pick up on. Two date attributes might be subtracted to give a third attribute representing age—an example of a semantic transformation driven by the meaning of the original attributes. Other transformations might be suggested by known properties of the machine learning algorithm. If a linear relationship involving two attributes A and B is suspected, and the algorithm is only capable of axis-parallel splits (as most decision tree and rule learners are), the ratio A/B might be defined as a new attribute. Although the definition of new attributes is a very important and powerful technique for practical data mining, we will not elaborate further because it depends intimately on the semantics of the particular data mining problem at hand.

Consider attribute selection, the first input transformation technique to be discussed. In many practical situations there are far too many attributes for learning schemes to handle, and some of them—perhaps the overwhelming majority—are clearly irrelevant or redundant. Consequently the data must be preprocessed to select a subset of the attributes to use in learning. Of course, learning schemes themselves try to select attributes appropriately and ignore irrelevant or redundant ones, but in practice their performance can frequently be improved by preselection. For example, experiments show that adding useless attributes causes the performance of learning schemes such as decision trees and rules, linear regression, instance-based learners, and clustering methods to deteriorate.

Discretization of numeric attributes is absolutely essential if the task involves numeric attributes but the chosen learning scheme can only handle categorical ones. And even schemes that can handle numeric attributes often produce better results, or work faster, if the attributes are prediscretized. The converse situation, where categorical attributes must be represented numerically, also occurs (though less often); and we discuss techniques for this case too.

Unclean data plagues data mining. We emphasized in Chapter 2 the necessity of getting to know your data: understanding the meaning of all the different attributes, the conventions used in coding them, the significance of missing values and duplicate data, measurement noise, typographical errors, and the presence of systematic errors—even deliberate ones. Various simple visualizations often help with this task. But there are also automatic methods of cleansing data, of detecting outliers, and of spotting anomalies, which we describe.

Next we turn to the question of engineering the output from machine learning schemes. In particular, we examine techniques for combining different models learned from the data. There are some surprises in store. For example, it is often advantageous to take the training data and derive several different training sets from it, learn a model from each, and combine the resulting models!

Indeed, techniques for doing this can be very powerful. It is, for example, possible to transform a relatively weak learning scheme into a rather strong one (in a precise sense that we will discuss). Moreover, if several learning schemes are available, it may be advantageous not to choose the best-performing one for your dataset (using cross-validation), but to use them all and combine the results. Finally, the standard, obvious way of modeling a multiclass learning situation as a two-class one can be improved using a simple but subtle technique.

7.1 Attribute selection

Most machine learning algorithms are designed to learn which are the most appropriate attributes to use for making their decisions. For example, decision tree methods choose the most promising attribute to split on at each point, and should—in theory—never select irrelevant or unhelpful attributes. Having more features should surely—in theory—result in more discriminating power, never less. "What's the difference between theory and practice?" an old question asks. "There is no difference between theory and practice," the answer goes, "—in theory. But in practice, there is." And here there is too: in practice, adding irrelevant or distracting attributes to a dataset often "confuses" machine learning systems.

Experiments with a decision tree learner (C4.5) have shown that adding to standard datasets a random binary attribute generated by tossing an unbiased coin impacts classification performance, causing it to deteriorate (typically by 5% to 10% in the situations tested). This happens because at some point in the trees that are learned, the irrelevant attribute is invariably chosen to branch on, causing random errors when test data is processed. How can this be, when decision tree learners are cleverly designed to choose the best attribute for splitting at each node? The reason is subtle. As you proceed further down the tree, less and less data is available to help make the selection decision. At some point, with little data, the random attribute will look good just by chance. And because the number of nodes at each level increases exponentially with depth, the chance of the rogue attribute looking good somewhere along the frontier multiplies up as the tree deepens. The real problem is that you inevitably reach depths at which only a small amount of data is available for attribute selection. And if the dataset were bigger it wouldn't necessarily help—you'd probably just go deeper.

Divide-and-conquer tree learners and separate-and-conquer rule learners both suffer from this effect because they inexorably reduce the amount of data on which they base judgments. Instance-based learners are very susceptible to irrelevant attributes because they always work in local neighborhoods, taking just a few training instances into account for each decision. Indeed, it has been shown that the number of training instances needed to produce a predetermined level of performance for instance-based learning increases exponentially with the number of irrelevant attributes present. Naive Bayes, by contrast, does not fragment the instance space and robustly ignores irrelevant attributes. It assumes by design that all attributes are independent of one another, an assumption that is just right for random "distracter" attributes. But through this very same assumption, Naive Bayes pays a heavy price in other ways, for its operation is damaged by adding redundant attributes.

The fact that irrelevant distracters degrade the performance of state-of-the-art decision tree and rule learners is, at first, surprising. Even more surprising is that *relevant* attributes can also be harmful. For example, suppose that in a two-class dataset, a new attribute were added which had the same value as the class to be predicted most of the time (65%) and the opposite value the rest of the time, randomly distributed among the instances. Experiments with standard datasets have shown that this can cause classification accuracy to deteriorate (by 1% to 5% in the situations tested). The problem is that the new attribute is (naturally) chosen for splitting high up in the tree. This has the effect of fragmenting the set of instances available at the nodes below, so that other choices are based on sparser data.

Because of the negative effect of irrelevant attributes on most machine learning schemes, it is common to precede learning with an attribute selection stage which strives to eliminate all but the most relevant attributes. The best way to select relevant attributes is manually, based on a deep understanding of the learning problem and what the attributes actually mean. However, automatic methods can also be useful. Reducing the dimensionality of the data by deleting unsuitable attributes improves the performance of learning algorithms. It also speeds them up, although this may be outweighed by the computation involved in attribute selection. More importantly, dimensionality reduction yields a more compact, more easily interpretable representation of the target concept, focusing the user's attention on the most relevant variables.

Scheme-independent selection

When selecting a good attribute subset there are two fundamentally different approaches. One is to make an independent assessment based on general characteristics of the data; the other is to evaluate the subset using the machine learning algorithm that will ultimately be employed for learning. The first is called the *filter* method, because the attribute set is filtered to produce the most promising subset before learning commences. The second is the *wrapper* method, because the learning algorithm is wrapped into the selection procedure. Making an independent assessment of an attribute subset would be easy if there were a good way of determining when an attribute was relevant to choosing the class. However, there is no universally accepted measure of "relevance," although several different ones have been proposed.

One simple scheme-independent method of attribute selection is to use just enough attributes to divide up the instance space in a way that separates all the training instances. For example, if just one or two attributes are used, there will generally be several instances that have the same combination of attribute values. At the other extreme, the full set of attributes will likely distinguish the instances uniquely, so that no two instances have the same values for all attributes. (This will not necessarily be the case, however; datasets sometimes contain instances with the same attribute values but different classes.) It makes intuitive sense to select the smallest attribute subset that serves to distinguish all instances uniquely. This can easily be found with an exhaustive search, though at considerable computational expense. Unfortunately, this strong bias toward consistency of the attribute set on the training data is statistically unwarranted and can lead to overfitting—the algorithm may go to unnecessary lengths to repair an inconsistency that was in fact merely caused by noise.

Machine learning algorithms can be used for attribute selection. For instance, you might first apply a decision tree algorithm to the full dataset, and then select only those attributes that are actually used in the tree. While this selection would have no effect at all if the second stage merely built another tree, it will have an effect on a different learning algorithm. For example, the nearest-neighbor algorithm is notoriously susceptible to irrelevant attributes, and its performance can be improved by using a decision tree builder as a filter for attribute selection first. The resulting nearest-neighbor scheme can also perform better than the decision tree algorithm used for filtering. As another example, the simple 1R scheme described in Chapter 4 has been used to select the attributes for a decision tree learner by evaluating the effect of branching on different attributes (although an error-based method like 1R may not be the optimal choice for ranking attributes, as we will see below when discussing the related problem of supervised discretization). Often the decision tree performs just as well when only the two or three top attributes are used for its construction—and it is much easier to understand. In this approach, the user determines how many attributes to use for building the decision tree.

Attributes can be selected using instance-based learning methods too. You could sample instances randomly from the training set and check neighboring records of the same and different classes—"near hits" and "near misses." If a near hit has a different value for a certain attribute, that attribute appears to be irrelevant and its weight should be decreased. On the other hand, if a near miss has a different value, the attribute appears to be relevant and its weight should be increased. Of course, this is the standard kind of procedure used for attribute weighting for instance-based learning, described in Section 6.4. After repeating this operation many times, selection takes place: only attributes with positive weights are chosen. As in the standard incremental formulation of instance-based learning, different results will be obtained each time the process is repeated, because of the different ordering of examples. This can be avoided by using all training instances and taking into account all near hits and near misses of each. A more serious disadvantage is that the method will not detect an attribute that is redundant because it is correlated with another attribute—for example, two identical attributes would be treated the same way, either both selected or both rejected.

Searching the attribute space

Most methods for attribute selection involve searching the space of attributes for the subset that is most likely to predict the class best. Figure 7.1 illustrates attribute space for the—by now all-too-familiar—weather dataset. The number of possible attribute subsets increases exponentially with the number of attributes, making exhaustive search impractical on all but the most simple problems.

Typically the space is searched greedily in one of two directions, top to bottom or bottom to top in the figure. At each stage, a local change is made to the current attribute subset by either adding or deleting a single attribute. The

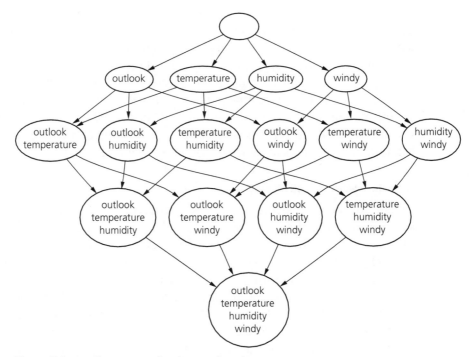

Figure 7.1 Attribute space for the weather dataset.

downward direction, where you start with no attributes and add them one at a time, is called *forward selection*. The upward one, where you start with the full set and delete attributes one at a time, is *backward elimination*.

In forward selection, each attribute that is not already in the current subset is tentatively added to it, and the resulting set of attributes is evaluated using, for example, cross-validation as discussed in the following section. This evaluation produces a numeric measure of the expected performance of the subset. The effect of adding each attribute in turn is quantified by this measure, the best one is chosen, and the procedure continues. However, if no attribute produces an improvement when added to the current subset, the search ends. This is a standard greedy search procedure, which is guaranteed to find a locally—but not necessarily globally—optimal set of attributes. Backward elimination operates in an entirely analogous fashion. In both cases a slight bias is often introduced toward smaller attribute sets. This can be done for forward selection by insisting that if the search is to continue, the evaluation measure must not only increase, but must increase by at least a small predetermined quantity. A similar modification works for backward elimination.

More sophisticated search schemes exist. Forward selection and backward elimination can be combined into a bidirectional search; again one can either begin with all the attributes or with none of them. Best-first search is a method that does not just terminate when the performance starts to drop but keeps a list of all attribute subsets evaluated so far, sorted in order of the performance measure, so that it can revisit an earlier configuration instead. Given enough time it will explore the entire space, unless this is prevented by some kind of stopping criterion. Beam search is similar but truncates its list of attribute subsets at each stage so that it only contains a fixed number—the beam width—of most promising candidates. Genetic algorithm search procedures are loosely based on the principal of natural selection: they "evolve" good feature subsets by using random perturbations of a current list of candidate subsets.

Scheme-specific selection

The performance of an attribute subset with scheme-specific selection is measured in terms of the learning scheme's classification performance using just those attributes. Given a subset of attributes, accuracy is estimated using the normal procedure of cross-validation described in Chapter 5 (Section 5.3). Of course, other evaluation methods such as performance on a holdout set (Section 5.3) or the bootstrap estimator (Section 5.4) could equally well be used.

The entire attribute selection process is rather computation-intensive. If each evaluation involves a tenfold cross-validation, the learning procedure must be executed ten times. With k attributes, the heuristic forward selection or backward elimination multiplies evaluation time by a factor of up to k^2—and for more sophisticated searches, the penalty will be far greater, up to $k \cdot 2^k$ for an exhaustive algorithm that examines the effect of adding every attribute to each of the 2^k possible subsets. No wonder computer manufacturers are getting into data mining in a big way!

Good results have been demonstrated on many datasets. In general terms, backward elimination produces larger attribute sets, and better classification accuracy, than forward selection. The reason for this is that the performance measure is only an estimate, and a single optimistic estimate will cause both of these search procedures to halt prematurely—backward elimination with too many attributes, and forward selection with not enough. But forward selection is useful if the focus is on understanding the decision structures involved, because it often reduces the number of attributes with only a very small effect on classification accuracy. Experience seems to show that more sophisticated search techniques are not generally justified—although they can produce much better results in certain cases.

But scheme-specific attribute selection by no means yields a uniform improvement in performance. Because of the complexity of the process, which is greatly increased by the feedback effect of including a target machine learning algorithm in the attribution selection loop, it is quite hard to predict the conditions under which it will turn out to be worthwhile. As in many machine learning situations, trial and error using your own particular source of data is the final arbiter.

There is one type of classifier for which scheme-specific attribute selection is an essential part of the learning process: the decision table. As mentioned in Section 3.1, the entire problem of learning decision tables consists of selecting the right attributes to be included. Usually this is done by measuring the table's cross-validation performance for different subsets of attributes and choosing the best-performing subset. Fortunately, leave-one-out cross-validation is very cheap for this kind of classifier. Obtaining the cross-validation error from a decision table derived from the training data is just a matter of manipulating the class counts associated with each of the table's entries, because the table's structure doesn't change when instances are added or deleted. The attribute space is generally searched by a best-first search because this strategy is less likely to get stuck in a local maximum than others such as forward selection.

Let's end our discussion with a success story. One learning method for which a simple scheme-specific attribute selection approach has shown good results is Naive Bayes. Although this method deals well with random attributes, it has the potential to be misled when there are dependencies between attributes, and particularly when redundant ones are added. However, good results have been reported using the forward selection algorithm—which is better able to detect when a redundant attribute is about to be added than the backward elimination approach—in conjunction with a very simple, almost "naive," metric that determines the quality of an attribute subset to be simply the performance of the learned algorithm on the *training* set. As was emphasized in Chapter 5, training set performance is certainly not a reliable indicator of test set performance. Nevertheless experiments show that this simple modification to Naive Bayes markedly improves its performance on those standard datasets for which it does not do as well as tree- or rule-based classifiers, and does not have any negative effect on results on datasets on which Naive Bayes already does well. *Selective Naive Bayes,* as this learning method is called, is a viable machine learning technique that performs reliably and well in practice.

7.2 Discretizing numeric attributes

Some classification and clustering algorithms deal with nominal attributes only and cannot handle ones measured on a numeric scale. To use them on general datasets, numeric attributes must first be "discretized" into a small number of distinct ranges. Even learning algorithms that do handle numeric attributes sometimes process them in ways that are not altogether satisfactory. Statistical clustering methods often assume that numeric attributes have a normal distribution—often not a very plausible assumption in practice—and the standard extension of the Naive Bayes classifier to numeric attributes adopts the same assumption. Although most decision tree and decision rule learners can handle numeric attributes, some implementations work much more slowly when numeric attributes are present because they repeatedly sort the attribute values. For all these reasons the question arises: what is a good way to discretize numeric attributes into ranges before any learning takes place?

We have already encountered some methods for discretizing numeric attributes. The 1R learning scheme described in Chapter 4 uses a simple but effective technique: sort the instances by the attribute's value and assign the value into ranges at the points that the class value changes—except that a certain minimum number of instances (6) must lie in each of the ranges, which means that any given range may include a mixture of class values. This is a "global" method of discretization that is applied to all continuous attributes before learning starts.

Decision tree learners, on the other hand, deal with numeric attributes on a local basis, examining attributes at each node of the tree, when it is being constructed, to see if they are worth branching on—and only at that point deciding on the best place to split continuous attributes. Although the tree-building method we examined in Chapter 6 only considers binary splits of continuous attributes, one can imagine a full discretization taking place at that point, yielding a multiway split on a numeric attribute. The pros and cons of the local versus global approach are clear. Local discretization is tailored to the actual context provided by each tree node and will produce different discretizations of the same attribute at different places in the tree if that seems appropriate. However, its decisions are based on less data as tree depth increases, which compromises their reliability. If trees are developed all the way out to single-instance leaves before being pruned back, as with the normal technique of backward pruning, it is clear that many discretization decisions will be based on data that is grossly inadequate.

When using global discretization prior to the application of a learning scheme, there are two possible ways of presenting the discretized data to the learner. The most obvious way is to treat discretized attributes like nominal ones: each discretization interval is represented by one value in the nominal attribute. However, since a discretized attribute is derived from a numeric one, its values are ordered, and treating it as nominal discards this potentially valuable ordering information. Of course, if a learning scheme can handle ordered attributes directly, the solution is obvious: each discretized attribute is declared to be of type "ordered."

If the learning scheme cannot handle ordered attributes, there is still a simple way of enabling it to exploit the ordering information: transform each discretized attribute into a set of binary attributes before the learning scheme is applied. Assuming the discretized attribute has k values, it is transformed into $k-1$ binary attributes, the first $i-1$ of which are set to *false* whenever the ith value of the discretized attribute is present in the data, and *true* otherwise. The remaining attributes are set to *false*. In other words, the $(i-1)$th binary attribute represents whether the discretized attribute is less than or equal to i. If a decision tree learner splits on this attribute, it implicitly utilizes the ordering information it encodes. Note that this transformation is independent of the particular discretization method being applied: it is simply a way of coding an ordered attribute using a set of binary attributes.

Unsupervised discretization

There are two basic approaches to the problem of discretization. One is to quantize each attribute in the absence of any knowledge of the classes of the instances in the training set—so-called unsupervised discretization. The other is to take the classes into account when discretizing—supervised discretization. The former is the only possibility when dealing with clustering problems where the classes are unknown or nonexistent.

The obvious way of discretizing a numeric attribute is to divide its range into a predetermined number of equal intervals: a fixed, data-independent yardstick. This is frequently done at the time when data is collected. But, like any unsupervised discretization method, it runs the risk of destroying distinctions that would have turned out to be useful in the learning process, by using gradations that are too coarse or by making unfortunate choices of boundary that needlessly lump together many instances of different classes.

Equal-interval binning often distributes instances very unevenly: some bins contain many instances while others contain none. This can seriously impair the ability of the attribute to help build good decision structures. It is often better to allow the intervals to be of different sizes, choosing them so that the same number of training examples fall into each one. This method, *equal-frequency binning,* divides the attribute's range into a predetermined number of bins based on the distribution of examples along that axis—sometimes called *histogram equalization* because if you take a histogram of the contents of the resulting bins it will be completely flat. If you view the number of bins as a resource, this method makes best use of it.

However, equal-frequency binning is still oblivious to the instances' classes, and this can cause bad boundaries. For example, if all instances in a bin have one class, and all instances in the next higher bin have another except for the first which has the original class, surely it makes sense to respect the class divisions and include that first instance in the previous bin, sacrificing the equal-frequency property for the sake of homogeneity. Supervised discretization—taking classes into account during the process—certainly has advantages.

Entropy-based discretization

Since the criterion used for splitting a numeric attribute during the formation of a decision tree works well in practice, it seems a good idea to extend it to more general discretization by recursively splitting intervals until it is time to stop. In Chapter 6 we saw how to sort the instances by the attribute's value and consider, for each possible splitting point, the information gain of the resulting split. To discretize the attribute, once the first split is determined the splitting process can be repeated in the upper and lower parts of the range, and so on recursively.

To see this working in practice, we revisit the example given on page 160 for discretizing the temperature attribute of the weather data, whose values are:

64	65	68	69	70	71	72	75	80	81	83	85
						no	yes				
yes	no	yes	yes	yes	no			no	yes	yes	no
						yes	yes				

(repeated values have been collapsed together). The information gain for each of the 11 possible positions for the breakpoint is calculated in the usual way. For example, the information value of the test `temperature < 71.5`, which splits the range into 4 yeses and 2 nos versus 5 yeses and 3 nos, is

$$\text{info}([4,2], [5,3]) = (6/14) \times \text{info}([4,2]) + (8/14) \times \text{info}([5,3]) = 0.939 \text{ bits.}$$

This represents the amount of information required to specify the individual values of yes and no given the split. We seek a discretization that makes the subintervals as pure as possible, and hence we choose to split at the point where the information value is smallest. (This is the same as splitting where the information *gain*, defined as the difference between the information value without the split and that with the split, is largest.) As before, we place numeric thresholds halfway between the values that delimit the boundaries of a concept.

The graph labeled A in Figure 7.2 shows the information values at each possible cut point at this first stage. The cleanest division—smallest information value—is at a temperature of 84 (0.827 bits), which separates off just the very final value, a no instance, from the list above. The instance classes are written below the horizontal axis, to make interpretation easier. Invoking the algorithm again on the lower range of temperatures, from 64 to 83, yields the graph labeled B. This has a minimum at 80.5 (0.800 bits), which splits off the next two values, both yes instances. Again invoking the algorithm on the lower range, now from 64 to 80, produces the graph labeled C (shown dotted to help distinguish it from the others). The minimum is at 77.5 (0.801 bits), splitting off another no instance. Graph D has a minimum at 73.5 (0.764 bits), splitting off

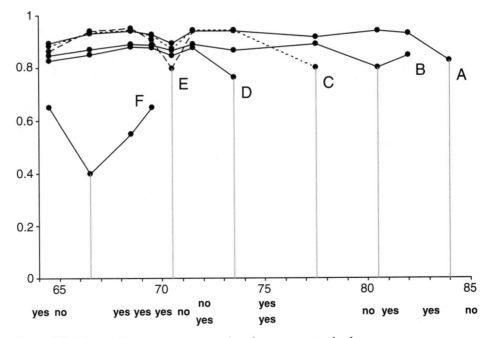

Figure 7.2 Discretizing temperature using the entropy method.

two yes instances. Graph E (again dashed, purely to make it more easily visible), for the temperature range 64 to 72, has a minimum at 70.5 (0.796 bits), which splits off two nos and a yes. Finally, graph F, for the range 64 to 70, has a minimum at 66.5 (0.4 bits).

The final discretization of the temperature attribute is shown in Figure 7.3. The fact that recursion only ever occurs in the first interval of each split is an artifact of this example: in general both the upper and lower intervals will have to be split further. Underneath each division is the label of the graph in Figure 7.2 that is responsible for it, and below that the actual value of the split point.

It can be shown theoretically that a cut point that minimizes the information value will never occur between two instances of the same class. This leads to a useful optimization: it is only necessary to consider potential divisions that separate instances of different classes. Notice that if class labels were assigned to the intervals based on the majority class in the interval, there would be no guarantee that adjacent intervals would receive different labels. You might be tempted to considering merging intervals with the same majority class (for example, the first two intervals of Figure 7.3), but as we will see below (page 244), this is not a good thing to do in general.

The only problem left to consider is the stopping criterion. In the temperature example, most of the intervals that were identified were "pure" in that all their instances had the same class, and there is clearly no point in trying to split such an interval. (Exceptions were the final interval, which we tacitly decided not to split, and the interval from 70.5 to 73.5.) In general, however, things are not so straightforward.

A good way to stop the entropy-based splitting discretization procedure turns out to be the minimum description length principle that we encountered in Chapter 5. In accordance with that principle, we want to minimize the size of the "theory" plus the size of the information necessary to specify all the data given that theory. In this case, if we do split, the theory is the splitting point, and we are comparing the situation when we split with that when we do not. In both cases we assume that the instances are known but their class labels are not. If we

64	65	68	69	70	71	72	75	80	81	83	85
yes	no	yes	yes	yes	no	no yes	yes yes	no	yes	yes	no

| | | F | | | | E | | D | C | B | | A | |
| | | 66.5 | | | | 70.5 | | 73.5 | 77.5 | 80.5 | | 84 | |

Figure 7.3 The result of discretizing temperature.

do not split, the classes can be transmitted by encoding each instance's label. If we do, we first encode the split point (in $\log_2[N{-}1]$ bits, where N is the number of instances), then the classes of the instances below that point, then the classes of those above it. You can imagine that if the split is a good one—say all the classes below it are yes and all those above are no—then there is much to be gained by splitting. If there is an equal number of yes and no instances, each instance costs one bit without splitting, but hardly more than zero bits with splitting—it is not quite zero because the class values associated with the split itself must be encoded, but this penalty is amortized across all the instances. In this case, if there are many examples, the penalty of having to encode the split point will be far outweighed by the information saved by splitting.

We emphasized in Section 5.9 that when applying the minimum description length principle, the devil is in the details. In the relatively straightforward case of discretization, the situation is tractable, although not simple. The amounts of information can be obtained exactly under certain reasonable assumptions. We will not go into the details, but the upshot is that the split dictated by a particular cut point is worthwhile if the information gain for that split exceeds a certain value that depends on the number of instances N, the number of classes k, the entropy of the instances E, the entropy of the instances in each subinterval E_1 and E_2, and the number of classes represented in each subinterval k_1 and k_2:

$$\text{gain} > \frac{\log_2(N - 1)}{N} + \frac{\log_2(3^k - 2) - kE + k_1E_1 + k_2E_2}{N}.$$

The first component is the information needed to specify the splitting point; the second is a correction due to the need to transmit which classes correspond to the upper and lower subintervals.

When applied to the temperature example, this criterion prevents any splitting at all. The first split removes just the final example, and as you can imagine very little actual information is gained by this when transmitting the classes—in fact, the MDL criterion will never create an interval containing just one example. Failure to discretize temperature effectively disbars it from playing any role in the final decision structure, since the same discretized value will be given to all instances. In this situation this is perfectly appropriate: temperature does not occur in good decision trees or rules for the weather data. In effect, failure to discretize is tantamount to attribute selection.

Other discretization methods

The entropy-based method with the MDL stopping criterion is one of the best general techniques for supervised discretization. However, many other methods have been investigated. For example, instead of proceeding top-down by recursively splitting intervals until some stopping criterion is satisfied, you could work bottom-up, first placing each instance into its own interval and then considering whether to merge adjacent intervals. You could apply a statistical criterion to see which would be the best two intervals to merge, and merge them if the statistic exceeds a certain preset confidence level, repeating the operation until no potential merge passes the test. The χ^2 test is a suitable one and has been used for this purpose. Instead of specifying a preset significance threshold, more complex techniques are available to determine an appropriate level automatically.

A rather different approach is to count the number of errors that a discretization makes when predicting each training instance's class, assuming that each interval receives the majority class. For example, the 1R method described earlier is error-based—it focuses on errors rather than the entropy. However, the best possible discretization in terms of error count is obtained by using the largest possible number of intervals, and this degenerate case should be avoided by restricting the number of intervals in advance. For example, you might ask what is the best way to discretize an attribute into k intervals in a way that minimizes the number of errors.

The brute-force method of finding the best way of partitioning an attribute into k intervals in a way that minimizes the error count is exponential in k, and hence infeasible. However, there are much more efficient schemes that are based on the idea of dynamic programming. Dynamic programming applies not just to the error count measure, but to any given impurity function, and can find the partitioning of N instances into k intervals in a way that minimizes the impurity in time proportional to kN^2. This gives a way of finding the best entropy-based discretization, yielding a potential speed improvement (but in practice a negligible one) over the recursive entropy-based method described above. And the news for error-based discretization is even better, for there is a way of using dynamic programming that minimizes the error count in time linear in N.

Entropy-based versus error-based discretization

Why not use error-based discretization, since the optimal discretization can be found very quickly? The answer is that there is a serious drawback to error-based discretization: it cannot produce adjacent intervals with the same label (like the first two of Figure 7.3). The reason is that merging two such intervals will not affect the error count, but it will free up an interval that can be used elsewhere to reduce the error count.

Why would anyone want to generate adjacent intervals with the same label? The reason is best illustrated with an example. Figure 7.4 shows the instance space for a simple two-class problem with two numeric attributes ranging from 0 to 1. Instances belong to one class (the dots) if their first attribute (a1) is less than 0.3, or if it is less than 0.7 *and* their second attribute (a2) is less than 0.5.

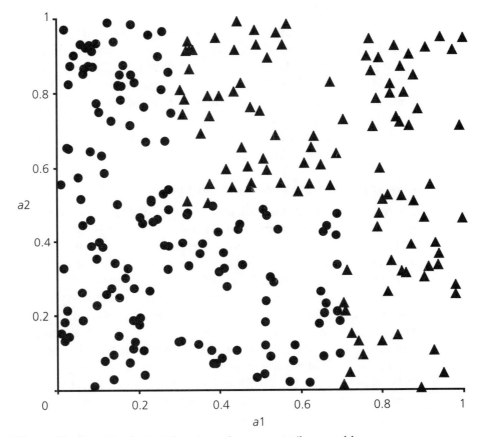

Figure 7.4 Class distribution for a two-class, two-attribute problem.

Otherwise they belong to the other class (triangles). The data in Figure 7.4 has been artificially generated according to this rule.

Now suppose we are trying to discretize both attributes with a view to learning the classes from the discretized attributes. The very best discretization splits a1 into three intervals, 0 through 0.3, 0.3 through 0.7, and 0.7 through 1; and a2 into two, 0 through 0.5 and 0.5 through 1. Given these nominal attributes, it will be easy to learn how to tell the classes apart with a simple decision tree or rule algorithm. Discretizing a2 is no problem. For a1, however, the first and last intervals will have opposite labels (dot and triangle, respectively). The second will have whichever label happens to occur most in the region from 0.3 through 0.7 (it is in fact dot for the data in Figure 7.4). Either way, this label must inevitably be the same as one of the adjacent labels—and of course this is true whatever the class probability happens to be in the middle region. Thus this discretization will not be achieved by any scheme that minimizes the error counts, for such a scheme cannot produce adjacent intervals with the same label.

The point is that what changes as the value of a1 crosses the boundary at 0.3 is not the majority class, but the class *distribution*. The majority class remains dot. The distribution, however, changes markedly, from 100% before the boundary to just over 50% after it. And the distribution changes again as the boundary at 0.7 is crossed, from 50% to 0%. Entropy-based discretization methods are sensitive to changes in the distribution even though the majority class does not change. Error-based methods are not.

Converting discrete to numeric attributes

There is a converse problem to discretization. Some learning algorithms—notably the nearest-neighbor instance-based method and numeric prediction techniques involving regression—naturally handle only attributes that are numeric. How can they be extended to nominal attributes?

In instance-based learning, as discussed in Chapter 4 (Section 4.7), discrete attributes can be treated as numeric by defining the "distance" between two nominal values that are the same as 0, and between two values that are different as 1—regardless of the actual values involved. Rather than modifying the distance function, this can be achieved by an attribute transformation: replace a k-valued nominal attribute by k synthetic binary attributes, one for each value indicating whether the attribute has that value or not. If the attributes have equal weight, this achieves the same effect on the distance function. The distance is insensitive to the attribute values because only "same" or "different" information is encoded, not the shades of difference that may be associated with the various possible values of the attribute. More subtle distinctions can be made if the attributes have weights reflecting their relative importance.

If the values of the attribute can be ordered, more possibilities arise. For a numeric prediction problem, the average class value corresponding to each value of a nominal attribute can be calculated from the training instances and used to determine an ordering—this technique was introduced for model trees in Chapter 6 (Section 6.5). (It is hard to come up with an analogous way of ordering attribute values for a classification problem.) An ordered nominal attribute can be replaced by an integer in the obvious way—but this implies not just an ordering but a metric on the attribute's values. The implication of a metric can be avoided by creating $k-1$ synthetic binary attributes for a k-valued nominal attribute, the ith being 0 if the value is one of the first i values, and 1 otherwise. This encoding still implies an ordering between different values of the attribute—adjacent values differ in just one of the synthetic attributes, whereas distant ones differ in several—but does not imply an equal distance between the attribute values.

7.3 Automatic data cleansing

A problem that plagues applications of data mining is poor data quality. Errors in large databases are extremely common. Attribute values, and class values as well, are frequently unreliable and corrupted. While one way of addressing this problem is to painstakingly check through the data, data mining techniques themselves can sometimes help to solve the problem.

Improving decision trees

It is a surprising fact that decision trees induced from training data can often be simplified, without loss of accuracy, by discarding misclassified instances from the training set and relearning, and then repeating until there are no misclassified instances. Experiments on standard datasets have shown that this hardly affects the classification accuracy of C4.5, a standard decision tree induction scheme. In some cases it improves slightly; in others it deteriorates slightly. The difference is rarely statistically significant—and even when it is, the advantage can go either way. What the technique does affect is decision tree size. The resulting trees are invariably much smaller than the original ones, even though they perform about the same.

What is the reason for this? When a decision tree induction method prunes away a subtree, it applies a statistical test that decides whether that subtree is "justified" by the data. The decision to prune accepts a small sacrifice in classification accuracy on the training set in the belief that this will improve test set performance. Some training instances that were classified correctly by the unpruned tree will now be misclassified by the pruned one. In effect, the decision has been taken to ignore these training instances.

But that decision has only been applied locally, in the pruned subtree. Its effect has not been allowed to percolate further up the tree, perhaps resulting in different choices being made of attributes to branch on. Removing the misclassified instances from the training set and relearning the decision tree is just taking the pruning decisions to their logical conclusion. If the pruning strategy is a good one, this should not harm performance. And it may improve it by allowing better attribute choices to be made.

It would no doubt be even better to consult a human expert. Misclassified training instances could be presented for verification, and those that were found to be wrong could be deleted—or better still, corrected.

Notice that we are assuming that the instances are not misclassified in any systematic way. If instances are systematically corrupted in both training and test sets—for example, one class value might be substituted for another—it is only to be expected that training on the erroneous training set would yield better performance on the—also erroneous—test set.

Interestingly enough, it has been shown that when artificial noise is added to attributes (rather than to classes), test set performance is improved if the same noise is added in the same way to the training set. In other words, when attribute noise is the problem, it is not a good idea to train on a "clean" set if performance is to be assessed on a "dirty" one. A learning scheme can learn to compensate for attribute noise, in some measure, if given a chance. In essence, it can learn which attributes are unreliable, and if they are all unreliable, how best to use them together to yield a more reliable result. To remove noise from attributes for the training set denies the opportunity to learn how best to combat that noise. But with class noise (rather than attribute noise), it is best to train on noise-free instances if possible.

Robust regression

The problems caused by noisy data have been known in linear regression for years. Statisticians often check data for outliers and remove them manually. In the case of linear regression, outliers can be identified visually—although it is never completely clear whether an outlier is an error or just a surprising, but correct, value. Outliers have a dramatic effect on the usual least-squares regression because the squared distance measure accentuates the influence of points far away from the regression line.

Statistical methods that address the problem of outliers are called *robust*. One way of making regression more robust is to use an absolute-value distance measure instead of the usual squared one. This weakens the effect of outliers. Another possibility is to try to identify outliers automatically and remove them from consideration. For example, one could form a regression line and then remove from consideration those 10% of points that lie farthest from the line. A third possibility is to minimize the *median* (rather than the mean) of the squares of the divergences from the regression line. It turns out that this estimator is very robust and actually copes with outliers in the *x* direction as well as outliers in the *y* direction—which is the normal direction one thinks of outliers.

A dataset that is often used to illustrate robust regression is the graph of international telephone calls made from Belgium during the years 1950 to 1973, shown in Figure 7.5. This data is taken from the Belgian Statistical Survey, published by the Ministry of Economy. The plot seems to show an upward trend over the years, but there is an anomalous group of points from 1964 to 1969. It turns out that during this period, results were mistakenly recorded in the total number of *minutes* of the calls. The years 1963 and 1970 are also partially affected. This error causes a large fraction of outliers in the *y* direction.

Not surprisingly, the usual least-squares regression line is seriously affected by this anomalous data. However, the least *median* of squares line remains remarkably unperturbed. This line has a simple and natural interpretation.

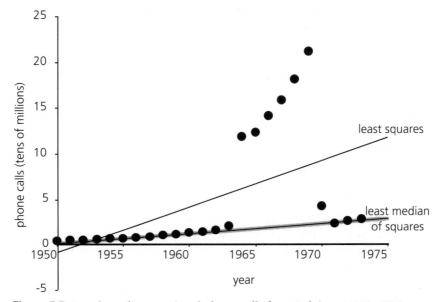

Figure 7.5 Number of international phone calls from Belgium, 1950–1973.

Geometrically, it corresponds to finding the narrowest strip covering half of the observations, where the thickness of the strip is measured in the vertical direction—this strip is marked in gray in Figure 7.5. The least median of squares line lies exactly at the center of this band. Note that this notion is often easier to explain and visualize than the normal least-squares definition of regression. Unfortunately, there is a serious disadvantage to median-based regression techniques: they incur high computational cost which often makes them infeasible for practical problems.

Detecting anomalies

One serious problem with any form of automatic detection of apparently incorrect data is that the baby may be thrown out with the bathwater. Short of consulting a human expert, there is really no way of telling whether a particular instance really is an error, or whether it just does not fit the type of model that is being applied. In statistical regression, visualizations help. It will usually be visually apparent, even to the nonexpert, if the wrong kind of curve is being fitted—a straight line is being fitted to data that lies on a parabola, for example. The outliers in Figure 7.5 certainly stand out to the eye. But most classification problems cannot be so easily visualized: the notion of "model type" is more subtle than a simple regression line. And although it is known that good results are obtained on most standard datasets by discarding instances that do not fit a decision tree model, this is not necessarily of great comfort when dealing with a particular new dataset. The suspicion will remain that perhaps the new dataset is simply unsuited to decision tree modeling.

One solution that has been tried is to use several different learning schemes—like a decision tree, and a nearest-neighbor learner, and a linear discriminant function—to filter the data. A conservative approach is to ask that all three schemes fail to classify an instance correctly before it is deemed erroneous and removed from the data. In some cases, filtering the data in this way and using the filtered data as input to a final learning scheme gives better performance than simply using the three learning schemes and letting them vote on the outcome. Training all three schemes on the *filtered* data and letting them vote can yield even better results. However, there is a danger to voting techniques: some learning algorithms are better suited to certain types of data than others, and the most appropriate scheme may simply get outvoted! We will examine a more subtle method of combining the output from different classifiers, called *stacking,* in the next section. The lesson, as usual, is to get to know your data and look at it in many different ways.

One possible danger with filtering approaches is that they might conceivably be sacrificing instances of a particular class (or group of classes) in order to improve accuracy on the remaining classes. Although there are no general ways that guard against this, it has not been found to be a problem in practice.

Finally, it is worth noting once again that automatic filtering is a poor substitute for getting the data right in the first place. And if this is too time-consuming and expensive to be practical, human inspection could be limited to those instances that are identified by the filter as suspect.

7.4 Combining multiple models

When wise people make critical decisions, they usually take into account the opinions of several experts rather than relying on their own judgment or that of a solitary trusted advisor. For example, before choosing an important new policy direction, a benign dictator consults widely: he or she would be ill advised to follow just one expert's opinion blindly. In a democratic setting, discussion of different viewpoints may produce a consensus; if not, a vote may be called for. In either case, different expert opinions are being combined.

In data mining, a model generated by machine learning can be regarded as an expert. *Expert* is probably too strong a word!—depending on the amount and quality of the training data, and whether the learning algorithm is appropriate to the problem at hand, the expert may in truth be regrettably ignorant—but we use the term nevertheless. An obvious approach to making decisions more reliable is to combine the output of several different models. The most prominent methods for combining models generated by machine learning are called *bagging, boosting, stacking,* and *error-correcting output codes.* They can all, more often than not, increase predictive performance over a single model. However, the combined models share the disadvantage of being rather hard to analyze: it is not easy to understand in intuitive terms what factors are contributing to the improved decisions.

Bagging, boosting, and stacking are general techniques that can be applied to numeric prediction problems as well as classification tasks. Bagging and boosting both use the same method of aggregating different models together. Error-correcting output codes are less general than the other techniques: they apply only to classification problems, and even then, just to ones that have more than two classes.

Bagging

Combining the decisions of different models means amalgamating the various outputs into a single prediction. The simplest way to do this in the case of classification is to take a vote (perhaps a weighted vote); in the case of numeric prediction it is to calculate the average (perhaps a weighted average). Bagging and boosting both adopt this approach, but they derive the individual models in different ways. In bagging, the models receive equal weight, whereas in boosting, weighting is used to give more influence to the more successful ones—just as an executive might place different values on the advice of different experts depending on how experienced they are.

To introduce bagging, suppose that several training datasets of the same size are chosen at random from the problem domain. Imagine using a particular machine learning technique to build a decision tree for each dataset. You might expect these trees to be practically identical and to make the same prediction for each new test instance. But, surprisingly, this assumption is usually quite wrong, particularly if the training datasets are fairly small. This is a rather disturbing fact and seems to cast a shadow over the whole enterprise! The reason for it is that decision tree induction (at least, the standard top-down method described in Chapter 4) is an unstable process: slight changes to the training data may easily result in a different attribute being chosen at a particular node, with significant ramifications for the structure of the subtree beneath that node. This automatically implies that there are test instances for which some of the decision trees produce correct predictions and others do not.

Returning to the experts analogy above, consider the experts to be the individual decision trees. We can combine the trees by having them vote on each test instance. If one class receives more votes than any of the others, it is taken as the correct one. Generally speaking, the more the merrier: predictions made by voting become more reliable as more votes are taken into account. Decisions rarely deteriorate if new training sets are discovered, trees are built for them, and their predictions participate in the vote as well. In particular, the combined classifier will seldom be less accurate than a decision tree constructed from just one of the datasets. (Improvement is not guaranteed, however. It can be shown theoretically that pathological situations exist where the combined decisions are worse.)

The effect of combining multiple hypotheses can be viewed through a theoretical device known as the *bias-variance decomposition*. Suppose we could have an infinite number of independent training sets of the same size, and use them to make an infinite number of classifiers. A test instance is processed by all classifiers and a single answer determined by majority vote. In this idealized situation, errors will still occur because no learning scheme is perfect: the error rate will depend on how well the machine learning method matches the problem at hand. Suppose the expected error rate were evaluated by averaging the error of the combined classifier over an infinite number of independently chosen test examples. The error rate for a particular learning algorithm is called its *bias* for the learning problem and measures how well the learning method matches the problem. This technical definition is a way of quantifying the vaguer notion of bias introduced in Section 1.5: it measures the "persistent" error of a learning algorithm that can't be eliminated even by taking an infinite number of training sets into account. Of course, it cannot be calculated exactly in practical situations, although it can be approximated.

A second source of error in a learned model, in a practical situation, stems from the particular training set used, which is inevitably finite and therefore not fully representative of the actual population of instances. The expected value of this component of the error, over all possible training sets of the given size and all possible test sets, is called the *variance* of the learning method for that problem. The total expected error of a classifier is made up of the sum of bias and variance: this is the bias-variance decomposition. Combining multiple classifiers decreases the expected error by reducing the variance component. The more classifiers that are included, the greater the reduction in variance.

Of course, a difficulty arises when putting this voting scheme into practice: usually there's only one training set, and obtaining more data is either impossible or expensive.

Bagging attempts to neutralize the instability of learning methods by simulating the process described above using a given training set. Instead of sampling a fresh, independent training dataset each time, the original training data is altered by deleting some instances and replicating others. Instances are randomly sampled, with replacement, from the original dataset to create a new one of the same size. This sampling procedure inevitably replicates some of the

---

model generation

```
Let n be the number of instances in the training data.
For each of t iterations:
    Sample n instances with replacement from training data.
    Apply the learning algorithm to the sample.
    Store the resulting model.
```

classification

```
For each of the t models:
    Predict class of instance using model.
Return class that has been predicted most often.
```

Figure 7.6 Algorithm for bagging.

instances and deletes others. If this idea strikes a chord, it is because we discussed it in Chapter 5 when describing the bootstrap method for estimating the generalization error of a learning method (Section 5.4): indeed, the term *bagging* stands for "bootstrap aggregating." Bagging applies the learning scheme—for example, a decision tree inducer—to each one of these artificially derived datasets, and the classifiers generated from them vote for the class to be predicted. The algorithm is summarized in Figure 7.6.

The difference between bagging and the idealized procedure described above is the way in which the training datasets are derived. Instead of obtaining independent datasets from the domain, bagging just resamples from the original training data. The datasets generated by resampling are different from each other but are certainly not independent because they are all based on one dataset. However, it turns out that bagging produces a combined model that often performs significantly better than the single model built from the original training data, and is never substantially worse.

Bagging can also be applied to learning schemes for numeric prediction—for example, model trees. The only difference is that instead of voting on the outcome, the individual predictions, being real numbers, are averaged. The bias-variance decomposition can be applied to numeric prediction as well, by decomposing the expected value of the mean-squared error of the predictions on fresh data. Bias is defined as the mean-squared error expected when averaging over models built from all possible training datasets of the same size, while variance is the component of the expected error of a single model that is due to the particular training data it was built from. It can be shown theoretically that averaging over multiple models always reduces the expected value of the mean-squared error. (As we mentioned above, the analogous result is not true for classification.)

Boosting

We have explained that bagging exploits the instability inherent in learning algorithms. As you might expect, it doesn't work for inducers that are stable, ones whose output is insensitive to small changes in the input. For example, it is pointless to use bagging in conjunction with the linear models discussed in Chapter 4 (Section 4.6), because their output changes very little if the training data is perturbed as described above. Intuitively, combining multiple models only helps when these models are significantly different from one another and each one treats a reasonable percentage of the data correctly. Ideally the models complement one another, each being a specialist in a part of the domain where the other models don't perform very well—just as human executives seek advisors whose skills and experience complement, rather than duplicate, one another.

The boosting method for combining multiple models exploits this insight by explicitly seeking models that complement one another. First, the similarities. Like bagging, boosting uses voting (for classification) or averaging (for prediction) to combine the output of individual models and, again like bagging, it combines models of the same type—for example, decision trees. However, boosting is iterative. Whereas in bagging individual models are built separately, in boosting each new model is influenced by the performance of those built previously. Boosting encourages new models to become experts for instances handled incorrectly by earlier ones. A final difference is that boosting weights a model's contribution by its performance, rather than giving equal weight to all models.

There are many variants on the idea of boosting. We describe a widely used method called *AdaBoost.M1* that is designed specifically for classification. Like bagging, it can be applied to any classification learning algorithm. However, to simplify matters we assume that the learning algorithm can handle weighted instances, where the weight of an instance is a positive number. (We explain later how to get around this restriction.) The presence of instance weights changes the way in which a classifier's error is calculated: it is the sum of the weights of the misclassified instances divided by the total weight of all instances, instead of the fraction of instances that are misclassified. By weighting instances, the learning algorithm can be forced to concentrate on a particular set of instances, namely those with high weight. Such instances become particularly important because there is a greater incentive to classify them correctly. The C4.5 algorithm, discussed in Chapter 6 (Section 6.1), is an example of a learning scheme that can accommodate weighted instances without modification because it already uses the notion of fractional instances to handle missing values.

The boosting algorithm, summarized in Figure 7.7, begins by assigning equal weight to all instances in the training data. It then calls the learning algorithm to

model generation
```
Assign equal weight to each training instance.
For each of t iterations:
  Apply learning algorithm to weighted dataset and store
    resulting model.
  Compute error e of model on weighted dataset and store error.
  If e equal to zero, or e greater or equal to 0.5:
    Terminate model generation.
  For each instance in dataset:
    If instance classified correctly by model:
      Multiply weight of instance by e / (1 - e).
  Normalize weight of all instances.
```

classification
```
Assign weight of zero to all classes.
For each of the t (or less) models:
  Add -log(e / (1 - e)) to weight of class predicted by model.
Return class with highest weight.
```

Figure 7.7 Algorithm for boosting.

form a classifier for this data, and reweights each instance according to the classifier's output. The weight of correctly classified instances is decreased, and that of misclassified ones is increased. This produces a set of "easy" instances with low weight, and a set of "hard" ones with high weight. In the next iteration—and all subsequent ones—a classifier is built for the reweighted data, which consequently focuses on classifying the hard instances correctly. Then the instances' weights are increased or decreased according to the output of this new classifier. As a result, some hard instances might become even harder and easier ones even easier; on the other hand, other hard instances might become easier, and easier ones harder—all possibilities can occur in practice. After each iteration, the weights reflect how often the instances have been misclassified by the classifiers produced so far. By maintaining a measure of "hardness" with each instance, this procedure provides an elegant way of generating a series of experts that complement one another.

How much should the weights be altered after each iteration? The answer depends on the current classifier's overall error. More specifically, if e denotes the classifier's error on the weighted data (a fraction between 0 and 1), then weights are updated by

$$weight \leftarrow weight \times e/(1-e)$$

for correctly classified instances, and the weights remain unchanged for misclassified ones. Of course, this does not increase the weight of misclassified instances as claimed above. However, after all weights have been updated they are renormalized so that their sum remains the same as it was before. Each instance's weight is divided by the sum of the new weights, and multiplied by the sum of the old ones. This automatically increases the weight of each misclassified instance and reduces that of each correctly classified one.

Whenever the error on the weighted training data exceeds or equals 0.5, the boosting procedure deletes the current classifier and does not perform any more iterations. The same thing happens when the error is 0, because then all instance weights become 0.

We have explained how the boosting method generates a series of classifiers. To form a prediction, their output is combined using a weighted vote. To determine the weights, note that a classifier that performs well on the weighted training data from which it was built (e close to 0) should receive a high weight, and a classifier that performs badly (e close to 0.5) should receive a low one. More specifically, we use

$$weight = -\log \frac{e}{1 - e},$$

which is a positive number between 0 and infinity. Incidentally, this formula explains why classifiers that perform perfectly on the training data must be deleted, for when e is 0 the weight is undefined. In order to make a prediction, the weights of all classifiers that vote for a particular class are summed, and the class with the greatest total is chosen.

We began by assuming that the learning algorithm can cope with weighted instances. If this is not the case, an unweighted dataset is generated from the weighted data by resampling—the same technique that bagging uses. Whereas for bagging each instance is chosen with equal probability, for boosting instances are chosen with probability proportional to their weight. As a result, instances with high weight are replicated frequently, while ones with low weight may never be selected. Once the new dataset becomes as large as the original one, it is fed into the learning scheme instead of the weighted data. It's as simple as that.

A disadvantage of this procedure is that some instances with low weight don't make it into the resampled dataset, and so information is lost before the learning scheme is applied. However, this can be turned to advantage. If the learning scheme produces a classifier whose error exceeds 0.5, boosting must terminate if the weighted data is used directly, whereas with resampling it might be possible to produce a classifier with error below 0.5 by discarding the resampled dataset and generating a new one from a different random seed. Sometimes more boosting iterations can be performed by resampling than when using the original weighted version of the algorithm.

The idea of boosting originated in a branch of machine learning research known as *computational learning theory*. Theoreticians are interested in boosting because it is possible to derive performance guarantees. For example, it can be shown that the error of the combined classifier on the training data approaches zero very quickly as more iterations are performed (exponentially quickly in the number of iterations). Unfortunately, as discussed in Chapter 5 (Section 5.1), guarantees for the training error are not very interesting because they do not necessarily indicate good performance on fresh data. However, it can be shown theoretically that boosting only fails on fresh data if the individual classifiers are too "complex" for the amount of training data present, or their training errors become too large too quickly (in a precise sense which is explained by Schapire et al. 1997). As usual, the problem lies in finding the right balance between the individual models' complexity and their fit to the data.

If boosting does succeed in reducing the error on fresh test data, it often does so in a spectacular way. One very surprising finding is that performing more boosting iterations can reduce the error on new data long after the error of the combined classifier on the training data has dropped to zero. Researchers were puzzled by this result because it seems to contradict Occam's razor, discussed in Section 5.9, which declares that, of two hypotheses that explain the empirical evidence equally well, the simpler one is to be preferred. Performing more boosting iterations without reducing training error does not explain the training data any better, and it certainly adds complexity to the combined classifier. Fortunately, the contradiction can be resolved by considering the classifier's confidence in its predictions. Confidence is measured by the difference between the estimated probability of the true class and that of the most likely predicted class other than the true class—a quantity known as the *margin*. The larger the margin, the more confident the classifier is in predicting the true class. It turns out that boosting can increase the margin long after the training error has dropped to zero. Hence, if the explanation of empirical evidence takes the margin into account, Occam's razor remains as sharp as ever.

The beautiful thing about boosting is that a powerful combined classifier can be built from very simple ones, so long as they achieve less than 50% error on the reweighted data. Usually this is easy—certainly for learning problems with two classes. Simple learning schemes are called *weak* learners, and boosting converts weak learners into strong ones. For example, good results for two-class problems can be obtained by boosting extremely simple decision trees that have only one level—called *decision stumps*. Of course, multiclass datasets make it more difficult to achieve error rates below 0.5. Decision trees can still be boosted, but they usually need to be more complex than decision stumps. More sophisticated algorithms have been developed that allow very simple models to be boosted successfully in multiclass situations. Although they are beyond the scope of this book, an implementation of one, LogitBoost, is included in the software discussed in Chapter 8.

Boosting often produces classifiers that are significantly more accurate on fresh data than ones generated by bagging. However, unlike bagging, boosting sometimes fails in practical situations: it can generate a classifier that is significantly less accurate than a single classifier built from the same data. This indicates that the combined classifier overfits the data.

Stacking

Stacked generalization, or stacking for short, is a different way of combining multiple models. Although developed some years ago, it is less widely used than bagging and boosting, partly because it is difficult to analyze theoretically, and partly because there is no generally accepted best way of doing it—the basic idea can be applied in many different variations.

Unlike bagging and boosting, stacking is not normally used to combine models of the same type—for example, a set of decision trees. Instead it is applied to models built by different learning algorithms. Suppose you have a decision tree inducer, a Naive Bayes learner, and an instance-based learning scheme, and you want to form a classifier for a given dataset. The usual procedure would be to estimate the expected error of each algorithm by cross-validation and to choose the best one to form a model for prediction on future data. But isn't there a better way? With three learning algorithms available, can't we use all three for prediction and combine the outputs together?

One way to combine outputs is by voting—the same mechanism used in bagging. However, (unweighted) voting only makes sense if the learning schemes perform comparably well. If two of the three classifiers make predictions that are grossly incorrect, we will be in trouble! Instead, stacking introduces the concept of a *meta learner*, which replaces the voting procedure. The problem with voting is that it's not clear which classifier to trust. Stacking tries to *learn* which classifiers are the reliable ones, using another learning algorithm—the meta learner—to discover how best to combine the output of the base learners.

The input to the meta model—also called the *level-1 model*—are the predictions of the base models, or *level-0 models*. A level-1 instance has as many attributes as there are level-0 learners, and the attribute values give the predictions of these learners on the corresponding level-0 instance. When the stacked learner is used for classification, an instance is first fed into the level-0 models, and each one guesses a class value. These guesses are fed into the level-1 model, which combines them into the final prediction.

There remains the problem of training the level-1 learner. To do this, we need to find a way of transforming the level-0 training data (used for training the level-0 learners) into level-1 training data (for training the level-1 learner). This seems straightforward: let each level-0 model classify a training instance, and attach to their predictions the instance's actual class value to yield a level-1 training instance. Unfortunately, this doesn't work well. It would allow rules to be learned such as *always believe the output of classifier A, and ignore B and C*. This rule may well be appropriate for particular base classifiers A, B, and C; and if so it will probably be learned. But just because it seems appropriate on the training data doesn't necessarily mean that it will work well on the test data— for it will inevitably learn to prefer classifiers that overfit the training data over ones that make decisions more realistically.

Consequently, stacking does not simply transform the level-0 training data into level-1 data in this manner. Recall from Chapter 5 that there are better methods of estimating a classifier's performance than using the error on the training set. One is to hold out some instances and use them for an independent evaluation. Applying this to stacking, we reserve some instances to form the training data for the level-1 learner, and build level-0 classifiers from the remaining data. Once the level-0 classifiers have been built, they are used to classify the instances in the holdout set, forming the level-1 training data as described above. Because the level-0 classifiers haven't been trained on these instances, their predictions are unbiased, and therefore the level-1 training data accurately reflects the true performance of the level-0 learning algorithms. Once the level-1 data has been generated by this holdout procedure, the level-0 learners can be reapplied to generate classifiers from the full training set, making slightly better use of the data and leading to better predictions.

The holdout method inevitably deprives the level-1 model of some of the training data. In Chapter 5, cross-validation was introduced as a means of circumventing this problem for error estimation. This can be applied in conjunction with stacking by performing a cross-validation for every level-0 learner. Each instance in the training data occurs in exactly one of the test folds of the cross-validation, and the predictions of the level-0 inducers built from the corresponding training fold are used to build a level-1 training instance from it. This generates a level-1 training instance for each level-0 training instance. Of course, it is slow because a level-0 classifier has to be trained for each fold of the cross-validation, but it does allow the level-1 classifier to make full use of the training data.

Given a test instance, most learning schemes are able to output probabilities for every class label, instead of making a single categorical prediction. This can be exploited to improve the performance of stacking by using the probabilities to form the level-1 data. The only difference to the standard procedure is that each nominal level-1 attribute—representing the class predicted by a level-0 learner—is replaced by several numeric attributes, each representing a class probability output by the level-0 learner. In other words, the number of attributes in the level-1 data is multiplied by the number of classes. This procedure has the advantage that the level-1 learner is privy to the confidence that each level-0 learner associates with its predictions, thereby amplifying communication between the two levels of learning.

An outstanding question remains: what algorithms are suitable for the level-1 inducer? In principle, any learning scheme can be applied. However, since most of the work is already done by the level-0 learners, the level-1 classifier is basically just an arbiter, and it makes sense to choose a rather simple algorithm for this purpose. In the words of David Wolpert, the inventor of stacking, it is reasonable that "relatively global, smooth" level-1 generalizers should perform well. And simple linear models—as discussed in Chapter 4 (Section 4.6)—have turned out best in practical situations.

Stacking can also be applied to numeric prediction. In that case, the level-0 models and the level-1 model all predict numeric values. The basic mechanism remains the same; the only difference lies in the nature of the level-1 data. In the numeric case, each level-1 attribute represents the numeric prediction made by one of the level-0 models, and instead of a class value the numeric target value is attached to level-1 training instances.

Error-correcting output codes

Error-correcting output codes are a technique for improving the performance of classification algorithms in multiclass learning problems. Recall from Chapter 6 that some learning algorithms—for example, support vector machines—only work with two-class problems. To apply such algorithms to multiclass datasets, the dataset is decomposed into several independent two-class problems, the algorithm is run on each one, and the outputs of the resulting classifiers are combined. Error-correcting output codes are a scheme for making the most of this transformation. In fact, the method works so well that it is often advantageous to apply it even when the learning algorithm can handle multiclass datasets directly.

In Section 4.6 (page 113) we learned how to transform a multiclass dataset into several two-class ones. For each class, a dataset is generated containing a copy of each instance in the original data, but with a modified class value. If the instance has the class associated with the corresponding dataset, it is tagged yes, otherwise no. Then classifiers are built for each of these binary datasets, classifiers that output a confidence figure with their predictions—for example, the estimated probability that the class is yes. During classification, a test instance is fed into each binary classifier, and the final class is the one associated with the classifier that pre-

Table 7.1 Transforming a multiclass problem into a two-class one: (a) standard method; (b) error-correcting code.

a	class	class vector	b	class	class vector
	a	1000		a	1111111
	b	0100		b	0000111
	c	0010		c	0011001
	d	0001		d	0101010

dicts yes most confidently. Of course, this method is sensitive to the accuracy of the confidence figures produced by the classifiers: if some classifiers have an exaggerated opinion of their own predictions, the overall result will suffer.

Consider a multiclass problem with four classes a, b, c, and d. The transformation can be visualized as shown in Table 7.1a, where yes and no are mapped to 1 and 0 respectively. Each of the original class values is converted into a four-bit code word, one bit per class, and the four classifiers predict the bits independently. Interpreting the classification process in terms of these code words, errors occur when the wrong binary bit receives the highest confidence.

However, we do not have to use the particular code words shown. Indeed there is no reason why each class must be represented by four bits. Look instead at the code of Table 7.1b, where classes are represented by seven bits. When applied to a dataset, seven classifiers must be built instead of four. To see what that might buy, consider the classification of a particular instance. Suppose it belongs to class a, and that the predictions of the individual classifiers are 1 0 1 1 1 1 1 (respectively). Obviously, comparing this code word with those in Table 7.1b, the second classifier has made a mistake: it predicted 0 instead of 1, no instead of yes. However, comparing the predicted bits with the code word associated with each class, the instance is clearly closer to a than to any other class. This can be quantified by the number of bits that must be changed to convert the predicted code word into those of Table 7.1b: the *Hamming distance,* or discrepancy between the bit strings, is 1, 3, 3, and 5 for the classes a, b, c, and d respectively. We can safely conclude that the second classifier made a mistake, and correctly identify a as the instance's true class.

The same kind of error correction is not possible with the code words of Table 7.1a, because any predicted string of four bits other than these four four-bit words has the same distance to at least two of them. The output codes are not "error-correcting."

What determines whether a code is error-correcting or not? Consider the Hamming distance between the code words representing different classes. The number of errors that can possibly be corrected depends on the minimum distance between any pair of code words, say d. The code can guarantee to correct up to $(d-1)/2$ single-bit errors, because if this number of bits of the correct code word are flipped, it will still be the closest and will therefore be identified correctly. In Table 7.1a the Hamming distance for each pair of code words is two. Hence the minimum distance d is also 2, and we can correct no more than 0 errors! However, in the code of Table 7.1b the minimum distance is 4 (in fact, the distance is 4 for all pairs). That means it is guaranteed to correct single-bit errors.

We have identified one property of a good error-correcting code: the code words must be well separated in terms of their Hamming distance. Because they comprise the rows of the code table, this property is called *row separation*. There is a second requirement that a good error-correcting code should fulfill: *column separation*. The Hamming distance between every pair of columns must be large, as must the distance between each column and the complement of every other column. In Table 7.1b, the seven columns are separated from each other (and their complements) by at least one bit.

Column separation is necessary because if two columns are identical (or if one is the complement of another), the corresponding classifiers will make the same errors. Error correction is weakened if the errors are correlated—in other words, if many bit positions are simultaneously incorrect. The greater the distance between columns, the more errors are likely to be corrected.

With fewer than four classes it is hard to construct a really effective error-correcting code because good row separation and good column separation cannot be achieved simultaneously. For example, with three classes there are only eight possible columns (2^3), four of which are complements of the other four. Moreover, columns with all zeroes or all ones provide no discrimination. This leaves just three possible columns, and the resulting code is not error-correcting at all. (In fact, it is the standard "one-per-class" encoding.)

If there are few classes, an exhaustive error-correcting code like the one in Table 7.1b can be built. In an exhaustive code for k classes, the columns comprise every possible k-bit string, except for complements and the trivial all-zero or all-one strings. Each codeword contains $2^{k-1}-1$ bits. The code is constructed as follows. The code word for the first class consists of all ones; that for the second class has 2^{k-2} zeroes followed by $2^{k-2}-1$ ones; the third has 2^{k-3} zeroes followed by 2^{k-3} ones followed by 2^{k-3} zeroes followed by $2^{k-3}-1$ ones; and so on. The ith code word consists of alternating runs of 2^{k-i} zeroes and ones, the last run being one short.

With more classes, exhaustive codes are infeasible because the number of columns increases exponentially and too many classifiers have to be built. In that case more sophisticated methods are employed, which can build a code with good error-correcting properties from a smaller number of columns.

Error-correcting output codes do not work for local learning algorithms, like instance-based learners, which predict the class of an instance by looking at nearby training instances. In the case of a nearest-neighbor classifier, all output bits would be predicted using the same training instance. The problem can be circumvented by using different attribute subsets to predict each output bit, decorrelating the predictions.

7.5 Further reading

Attribute selection, under the term *feature selection,* has been investigated in the field of pattern recognition for decades. Backward elimination, for example, was introduced in the early 1960s (Marill and Green 1963). Kittler (1978) surveys the feature selection algorithms that have been developed for pattern recognition. Best-first search and genetic algorithms are standard artificial intelligence techniques (Winston 1992; Goldberg 1989).

The experiments that show the performance of decision tree learners deteriorating as new attributes are added are reported by John (1997), who gives a nice discussion of attribute selection. The idea of finding the smallest attribute set that carves up the instances uniquely is from Almuallin and Dietterich (1991, 1992) and was further developed by Liu and Setiono (1996). Kibler and Aha (1987) and Cardie (1993) both investigated the use of decision tree algorithms to identify features for nearest-neighbor learning; Holmes and Nevill-Manning (1995) used 1R to order features for selection; Kira and Rendell (1992) used instance-based methods to select features.

The use of wrapper methods for feature selection is from John et al. (1994) and Kohavi and John (1997), while genetic algorithms have been applied within a wrapper framework by Vafaie and DeJong (1992) and Cherkauer and Shavlik (1996). The selective Naive Bayes learning scheme is from Langley and Sage (1994).

Dougherty et al. (1995) give a brief account of supervised and unsupervised discretization, along with experimental results comparing the entropy-based method with equal-width binning and the 1R method. Frank and Witten (1999) discuss the effect of using the ordering information in discretized attributes. The entropy-based method for discretization, including the use of the Minimum Description Length stopping criterion, was developed by Fayyad and Irani (1993). The bottom-up statistical method using the X^2 test is from Kerber (1992), and its extension to an automatically determined significance level is discussed by Liu and Setiono (1997). Fulton et al. (1995) investigate the use of dynamic programming for discretization and derive the quadratic time bound for a general impurity function (e.g., entropy) and the linear one for error-based discretization. The example used for showing the weakness of error-based discretization is adapted from Kohavi and Sahami (1996), who were the first to clearly identify this phenomenon.

The experiments on using C4.5 to filter its own training data were reported by John (1995). The more conservative approach of a consensus filter involving several different learning algorithms has been investigated by Brodley and Friedl (1996). Rousseeuw and Leroy (1987) discuss the detection of outliers in statistical regression, including the least median of squares method; they also present the telephone data of Figure 7.5. It was Quinlan (1986) who noticed that removing noise from the training instance's attributes can decrease a classifier's performance on similarly noisy test instances, particularly at higher noise levels.

Combining multiple models is a popular research topic in machine learning research, with many related publications. As well as the methods discussed above, there are other procedures for combining multiple models—for example, Bayesian model averaging (Madigan et al. 1996), and averaging over models output by a randomized learning algorithm.

The term *bagging* (for "bootstrap aggregating") was coined by Breiman (1996b), who investigated the properties of bagging theoretically and empirically for both classification and numeric prediction. Freund and Schapire (1996) developed the AdaBoost.M1 boosting algorithm, and derived theoretical bounds for its performance. Later, they improved these bounds using the concept of margins (Schapire et al. 1997). Drucker (1997) adapted AdaBoost.M1 for numeric prediction. Other boosting algorithms have been described, but their performance is either very similar to AdaBoost.M1, or they work only with specifically adapted learners. A notable exception is LogitBoost (Friedman et al. 1998), derived from the statistical framework of additive logistic regression, which takes a learning algorithm for numeric prediction and forms a combined model that can be used for classification. Although it lies beyond the scope of this book, an implementation of LogitBoost is included in the software described in the next chapter. Friedman (1999) has also developed a way of making boosting less likely to overfit, thereby improving its performance on noisy data.

Stacked generalization originated with Wolpert (1992), who presented the idea in the neural network literature, and was applied to numeric prediction by Breiman (1996a). Ting and Witten (1997a) compared different level-1 models empirically and found that a simple linear model performs best; they also demonstrated the advantage of using probabilities as level-1 data. A combination of stacking and bagging has also been investigated (Ting and Witten 1997b).

The idea of using error-correcting output codes for classification gained wide acceptance after a paper by Dietterich and Bakiri (1995); Ricci and Aha (1998) showed how to apply such codes to nearest-neighbor classifiers.

chapter eight

Nuts and bolts: Machine learning algorithms in Java

All the algorithms discussed in this book have been implemented and made freely available on the World Wide Web (*www.cs.waikato. ac.nz/ml/weka*) for you to experiment with. This will allow you to learn more about how they work and what they do. The implementations are part of a system called Weka, developed at the University of Waikato in New Zealand. "Weka" stands for the Waikato Environment for Knowledge Analysis. (Also, the *weka,* pronounced to rhyme with *Mecca,* is a flightless bird with an inquisitive nature found only on the islands of New Zealand.) The system is written in Java, an object-oriented programming language that is widely available for all major computer platforms, and Weka has been tested under Linux, Windows, and Macintosh operating systems. Java allows us to provide a uniform interface to many different learning algorithms, along with methods for pre- and postprocessing and for evaluating the result of learning schemes on any given dataset. The interface is described in this chapter.

There are several different levels at which Weka can be used. First of all, it provides implementations of state-of-the-art learning algorithms that you can apply to your dataset from the command line. It also includes a variety of tools for transforming datasets, like the algorithms for discretization discussed in Chapter 7. You can preprocess a dataset, feed it into a learning scheme, and analyze the resulting classifier and its performance—all without writing any program code at all. As an example to get you started, we will explain how to transform a spreadsheet into a dataset with the right format for this process, and how to build a decision tree from it.

Learning how to build decision trees is just the beginning: there are many other algorithms to explore. The most important resource for navigating through the software is the online documentation, which has been automatically generated from the source code and concisely reflects its structure. We will explain how to use this documentation and identify Weka's major building blocks, highlighting which parts contain supervised learning methods, which contain tools for data preprocessing, and which contain methods for other learning schemes. The online documentation is very helpful even if you do no more than process datasets from the command line, because it is the only complete list of available algorithms. Weka is continually growing, and—being generated automatically from the source code—the online documentation is always up to date. Moreover, it becomes essential if you want to proceed to the next level and access the library from your own Java programs, or to write and test learning schemes of your own.

One way of using Weka is to apply a learning method to a dataset and analyze its output to extract information about the data. Another is to apply several learners and compare their performance in order to choose one for prediction. The learning methods are called *classifiers*. They all have the same command-line interface, and there is a set of generic command-line options—as well as some scheme-specific ones. The performance of all classifiers is measured by a common evaluation module. We explain the command-line options and show how to interpret the output of the evaluation procedure. We describe the output of decision and model trees. We include a list of the major learning schemes and their most important scheme-specific options. In addition, we show you how to test the capabilities of a particular learning scheme, and how to obtain a bias-variance decomposition of its performance on any given dataset.

Implementations of actual learning schemes are the most valuable resource that Weka provides. But tools for preprocessing the data, called *filters,* come a close second. Like classifiers, filters have a standardized command-line interface, and there is a basic set of command-line options that they all have in common. We will show how different filters can be used, list the filter algorithms, and describe their scheme-specific options.

The main focus of Weka is on classifier and filter algorithms. However, it also includes implementations of algorithms for learning association rules and for clustering data for which no class value is specified. We briefly discuss how to use these implementations, and point out their limitations.

In most data mining applications, the machine learning component is just a small part of a far larger software system. If you intend to write a data mining application, you will want to access the programs in Weka from inside your own code. By doing so, you can solve the machine learning subproblem of your application with a minimum of additional programming. We show you how to do that by presenting an example of a simple data mining application in Java. This will enable you to become familiar with the basic data structures in Weka, representing instances, classifiers, and filters.

If you intend to become an expert in machine learning algorithms (or, indeed, if you already are one), you'll probably want to implement your own algorithms without having to address such mundane details as reading the data from a file, implementing filtering algorithms, or providing code to evaluate the results. If so, we have good news for you: Weka already includes all this. In order to make full use of it, you must become acquainted with the basic data structures. To help you reach this point, we discuss these structures in more detail and explain example implementations of a classifier and a filter.

8.1   Getting started

Suppose you have some data and you want to build a decision tree from it. A common situation is for the data to be stored in a spreadsheet or database. However, Weka expects it to be in ARFF format, introduced in Section 2.4, because it is necessary to have type information about each attribute which cannot be automatically deduced from the attribute values. Before you can apply any algorithm to your data, is must be converted to ARFF form. This can be done very easily. Recall that the bulk of an ARFF file consists of a list of all the instances, with the attribute values for each instance being separated by commas (Figure 2.2). Most spreadsheet and database programs allow you to export your data into a file in comma-separated format—as a list of records where the items are separated by commas. Once this has been done, you need only load the file into a text editor or a word processor; add the dataset's name using the `@rela-tion` tag, the attribute information using `@attribute`, and a `@data` line; save the file as raw text—and you're done!

In the following example we assume that your data is stored in a Microsoft Excel spreadsheet, and you're using Microsoft Word for text processing. Of course, the process of converting data into ARFF format is very similar for other software packages. Figure 8.1a shows an Excel spreadsheet containing the weather data from Section 1.2. It is easy to save this data in comma-separated format. First, select the *Save As...* item from the *File* pull-down menu. Then, in

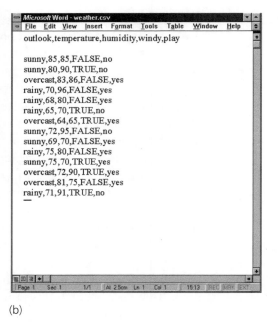

	A	B	C	D	E
1	outlook	temperatur	humidity	windy	play
2					
3	sunny	85	85	FALSE	no
4	sunny	80	90	TRUE	no
5	overcast	83	86	FALSE	yes
6	rainy	70	96	FALSE	yes
7	rainy	68	80	FALSE	yes
8	rainy	65	70	TRUE	no
9	overcast	64	65	TRUE	yes
10	sunny	72	95	FALSE	no
11	sunny	69	70	FALSE	yes
12	rainy	75	80	FALSE	yes
13	sunny	75	70	TRUE	yes
14	overcast	72	90	TRUE	yes
15	overcast	81	75	FALSE	yes
16	rainy	71	91	TRUE	no
17					
18					
19					
20					

(a)

Microsoft Word - weather.csv

outlook,temperature,humidity,windy,play

sunny,85,85,FALSE,no
sunny,80,90,TRUE,no
overcast,83,86,FALSE,yes
rainy,70,96,FALSE,yes
rainy,68,80,FALSE,yes
rainy,65,70,TRUE,no
overcast,64,65,TRUE,yes
sunny,72,95,FALSE,no
sunny,69,70,FALSE,yes
rainy,75,80,FALSE,yes
sunny,75,70,TRUE,yes
overcast,72,90,TRUE,yes
overcast,81,75,FALSE,yes
rainy,71,91,TRUE,no
—

(b)

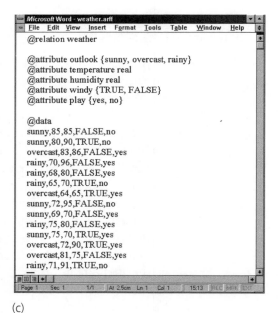

Microsoft Word - weather.arff

@relation weather

@attribute outlook {sunny, overcast, rainy}
@attribute temperature real
@attribute humidity real
@attribute windy {TRUE, FALSE}
@attribute play {yes, no}

@data
sunny,85,85,FALSE,no
sunny,80,90,TRUE,no
overcast,83,86,FALSE,yes
rainy,70,96,FALSE,yes
rainy,68,80,FALSE,yes
rainy,65,70,TRUE,no
overcast,64,65,TRUE,yes
sunny,72,95,FALSE,no
sunny,69,70,FALSE,yes
rainy,75,80,FALSE,yes
sunny,75,70,TRUE,yes
overcast,72,90,TRUE,yes
overcast,81,75,FALSE,yes
rainy,71,91,TRUE,no

Figure 8.1 Weather data: (a) in spreadsheet; (b) comma-separated; (c) in ARFF format.

(c)

the ensuing dialog box, select *CSV (Comma Delimited)* from the file type popup menu, enter a name for the file, and click the *Save* button. (A message will warn you that this will only save the active sheet: just ignore it by clicking *OK*.)

Now load this file into Microsoft Word. Your screen will look like Figure 8.1b. The rows of the original spreadsheet have been converted into lines of text, and the elements are separated from each other by commas. All you have to do is convert the first line, which holds the attribute names, into the header structure that makes up the beginning of an ARFF file.

Figure 8.1c shows the result. The dataset's name is introduced by a `@relation` tag, and the names, types, and values of each attribute are defined by `@attribute` tags. The data section of the ARFF file begins with a `@data` tag. Once the structure of your dataset matches Figure 8.1c, you should save it as a text file. Choose *Save as...* from the *File* menu, and specify *Text Only with Line Breaks* as the file type by using the corresponding popup menu. Enter a file name, and press the *Save* button. We suggest that you rename the file to *weather.arff* to indicate that it is in ARFF format. Note that the classification schemes in Weka assume by default that the class is the last attribute in the ARFF file, which fortunately it is in this case. (We explain in Section 8.3 below how to override this default.)

Now you can start analyzing this data using the algorithms provided. In the following we assume that you have downloaded Weka to your system, and that your Java environment knows where to find the library. (More information on how to do this can be found at the Weka Web site.)

To see what the C4.5 decision tree learner described in Section 6.1 does with this dataset, we use the J4.8 algorithm, which is Weka's implementation of this decision tree learner. (J4.8 actually implements a later and slightly improved version called C4.5 Revision 8, which was the last public version of this family of algorithms before C5.0, a commercial implementation, was released.) Type

```
java weka.classifiers.j48.J48 -t weather.arff
```

at the command line. This incantation calls the Java virtual machine and instructs it to execute the J48 algorithm from the *j48* package—a subpackage of *classifiers*, which is part of the overall *weka* package. Weka is organized in "packages" that correspond to a directory hierarchy. We'll give more details of the package structure in the next section: in this case, the subpackage name is *j48* and the program to be executed from it is called J48. The -t option informs the algorithm that the next argument is the name of the training file.

After pressing *Return,* you'll see the output shown in Figure 8.2. The first part is a pruned decision tree in textual form. As you can see, the first split is on the `outlook` attribute, and then, at the second level, the splits are on `humidity` and `windy`, respectively. In the tree structure, a colon introduces the class label that has been assigned to a particular leaf, followed by the number of instances that reach that leaf, expressed as a decimal number because of the way the algorithm uses fractional instances to handle missing values. Below the tree structure, the

```
J48 pruned tree
------

outlook = sunny
|   humidity <= 75: yes (2.0)
|   humidity > 75: no (3.0)
outlook = overcast: yes (4.0)
outlook = rainy
|   windy = TRUE: no (2.0)
|   windy = FALSE: yes (3.0)

Number of Leaves  :      5
Size of the tree :      8


=== Error on training data ===

Correctly Classified Instances          14              100      %
Incorrectly Classified Instances         0                0      %
Mean absolute error                      0
Root mean squared error                  0
Total Number of Instances               14

=== Confusion Matrix ===

 a b   <-- classified as
 9 0 | a = yes
 0 5 | b = no

=== Stratified cross-validation ===

Correctly Classified Instances           9           64.2857 %
Incorrectly Classified Instances         5           35.7143 %
Mean absolute error                  0.3036
Root mean squared error              0.4813
Total Number of Instances               14

=== Confusion Matrix ===

 a b   <-- classified as
 7 2 | a = yes
 3 2 | b = no
```

Figure 8.2 Output from the J4.8 decision tree learner.

number of leaves is printed, then the total number of nodes in the tree (Size of the tree).

The second part of the output gives estimates of the tree's predictive performance, generated by Weka's evaluation module. The first set of measurements is derived from the training data. As discussed in Section 5.1, such measurements are highly optimistic and very likely to overestimate the true predictive performance. However, it is still useful to look at these results, for they generally represent an upper bound on the model's performance on fresh data. In this case, all fourteen training instances have been classified correctly, and none were left unclassified. An instance can be left unclassified if the learning scheme refrains from assigning any class label to it, in which case the number of unclassified instances will be reported in the output. For most learning schemes in Weka, this never occurs.

In addition to the classification error, the evaluation module also outputs measurements derived from the class probabilities assigned by the tree. More specifically, it outputs the mean absolute error and the root mean-squared error of the probability estimates. The root mean-squared error is the square root of the average quadratic loss, discussed in Section 5.6. The mean absolute error is calculated in a similar way by using the absolute instead of the squared difference. In this example, both figures are 0 because the output probabilities for the tree are either 0 or 1, due to the fact that all leaves are pure and all training instances are classified correctly.

The summary of the results from the training data ends with a confusion matrix, mentioned in Chapter 5 (Section 5.7), showing how many instances of each class have been assigned to each class. In this case, only the diagonal elements of the matrix are non-zero because all instances are classified correctly.

The final section of the output presents results obtained using stratified ten-fold cross-validation. The evaluation module automatically performs a ten-fold cross-validation if no test file is given. As you can see, more than 30% of the instances (5 out of 14) have been misclassified in the cross-validation. This indicates that the results obtained from the training data are very optimistic compared with what might be obtained from an independent test set from the same source. From the confusion matrix you can observe that two instances of class yes have been assigned to class no, and three of class no are assigned to class yes.

8.2 Javadoc and the class library

Before exploring other learning algorithms, it is useful to learn more about the structure of Weka. The most detailed and up-to-date information can be found in the online documentation on the Weka Web site. This documentation is generated directly from comments in the source code using Sun's Javadoc utility. To understand its structure, you need to know how Java programs are organized.

Classes, instances, and packages

Every Java program is implemented as a *class*. In object-oriented programming, a class is a collection of variables along with some *methods* that operate on those variables. Together, they define the behavior of an *object* belonging to the class. An object is simply an instantiation of the class that has values assigned to all the class's variables. In Java, an object is also called an *instance* of the class. Unfortunately this conflicts with the terminology used so far in this book, where the terms *class* and *instance* have appeared in the quite different context of machine learning. From now on, you will have to infer the intended meaning of these terms from the context in which they appear. This is not difficult—though sometimes we'll use the word *object* instead of Java's *instance* to make things clear.

In Weka, the implementation of a particular learning algorithm is represented by a class. We have already met one, the J48 class described above that builds a C4.5 decision tree. Each time the Java virtual machine executes J48, it creates an instance of this class by allocating memory for building and storing a decision tree classifier. The algorithm, the classifier it builds, and a procedure for outputting the classifier, are all part of that instantiation of the J48 class.

Larger programs are usually split into more than one class. The J48 class, for example, does not actually contain any code for building a decision tree. It includes references to instances of other classes that do most of the work. When there are a lot of classes—as in Weka—they can become difficult to comprehend and navigate. Java allows classes to be organized into *packages*. A package is simply a directory containing a collection of related classes. The *j48* package mentioned above contains the classes that implement J4.8, our version of C4.5, and PART, which is the name we use for the scheme for building rules from partial decision trees that was explained near the end of Section 6.2 (page 181). Not surprisingly, these two learning algorithms share a lot of functionality, and most of the classes in this package are used by both algorithms, so it is logical to put them in the same place. Because each package corresponds to a directory, packages are organized in a hierarchy. As already mentioned, the *j48* package is a subpackage of the *classifiers* package, which is itself a subpackage of the overall *weka* package.

When you consult the online documentation generated by Javadoc from your Web browser, the first thing you see is a list of all the packages in Weka (Figure 8.3a). In the following we discuss what each one contains. On the Web page they are listed in alphabetical order; here we introduce them in order of importance.

The weka.core package

The *core* package is central to the Weka system. It contains classes that are accessed from almost every other class. You can find out what they are by clicking on the hyperlink underlying *weka.core*, which brings up Figure 8.3b.

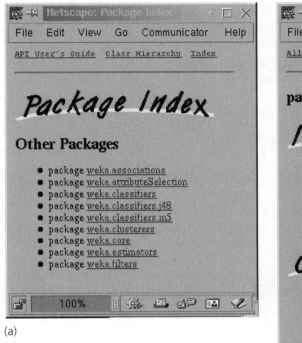

(a)

Figure 8.3 Using Javadoc: (a) the front page; (b) the *weka.core* package.

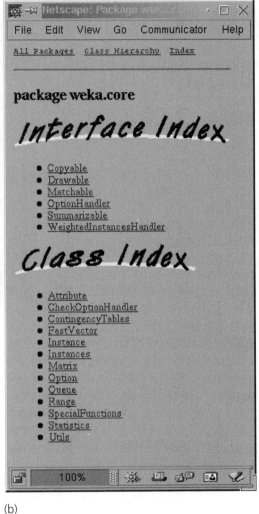

(b)

The Web page in Figure 8.3b is divided into two parts: the *Interface Index* and the *Class Index*. The latter is a list of all classes contained within the package, while the former lists all the interfaces it provides. An *interface* is very similar to a class, the only difference being that it doesn't actually do anything by itself—it is merely a list of methods without actual implementations. Other classes can declare that they "implement" a particular interface, and then provide code for its methods. For example, the OptionHandler interface defines those methods that are implemented by all classes that can process command-line options—including all classifiers.

The key classes in the *core* package are called `Attribute`, `Instance`, and `Instances`. An object of class `Attribute` represents an attribute. It contains the attribute's name, its type and, in the case of a nominal attribute, its possible values. An object of class `Instance` contains the attribute values of a particular instance; and an object of class `Instances` holds an ordered set of instances, in other words, a dataset. By clicking on the hyperlinks underlying the classes, you can find out more about them. However, you need not know the details just to use Weka from the command line. We will return to these classes in Section 8.4 when we discuss how to access the machine learning routines from other Java code.

Clicking on the *All Packages* hyperlink in the upper left corner of any documentation page brings you back to the listing of all the packages in Weka (Figure 8.3a).

The weka.classifiers package

The *classifiers* package contains implementations of most of the algorithms for classification and numeric prediction that have been discussed in this book. (Numeric prediction is included in *classifiers:* it is interpreted as prediction of a continuous class.) The most important class in this package is `Classifier`, which defines the general structure of any scheme for classification or numeric prediction. It contains two methods, `buildClassifier()` and `classifyInstance()`, which all of these learning algorithms have to implement. In the jargon of object-oriented programming, the learning algorithms are represented by subclasses of `Classifier`, and therefore automatically inherit these two methods. Every scheme redefines them according to how it builds a classifier and how it classifies instances. This gives a uniform interface for building and using classifiers from other Java code. Hence, for example, the same evaluation module can be used to evaluate the performance of any classifier in Weka.

Another important class is `DistributionClassifier`. This subclass of `Classifier` defines the method `distributionForInstance()`, which returns a probability distribution for a given instance. Any classifier that can calculate class probabilities is a subclass of `DistributionClassifier` and implements this method.

To see an example, click on `DecisionStump`, which is a class for building a simple one-level binary decision tree (with an extra branch for missing values). Its documentation page, shown in Figure 8.4, begins with the fully qualified name of this class: `weka.classifiers.DecisionStump`. You have to use this rather lengthy expression if you want to build a decision stump from the command line. The page then displays a tree structure showing the relevant part of the class hierarchy. As you can see, `DecisionStump` is a subclass of `DistributionClassifier`, and therefore produces class probabilities. `DistributionClassifier`, in turn, is a subclass of `Classifier`, which is itself a subclass of

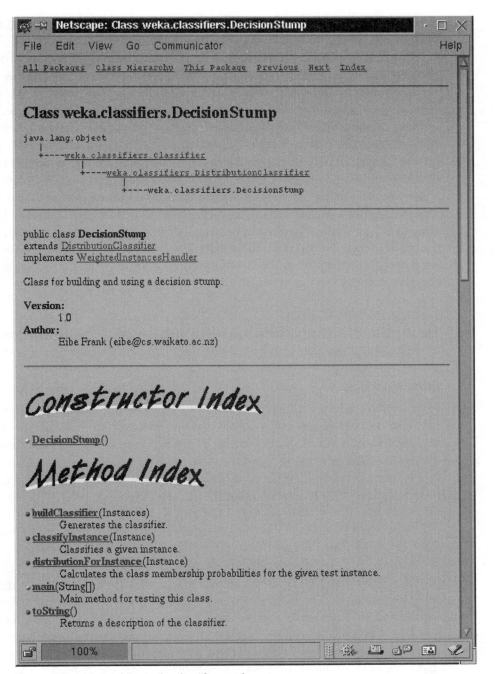

Figure 8.4 A class of the *weka.classifiers* package.

Object. The Object class is the most general one in Java: all classes are automatically subclasses of it.

After some generic information about the class, its author, and its version, Figure 8.4 gives an index of the constructors and methods of this class. A *constructor* is a special kind of method that is called whenever an object of that class is created, usually initializing the variables that collectively define its state. The index of methods lists the name of each one, the type of parameters it takes, and a short description of its functionality. Beneath those indexes, the Web page gives more details about the constructors and methods. We return to those details later.

As you can see, DecisionStump implements all methods required by both a Classifier and a DistributionClassifier. In addition, it contains toString() and main() methods. The former returns a textual description of the classifier, used whenever it is printed on the screen. The latter is called every time you ask for a decision stump from the command line, in other words, every time you enter a command beginning with

```
java weka.classifiers.DecisionStump
```

The presence of a main() method in a class indicates that it can be run from the command line, and all learning methods and filter algorithms implement it.

Other packages

Several other packages listed in Figure 8.3a are worth mentioning here: *weka.classifiers.j48, weka.classifiers.m5, weka.associations, weka.clusterers, weka.estimators, weka.filters,* and *weka.attributeSelection.* The *weka.classifiers.j48* package contains the classes implementing J4.8 and the PART rule learner. They have been placed in a separate package (and hence in a separate directory) to avoid bloating the *classifiers* package. The *weka.classifiers.m5* package contains classes implementing the model tree algorithm of Section 6.5, which is called M5′.

In Chapter 4 (Section 4.5) we discussed an algorithm for mining association rules, called APRIORI. The *weka.associations* package contains two classes, Item-Set and Apriori, which together implement this algorithm. They have been placed in a separate package because association rules are fundamentally different from classifiers. The *weka.clusterers* package contains an implementation of two methods for unsupervised learning: COBWEB and the EM algorithm (Section 6.6). The *weka.estimators* package contains subclasses of a generic Estimator class, which computes different types of probability distribution. These subclasses are used by the Naive Bayes algorithm.

Along with actual learning schemes, tools for preprocessing a dataset, which we call *filters,* are an important component of Weka. In *weka.filters,* the Filter class is the analog of the Classifier class described above. It defines the general structure of all classes containing filter algorithms—they are all implemented as subclasses of `Filter`. Like classifiers, filters can be used from the command line; we will see later how this is done. It is easy to identify classes that implement filter algorithms: their names end in *Filter*.

Attribute selection is an important technique for reducing the dimensionality of a dataset. The *weka.attributeSelection* package contains several classes for doing this. These classes are used by the `AttributeSelectionFilter` from *weka.filters*, but they can also be used separately.

Indexes

As mentioned above, all classes are automatically subclasses of `Object`. This makes it possible to construct a tree corresponding to the hierarchy of all classes in Weka. You can examine this tree by selecting the *Class Hierarchy* hyperlink from the top of any page of the online documentation. This shows very concisely which classes are subclasses or superclasses of a particular class—for example, which classes inherit from `Classifier`.

The online documentation contains an index of all publicly accessible variables (called *fields*) and methods in Weka—in other words, all fields and methods that you can access from your own Java code. To view it, click on the *Index* hyperlink located at the top of every documentation page.

8.3 Processing datasets using the machine learning programs

We have seen how to use the online documentation to find out which learning methods and other tools are provided in the Weka system. Now we show how to use these algorithms from the command line, and then discuss them in more detail.

Using M5´

Section 8.1 explained how to interpret the output of a decision tree learner and showed the performance figures that are automatically generated by the evaluation module. The interpretation of these is the same for all models that predict a categorical class. However, when evaluating models for numeric prediction, Weka produces a different set of performance measures.

As an example, suppose you have a copy of the CPU performance dataset from Table 1.5 of Chapter 1 named *cpu.arff* in the current directory. Figure 8.5 shows the output obtained if you run the model tree inducer M5´ on it by typing

```
java weka.classifiers.m5.M5Prime -t cpu.arff
```

```
Pruned training model tree:

MMAX <= 14000 : LM1 (141/4.18%)
MMAX >  14000 : LM2 (68/51.8%)

Models at the leaves (smoothed):

  LM1:  class = 4.15
               - 2.05vendor=honeywell,ipl,ibm,cdc,ncr,basf,
                   gould,siemens,nas,adviser,sperry,amdahl
               + 5.43vendor=adviser,sperry,amdahl
               - 5.78vendor=amdahl + 0.00638MYCT
               + 0.00158MMIN + 0.00345MMAX
               + 0.552CACH + 1.14CHMIN + 0.0945CHMAX
  LM2:  class = -113
               - 56.1vendor=honeywell,ipl,ibm,cdc,ncr,basf,
                   gould,siemens,nas,adviser,sperry,amdahl
               + 10.2vendor=adviser,sperry,amdahl
               - 10.9vendor=amdahl
               + 0.012MYCT + 0.0145MMIN + 0.0089MMAX
               + 0.808CACH + 1.29CHMAX

=== Error on training data ===

Correlation coefficient                0.9853
Mean absolute error                   13.4072
Root mean squared error               26.3977
Relative absolute error               15.3431 %
Root relative squared error           17.0985 %
Total Number of Instances            209

=== Cross-validation ===

Correlation coefficient                0.9767
Mean absolute error                   13.1239
Root mean squared error               33.4455
Relative absolute error               14.9884 %
Root relative squared error           21.6147 %
Total Number of Instances            209
```

Figure 8.5 Output from the M5′ program for numeric prediction.

and pressing *Return*. The structure of the pruned model tree is surprisingly simple. It is a decision stump, a binary 1-level decision tree, with a split on the MMAX attribute. Attached to that stump are two linear models, one for each leaf. Both involve one nominal attribute, called vendor. The expression vendor=adviser, sperry,amdahl is interpreted as follows: if vendor is either adviser, sperry, or amdahl, then substitute 1, otherwise 0.

The description of the model tree is followed by several figures that measure its performance. As with decision tree output, the first set is derived from the training data and the second uses tenfold cross-validation (this time not stratified, of course, because that doesn't make sense for numeric prediction). The meaning of the different measures is explained in Section 5.8.

Generic options

In the examples above, the -t option was used to communicate the name of the training file to the learning algorithm. There are several other options that can be used with any learning scheme, and also scheme-specific ones that apply only to particular schemes. If you invoke a scheme without any command-line options at all, it displays all options that can be used. First the general options are listed, then the scheme-specific ones. Try, for example,

```
java weka.classifiers.j48.J48
```

You'll see a listing of the options common to all learning schemes, shown in Table 8.1, followed by a list of those that just apply to J48, shown in Table 8.2. We will explain the generic options and then briefly review the scheme-specific ones.

The options in Table 8.1 determine which data is used for training and testing, how the classifier is evaluated, and what kind of statistics are displayed. You might want to use an independent test set instead of performing a cross-validation on the training data to evaluate a learning scheme. The -T option allows just that: if you provide the name of a file, the data in it is used to derive performance statistics, instead of cross-validation. Sometimes the class is not the last attribute in an ARFF file: you can declare that another one is the class using -c. This option requires you to specify the position of the desired attribute in the file, 1 for the first attribute, 2 for the second, and so on. When tenfold cross-validation is performed (the default if a test file is not provided), the data is randomly shuffled first. If you want to repeat the cross-validation several times, each time reshuffling the data in a different way, you can set the random number seed with -s (default value 1). With a large dataset you may want to reduce the number of folds for the cross-validation from the default value of 10 using -x.

Weka also implements cost-sensitive classification. If you provide the name of a file containing a cost matrix using the -m option, the dataset will be

Table 8.1	Generic options for learning schemes in Weka.
option	function
-t <training file>	Specify training file
-T <test file>	Specify test file. If none, a cross-validation is performed on the training data
-c <class index>	Specify index of class attribute
-x <number of folds>	Specify number of folds for cross-validation
-s <random number seed>	Specify random number seed for cross-validation
-m <cost matrix file>	Specify file containing cost matrix
-v	Output no statistics for training data
-l <input file>	Specify input file for model
-d <output file>	Specify output file for model
-o	Output statistics only, not the classifier
-i	Output information retrieval statistics for two-class problems
-k	Output information-theoretic statistics
-p	Only output predictions for test instances
-r	Only output cumulative margin distribution

reweighted (or resampled, depending on the learning scheme) according to the information in this file. Here is a cost matrix for the weather data above:

```
0 1 10 % If true class yes and prediction no, penalty is 10
1 0 1  % If true class no and prediction yes, penalty is 1
```

Each line must contain three numbers: the index of the true class, the index of the incorrectly assigned class, and the penalty, which is the amount by which that particular error will be weighted (the penalty must be a positive number). Not all combinations of actual and predicted classes need be listed: the default penalty is 1. (In all Weka input files, comments introduced by % can be appended to the end of any line.)

To illustrate cost-sensitive classification, let's apply J4.8 to the weather data, with a heavy penalty if the learning scheme predicts no when the true class is yes. Save the cost matrix above in a file called *costs* in the same directory as *weather.arff*. Assuming that you want the cross-validation performance only, not the error on the training data, enter

```
java weka.classifiers.j48.J48 -t weather.arff -m costs -v
```

```
J48 pruned tree
————

: yes (14.0/0.74)

Number of Rules   :        1
Size of the tree :        1

=== Confusion Matrix ===

 a b    <-- classified as
 9 0  | a = yes
 5 0  | b = no


=== Stratified cross-validation ===

Correctly Classified Instances          9              64.2857 %
Incorrectly Classified Instances        5              35.7143 %
Correctly Classified With Cost         90              94.7368 %
Incorrectly Classified With Cost        5               5.2632 %
Mean absolute error                  0.3751
Root mean squared error              0.5714
Total Number of Instances              14
Total Number With Cost                 95

=== Confusion Matrix ===

 a b    <-- classified as
 9 0  | a = yes
 5 0  | b = no
```

Figure 8.6 Output from J4.8 with cost-sensitive classification.

The output, shown in Figure 8.6, is quite different from that given earlier in Figure 8.2. To begin with, the decision tree has been reduced to its root! Also, four new performance measures are included, each one ending in With Cost. These are calculated by weighting the instances according to the weights given in the cost matrix. As you can see, the learner has decided that it's best to always predict yes in this situation—which is not surprising, given the heavy penalty for erroneously predicting no.

Returning to Table 8.1, it is also possible to save and load models. If you provide the name of an output file using –d, Weka will save the classifier generated from the training data into this file. If you want to evaluate the same classifier on a new batch of test instances, you can load it back using –l instead of rebuilding it. If the classifier can be updated incrementally (and you can determine this by checking whether it implements the UpdateableClassifier interface), you can provide both a training file and an input file, and Weka will load the classifier and update it with the given training instances.

If you only wish to assess the performance of a learning scheme and are not interested in the model itself, use –o to suppress output of the model. To see the information-retrieval performance measures of precision, recall, and the F-measure that were introduced in Section 5.7, use –i (note that these can only be calculated for two-class datasets). Information-theoretic measures computed from the probabilities derived by a learning scheme—such as the informational loss function discussed in Section 5.6—can be obtained with –k.

Users often want to know which class values the learning scheme actually predicts for each test instance. The –p option, which only applies if you provide a test file, prints the number of each test instance, its class, the confidence of the scheme's prediction, and the predicted class value. Finally, you can output the cumulative margin distribution for the training data. This allows you to investigate how the distribution of the margin measure from Section 7.4 (in the subsection *Boosting*) changes with the number of iterations performed when boosting a learning scheme.

Scheme-specific options

Table 8.2 shows the options specific to J4.8. You can force the algorithm to use the unpruned tree instead of the pruned one. You can suppress subtree raising, which results in a more efficient algorithm. You can set the confidence threshold for the pruning procedure, and the minimum number of instances permissible at any leaf—both parameters were discussed in Section 6.1 (p. 169). In addition

Table 8.2	Scheme-specific options for the J4.8 decision tree learner.
option	function
–U	Use unpruned tree
–C <pruning confidence>	Specify confidence threshold for pruning
–M <number of instances>	Specify minimum number of instances in a leaf
–R	Use reduced-error pruning
–N <number of folds>	Specify number of folds for reduced error pruning. One fold is used as pruning set
–B	Use binary splits only
	Don't perform subtree raising

to C4.5's standard pruning procedure, reduced-error pruning (Section 6.2) can be performed, which prunes the decision tree to optimize performance on a holdout set. The -N option governs how large this set is: the dataset is divided equally into that number of parts, and the last is used as the holdout set (default value 3). Finally, to build a binary tree instead of one with multiway branches for nominal attributes, use -B.

Classifiers

J4.8 is just one of many practical learning schemes that you can apply to your dataset. Table 8.3 lists them all, giving the name of the class implementing the scheme along with its most important scheme-specific options and their effects. It also indicates whether the scheme can handle weighted instances (W column), whether it can output a class distribution for datasets with a categorical class (D column), and whether it can be updated incrementally (I column). Table 8.3 omits a few other schemes designed mainly for pedagogical purposes that implement some of the basic methods covered in Chapter 4—a rudimentary implementation of Naive Bayes, a divide-and-conquer decision tree algorithm (ID3), a covering algorithm for generating rules (PRISM), and a nearest-neighbor instance-based learner (IB1); we will say something about these in Section 8.5 when we explain how to write new machine learning schemes. Of course, Weka is a growing system: other learning algorithms will be added in due course, and the online documentation must be consulted for a definitive list.

The most primitive of the schemes in Table 8.3 is called ZeroR: it simply predicts the majority class in the training data if the class is categorical and the average class value if it is numeric. Although it makes little sense to use this scheme for prediction, it can be useful for determining a baseline performance as a benchmark for other learning schemes. (Sometimes other schemes actually perform worse than ZeroR: this indicates serious overfitting.)

Ascending the complexity ladder, the next learning scheme is OneR, discussed in Section 4.1, which produces simple rules based on one attribute only. It takes a single parameter: the minimum number of instances that must be covered by each rule that is generated (default value 6).

NaiveBayes implements the probabilistic Naive Bayesian classifier from Section 4.2. By default it uses the normal distribution to model numeric attributes; however, the -K option instructs it to use kernel density estimators instead. This can improve performance if the normality assumption is grossly incorrect.

The next scheme in Table 8.3, DecisionTable, produces a decision table using the wrapper method of Section 7.1 to find a good subset of attributes for inclusion in the table. This is done using a best-first search. The number of non-improving attribute subsets that are investigated before the search terminates can be controlled using -S (default value 5). The number of cross-validation folds

Table 8.3   The learning schemes in Weka.

scheme	book section	class	W	D	I	option	function
Majority/average predictor		weka.classifiers.ZeroR	y	y	n	None	
1R	4.1	weka.classifiers.OneR	n	n	n	-B <>	Specify minimum bucket size
Naive Bayes	4.2	weka.classifiers.NaiveBayes	y	y	n	-K	Use kernel density estimator
Decision table	3.1	weka.classifiers.DecisionTable	y	y	n	-X <>	Specify number of folds for cross-validation
						-S <>	Specify threshold for stopping search
Instance-based learner	4.7	weka.classifiers.IBk	y	y	y	-I	Use nearest-neighbor classifier
						-D	Weight by inverse of distance
						-F	Weight by 1-distance
						-K <>	Specify number of neighbors
						-W <>	Specify window size
						-X	Use cross-validation
C4.5	6.1	weka.classifiers.j48.J48	y	y	n	Table 8.2	Already discussed
PART rule learner	6.2	weka.classifiers.j48.PART	y	y	n	Table 8.2	As for J4.8, except that $-U$ and $-S$ are not available
Support vector machine	6.3	weka.classifiers.SMO	n	y	n	-C <>	Specify upper bound for weights
						-E <>	Specify degree of polynomials
						-S <>	Specify attribute selection method
Linear regression	4.6	weka.classifiers.LinearRegression	y	–	n	-S <>	Specify attribute selection method
M5' model tree learner	6.5	weka.classifiers.m5.M5Prime	n	–	n	-O <>	Specify type of model
						-U	Use unsmoothed tree
						-F <>	Specify pruning factor
						-V <>	Specify verbosity of output
Locally weighted regression	6.5	weka.classifiers.LWR	y	–	y	-K <>	Specify number of neighbors
						-W <>	Specify kernel shape
One-level decision trees	7.4	weka.classifiers.DecisionStump	y	y	n	None	

performed by the wrapper can be changed using -X (default: leave-one-out). Usually, a decision table assigns the majority class from the training data to a test instance if it does not match any entry in the table. However, if you specify the -I option, the nearest match will be used instead. This often improves performance significantly.

IBk is an implementation of the k-nearest-neighbors classifier that employs the distance metric discussed in Section 4.7. By default it uses just one nearest neighbor ($k = 1$), but the number can be specified manually with -K or determined automatically using leave-one-out cross-validation. The -X option instructs IBk to use cross-validation to determine the best value of k between 1 and the number given by -K. If more than one neighbor is selected, the predictions of the neighbors can be weighted according to their distance to the test instance, and two different formulas are implemented for deriving the weight from the distance (-D and -F). The time taken to classify a test instance with a nearest-neighbor classifier increases linearly with the number of training instances. Consequently it is sometimes necessary to restrict the number of training instances that are kept in the classifier, which is done by setting the window size option.

We have already discussed the options for J4.8; those for PART, which forms rules from pruned partial decision trees built using C4.5's heuristics as described near the end of Section 6.2 (page 181), are a subset of these. Just as reduced-error pruning can reduce the size of a J4.8 decision tree, it can also reduce the number of rules produced by PART—with the side effect of decreasing run time because complexity depends on the number of rules that are generated. However, reduced-error pruning often reduces the accuracy of the resulting decision trees and rules because it reduces the amount of data that can be used for training. With large enough datasets, this disadvantage vanishes.

In Section 6.3 we introduced support vector machines. The SMO class implements the *sequential minimal optimization* algorithm, which learns this type of classifier. Despite being one of the fastest methods for learning support vector machines, sequential minimal optimization is often slow to converge to a solution—particularly when the data is not linearly separable in the space spanned by the nonlinear mapping. Because of noise, this often happens. Both run time and accuracy depend critically on the values that are given to two parameters: the upper bound on the coefficients' values in the equation for the hyperplane (-C), and the degree of the polynomials in the non-linear mapping (-E). Both are set to 1 by default. The best settings for a particular dataset can be found only by experimentation.

The next three learning schemes in Table 8.3 are for numeric prediction. The simplest is linear regression, whose only parameter controls how attributes to be included in the linear function are selected. By default, the heuristic employed by the model tree inducer M5′ is used, whose run time is linear in the number of attributes. However, it is possible to suppress all attribute selection by setting -s to 1, and to use greedy forward selection, whose run time is quadratic in the number of attributes, by setting -s to 2.

The class that implements M5′ has already been described in the example on page 277. It implements the algorithm explained in Section 6.5 except that a simpler method is used to deal with missing values: they are replaced by the global mean or mode of the training data before the model tree is built. Several different forms of model output are provided, controlled by the -o option: a model tree (-o m), a regression tree without linear models at the leaves (-o r), and a simple linear regression (-o l). The automatic smoothing procedure described in Section 6.5 can be disabled using -U. The amount of pruning that this algorithm performs can be controlled by setting the pruning factor to a value between 0 and 10. Finally, the verbosity of the output can be set to a value from 0 to 3.

Locally weighted regression, the second scheme for numeric prediction described in Section 6.5, is implemented by the LWR class. Its performance depends critically on the correct choice of kernel width, which is determined by calculating the distance of the test instance to its kth nearest neighbor. The value of k can be specified using -K. Another factor that influences performance is the shape of the kernel: choices are 0 for a linear kernel (the default), 1 for an inverse one, and 2 for the classic Gaussian kernel.

The final scheme in Table 8.3, DecisionStump, builds binary decision stumps—one-level decision trees—for datasets with either a categorical or a numeric class. It copes with missing values by extending a third branch from the stump, in other words, by treating missing as a separate attribute value. It is designed for use with the boosting methods discussed later in this section.

Meta-learning schemes

Chapter 7 described methods for enhancing the performance and extending the capabilities of learning schemes. We call these *meta-learning schemes* because they incorporate other learners. Like ordinary learning schemes, meta learners belong to the *classifiers* package: they are summarized in Table 8.4.

The first is an implementation of the bagging procedure discussed in Section 7.4. You can specify the number of bagging iterations to be performed (default value 10) and the random number seed for resampling. The name of the learning scheme to be bagged is declared using the -W option. Here is the beginning of a command line for bagging unpruned J4.8 decision trees:

```
java weka.classifiers.bagging -W weka.classifiers.j48.J48...-- -U
```

There are two lists of options, those intended for bagging and those for the base learner itself, and a double minus sign (--) is used to separate the lists. Thus the

Table 8.4	The meta-learning schemes in Weka.	
scheme	option	function
weka.classifiers.Bagging	-I <>	Specify number of iterations
	-W <>	Specify base learner
	-S <>	Specify random number seed
weka.classifiers.AdaBoostM1	-I <>	Specify number of iterations
	-P <>	Specify weight mass to be used
	-W <>	Specify base learner
	-Q	Use resampling
	-S <>	Specify random number seed
weka.classifiers.LogitBoost	-I <>	Specify number of iterations
	-P <>	Specify weight mass to be used
	-W <>	Specify base learner
weka.classifiers. MultiClassClassifier	-W <>	Specify base learner
weka.classifiers. CVParameterSelection	-W <>	Specify base learner
	-P <>	Specify option to be optimized
	-X <>	Specify number of cross-validation folds
	-S <>	Specify random number seed
weka.classifiers. Stacking	-B <>	Specify level-0 learner and options
	-M <>	Specify level-1 learner and options
	-X <>	Specify number of cross-validation folds
	-S <>	Specify random number seed

–U in the above command line is directed to the J48 program, where it will cause the use of unpruned trees (see Table 8.2). This convention avoids the problem of conflict between option letters for the meta learner and those for the base learner.

AdaBoost.M1, also discussed in Section 7.4, is handled in the same way as bagging. However, there are two additional options. First, if –Q is used, boosting with resampling will be performed instead of boosting with reweighting. Second, the –P option can be used to accelerate the learning process: in each iteration only the percentage of the weight mass specified by –P is passed to the base learner, instances being sorted according to their weight. This means that the base learner has to process fewer instances because often most of the weight is concentrated on a fairly small subset, and experience shows that the consequent reduction in classification accuracy is usually negligible.

Another boosting procedure is implemented by LogitBoost. A detailed discussion of this method is beyond the scope of this book; suffice to say that it is based on the concept of additive logistic regression (Friedman et al. 1998). In contrast to AdaBoost.M1, LogitBoost can successfully boost very simple learning schemes, (like DecisionStump, that was introduced above), even in multiclass situations. From a user's point of view, it differs from AdaBoost.M1 in an important way because it boosts schemes for numeric prediction in order to form a combined classifier that predicts a categorical class.

Weka also includes an implementation of a meta learner which performs stacking, as explained in Chapter 7 (Section 7.4). In stacking, the result of a set of different level-0 learners is combined by a level-1 learner. Each level-0 learner must be specified using -B, followed by any relevant options—and the entire specification of the level-0 learner, including the options, must be enclosed in double quotes. The level-1 learner is specified in the same way, using -M. Here is an example:

```
java weka.classifiers.Stacking -B "weka.classifiers.j48.J48 -U"
   -B "weka.classifiers.IBk -K 5" -M "weka.classifiers.j48.J48" ...
```

By default, tenfold cross-validation is used; this can be changed with the -X option.

Some learning schemes can only be used in two-class situations—for example, the SMO class described above. To apply such schemes to multiclass datasets, the problem must be transformed into several two-class ones and the results combined. MultiClassClassifier does exactly that: it takes a base learner that can output a class distribution or a numeric class, and applies it to a multiclass learning problem using the simple one-per-class coding introduced in Section 4.6 (p. 114).

Often, the best performance on a particular dataset can only be achieved by tedious parameter tuning. Weka includes a meta learner that performs optimization automatically using cross-validation. The -W option of CVParameterSelection takes the name of a base learner, and the -P option specifies one parameter in the format

```
"<option name> <starting value> <last value> <number of steps>"
```

An example is:

```
java...CVParameterSelection -W...OneR -P "B 1 10 10" -t
   weather.arff
```

which evaluates integer values between 1 and 10 for the B parameter of 1R. Multiple parameters can be specified using several -P options.

CVParameterSelection causes the space of all possible combinations of the given parameters to be searched exhaustively. The parameter set with the best cross-validation performance is chosen, and this is used to build a classifier from the full training set. The -x option allows you to specify the number of folds (default 10).

Suppose you are unsure of the capabilities of a particular classifier—for example, you might want to know whether it can handle weighted instances. The `weka.classifiers.CheckClassifier` tool prints a summary of any classifier's properties. For example,

```
java weka.classifiers.CheckClassifier -W weka.classifiers.IBk
```

prints a summary of the properties of the IBk class discussed above.

In Section 7.4 we discussed the bias-variance decomposition of a learning algorithm. Weka includes an algorithm that estimates the bias and variance of a particular learning scheme with respect to a given dataset. BVDecompose takes the name of a learning scheme and a training file and performs a bias-variance decomposition. It provides options for setting the index of the class attribute, the number of iterations to be performed, and the random number seed. The more iterations that are performed, the better the estimate.

Filters

Having discussed the learning schemes in the *classifiers* package, we now turn to the next important package for command-line use, *filters*. We begin by examining a simple filter that can be used to delete specified attributes from a dataset, in other words, to perform manual attribute selection. The following command line

```
java weka.filters.AttributeFilter -R 1,2 -i weather.arff
```

yields the output in Figure 8.7. As you can see, attributes 1 and 2, namely outlook and temperature, have been deleted. Note that no spaces are allowed in the

```
@relation weather-weka.filters.AttributeFilter-R1_2

@attribute humidity real
@attribute windy {TRUE,FALSE}
@attribute play {yes,no}

@data

85,FALSE,no
90,TRUE,no
...
```

Figure 8.7 Effect of `AttributeFilter` on the weather dataset.

Table 8.5   The filter algorithms in Weka.

filter	option	function
weka.filters.AddFilter	-C <>	Specify index of new attribute
	-L <>	Specify labels for nominal attribute
	-N <>	Specify name of new attribute
weka.filters. AttributeSelectionFilter	-E <>	Specify evaluation class
	-S <>	Specify search class
	-T <>	Set threshold by which to discard attributes
weka.filters.AttributeFilter	-R <>	Specify attributes to be deleted
	-V	Invert matching sense
weka.filters.DiscretizeFilter	-B <>	Specify number of bins
	-O	Optimize number of bins
	-R <>	Specify attributes to be discretized
	-V	Invert matching sense
	-D	Output binary attributes
weka.filter.MakeIndicatorFilter	-C <>	Specify attribute index
	-V <>	Specify value index
	-N	Output nominal attribute
weka.filter.MergeTwoValuesFilter	-C <>	Specify attribute index
	-F <>	Specify first value index
	-S <>	Specify second value index

list of attribute indices. The resulting dataset can be placed in the file *weather.new.arff* by typing:

```
java...AttributeFilter -R 1,2 -i weather.arff -o weather.new.arff
```

All filters in Weka are used in the same way. They take an input file specified using the -i option and an optional output file specified with -o. A class index can be specified using -c. Filters read the ARFF file, transform it, and write it out. (If files are not specified, they read from standard input and write to standard output, so that they can be used as a "pipe" in Unix systems.) All filter algorithms provide a list of available options in response to -h, as in

```
java weka.filters.AttributeFilter -h
```

Table 8.5 lists the filters implemented in Weka, along with their principal options.

The first, AddFilter, inserts an attribute at the given position. For all instances in the dataset, the new attribute's value is declared to be missing. If a

Table 8.5	The filter algorithms in Weka. (continued)	
filter	option	function
weka.filters. NominalToBinaryFilter	-N	Output nominal attributes
weka.filters. ReplaceMissingValuesFilter		
weka.filters.InstanceFilter	-C <>	Specify attribute index
	-S <>	Specify numeric value
	-L <>	Specify nominal values
	-V	Invert matching sense
weka.filters. SwapAttributeValuesFilter	-C <>	Specify attribute index
	-F <>	Specify first value index
	-S <>	Specify second value index
weka.filters. NumericTransformFilter	-R <>	Specify attributes to be transformed
	-V	Invert matching sense
	-C <>	Specify Java class
	-M <>	Specify transformation method
weka.filters. SplitDatasetFilter	-R <>	Specify range of instances to be split
	-V	Invert matching sense
	-N <>	Specify number of folds
	-F <>	Specify fold to be returned
	-S <>	Specify random number seed

list of comma-separated nominal values is given using the -L option, the new attribute will be a nominal one, otherwise it will be numeric. The attribute's name can be set with -N.

AttributeSelectionFilter allows you to select a set of attributes using different methods: since it is rather complex we will leave it to last.

AttributeFilter has already been used above. However, there is a further option: if -V is used the matching set is inverted—that is, only attributes *not* included in the -R specification are deleted.

An important filter for practical applications is DiscretizeFilter. It contains an unsupervised and a supervised discretization method, both discussed in Section 7.2. The former implements equal-width binning, and the number of bins can be set manually using -B. However, if -O is present, the number of bins will be chosen automatically using a cross-validation procedure that maximizes the estimated likelihood of the data. In that case, -B gives an upper bound to the possible number of bins. If the index of a class attribute is specified using -C, supervised discretization will be performed using the MDL method of Fayyad and Irani (1993). Usually, discretization loses the ordering implied by the original numeric attribute when it is transformed into a nominal one. However, this information is preserved if the discretized attribute with k values is transformed into k-1 binary attributes. The -D option does this automatically by producing one binary attribute for each split point (described in Section 7.2 [p. 239]).

MakeIndicatorFilter is used to convert a nominal attribute into a binary indicator attribute and can be used to transform a multiclass dataset into several two-class ones. The filter substitutes a binary attribute for the chosen nominal one, setting the corresponding value for each instance to 1 if a particular original value was present and to 0 otherwise. Both the attribute to be transformed and the original nominal value are set by the user. By default the new attribute is declared to be numeric, but if -N is given it will be nominal.

Suppose you want to merge two values of a nominal attribute into a single category. This is done by MergeAttributeValuesFilter. The name of the new value is a concatenation of the two original ones, and every occurrence of either of the original values is replaced by the new one. The index of the new value is the smaller of the original indexes.

Some learning schemes, like support vector machines, can handle only binary attributes. The advantage of binary attributes is that they can be treated as either nominal or numeric. NominalToBinaryFilter transforms all multivalued nominal attributes in a dataset into binary ones, replacing each attribute with k values by $k-1$ binary attributes. If a class is specified using the -c option, it is left untouched. The transformation used for the other attributes depends on whether the class is numeric. If the class is numeric, the M5′ transformation method is employed for each attribute; otherwise a simple one-per-value encoding is used. If the -N option is used, all new attributes will be nominal, otherwise they will be numeric.

One way of dealing with missing values is to replace them globally before applying a learning scheme. ReplaceMissingValuesFilter substitutes the mean, for numeric attributes, or the mode, for nominal ones, for each occurrence of a missing value.

To remove from a dataset all instances that have certain values for nominal attributes, or numeric values above or below a certain threshold, use Instance-Filter. By default all instances are deleted that exhibit one of a given set of nominal attribute values (if the specified attribute is nominal), or a numeric value below a given threshold (if it is numeric). However, the matching criterion can be inverted using -V.

The SwapAttributeValuesFilter is a simple one: all it does is swap the positions of two values of a nominal attribute. Of course, this could also be accomplished by editing the ARFF file in a word processor. The order of attribute values is entirely cosmetic: it does not affect machine learning at all. If the selected attribute is the class, changing the order affects the layout of the confusion matrix.

In some applications it is necessary to transform a numeric attribute before a learning scheme is applied—for example, replacing each value with its square root. This is done using `NumericTransformFilter`, which transforms all of the selected numeric attributes using a given function. The transformation can be any Java function that takes a `double` as its argument and returns another `double`, for example, `sqrt()` in `java.lang.Math`. The name of the class that implements the function (which must be a fully qualified name) is set using –c, and the name of the transformation method is set using –M: thus to take the square root use:

```
java weka.filters.NumericTransformFilter -C java.lang.Math -M sqrt...
```

Weka also includes a filter with which you can generate subsets of a dataset, `SplitDatasetFilter`. You can either supply a range of instances to be selected using the –R option, or generate a random subsample whose size is determined by the –N option. The dataset is split into the given number of folds, and one of them (indicated by –F) is returned. If a random number seed is provided (with –S), the dataset will be shuffled before the subset is extracted. Moreover, if a class attribute is set using –c the dataset will be stratified, so that the class distribution in the subsample is approximately the same as in the full dataset.

It is often necessary to apply a filter algorithm to a training dataset and then, using settings derived from the training data, apply the same filter to a test file. Consider a filter that discretizes numeric attributes. If the discretization method is supervised—that is, if it uses the class values to derive good intervals for the discretization—the results will be biased if it is applied directly to the test data. It is the discretization intervals derived from the *training* data that must be applied to the test data. More generally, the filter algorithm must optimize its internal settings according to the training data and apply these same settings to the test data. This can be done in a uniform way with all filters by adding –b as a command-line option and providing the name of input and output files for the test data using –r and –s respectively. Then the filter class will derive its internal settings using the training data provided by –i and use these settings to transform the test data.

Finally, we return to `AttributeSelectionFilter`. This lets you select a set of attributes using attribute selection classes in the `weka.attributeSelection` package. The –c option sets the class index for supervised attribute selection. With –E you provide the name of an evaluation class from `weka.attributeSe-lection` that determines how the filter evaluates attributes, or sets of attributes; in addition you may need to use –S to specify a search technique. Each feature evaluator, subset evaluator, and search method has its own options. They can be printed with –h.

There are two types of evaluators that you can specify with –E: ones that consider one attribute at a time, and ones that consider sets of attributes together. The former are subclasses of weka.attributeSelection.AttributeEvaluator— an example is weka.attributeSelection.InfoGainAttributeEval, which evaluates attributes according to their information gain. The latter are subclasses of weka.attributeSelection.SubsetEvaluator—like weka.attributeSelection. CfsSubsetEval, which evaluates subsets of features by the correlation among them. If you give the name of a subclass of AttributeEvaluator, you must also provide, using –T, a threshold by which the filter can discard low-scoring attributes. On the other hand, if you give the name of a subclass of SubsetEvaluator, you must provide the name of a search class using –S, which is used to search through possible subsets of attributes. Any subclass of weka.attribute-Selection.ASSearch can be used for this option—for example weka.attribute-Selection.BestFirst, which implements a best-first search.

Here is an example showing AttributeSelectionFilter being used with correlation-based subset evaluation and best-first search for the weather data:

```
java weka.filters.AttributeSelectionFilter
    -S weka.attributeSelection.BestFirst
    -E weka.attributeSelection.CfsSubsetEval
    -i weather.arff -c5
```

To provide options for the evaluator, you must enclose both the name of the evaluator and its options in double quotes (e.g., –S "<evaluator> <options>"). Options for the search class can be specified in the same way.

Association rules

Weka includes an implementation of the APRIORI algorithm for generating association rules: the class for this is weka.associations.Apriori. To see what it does, try

```
java weka.associations.Apriori -t weather.nominal.arff
```

where weather.nominal.arff is the nominal version of the weather data from Section 1.2. (The APRIORI algorithm can only deal with nominal attributes.)

The output is shown in Figure 8.8. The last part gives the association rules that are found. The number preceding the ==> symbol indicates the rule's support, that is, the number of items covered by its premise. Following the rule is the number of those items for which the rule's consequent holds as well. In parentheses is the confidence of the rule—in other words, the second figure divided by the first. In this simple example, the confidence is 1 for every rule. APRIORI orders rules according to their confidence and uses support as a tiebreaker. Preceding the rules are the numbers of item sets found for each sup-

```
Apriori
=======

Minimum support: 0.2
Minimum confidence: 0.9
Number of cycles performed: 17

Generated sets of large itemsets:

Size of set of large itemsets L(1): 12
Size of set of large itemsets L(2): 47
Size of set of large itemsets L(3): 39
Size of set of large itemsets L(4): 6

Best rules found:

1 . humidity=normal windy=FALSE 4 ==> play=yes 4 (1)
2 . temperature=cool 4 ==> humidity=normal 4 (1)
3 . outlook=overcast 4 ==> play=yes 4 (1)
4 . temperature=cool play=yes 3 ==> humidity=normal 3 (1)
5 . outlook=rainy windy=FALSE 3 ==> play=yes 3 (1)
6 . outlook=rainy play=yes 3 ==> windy=FALSE 3 (1)
7 . outlook=sunny humidity=high 3 ==> play=no 3 (1)
8 . outlook=sunny play=no 3 ==> humidity=high 3 (1)
9 . temperature=cool windy=FALSE 2 ==> humidity=normal play=yes 2 (1)
10. temperature=cool humidity=normal windy=FALSE 2 ==> play=yes 2 (1)
```

Figure 8.8 Output from the APRIORI association rule learner.

port size considered. In this case six item sets of four items were found to have the required minimum support.

By default, APRIORI tries to generate ten rules. It begins with a minimum support of 100% of the data items and decreases this in steps of 5% until there are at least ten rules with the required minimum confidence, or until the support has reached a lower bound of 10%, whichever occurs first. The minimum confidence is set to 0.9 by default. As you can see from the beginning of Figure 8.8, the minimum support decreased to 0.2, or 20%, before the required number of rules could be generated; this involved a total of 17 iterations.

All of these parameters can be changed by setting the corresponding options. As with other learning algorithms, if the program is invoked without any command-line arguments, all applicable options are listed. The principal ones are summarized in Table 8.6.

Table 8.6	Principal options for the APRIORI association rule learner.

option	function
-t <training file>	Specify training file
-N <required number of rules>	Specify required number of rules
-C <minimum confidence of a rule>	Specify minimum confidence of a rule
-D <delta for minimum support>	Specify delta for decrease of minimum support
-M <lower bound for minimum support>	Specify lower bound for minimum support

Clustering

Weka includes a package that contains clustering algorithms, *weka.clusterers*. These operate in a similar way to the classification methods in *weka.classifiers*. The command-line options are again split into generic and scheme-specific options. The generic ones, summarized in Table 8.7, are just the same as for classifiers except that a cross-validation is not performed by default if the test file is missing.

It may seem strange that there is an option for providing test data. However, if clustering is accomplished by modeling the distribution of instances probabilistically, it is possible to check how well the model fits the data by computing the likelihood of a set of test data given the model. Weka measures goodness-of-fit by the logarithm of the likelihood, or log-likelihood: and the larger this quantity, the better the model fits the data. Instead of using a single test set, it is also possible to compute a cross-validation estimate of the log-likelihood using –x.

Weka also outputs how many instances are assigned to each cluster. For clustering algorithms that do not model the instance distribution probabilistically, these are the only statistics that Weka outputs. It's easy to find out which clusterers generate a probability distribution: they are subclasses of weka.clusterers.DistributionClusterer.

Table 8.7	Generic options for clustering schemes in Weka.

option	function
-t <training file>	Specify training file
-T <test file>	Specify test file
-x <number of folds>	Specify number of folds for cross-validation
-s <random number seed>	Specify random number seed for cross-validation
-l <input file>	Specify input file for model
-d <output file>	Specify output file for model
-p	Only output predictions for test instances

There are two clustering algorithms in *weka.clusterers:* `weka.clusterers.EM` and `weka.clusterers.Cobweb`. The former is an implementation of the EM algorithm and the latter implements the incremental clustering algorithm (both are described in Chapter 6, Section 6.6). They can handle both numeric and nominal attributes.

Like Naive Bayes, EM makes the assumption that the attributes are independent random variables. The command line

```
java weka.clusterers.EM -t weather.arff -N 2
```

results in the output shown in Figure 8.9. The -N options forces EM to generate two clusters. As you can see, the number of clusters is printed first, followed by a description of each one: the cluster's prior probability and a probability distribution for all attributes in the dataset. For a nominal attribute, the distribution is represented by the count associated with each value (plus one); for a numeric attribute it is a standard normal distribution. EM also outputs the number of training instances in each cluster, and the log-likelihood of the training data with respect to the clustering that it generates.

By default, EM selects the number of clusters automatically by maximizing the logarithm of the likelihood of future data, estimated using cross-validation. Beginning with one cluster, it continues to add clusters until the estimated log-likelihood decreases. However, if you have access to prior knowledge about the number of clusters in your data, it makes sense to force EM to generate the desired number of clusters. Apart from -N, EM recognizes two additional scheme-specific command-line options: -I sets the maximum number of iterations performed by the algorithm, and -s sets the random number seed used to initialize the cluster membership probabilities.

The cluster hierarchy generated by COBWEB is controlled by two parameters: the acuity and the cutoff (see Chapter 6, page 216). They can be set using the command-line options -A and -C, and are given as a percentage. COBWEB's output is very sensitive to these parameters, and it pays to spend some time experimenting with them.

8.4 Embedded machine learning

When invoking learning schemes and filter algorithms from the command line, there is no need to know anything about programming in Java. In this section we show how to access these algorithms from your own code. In doing so, the advantages of using an object-oriented programming language will become clear. From now on, we assume that you have at least some rudimentary knowledge of Java. In most practical applications of data mining, the learning component is an integrated part of a far larger software environment. If the environ-

```
EM
==

Number of clusters: 2

Cluster: 0 Prior probability: 0.2816

Attribute: outlook
Discrete Estimator. Counts =  2.96 2.98 1   (Total = 6.94)
Attribute: temperature
Normal Distribution. Mean =  82.2692 StdDev =    2.2416
Attribute: humidity
Normal Distribution. Mean =  83.9788 StdDev =    6.3642
Attribute: windy
Discrete Estimator. Counts =  1.96 3.98   (Total = 5.94)
Attribute: play
Discrete Estimator. Counts =  2.98 2.96   (Total = 5.94)

Cluster: 1 Prior probability: 0.7184

Attribute: outlook
Discrete Estimator. Counts =  4.04 3.02 6   (Total = 13.06)
Attribute: temperature
Normal Distribution. Mean =  70.1616 StdDev =    3.8093
Attribute: humidity
Normal Distribution. Mean =  80.7271 StdDev =   11.6349
Attribute: windy
Discrete Estimator. Counts =  6.04 6.02   (Total = 12.06)
Attribute: play
Discrete Estimator. Counts =  8.02 4.04   (Total = 12.06)


=== Clustering stats for training data ===

Cluster Instances
      0        4   (29 %)
      1       10   (71 %)

Log likelihood: -9.01881
```

Figure 8.9 Output from the EM clustering scheme.

ment is written in Java, you can use Weka to solve the learning problem without writing any machine learning code yourself.

A simple message classifier

We present a simple data mining application, automatic classification of email messages, to illustrate how to access classifiers and filters. Because its purpose is educational, the system has been kept as simple as possible, and it certainly doesn't perform at the state of the art. However, it will give you an idea how to use Weka in your own application. Furthermore, it is straightforward to extend the system to make it more sophisticated.

The first problem faced when trying to apply machine learning in a practical setting is selecting attributes for the data at hand. This is probably also the most important problem: if you don't choose meaningful attributes—attributes which together convey sufficient information to make learning tractable—any attempt to apply machine learning techniques is doomed to fail. In truth, the choice of a learning scheme is usually far less important than coming up with a suitable set of attributes.

In the example application, we do not aspire to optimum performance, so we use rather simplistic attributes: they count the number of times specific keywords appear in the message to be classified. We assume that each message is stored in an individual file, and the program is called every time a new message is to be processed. If the user provides a class label for the message, the system will use the message for training; if not, it will try to classify it. The instance-based classifier IBk is used for this example application.

Figure 8.10 shows the source code for the application program, implemented in a class called MessageClassifier. The main() method accepts the following command-line arguments: the name of a message file (given by -m), the name of a file holding an object of class MessageClassifier (-t) and, optionally, the classification of the message (-c). The message's class can be hit or miss. If the user provides a classification using -c, the message will be added to the training data; if not, the program will classify the message as either hit or miss.

Main()

The main() method reads the message into an array of characters and checks whether the user has provided a classification for it. It then attempts to read an existing MessageClassifier object from the file given by -t. If this file does not exist, a new object of class MessageClassifier will be created. In either case the resulting object is called messageCl. After checking for illegal command-line options, the given message is used to either update messageCl by calling the method updateModel() on it, or classify it by calling classifyMessage(). Finally, if messageCl has been updated, the object is saved back into the file. In the fol-

```
/**
 * Java program for classifying short text messages into two classes.
 */

import weka.core.*;
import weka.classifiers.*;
import weka.filters.*;
import java.io.*;
import java.util.*;

public class MessageClassifier implements Serializable {

  /* Our (rather arbitrary) set of keywords. */
  private final String[] m_Keywords = {"product", "only", "offer", "great", "amazing",
    "phantastic", "opportunity", "buy", "now"};

  /* The training data. */
  private Instances m_Data = null;

  /* The filter. */
  private Filter m_Filter = new DiscretizeFilter();

  /* The classifier. */
  private Classifier m_Classifier = new IBk();

  /**
   * Constructs empty training dataset.
   */
  public MessageClassifier() throws Exception {

    String nameOfDataset = "MessageClassificationProblem";

    // Create numeric attributes.
    FastVector attributes = new FastVector(m_Keywords.length + 1);
    for (int i = 0 ; i < m_Keywords.length; i++) {
      attributes.addElement(new Attribute(m_Keywords[i]));
    }

    // Add class attribute.
    FastVector classValues = new FastVector(2);
    classValues.addElement("miss");
    classValues.addElement("hit");
    attributes.addElement(new Attribute("Class", classValues));

    // Create dataset with initial capacity of 100, and set index of class.
    m_Data = new Instances(nameOfDataset, attributes, 100);
    m_Data.setClassIndex(m_Data.numAttributes() - 1);
  }

  /**
   * Updates model using the given training message.
   */
  public void updateModel(String message, String classValue)
    throws Exception {
```

Figure 8.10 Source code for the message classifier.

```
    // Convert message string into instance.
    Instance instance = makeInstance(cleanupString(message));

    // Add class value to instance.
    instance.setClassValue(classValue);

    // Add instance to training data.
    m_Data.add(instance);

    // Use filter.
    m_Filter.inputFormat(m_Data);
    Instances filteredData = Filter.useFilter(m_Data, m_Filter);

    // Rebuild classifier.
    m_Classifier.buildClassifier(filteredData);
  }

  /**
   * Classifies a given message.
   */
  public void classifyMessage(String message) throws Exception {

    // Check if classifier has been built.
    if (m_Data.numInstances() == 0) {
      throw new Exception("No classifier available.");
    }

    // Convert message string into instance.
    Instance instance = makeInstance(cleanupString(message));

    // Filter instance.
    m_Filter.input(instance);
    Instance filteredInstance = m_Filter.output();

    // Get index of predicted class value.
    double predicted = m_Classifier.classifyInstance(filteredInstance);

    // Classify instance.
    System.err.println("Message classified as : " +
                  m_Data.classAttribute().value((int)predicted));
  }

  /**
  * Method that converts a text message into an instance.
   */
  private Instance makeInstance(String messageText) {

    StringTokenizer tokenizer = new StringTokenizer(messageText);
    Instance instance = new Instance(m_Keywords.length + 1);
    String token;

    // Initialize counts to zero.
    for (int i = 0; i < m_Keywords.length; i++) {
```

Figure 8.10 (continued)

```
      instance.setValue(i, 0);
    }

    // Compute attribute values.
    while (tokenizer.hasMoreTokens()) {
      token = tokenizer.nextToken();
      for (int i = 0; i < m_Keywords.length; i++) {
        if (token.equals(m_Keywords[i])) {
          instance.setValue(i, instance.value(i) + 1.0);
          break;
        }
      }
    }

    // Give instance access to attribute information from the dataset.
    instance.setDataset(m_Data);

    return instance;
  }

  /**
   * Method that deletes all non-letters from a string, and lowercases it.
   */
  private String cleanupString(String messageText) {

    char[] result = new char[messageText.length()];
    int position = 0;

    for (int i = 0; i < messageText.length(); i++) {
      if (Character.isLetter(messageText.charAt(i)) ||
        Character.isWhitespace(messageText.charAt(i))) {
        result[position++] = Character.toLowerCase(messageText.charAt(i));
      }
    }
    return new String(result);
  }

  /**
   * Main method.
   */
  public static void main(String[] options) {

    MessageClassifier messageCl;
    byte[] charArray;

    try {

      // Read message file into string.
      String messageFileString = Utils.getOption('m', options);
      if (messageFileString.length() != 0) {
        FileInputStream messageFile = new FileInputStream(messageFileString);
        int numChars = messageFile.available();
```

Figure 8.10 (continued)

```
        charArray = new byte[numChars];
        messageFile.read(charArray);
        messageFile.close();
      } else {
        throw new Exception ("Name of message file not provided.");
      }

      // Check if class value is given.
      String classValue = Utils.getOption('c', options);

      // Check for model file. If existent, read it, otherwise create new
      // one.
      String modelFileString = Utils.getOption('t', options);
      if (modelFileString.length() != 0) {
        try {
          FileInputStream modelInFile = new FileInputStream(modelFileString);
          ObjectInputStream modelInObjectFile =
            new ObjectInputStream(modelInFile);
          messageCl = (MessageClassifier) modelInObjectFile.readObject();
          modelInFile.close();
        } catch (FileNotFoundException e) {
          messageCl = new MessageClassifier();
        }
      } else {
        throw new Exception ("Name of data file not provided.");
      }

      // Check if there are any options left
      Utils.checkForRemainingOptions(options);

      // Process message.
      if (classValue.length() != 0) {
        messageCl.updateModel(new String(charArray), classValue);
      } else {
        messageCl.classifyMessage(new String(charArray));
      }
    // If class has been given, updated message classifier must be saved
      if (classValue.length() != 0) {
        FileOutputStream modelOutFile =
          new FileOutputStream(modelFileString);
        ObjectOutputStream modelOutObjectFile =
          new ObjectOutputStream(modelOutFile);
        modelOutObjectFile.writeObject(messageCl);
        modelOutObjectFile.flush();
        modelOutFile.close();
      }
    } catch (Exception e) {
      e.printStackTrace();
    }
  }
}
```

Figure 8.10

lowing, we first discuss how a new MessageClassifier object is created by the constructor MessageClassifier(), and then explain how the two methods updateModel() and classifyMessage() work.

MessageClassifier()

Each time a new MessageClassifier is created, objects for holding a dataset, a filter, and a classifier are generated automatically. The only nontrivial part of the process is creating a dataset, which is done by the constructor MessageClassifier(). First the dataset's name is stored as a string. Then an Attribute object is created for each of the attributes—one for each keyword, and one for the class. These objects are stored in a dynamic array of type FastVector. (FastVector is Weka's own fast implementation of the standard Java Vector class. Vector is implemented in a way that allows parallel programs to synchronize access to them, which was very slow in early Java implementations.)

Attributes are created by invoking one of the two constructors in the class Attribute. The first takes one parameter—the attribute's name—and creates a numeric attribute. The second takes two parameters: the attribute's name and a FastVector holding the names of its values. This latter constructor generates a nominal attribute. In MessageClassifier, the attributes for the keywords are numeric, so only their names need be passed to Attribute(). The keyword itself is used to name the attribute. Only the class attribute is nominal, with two values: hit and miss. Hence, MessageClassifier() passes its name ("class") and the values—stored in a FastVector—to Attribute().

Finally, to create a dataset from this attribute information, MessageClassifier() must create an object of the class Instances from the *core* package. The constructor of Instances used by MessageClassifier() takes three arguments: the dataset's name, a FastVector containing the attributes, and an integer indicating the dataset's initial capacity. We set the initial capacity to 100; it is expanded automatically if more instances are added to the dataset. After constructing the dataset, MessageClassifier() sets the index of the class attribute to be the index of the last attribute.

UpdateModel()

Now that you know how to create an empty dataset, consider how the MessageClassifier object actually incorporates a new training message. The method updateModel() does this job. It first calls cleanupString() to delete all nonletters and non-whitespace characters from the message. Then it converts the message into a training instance by calling makeInstance(). The latter method counts the number of times each of the keywords in m_Keywords appears in the message, and stores the result in an object of the class Instance from the *core* package. The constructor of `Instance` used in `makeInstance()` sets all the instance's values to be missing, and its weight to 1. Therefore `makeInstance()` must set all attribute values other than the class to 0 before it starts to calculate keyword frequencies.

Once the message has been processed, `makeInstance()` gives the newly created instance access to the data's attribute information by passing it a reference to the dataset. In Weka, an `Instance` object does not store the type of each attribute explicitly; instead it stores a reference to a dataset with the corresponding attribute information.

Returning to `updateModel()`, once the new instance has been returned from `makeInstance()` its class value is set and it is added to the training data. In the next step a filter is applied to this data. In our application the `DiscretizeFilter` is used to discretize all numeric attributes. Because a class index has been set for the dataset, the filter automatically uses supervised discretization (otherwise equal-width discretization would be used). Before the data can be transformed, we must first inform the filter of its format. This is done by passing it a reference to the corresponding input dataset via `inputFormat()`. Every time this method is called, the filter is initialized—that is, all its internal settings are reset. In the next step, the data is transformed by `useFilter()`. This generic method from the `Filter` class applies a given filter to a given dataset. In this case, because the `DiscretizeFilter` has just been initialized, it first computes discretization intervals from the training dataset, then uses these intervals to discretize it. After returning from `useFilter()`, all the filter's internal settings are fixed until it is initialized by another call of `inputFormat()`. This makes it possible to filter a test instance without updating the filter's internal settings.

In the last step, `updateModel()` rebuilds the classifier—in our program, an instance-based `IBk` classifier—by passing the training data to its `buildClassifier()` method. It is a convention in Weka that the `buildClassifier()` method completely initializes the model's internal settings before generating a new classifier.

ClassifyMessage()

Now we consider how `MessageClassifier` processes a test message—a message for which the class label is unknown. In `classifyMessage()`, our program first checks that a classifier has been constructed by seeing if any training instances are available. It then uses the methods described above—`cleanupString()` and `makeInstance()`—to transform the message into a test instance. Because the classifier has been built from filtered training data, the test instance must also be processed by the filter before it can be classified. This is very easy: the `input()` method enters the instance into the filter object, and the transformed instance is obtained by calling `output()`. Then a prediction is produced by passing the instance to the classifier's `classifyInstance()` method. As you can see, the prediction is coded as a `double` value. This allows Weka's evaluation module to treat models for categorical and numeric prediction similarly. In the case of categorical prediction, as in this example, the `double` variable holds the index of the predicted class value. In order to output the string corresponding to this class value, the program calls the `value()` method of the dataset's class attribute.

8.5 Writing new learning schemes

Suppose you need to implement a special-purpose learning algorithm that is not included in Weka, or a filter that performs an unusual data transformation. Or suppose you are engaged in machine learning research and want to investigate a new learning scheme or data preprocessing operation. Or suppose you just want to learn more about the inner workings of an induction algorithm by actually programming it yourself. This section shows how to make full use of Weka's class hierarchy when writing classifiers and filters, using a simple example of each.

Several elementary learning schemes, not mentioned above, are included in Weka mainly for educational purposes: they are listed in Table 8.8. None of them takes any scheme-specific command-line options. All these implementations are useful for understanding the inner workings of a classifier. As an example, we discuss the `weka.classifiers.Id3` scheme, which implements the ID3 decision tree learner from Section 4.3.

An example classifier

Figure 8.11 gives the source code of `weka.classifiers.Id3`, which, as you can see from the code, extends the `DistributionClassifier` class. This means that in addition to the `buildClassifier()` and `classifyInstance()` methods from the `Classifier` class it also implements the `distributionForInstance()` method, which returns a predicted distribution of class probabilities for an instance. We will study the implementation of these three methods in turn.

Table 8.8	Simple learning schemes in Weka.	
scheme	description	book section
weka.classifiers.NaiveBayesSimple	Probabilistic learner	4.2
weka.classifiers.Id3	Decision tree learner	4.3
weka.classifiers.Prism	Rule learner from	4.4
weka.classifiers.IB1	Instance-based learner	4.7

```
import weka.classifiers.*;
import weka.core.*;
import java.io.*;
import java.util.*;

/**
 * Class implementing an Id3 decision tree classifier.
 */
public class Id3 extends DistributionClassifier {

  /** The node's successors. */
  private Id3[] m_Successors;

  /** Attribute used for splitting. */
  private Attribute m_Attribute;

  /** Class value if node is leaf. */
  private double m_ClassValue;

  /** Class distribution if node is leaf. */
  private double[] m_Distribution;

  /** Class attribute of dataset. */
  private Attribute m_ClassAttribute;

  /**
   * Builds Id3 decision tree classifier.
   */
  public void buildClassifier(Instances data) throws Exception {

    if (!data.classAttribute().isNominal()) {
      throw new Exception("Id3: nominal class, please.");
    }
    Enumeration enumAtt = data.enumerateAttributes();
    while (enumAtt.hasMoreElements()) {
      Attribute attr = (Attribute) enumAtt.nextElement();
      if (!attr.isNominal()) {
        throw new Exception("Id3: only nominal attributes, please.");
      }
      Enumeration enum = data.enumerateInstances();
      while (enum.hasMoreElements()) {
        if (((Instance) enum.nextElement()).isMissing(attr)) {
          throw new Exception("Id3: no missing values, please.");
        }
      }
    }
    data = new Instances(data);
    data.deleteWithMissingClass();
    makeTree(data);
  }

  /**
   * Method building Id3 tree.
   */
  private void makeTree(Instances data) throws Exception {

    // Check if no instances have reached this node.
```

Figure 8.11 Source code for the ID3 decision tree learner.

```
    if (data.numInstances() == 0) {
      m_Attribute = null;
      m_ClassValue = Instance.missingValue();
      m_Distribution = new double[data.numClasses()];
      return;
    }

    // Compute attribute with maximum information gain.
    double[] infoGains = new double[data.numAttributes()];
    Enumeration attEnum = data.enumerateAttributes();
    while (attEnum.hasMoreElements()) {
      Attribute att = (Attribute) attEnum.nextElement();
      infoGains[att.index()] = computeInfoGain(data, att);
    }
    m_Attribute = data.attribute(Utils.maxIndex(infoGains));

    // Make leaf if information gain is zero.
    // Otherwise create successors.
    if (Utils.eq(infoGains[m_Attribute.index()], 0)) {
      m_Attribute = null;
      m_Distribution = new double[data.numClasses()];
      Enumeration instEnum = data.enumerateInstances();
      while (instEnum.hasMoreElements()) {
        Instance inst = (Instance) instEnum.nextElement();
        m_Distribution[(int) inst.classValue()]++;
      }
      Utils.normalize(m_Distribution);
      m_ClassValue = Utils.maxIndex(m_Distribution);
      m_ClassAttribute = data.classAttribute();
    } else {
      Instances[] splitData = splitData(data, m_Attribute);
      m_Successors = new Id3[m_Attribute.numValues()];
      for (int j = 0; j < m_Attribute.numValues(); j++) {
        m_Successors[j] = new Id3();
        m_Successors[j].buildClassifier(splitData[j]);
      }
    }
  }
}

/**
 * Classifies a given test instance using the decision tree.
 */
public double classifyInstance(Instance instance) {

  if (m_Attribute == null) {
    return m_ClassValue;
  } else {
    return m_Successors[(int) instance.value(m_Attribute)].
        classifyInstance(instance);
  }
}

/**
 * Computes class distribution for instance using decision tree.
 */
public double[] distributionForInstance(Instance instance) {
```

Figure 8.11 (continued)

```
      if (m_Attribute == null) {
        return m_Distribution;
      } else {
        return m_Successors[(int) instance.value(m_Attribute)].
            distributionForInstance(instance);
      }
    }

    /**
     * Prints the decision tree using the private toString method from below.
     */
    public String toString() {

      return "Id3 classifier\n==============\n" + toString(0);
    }

    /**
     * Computes information gain for an attribute.
     */
    private double computeInfoGain(Instances data, Attribute att)
      throws Exception {

      double infoGain = computeEntropy(data);
      Instances[] splitData = splitData(data, att);
      for (int j = 0; j < att.numValues(); j++) {
        if (splitData[j].numInstances() > 0) {
          infoGain -= ((double) splitData[j].numInstances() /
                       (double) data.numInstances()) *
            computeEntropy(splitData[j]);
        }
      }
      return infoGain;
    }

  /**
   * Computes the entropy of a dataset.
   */
   private double computeEntropy(Instances data) throws Exception {

     double [] classCounts = new double[data.numClasses()];
     Enumeration instEnum = data.enumerateInstances();
     while (instEnum.hasMoreElements()) {
       Instance inst = (Instance) instEnum.nextElement();
       classCounts[(int) inst.classValue()]++;
     }
     double entropy = 0;
     for (int j = 0; j < data.numClasses(); j++) {
       if (classCounts[j] > 0) {
         entropy -= classCounts[j] * Utils.log2(classCounts[j]);
       }
     }
     entropy /= (double) data.numInstances();
     return entropy + Utils.log2(data.numInstances());
   }

    /**
     * Splits a dataset according to the values of a nominal attribute.
```

Figure 8.11 (continued)

```java
    */
  private Instances[] splitData(Instances data, Attribute att) {

    Instances[] splitData = new Instances[att.numValues()];
    for (int j = 0; j < att.numValues(); j++) {
      splitData[j] = new Instances(data, data.numInstances());
    }
    Enumeration instEnum = data.enumerateInstances();
    while (instEnum.hasMoreElements()) {
      Instance inst = (Instance) instEnum.nextElement();
      splitData[(int) inst.value(att)].add(inst);
    }
    return splitData;
  }

  /**
   * Outputs a tree at a certain level.
   */
  private String toString(int level) {

    StringBuffer text = new StringBuffer();

    if (m_Attribute == null) {
      if (Instance.isMissingValue(m_ClassValue)) {
        text.append(": null");
      } else {
        text.append(": "+m_ClassAttribute.value((int) m_ClassValue));
      }
    } else {
      for (int j = 0; j < m_Attribute.numValues(); j++) {
        text.append("\n");
        for (int i = 0; i < level; i++) {
          text.append("|  ");
        }
        text.append(m_Attribute.name() + " = " + m_Attribute.value(j));
        text.append(m_Successors[j].toString(level + 1));
      }
    }
    return text.toString();
  }

  /**
   * Main method.
   */
  public static void main(String[] args) {

    try {
      System.out.println(Evaluation.evaluateModel(new Id3(), args));
    } catch (Exception e) {
      System.out.println(e.getMessage());
    }
  }
}
```

Figure 8.11

BuildClassifier()

The `buildClassifier()` method constructs a classifier from a set of training data. In our implementation it first checks the training data for a non-nominal class, missing values, or any other attribute that is not nominal, because the ID3 algorithm can't handle these. It then makes a copy of the training set (to avoid changing the original data) and calls a method from `weka.core.Instances` to delete all instances with missing class values, because these instances are useless in the training process. Finally it calls `makeTree()`, which actually builds the decision tree by recursively generating all subtrees attached to the root node.

MakeTree()

In `makeTree()`, the first step is to check whether the dataset is empty. If not, a leaf is created by setting `m_Attribute` to null. The class value `m_ClassValue` assigned to this leaf is set to be missing, and the estimated probability for each of the dataset's classes in `m_Distribution` is initialized to zero. If training instances are present, `makeTree()` finds the attribute that yields the greatest information gain for them. It first creates a Java `Enumeration` of the dataset's attributes. If the index of the class attribute is set—as it will be for this dataset—the class is automatically excluded from the enumeration. Inside the enumeration, the information gain for each attribute is computed by `computeInfoGain()` and stored in an array. We will return to this method later. The `index()` method from `weka.core.Attribute` returns the attribute's index in the dataset, which is used to index the array. Once the enumeration is complete, the attribute with greatest information gain is stored in the class variable `m_Attribute`. The `maxIndex()` method from `weka.core.Utils` returns the index of the greatest value in an array of integers or doubles. (If there is more than one element with maximum value, the first is returned.) The index of this attribute is passed to the `attribute()` method from `weka.core.Instances`, which returns the corresponding attribute.

You might wonder what happens to the array field corresponding to the class attribute. We need not worry about this because Java automatically initializes all elements in an array of numbers to zero, and the information gain is always greater than or equal to zero. If the maximum information gain is zero, `makeTree()` creates a leaf. In that case `m_Attribute` is set to null, and `makeTree()` computes both the distribution of class probabilities and the class with greatest probability. (The `normalize()` method from `weka.core.Utils` normalizes an array of doubles so that its sum is 1.)

When it makes a leaf with a class value assigned to it, `makeTree()` stores the class attribute in `m_ClassAttribute`. This is because the method that outputs the decision tree needs to access this in order to print the class label.

If an attribute with nonzero information gain is found, `makeTree()` splits the dataset according to the attribute's values and recursively builds subtrees for each of the new datasets. To make the split it calls the method `splitData()`. This first creates as many empty datasets as there are attribute values and stores them in an array (setting the initial capacity of each dataset to the number of instances in the original dataset), then iterates through all instances in the original dataset and allocates them to the new dataset that corresponds to the attribute's value. Returning to `makeTree()`, the resulting array of datasets is used for building subtrees. The method creates an array of `Id3` objects, one for each attribute value, and calls `buildClassifier()` on each by passing it the corresponding dataset.

ComputeInfoGain()

Returning to `computeInfoGain()`, this calculates the information gain associated with an attribute and a dataset using a straightforward implementation of the method in Section 4.3 (pp. 92–94). First it computes the entropy of the dataset. Then it uses `splitData()` to divide it into subsets, and calls `computeEntropy()` on each one. Finally it returns the difference between the former entropy and the weighted sum of the latter ones—the information gain. The method `computeEntropy()` uses the `log2()` method from `weka.core.Utils` to compute the logarithm (to base 2) of a number.

ClassifyInstance()

Having seen how ID3 constructs a decision tree, we now examine how it uses the tree structure to predict class values and probabilities. Let's first look at `classifyInstance()`, which predicts a class value for a given instance. In Weka, nominal class values—like the values of all nominal attributes—are coded and stored in `double` variables, representing the index of the value's name in the attribute declaration. We chose this representation in favor of a more elegant object-oriented approach to increase speed of execution and reduce storage requirements. In our implementation of ID3, `classifyInstance()` recursively descends the tree, guided by the instance's attribute values, until it reaches a leaf. Then it returns the class value `m_ClassValue` stored at this leaf. The method `distributionForInstance()` works in exactly the same way, returning the probability distribution stored in `m_Distribution`.

Most machine learning models, and in particular decision trees, serve as a more or less comprehensible explanation of the structure found in the data. Accordingly each of Weka's classifiers, like many other Java objects, implements a `toString()` method that produces a textual representation of itself in the form of a `String` variable. ID3's `toString()` method outputs a decision tree in roughly the same format as J4.8 (Figure 8.2). It recursively prints the tree structure into a `String` variable by accessing the attribute information stored at the nodes. To obtain each attribute's name and values, it uses the `name()` and `value()` methods from `weka.core.Attribute`.

Main()

The only method in `Id3` that hasn't been described is `main()`, which is called whenever the class is executed from the command line. As you can see, it's simple: it basically just tells Weka's `Evaluation` class to evaluate `Id3` with the given command-line options, and prints the resulting string. The one-line expression that does this is enclosed in a `try-catch` statement, which catches the various exceptions that can be thrown by Weka's routines or other Java methods.

The `evaluation()` method in `weka.classifiers.Evaluation` interprets the generic scheme-independent command-line options discussed in Section 8.3, and acts appropriately. For example, it takes the `-t` option, which gives the name of the training file, and loads the corresponding dataset. If no test file is given, it performs a cross-validation by repeatedly creating classifier objects and calling `buildClassifier()`, `classifyInstance()`, and `distributionForInstance()` on different subsets of the training data. Unless the user suppresses output of the model by setting the corresponding command-line option, it also calls the `toString()` method to output the model built from the full training dataset.

What happens if the scheme needs to interpret a specific option such as a pruning parameter? This is accomplished using the `OptionHandler` interface in `weka.classifiers`. A classifier that implements this interface contains three methods, `listOptions()`, `setOptions()`, and `getOptions()`, which can be used to list all the classifier's scheme-specific options, to set some of them, and to get the options that are currently set. The `evaluation()` method in `Evaluation` automatically calls these methods if the classifier implements the `Option-Handler` interface. Once the scheme-independent options have been processed, it calls `setOptions()` to process the remaining options before using `buildClassifier()` to generate a new classifier. When it outputs the classifier, it uses `getOptions()` to output a list of the options that are currently set. For a simple example of how to implement these methods, look at the source code for `weka.classifiers.OneR`.

Some classifiers are incremental, that is, they can be incrementally updated as new training instances arrive and don't have to process all the data in one batch. In Weka, incremental classifiers implement the `UpdateableClassifier` interface in `weka.classifiers`. This interface declares only one method, namely `update-Classifier()`, which takes a single training instance as its argument. For an example of how to use this interface, look at the source code for `weka.classifiers.IBk`.

If a classifier is able to make use of instance weights, it should implement the `WeightedInstancesHandler()` interface from *weka.core*. Then other algorithms, such as the boosting algorithms, can make use of this property.

Conventions for implementing classifiers

There are some conventions that you must obey when implementing classifiers in Weka. If you do not, things will go awry—for example, Weka's evaluation module might not compute the classifier's statistics properly when evaluating it.

The first convention has already been mentioned: each time a classifier's buildClassifier() method is called, it must reset the model. The CheckClassifier class described in Section 8.3 performs appropriate tests to ensure that this is the case. When buildClassifier() is called on a dataset, the same result must always be obtained, regardless of how often the classifier has been applied before to other datasets. However, buildClassifier() must not reset class variables that correspond to scheme-specific options, because these settings must persist through multiple calls of buildClassifier(). Also, a call of buildClassifier() must never change the input data.

The second convention is that when the learning scheme can't make a prediction, the classifier's classifyInstance() method must return Instance.missingValue() and its distributionForInstance() method must return zero probabilities for all classes. The ID3 implementation in Figure 8.11 does this.

The third convention concerns classifiers for numeric prediction. If a Classifier is used for numeric prediction, classifyInstance() just returns the numeric value that it predicts. In some cases, however, a classifier might be able to predict nominal classes and their class probabilities, as well as numeric class values—weka.classifiers.IBk is an example. In that case, the classifier is a DistributionClassifier and implements the distributionForInstance() method. What should distributionForInstance() return if the class is numeric? Weka's convention is that it returns an array of size one whose only element contains the predicted numeric value.

Another convention—not absolutely essential, but very useful nonetheless—is that every classifier implements a toString() method that outputs a textual description of itself.

Writing filters

There are two kinds of filter algorithms in Weka, depending on whether, like DiscretizeFilter, they must accumulate statistics from the whole input dataset before processing any instances, or, like AttributeFilter, they can process each instance immediately. We present an implementation of the first kind, and point out the main differences from the second kind, which is simpler.

The Filter superclass contains several generic methods for filter construction, listed in Table 8.9, that are automatically inherited by its subclasses. Writing a new filter essentially involves overriding some of these. Filter also documents the purpose of these methods, and how they need to be changed for particular types of filter algorithm.

Table 8.9	Public methods in the `Filter` class.

method	description
`boolean inputFormat(Instances)`	Set input format of data, returning `true` if output format can be collected immediately
`Instances outputFormat()`	Return output format of data
`boolean input(Instance)`	Input instance into filter, returning `true` if instance can be output immediately
`boolean batchFinished()`	Inform filter that all training data has been input, returning `true` if instances are pending output
`Instance output()`	Output instance from the filter
`Instance outputPeek()`	Output instance without removing it from output queue
`int numPendingOutput()`	Return number of instances waiting for output
`boolean isOutputFormatDefined()`	Return `true` if output format can be collected

The first step in using a filter is to inform it of the input data format, accomplished by the method `inputFormat()`. This takes an object of class `Instances` and uses its attribute information to interpret future input instances. The filter's output data format can be determined by calling `outputFormat()`—also stored as an object of class `Instances`. For filters that process instances at once, the output format is determined as soon as the input format has been specified. However, for those that must see the whole dataset before processing any individual instance, the situation depends on the particular filter algorithm. For example, `DiscretizeFilter` needs to see all training instances before determining the output format, because the number of discretization intervals is determined by the data. Consequently the method `inputFormat()` returns `true` if the output format can be determined as soon as the input format has been specified, and `false` otherwise. Another way of checking whether the output format exists is to call `isOutputFormatDefined()`.

Two methods are used for piping instances through the filter: `input()` and `output()`. As its name implies, the former gets an instance into the filter; it returns `true` if the processed instance is available immediately and `false` otherwise. The latter outputs an instance from the filter and removes it from its output queue. The `outputPeek()` method outputs a filtered instance without removing it from the output queue, and the number of instances in the queue can be obtained with `numPendingOutput()`.

Filters that must see the whole dataset before processing instances need to be notified when all training instances have been input. This is done by calling batchFinished(), which tells the filter that the statistics obtained from the input data gathered so far—the training data—should not be updated when further data is received. For all filter algorithms, once batchFinished() has been called, the output format can be read and the filtered training instances are ready for output. The first time input() is called after batchFinished(), the output queue is reset—that is, all training instances are removed from it. If there are training instances awaiting output, batchFinished() returns true, otherwise false.

An example filter

It's time for an example. The ReplaceMissingValuesFilter takes a dataset and replaces missing values with a constant. For numeric attributes, the constant is the attribute's mean value; for nominal ones, its mode. This filter must see all the training data before any output can be determined, and once these statistics have been computed. they must remain fixed when future test data is filtered. Figure 8.12 shows the source code.

InputFormat()

ReplaceMissingValuesFilter overwrites three of the methods defined in Filter: inputFormat(), input(), and batchFinished(). In inputFormat(), as you can see from Figure 8.12, a dataset m_InputFormat is created with the required input format and capacity zero; this will hold incoming instances. The method setOutputFormat(), which is a protected method in Filter, is called to set the output format. Then the variable b_NewBatch, which indicates whether the next incoming instance belongs to a new batch of data, is set to true because a new dataset is to be processed; and m_ModesAndMeans, which will hold the filter's statistics, is initialized. The variables b_NewBatch and m_InputFormat are the only fields declared in the superclass Filter that are visible in ReplaceMissingValuesFilter, and they must be dealt with appropriately. As you can see from Figure 8.12, the method inputFormat() returns true because the output format can be collected immediately—replacing missing values doesn't change the dataset's attribute information.

Input()

An exception is thrown in input() if the input format is not set. Otherwise, if b_NewBatch is true—that is, if a new batch of data is to be processed—the filter's output queue is initialized, causing all instances awaiting output to be deleted, and the flag b_NewBatch is set to false, because a new instance is about to be processed. Then, if statistics have not yet been accumulated from the training data (that is, if m_ModesAndMeans is null), the new instance is added to m_Input-Format and input() returns false because the instance is not yet available for output. Otherwise, the instance is converted using convertInstance(), and true is returned. The method convertInstance() transforms an instance to the output format by replacing missing values with the modes and means, and appends it to the output queue by calling `push()`, a protected method defined in `Filter`. Instances in the filter's output queue are ready for collection by `output()`.

BatchFinished()

In `batchFinished()`, the filter first checks whether the input format is defined. Then, if no statistics have been stored in `m_ModesAndMeans` by a previous call, the modes and means are computed and the training instances are converted using `convertInstance()`. Finally, regardless of the status of `m_ModesAndMeans`, `b_New-Batch` is set to `true` to indicate that the last batch has been processed, and `true` is returned if instances are available in the output queue.

Main()

The `main()` method evaluates the command-line options and applies the filter. It does so by calling two methods from `Filter`: `batchFilterFile()` and `filter-File()`. The former is called if a test file is provided as well as a training file (using the `-b` command-line option); otherwise the latter is called. Both methods interpret the command-line options. If the filter implements the `Option-Handler` interface, its `setOptions()`, `getOptions()`, and `listOptions()` methods are called to deal with any filter-specific options, just as in the case of classifiers.

In general, as in this particular example of `ReplaceMissingValuesFilter`, only the three routines `inputFormat()`, `input()`, and `batchFinished()` need be changed in order to implement a filter with new functionality. The method `out-putFormat()` from `Filter` is actually declared final and can't be overwritten anyway. Moreover, if the filter can process each instance immediately, `batch Finished()` need not be altered—the default implementation will do the job. A simple (but not very useful) example of such a filter is `weka.filters.AllFilter`, which passes all instances through unchanged.

Conventions for writing filters

By now, most of the requirements for implementing filters should be clear. However, some deserve explicit mention. First, filters must never change the input data, nor add instances to the dataset used to provide the input format. `ReplaceMissingValuesFilter()` avoids this by storing an empty copy of the dataset in `m_InputFormat`. Second, calling `inputFormat()` should initialize the filter's internal state, but not alter any variables corresponding to user-provided command-line options. Third, instances input to the filter should never be pushed directly on to the output queue: they must be replaced by brand new objects of class `Instance`. Otherwise, anomalies will appear if the input instances are changed outside the filter later on. For example, `AllFilter` calls the `copy()` method in `Instance` to create a copy of each instance before pushing it on to the output queue.

```java
import weka.filters.*;
import weka.core.*;
import java.io.*;

/**
 * Replaces all missing values for nominal and numeric attributes in a
 * dataset with the modes and means from the training data.
 */
public class ReplaceMissingValuesFilter extends Filter {

  /** The modes and means */
  private double[] m_ModesAndMeans = null;

  /**
   * Sets the format of the input instances.
   */
  public boolean inputFormat(Instances instanceInfo)
       throws Exception {

    m_InputFormat = new Instances(instanceInfo, 0);
    setOutputFormat(m_InputFormat);
    b_NewBatch = true;
    m_ModesAndMeans = null;
    return true;
  }

  /**
   * Input an instance for filtering. Filter requires all
   * training instances be read before producing output.
   */
  public boolean input(Instance instance) throws Exception {

    if (m_InputFormat == null) {
      throw new Exception("No input instance format defined");
    }
    if (b_NewBatch) {
      resetQueue();
      b_NewBatch = false;
    }
    if (m_ModesAndMeans == null) {
      m_InputFormat.add(instance);
      return false;
    } else {
      convertInstance(instance);
      return true;
    }
  }

  /**
   * Signify that this batch of input to the filter is finished.
   */

  public boolean batchFinished() throws Exception {

    if (m_InputFormat == null) {
      throw new Exception("No input instance format defined");
    }
```

Figure 8.12 Source code for a filter that replaces the missing values in a dataset.

```
    if (m_ModesAndMeans == null) {

      // Compute modes and means
      m_ModesAndMeans = new double[m_InputFormat.numAttributes()];
      for (int i = 0; i < m_InputFormat.numAttributes(); i++) {
        if (m_InputFormat.attribute(i).isNominal() ||
            m_InputFormat.attribute(i).isNumeric()) {
          m_ModesAndMeans[i] = m_InputFormat.meanOrMode(i);
        }
      }

      // Convert pending input instances
      for(int i = 0; i < m_InputFormat.numInstances(); i++) {
        Instance current = m_InputFormat.instance(i);
        convertInstance(current);
      }
    }

    b_NewBatch = true;
    return (numPendingOutput() != 0);
  }

  /**
   * Convert a single instance over. The converted instance is
   * added to the end of the output queue.
   */
  private void convertInstance(Instance instance) throws Exception {

    Instance newInstance = new Instance(instance);

    for(int j = 0; j < m_InputFormat.numAttributes(); j++){
      if (instance.isMissing(j) &&
          (m_InputFormat.attribute(j).isNominal() ||
           m_InputFormat.attribute(j).isNumeric())) {
        newInstance.setValue(j, m_ModesAndMeans[j]);
      }
    }
    push(newInstance);
  }

  /**
   * Main method.
   */
  public static void main(String [] argv) {

    try {
      if (Utils.getFlag('b', argv)) {
        Filter.batchFilterFile(new ReplaceMissingValuesFilter(),argv);
      } else {
        Filter.filterFile(new ReplaceMissingValuesFilter(),argv);
      }
    } catch (Exception ex) {
      System.out.println(ex.getMessage());
    }
  }
}
```

Figure 8.12

chapter nine

Looking forward

Machine learning is a burgeoning new technology for mining knowledge from data, a technology that a lot of people are starting to take seriously. We don't want to oversell it. The kind of machine learning we know is not about the big problems: futuristic visions of autonomous robot servants, philosophical conundrums of consciousness, metaphysical issues of free will, evolutionary—or theological—questions of where intelligence comes from, linguistic debates over language learning, psychological theories of child development, or cognitive explanations of what intelligence is and how it works. For us, it's far more prosaic: machine learning is about algorithms for inferring structure from data, and ways of validating that structure. These algorithms are not abstruse and complicated, but they're not completely obvious and trivial either.

Looking forward, the main challenge ahead is applications. Opportunities abound. Wherever there is data, information can be gleaned from it. Whenever there is too much data for people to pore over themselves, the mechanics of learning will have to be automatic. But the inspiration will certainly not be automatic. Applications will come not from computer programs, nor from machine learning experts, nor from the data itself, but from the people who work with the data and the problems from which it arises. That is why we have written this book—and the Weka system—to empower those who are not machine learning experts to apply these techniques to the problems that arise in daily working life. The ideas are simple. The algorithms are here. The rest is really up to you!

Of course, development of the technology is certainly not finished. Machine learning is a hot research topic, and new ideas and techniques continually emerge. To give a flavor of the scope and variety of research fronts, we close by looking at four topical areas in the world of machine learning.

9.1   Learning from massive datasets

The enormous proliferation of very large databases in today's companies and scientific institutions makes it necessary for machine learning algorithms to operate on massive datasets. Two separate dimensions become critical when any algorithm is applied to very large datasets: space and time.

Suppose the dataset is so large that it can't be held in main memory. This causes no difficulty if the learning scheme works in an incremental fashion, processing one instance at a time when generating the model. An instance can be read from the input file, the model updated, the next instance read, and so on—without ever holding more than one training instance in main memory. Normally the resulting model is small compared to the dataset size, and the amount of available memory does not impose any serious constraint on it. The Naive Bayes method is an excellent example of this kind of algorithm; there are also incremental versions of decision tree inducers and rule learning schemes. However, incremental algorithms for some of the learning methods discussed in this book have not yet been developed—for example, model tree inducers. Other methods, like basic instance-based schemes and locally weighted regression, need access to all the training instances at prediction time. In that case, sophisticated caching and indexing mechanisms have to be employed to keep only the most frequently used parts of a dataset in memory and to provide rapid access to relevant instances in the file.

The other critical dimension when applying learning algorithms to massive datasets is time. If the learning time does not scale linearly (or almost linearly) with the number of training instances, it will eventually become infeasible to process very large datasets. In some applications the number of attributes is a critical factor, and only methods that scale linearly in the number of attributes are acceptable. Alternatively, prediction time might be the crucial issue. With a simple nearest-neighbor learning algorithm, for example, the entire database must be scanned to derive a single prediction. Fortunately, there are many learning algorithms that scale gracefully during both training and testing. For example, the training time for Naive Bayes is linear in both the number of instances and the number of attributes. For top-down decision tree inducers, we saw in Section 6.1 (pages 167–168) that training time is linear in the number of attributes and, if the tree is uniformly bushy, log-linear in the number of instances (if subtree raising is not used, with a further log factor if it is). In both cases, testing time per instance is linear in the number of attributes.

When a dataset is too large for a particular learning algorithm to be applied, there are three ways to make learning feasible. The first is trivial: instead of applying the scheme to the full dataset, use just a small subset for training. Of course, information is lost when subsampling is employed. However, the loss may be negligible because the predictive performance of a learned model often flattens out long before all the training data is incorporated into it. If this is the case, it can easily be verified by observing the model's performance on a holdout test set for training sets of different size.

This kind of behavior, often called the *law of diminishing returns,* may arise because the learning problem is a simple one, so that a small volume of training data is sufficient to learn an accurate model. Alternatively, the learning algorithm might be incapable of grasping the detailed structure of the underlying domain. This is often observed when Naive Bayes is employed in a complex domain: additional training data may not improve the performance of the model, whereas a decision tree's accuracy may continue to climb. In this case, of course, if predictive performance is the main objective, you should switch to the more complex learning algorithm. But beware of overfitting! Take care not to assess performance on the training data.

Parallelization is another way of reducing the time complexity of learning. The idea is to split the problem into smaller parts, solve each using a separate processor, and combine the results together. To do this, a parallelized version of the learning algorithm must be created. Some algorithms lend themselves naturally to parallelization. Nearest-neighbor methods, for example, can easily be distributed among several processors by splitting the data into several parts and letting each processor find the nearest neighbor in its part of the training set. Decision tree learners can be parallelized by letting each processor build a subtree of the complete tree. Bagging and stacking (though not boosting) are naturally parallel algorithms. However, parallelization is only a partial remedy because with a fixed number of processors, the algorithm's asymptotic time complexity cannot be improved.

The best but most challenging way to enable a learning paradigm to deal with very large datasets would be to develop a new algorithm with lower computational complexity. In some cases, it is provably impossible to derive exact algorithms with lower complexity. Decision tree learners that deal with numeric attributes fall into this category. Their asymptotic time complexity is dominated by the sorting process for the numeric attribute values, a procedure that must be performed at least once for any given dataset. However, stochastic algorithms can sometimes be derived that approximate the true solution but require a much smaller amount of time.

Background knowledge can make it possible to vastly reduce the amount of data that needs to be processed by a learning algorithm. Depending on which attribute is the class, most of the attributes in a huge dataset might turn out to be irrelevant when background knowledge is taken into account. As usual, it pays to carefully engineer the data that is passed to the learning scheme and to make the greatest possible use of any prior information about the learning problem at hand. If insufficient background knowledge is available, the attribute filtering algorithms discussed in Section 7.1 can often drastically reduce the amount of data—possibly at the expense of a minor loss in predictive performance. Some of these—for example, attribute selection using decision trees or the 1R learning scheme—are linear in the number of attributes.

As you can see, there are several possibilities for adapting machine learning algorithms to deal with massive datasets. And commercial products exist that already use parallelism to reach well beyond the capabilities of straightforward implementations of the algorithms. Some are capable of successfully mining datasets with millions of instances, and one claims to be capable of mining datasets with tens of thousands of attributes.

Just to give you a feeling for the amount of data that can be handled by straightforward implementations of machine learning algorithms on ordinary microcomputers, we ran the decision tree learner J4.8 on a dataset with 600,000 instances, 54 attributes (10 numeric, 44 binary) and a class with 7 values. We used a Pentium Pro with a 200 MHz clock and 1 Gbyte main memory, and a commercial Java compiler. It took seven hours to load the data file, build the tree using reduced-error pruning, and classify all the training instances. The tree had 20,000 nodes. Note that this implementation is written in Java, and executing a Java program is several times slower than running a corresponding program written in C because the Java byte-code must be translated into machine code before it can be executed. (In our experience the difference is a factor of 3 to 5 if the virtual machine uses a just-in-time compiler.) But Java byte-code processors in machines with many gigabytes of main memory are only a couple of years away, and these will considerably increase the scale on which the implementations accompanying this book can be used.

There are datasets today that truly deserve the adjective *massive*. Scientific datasets from astrophysics, nuclear physics, earth science, and molecular biology are measured in hundreds of gigabytes—or even terabytes. So are datasets containing records of financial transactions. Application of standard programs for machine learning to such datasets in their entirety is clearly out of the question.

9.2   Visualizing machine learning

The human mind is at its best when processing images. Pictures can convey information far more succinctly than textual descriptions. This applies to data mining too: visualization tools are extremely useful when preparing the input to a learning scheme and when trying to understand its output.

Visualizing the input

Interactive visualization is a powerful tool for attribute selection and outlier detection. It is true that in most practical data mining situations there are far too many attributes to visualize simultaneously, and there is no alternative to automatic algorithms for attribute selection. Nevertheless, even here visualizations can be very useful to gain better understanding of what the algorithms find. Moreover, they can provide useful clues about which learning methods are likely to produce good results for the data.

Figure 9.1a shows a visualization of the Iris dataset from Section 1.2, using just the petal-length attribute. Each training instance is represented as a point, and different symbols are used to differentiate between the three classes Iris setosa, Iris virginica, and Iris versicolor. The display projects the dataset onto one of the attributes and plots it in histogram style: the horizontal axis has no meaning in terms of the problem domain. It is immediately clear that the class Iris setosa is separable from the other two using just the petal-length attribute. It is also clear that the other two classes overlap if just this one attribute is considered. As you can see, this type of display is very useful to eyeball if the attribute provides any relevant information about the variable of interest—particularly if this finding is backed up by the user's domain knowledge. And it works just as well on a massive scale as it does on the tiny Iris dataset.

Figure 9.1b shows what happens when the petal-width attribute is added to create a two-dimensional projection of the dataset. This representation makes it obvious that these two attributes are sufficient to discriminate quite well between the three classes. The figure also shows that axis-parallel splits, like those produced by a decision tree, are not ideally suited to modeling the class boundary between the classes Iris virginica and Iris versicolor (although the effect is not as pronounced as it might be in other datasets). A nearest-neighbor classifier might deliver better predictive performance.

One- or two-dimensional representations like these have the advantage that they are very easy to understand. However, important interactions often occur between three or more attributes. Some visualization tools provide animated three-dimensional displays of datasets, but beyond this there are no straightforward representations. Sophisticated visualization software sometimes incorpo-

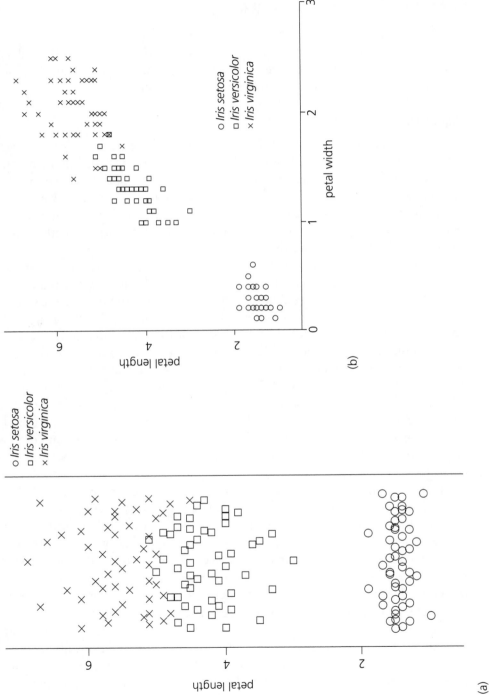

Figure 9.1 Representation of Iris data: (a) one dimension; (b) two dimensions.

rates complex geometrical techniques that project high-dimensional spaces into three dimensions; however, special skills and experience are needed to interpret these.

Visualizing the output

Visualizing the output of a learning scheme can be equally useful. Some models lend themselves naturally to a graphical representation. Early in this book we saw decision trees represented as tree-structured graphs (for instance, Figure 1.2). These graphs were rather primitive, and it is possible to convey significantly more information in a richer and more complex representation. The thickness of the graph's edges can be varied according to the relative number of instances that traverse them, and each node can be associated with a diagram displaying its class distribution.

Figure 9.2 shows output produced automatically from a decision tree in a study aimed at determining the factors that influence the growth of white clover in dry hill country in New Zealand. The predicted attribute is the predominant

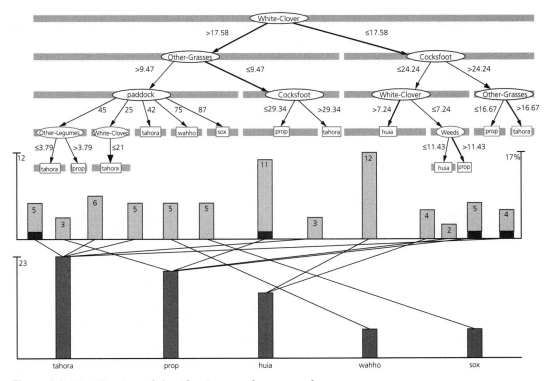

Figure 9.2 Visualization of classification tree for grasses data.

type of grass that is growing on the plot—tahora, prop, huia, wahho, or sox. The upper region is an augmented version of the decision tree. The nodes are types of grass and the thickness of the branches represent the number of examples—in this case training examples. Although, as we will see below, this information is redundant, it provides a convenient view of paths through the tree. The thickest ones stand out, giving a structural overview of the data. The branches (and hence children) of each node are ordered in size: the left one represents the largest branch and the rightmost the smallest. Each node is centered in a horizontal bar whose length is determined by the number of examples it classifies. The root node occupies the full horizontal stretch, and every other node occupies a fraction of its parent's allocation. This makes it possible to see immediately the size of any node relative either to the total population or to the population of the parent or indeed any ancestor. For example, paddock grass contains about two-fifths of the training examples, and represents about two-thirds of the OtherGrasses92 class.

The middle part of Figure 9.2 is a histogram of leaf node occupancy. The column underneath each leaf represents the number of examples that reach it (also written at the top of the bar). This makes it easy to pick out the largest and smallest leaves and relate them to the structure of the tree. In this example, the largest leaf has type huia. It is apparent that this emanates from a secondary branch of the root node: it represents the majority of the root minority. The other sizable node, to its left, is of type prop. Although the path to this leaf takes the root majority, it is still a minority path. The examples that are incorrectly classified are represented by gray regions at the bottom of the bars.

The lower part of Figure 9.2 shows each class as a single column, in decreasing order of size. Lines connect the classes back to the leaf nodes that comprise them. For example, you can see that tahora, the largest class, comprises many terminal classes, while the two smallest classes only occur once each. We also see that the largest leaf node corresponds to the third-ranked class, not the largest one.

There are visualization techniques for other learning methods that produce structured descriptions. Decision tables, for example, have a natural representation as a two-dimensional grid structure, each cell representing one table entry. The class distribution and number of instances corresponding to a cell can also be included in the visualization.

Ideally, knowledge discovery takes place in an iterative cycle in which the machine learning component is embedded in a system that visualizes both input and output. Then, users can conveniently analyze the model generated by the learning scheme and refine the input data until the desired kind of result is obtained. The degree of interaction can be increased by allowing the user to alter the model directly, which can be very useful when the model conflicts with the user's domain knowledge in some obvious way.

9.3 Incorporating domain knowledge

Throughout this book we have emphasized the importance of getting to know your data when undertaking practical data mining. Knowledge of the domain is absolutely essential for success. Data about data is often called *metadata,* and one of the frontiers in machine learning is the development of schemes to allow learning schemes to take metadata into account in a useful way.

You don't have to look far for examples of how metadata might be applied. In Chapter 2 we divided attributes into nominal and numeric. But we also noted that many finer distinctions are possible. If an attribute is numeric, an ordering is implied, but sometimes there is a zero point and sometimes not (for time intervals there is, but for dates there is not). Even the ordering may be nonstandard: angular degrees have a different ordering to integers because 360° is the same as 0°, and 180° is the same as −180° or indeed 900°. Discretization schemes assume ordinary linear ordering, as do learning schemes that accommodate numeric attributes, but it would be a routine matter to extend them to circular orderings. Categorical data may also be ordered. Imagine how much more difficult our lives would be if there were no conventional ordering for letters of the alphabet (looking up a listing in the Hong Kong telephone directory presents an interesting and nontrivial problem!). And the rhythms of everyday life are reflected in circular orderings: days of the week, months of the year. To further complicate matters there are many other kinds of ordering, such as partial orderings on subsets: subset A may include subset B, or B may include A, or neither may include the other. Extending ordinary learning schemes to take account of this kind of information in a satisfactory and general way is an open research problem.

Metadata often involves relations among attributes. Three kinds of relation can be distinguished: semantic, causal, and functional. A *semantic* relation between two attributes indicates that if the first is included in a rule, the second should be too. In this case, it is known a priori that the attributes only make sense together. For example, in agricultural data that we have analyzed, an attribute called `milk production` measures how much milk an individual cow produces, and the purpose of our investigation meant that this attribute had a semantic relationship with three other attributes, `cow-identifier`, `herd-identifier`, and `farmer-identifier`. In other words, a milk production value can only be understood in the context of the cow that produced the milk, and the cow is further linked to a specific herd owned by a given farmer. Semantic relations are, of course, problem-dependent: they depend not just on the dataset but also on what you are trying to do with it.

Causal relations occur when one attribute causes another. In a system that is trying to predict an attribute that is caused by another, we know that the other attribute must be included in order to make the prediction meaningful. For example, in the agricultural data mentioned above, there is a chain from the farmer, herd, and cow identifiers, through measured attributes such as milk production, down to the attribute that records whether a particular cow was retained or sold by the farmer. Rules that fail to recognize this chain are meaningless, no matter how well they seem to fit the data.

Functional dependencies occur in many databases, and the people who create databases strive to identify them for the purpose of normalizing the relations in the database. When learning from the data, the significance of a functional dependency of one attribute on another is that if the latter is used in a rule, there is no need to consider the former. Learning schemes often rediscover functional dependencies that are already known. Not only does this generate meaningless, or more accurately tautological, rules but other, more interesting, patterns may be obscured by the functional relationships. However, there has been much work in automatic database design on the problem of inferring functional dependencies from example queries, and the methods developed should prove useful in weeding out tautological rules generated by learning schemes.

Taking these kinds of metadata, or prior domain knowledge, into account when doing induction using any of the algorithms we have met does not seem to present any deep or difficult technical challenges. The only real problem—and it is a big one—is how to express the metadata in a general and easily understandable way so that it can be generated by a person and used by the algorithm.

It seems attractive to couch the metadata knowledge in just the same representation as the machine learning scheme generates. We focus on rules, which are the norm for this kind of work. The rules that specify metadata correspond to prior knowledge of the domain. Given training examples, additional rules can be derived by one of the rule induction schemes we have already met. In this way, the system might be able to combine "experience" (from examples) with "theory" (from domain knowledge). It would be capable of confirming and modifying its programmed-in knowledge based on empirical evidence. Loosely put, the user tells the system what he or she knows, gives it some examples, and it figures the rest out for itself!

In order to make use of prior knowledge expressed as rules in a sufficiently flexible way, it is necessary for the system to be able to perform logical deduction. Otherwise, the knowledge has to expressed in precisely the right form for the learning algorithm to take advantage of it, which is likely to be too demanding for practical use. Consider causal metadata: if attribute A causes B and B causes C, then we would like the system to deduce that A causes C rather than having to state that fact explicitly. Although in this simple example explicitly stating the new fact presents little problem, in practice, with extensive metadata, it will be unrealistic to expect users to express all logical consequences of their prior knowledge.

A combination of deduction from prespecified domain knowledge and induction from training examples seems like a flexible way of accommodating metadata. At one extreme, when examples are scarce (or nonexistent), deduction is the prime (or only) means of generating new rules. At the other, when examples are abundant but metadata is scarce (or nonexistent), the standard machine learning techniques described in this book suffice. Practical situations span the territory in between.

This is a compelling vision, and methods of inductive logic programming, mentioned in Section 3.6, do offer a general way of specifying domain knowledge explicitly through statements in a formal logic language. However, current logic-programming solutions suffer serious shortcomings in real-world environments. They tend to be brittle and lack robustness, and they may be so computation-intensive as to be completely infeasible on datasets of any practical size. Perhaps this stems from the fact that they use first-order logic, that is, they allow variables to be introduced into the rules. The machine learning schemes we have seen, whose input and output are represented in terms of attributes and constant values, perform their machinations in propositional logic, without variables—greatly reducing the search space and avoiding all sorts of difficult problems of circularity and termination. Perhaps it is possible to realize the vision without the accompanying brittleness and computational infeasibility of standard logic-programming solutions by adopting simplified reasoning systems. It will be interesting to see whether these problems are overcome, so that systems that allow flexible specification of different types of metadata can be more widely deployed in the future.

9.4   Text mining

Data mining is about looking for patterns in data. Likewise, text mining is about looking for patterns in text: the process of analyzing text to extract information that is useful for particular purposes. Compared to the kind of data we have been talking about in this book, text is unstructured, amorphous, and difficult to deal with. Nevertheless, in modern Western culture, text is the most common vehicle for the formal exchange of information. The motivation for trying to extract information from it is compelling—even if success is only partial.

Text mining is possible because you do not have to understand text in order to extract useful information from it. We have already seen an example, though admittedly a very simple one: the scheme for automatic classification of email messages in Section 8.4. Here are some more possibilities.

Finding key phrases for documents

Imagine a large set of documents to which pertinent key phrases have been assigned. Professional indexers often choose phrases from a predefined "controlled vocabulary" relevant to the domain at hand. However, the great majority of documents come without key phrases, and assigning them manually is a tedious process that requires extensive knowledge of the subject matter. However, with a sufficient quantity of training data that includes several documents for each term in the controlled vocabulary, a machine learning solution is possible.

Each document is a training instance: a positive instance for the terms that are associated with it and a negative instance for all the other terms. Using words as features—perhaps a small number of well-chosen words as in Figure 8.10, or perhaps all words that appear in the document except the most common words like *the* and *and*—and word counts as feature values, a model could be built for each of the terms. The documents containing that term would be positive examples and the remaining documents negative ones. The model predicts whether or not that term is assigned to a new document based on the words in it, and their counts. Given a new document, each model would be applied to it to see which terms to assign. Alternatively, the learning method may produce a likelihood of the term being assigned, and if, say, five terms were sought for the new document, the five with the highest likelihoods could be chosen. Such models have been built and used to assign key phrases to short medical abstracts with quite high accuracy; the methods that currently perform best use linear support vector machines, described in Section 6.3.

Suppose the key phrases do not come from a fixed vocabulary, but are likely to be phrases that occur in the text of the document itself. Maybe only a much smaller training set is available—after all, assigning phrases to documents involves expensive intellectual labor. The above technique is inapplicable because it can only form models for the key phrases that are used in the training data. But instead the key phrases could be chosen from the text itself. Given a document, rudimentary lexical techniques based on punctuation and common words could be used to extract a set of candidate key phrases. Then, features could be computed for each phrase, like how often it appears in that document (normalized by how often that phrase appears in other documents in the corpus), how close to the beginning of the document it first occurs (for key phrases tend to occur early on), how often it has been used as a key phrase in other training documents, whether it occurs in the title, abstract, or section headings, whether it occurs in the title of papers cited in the reference list, and so on.

The training data could be used to form a model that takes these features and predicts whether or not a candidate key phrase will actually appear as a key phrase—this information is known for the training documents. Then the model could be applied to extract likely key phrases from new documents. Such models have been built and used to assign key phrases to technical papers; simple schemes like Naive Bayes seem adequate for this task.

So that you can judge for yourself the success of machine learning on this problem, Table 9.1 shows the titles of three research articles and two sets of key

Table 9.1   Author- and machine-assigned key phrases for three papers.

Protocols for secure, atomic transaction execution in electronic commerce		Neural multigrid for gauge theories and other disordered systems		Proof nets, garbage, and computations	
anonymity	*atomicity*	disordered systems	disordered	*cut-elimination*	cut
atomicity	*auction*	*gauge fields*	gauge	linear logic	cut elimination
auction	customer	*multigrid*	*gauge fields*	*proof nets*	garbage
electronic commerce	*electronic commerce*	neural multigrid	interpolation kernels	sharing graphs	*proof net*
privacy	intruder	neural networks	length scale	typed lambda-calculus	weakening
real-time	merchant		*multigrid*		
security	protocol		smooth		
transaction	*security*				
	third party				
	transaction				

phrases for each one. One set contains the key phrases assigned by the article's author; the other was determined automatically from its full text. Phrases in common between the two sets are italicized. In each case, the author's key phrases and the automatically extracted key phrases are quite similar, but it is not too difficult to guess which ones are the author's. The giveaway is that the machine learning scheme, in addition to choosing several good key phrases, also chooses some that authors are unlikely to use—for example, *gauge*, *smooth*, and especially *garbage*! Despite the anomalies, the automatically extracted lists seem to provide reasonable tags for the three papers. If no author-specified key phrases were available, they could prove useful for someone scanning quickly for relevant information.

Finding information in running text

A rather different kind of text mining is the automatic identification of particular kinds of information in running text. For example, suppose people's names could be identified wherever they occurred in a piece of text. Then, hyperlinks could be inserted automatically to other places that mention the same person—links that are "dynamically evaluated" by calling upon a search engine to bind them at click time. Or if different kinds of data could be identified, actions could be associated with them. A day/time specification appearing anywhere within your email could be associated with diary actions such as updating a personal organizer or creating an automatic reminder, and each mention of a day/time in the text could raise a popup menu of calendar-based actions. Or text could be mined for data in tabular format, allowing databases to be created from formatted tables such as stock market information on Web pages. Or an agent could monitor incoming newswire stories for company names and collect documents that mention them—an automated press clipping service.

How can such items be identified automatically? One promising way is to use statistical techniques based on language models. Given training data of different types of text—plain text, names, dates, dollar amounts, and so on—statistical character-based models are built for each type. Then, tokens of unknown type can be assigned to the model that predicts them with highest probability. Note that there is a close connection with prediction and compression: the number of bits required to compress an item with respect to a model can be interpreted as the negative logarithm of the probability with which that item is produced by the model. We encountered this relationship between probability and bits of information in Section 4.3 (pages 93–94).

The problem is not only to be able to identify items as being of certain types, but to locate these items where they occur in running text. To do this, consider the text to be a sequence of information from different sources. Posit the existence of begin-item and end-item symbols in the text and evaluate the probability of the entire string using the indicated models for the appropriate portions. The *begin* and *end* symbols identify the type of the item concerned; we have begin-name and end-name, begin-date and end-date, and so on. Competing interpretations, represented by different positioning of begin-item and end-item symbols, can be compared on the basis of their probability. In order to generate candidate interpretations, a tree structure of alternative interpretations of the text so far can be built and expanded by developing the most promising nodes. Although we have only sketched the process here, dynamic-programming-style algorithms can be developed that take a string of text and work out the optimal sequence of models that would produce it, along with their placement.

Soft parsing

This scheme can, without any extra technical difficulty, be applied hierarchically in situations where each token can contain subtokens—just as a name comprises first name, middle initial, and surname; and a street address is made up of different components. The term *soft parsing* has been used to denote the inference of what is effectively a hierarchical grammar from example strings using this probabilistic learning technique, and its application to test strings. To take a more complex example, a bibliographic reference might consist of a name, date, title, journal, volume number, issue number, and page numbers, along with appropriate intervening characters. These characters are very highly determined: names are separated by , • or •and•; between the name and date field comes • (; etc. (bullets are used here to make spaces visible). Many different forms of reference exist, of course, and examples of each must appear in the training data.

Training data for the individual models, like name, date, title, and so on, is very easy to come by: bibliography files are a convenient source. Some fields—such as author and editor—will be impossible to distinguish on the basis of their probability models alone, but the higher-level model for references as a whole will contain well-determined clues (such as the phrase *edited by*) that allows them to be accurately identified. Unlike standard language parsing, this technique is "soft" in that it generates alternative interpretations of test strings and selects the most likely one, rather than checking that the string conforms to the grammar and producing only a single interpretation.

Extending the soft parsing model to extract metadata such as author and title from plain text seems straightforward. Title pages have a characteristic structure that is easy to capture. It may be necessary to add features such as the distance from the start of the document (to help distinguish the author's name from other names that appear in the document's body); this seems easy to do using a machine learning model trained on example occurrences. Indeed, the algorithm for key phrase extraction by determining candidate key phrases and calculating appropriate features, described in the previous subsection, fits into the same soft parsing framework.

9.5 Mining the World Wide Web

We began this book by pointing out that we are overwhelmed with data. The amount of data in the world, in our lives, goes on and on increasing—and there's no end in sight. Nowhere does this impact the lives of ordinary people more than on the World Wide Web. At present, there are an estimated 4,000 Gbytes of data on the Web, and it continues to grow exponentially, doubling every six months. As we write this (in 1999), the percentage of U.S. consumers using the Internet is just reaching 50%. And none of them can keep pace with the information explosion.

Whereas data mining belongs in the corporate world because that's where most databases are, text mining promises to move machine learning technology out of the companies and into the home. Whenever we are overwhelmed by data on the Web, text mining could provide tools to tame it. Applications are legion. Finding names, addresses, and phone numbers on Web pages, locating information like stock prices in tables expressed in either HTML or plain text, shopping for bargains in an electronic world where each store presents its wares in its own house style, data detectors of any kind—all of these could be accomplished without any explicit programming. Already text mining techniques are being used to predict what link you're going to click next, to organize documents into hierarchies to make it easier for you to find what you want, to filter your email—both by screening out unwanted items like junk mail and by selecting high-priority items so that you can be alerted on your email pager. In a world where information is overwhelming, disorganized, and anarchic, text mining may be the solution we so desperately need.

Data mining is already widely used at work. Although in its infancy, text mining may turn out to bring the techniques in this book into our own lives.

9.6 Further reading

There is a substantial amount of literature that treats the topic of massive datasets, and we can only point to a few references here. Fayyad and Smyth (1995) discuss the application of data mining to voluminous data from scientific experiments. Shafer et al. (1996) describe a parallel version of a top-down decision tree inducer. A sequential decision tree algorithm for massive disk-resident datasets has been developed by Mehta et al. (1996). Bennett et al. (1998) present a sophisticated indexing technique that speeds up nearest-neighbor queries. A data structure for caching class counts from large datasets—needed by many learning schemes—has been developed by Moore and Lee (1998).

Bellcore's XGobi software, described by Swayne et al. (1998), is an excellent example of a sophisticated visualization tool. It was used to produce the pictures in Figure 9.1, and it is capable of far more than these simple examples show. Berchtold et al. (1998) have developed a technique for visualizing dependencies between pairs of attributes, another for analyzing the input data. Fly-through decision trees and three-dimensional representations of decision tables are included in SGI's MineSet data mining software (Brunk et al. 1997). Humphrey et al. (1998) developed the system for visualizing decision trees that we have described, and it was this system that produced Figure 9.2.

Despite its importance, little seems to have been written about the general problem of incorporating metadata into practical data mining. A scheme for encoding domain knowledge into propositional rules and its use for both deduction and induction has been investigated by Giraud-Carrier (1996). The related area of inductive logic programming, which deals with knowledge represented by first-order logic rules, is covered by Bergadano and Gunetti (1996).

Text mining is an emerging new area, and there are as yet no comprehensive sources of information. The use of support vector machines to assign key phrases from a controlled vocabulary to documents on the basis of a large number of training documents is described by Dumais et al. (1998). The use of machine learning to extract key phrases from the document text has been investigated by Turney (1999) and Frank et al. (1999). An approach to finding information in running text has been reported by Witten et al. (1999). The statistic on the percentage of U.S. consumers using the Internet is from a poll by Market Opinion Research International (Fox 1999).

References

Adriaans, P., and D. Zantige. 1996. *Data mining.* Harlow, England: Addison-Wesley.

Agrawal, R., and R. Srikant. 1994. Fast algorithms for mining association rules in large databases. In Bocca, J., M. Jarke, and C. Zaniolo, editors, *Proc. International Conference on Very Large Data Bases*, Santiago, Chile. San Francisco: Morgan Kaufmann, pp. 478–499.

Agrawal, R., T. Imielinski, and A. Swami. 1993a. Database mining: a performance perspective. *IEEE Trans. Knowledge and Data Engineering* 5(6):914–925.

———. 1993b. Mining association rules between sets of items in large databases. In Buneman, P., and S. Jajodia, editors, *Proc. ACM SIGMOD International Conference on Management of Data*, Washington, DC. New York: ACM, pp. 207–216.

Aha, D. 1992. Tolerating noisy, irrelevant, and novel attributes in instance-based learning algorithms. *International Journal of Man-Machine Studies* 36(2):267–287.

Almuallin, H., and T. G. Dietterich. 1991. Learning with many irrelevant features. In *Proc. Ninth National Conference on Artificial Intelligence*, Anaheim, CA. Menlo Park, CA: AAAI Press, pp. 547–552.

———. 1992. Efficient algorithms for identifying relevant features. In *Proc. Ninth Canadian Conference on Artificial Intelligence*, Vancouver, BC. San Francisco: Morgan Kaufmann, pp. 38–45.

Asmis, E. 1984. *Epicurus' scientific method.* Ithaca, NY: Cornell University Press.

Atkeson, C. G., S. A. Schaal, and A. W. Moore. 1997. Locally weighted learning. *AI Review* 11:11–71.

Bayes, T. 1763. An essay towards solving a problem in the doctrine of chances. *Philosophical Transactions of the Royal Society of London* 53:370–418.

Beck, J. R., and E. K. Schultz. 1986. The use of ROC curves in test performance evaluation. *Archives of Pathology and Laboratory Medicine* 110:13–20.

Bennett, K. P., U. Fayyad, and D. Geiger. 1998. Density-based indexing for nearest-neighbor queries. Technical Report MR-TR-98-58. Seattle: Microsoft Research.

Berchtold, S., H. V. Jagadish, and K. A. Ross. 1998. Independence diagrams: A technique for visual data mining. In Agrawal, R., P. E. Stolorz, and G. Piatetsky-Shapiro, editors, *Proc. Fourth International Conference on Knowledge Discovery and Data Mining*, New York. Menlo Park, CA: AAAI Press, pp. 139–143.

Bergadano, F., and D. Gunetti. 1996. *Inductive logic programming: From machine learning to software engineering.* Cambridge, MA: MIT Press.

Berry, M. J. A., and G. Linoff. 1997. *Data mining techniques for marketing, sales, and customer support.* New York: John Wiley.

Bigus, J. P. 1996. *Data mining with neural networks.* New York: McGraw Hill.

Blake, C., E. Keogh, and C. J. Merz. 1998. *UCI Repository of machine learning databases* [http://www. ics. uci. edu/~mlearn/MLRepository. html]. Department of Information and Computer Science, University of California, Irvine.

BLI (Bureau of Labour Information). 1988. *Collective Bargaining Review* (November). Ottawa, Ontario, Canada: Labour Canada, Bureau of Labour Information.

Brachman, R. J., and H. J. Levesque, editors. 1985. *Readings in knowledge representation.* San Francisco: Morgan Kaufmann.

Breiman, L. 1996a. Stacked regression. *Machine Learning* 24(1):49–64.

———. 1996b. Bagging predictors. *Machine Learning* 24(2):123–140.

Breiman, L., J. H. Friedman, R. A. Olshen, and C. J. Stone. 1984. *Classification and regression trees.* Monterey, CA: Wadsworth.

Brodley, C. E., and M. A. Friedl. 1996. Identifying and eliminating mislabeled training instances. In *Proc. Thirteenth National Conference on Artificial Intelligence*, Portland, OR. Menlo Park, CA: AAAI Press, pp. 799–805.

Brownstown, L., R. Farrell, E. Kant, and N. Martin. 1985. *Programming expert systems in OPS5.* Reading, MA: Addison-Wesley.

Brunk, C., J. Kelly, and R. Kohavi. 1997. MineSet: An integrated system for data mining. In Heckerman, D., H. Mannila, D. Pregibon, and R. Uthurusamy, editors, *Proc. Third International Conference on Knowledge Discovery and Data Mining*, Newport Beach, CA. Menlo Park, CA: AAAI Press.

Burges, C. J. C. 1998. A tutorial on support vector machines for pattern recognition. *Data Mining and Knowledge Discovery* 2(2).

Cabena, P., P. Hadjinian, R. Stadler, J. Verhees, and A. Zanasi. 1998. *Discovering data mining: From concept to implementation.* Upper Saddle River, NJ: Prentice Hall.

Cardie, C. 1993. Using decision trees to improve case-based learning. In Utgoff, P., editor, *Proc. Tenth International Conference on Machine Learning*, Amherst, MA. San Francisco: Morgan Kaufmann, pp. 25–32.

Cendrowska, J. 1987. PRISM: An algorithm for inducing modular rules. *International Journal of Man-Machine Studies* 27(4):349–370.

Cheeseman, P., and J. Stutz. 1995. Bayesian classification (AutoClass): Theory and results. In U. M. Fayyad, G. Piatetsky-Shapiro, P. Smyth, and R. Uthurusamy, editors, *Advances in Knowledge Discovery and Data Mining.* Menlo Park, CA: AAAI Press, pp. 153–180.

Chen, M.-S., J. Jan, and P. S. Yu. 1996. Data mining: An overview from a database perspective. *IEEE Trans. Knowledge and Data Engineering* 8(6):866–883.

Cherkauer, K. J., and J. W. Shavlik. 1996. Growing simpler decision trees to facilitate knowledge discovery. In Simoudis, E., J. W. Han, and U. Fayyad, editors, *Proc. Second International Conference on Knowledge Discovery and Data Mining*, Portland, OR. Menlo Park, CA: AAAI Press, pp. 315–318.

Cleary, J. G., and L. E. Trigg. 1995. K*: An instance-based learner using an entropic distance measure. In Prieditis, A., and S. Russell, editors, *Proc. Twelfth International Conference on Machine Learning*, Tahoe City, CA. San Francisco: Morgan Kaufmann, pp. 108–114.

Cohen, W. W. 1995. Fast effective rule induction. In Prieditis, A., and S. Russell, editors, *Proc. Twelfth International Conference on Machine Learning*, Tahoe City, CA. San Francisco: Morgan Kaufmann, pp. 115–123.

Cortes, C., and V. Vapnik. 1995. Support vector networks. *Machine Learning* 20(3):273–297.

Dhar, V., and R. Stein. 1997. *Seven methods for transforming corporate data into business intelligence.* Upper Saddle River, NJ: Prentice Hall.

Dietterich, T. G., and G. Bakiri. 1995. Solving multiclass learning problems via error-correcting output codes. *Journal Artificial Intelligence Research* 2:263–286.

Dougherty, J., R. Kohavi, and M. Sahami. 1995. Supervised and unsupervised discretization of continuous features. In Prieditis, A., and S. Russell, editors, *Proc.*

Twelfth International Conference on Machine Learning, Tahoe City, CA. San Francisco: Morgan Kaufmann, pp. 194–202.

Drucker, H. 1997. Improving regressors using boosting techniques. In Fisher, D. H., *Proc. Fourteenth International Conference on Machine Learning,* Nashville, TN. San Francisco: Morgan Kaufmann, pp. 107–115.

Duda, R. O., and P. E. Hart. 1973. *Pattern classification and scene analysis.* New York: John Wiley.

Dumais, S. T., J. Platt, D. Heckerman, and M. Sahami. 1998. Inductive learning algorithms and representations for text categorization. In *Proc. ACM Seventh International Conference on Information and Knowledge Management,* Bethesda, MD. New York: ACM, pp. 148–155.

Efron, B., and R. Tibshirani. 1993. *An introduction to the bootstrap.* London: Chapman and Hall.

Egan, J. P. 1975. *Signal detection theory and ROC analysis.* Series in Cognition and Perception. New York: Academic Press.

Fayyad, U. M., and K. B. Irani. 1993. Multi-interval discretization of continuous-valued attributes for classification learning. In *Proc. Thirteenth International Joint Conference on Artificial Intelligence,* Chambery, France. San Francisco: Morgan Kaufmann, pp. 1022–1027.

Fayyad, U. M., and P. Smyth. 1995. From massive datasets to science catalogs: Applications and challenges. In *Proc. Workshop on Massive Datasets.* Washington, DC: NRC, Committee on Applied and Theoretical Statistics.

Fayyad, U. M., G. Piatetsky-Shapiro, P. Smyth, and R. Uthurusamy, editors. 1996. *Advances in knowledge discovery and data mining.* Menlo Park, CA: AAAI Press/MIT Press.

Fisher, D. 1987. Knowledge acquisition via incremental conceptual clustering. *Machine Learning* 2(2):139–172.

Fisher, R. A. 1936. The use of multiple measurements in taxonomic problems. *Annual Eugenics* 7(part II):179–188. Reprinted in *Contributions to Mathematical Statistics,* 1950. New York: John Wiley.

Fix, E., and J. L. Hodges Jr. 1951. Discriminatory analysis; non-parametric discrimination: Consistency properties. Technical Report 21-49-004(4), USAF School of Aviation Medicine, Randolph Field, Texas.

Fletcher, R. 1987. *Practical methods of optimization,* second edition. New York: John Wiley.

Fox, R. 1999. News track. *Communications of the ACM* 42(2):9–11.

Frank, E., and I. H. Witten. 1998. Generating accurate rule sets without global optimization. In Shavlik, J., editor, *Proc. Fifteenth International Conference on Machine Learning*, Madison, WI. San Francisco: Morgan Kaufmann, pp. 144–151.

———. 1999. Making better use of global discretization. In Bratko, I., and S. Dzeroski, editors, *Proc. Sixteenth International Conference on Machine Learning*, Bled, Slovenia. San Francisco: Morgan Kaufmann, pp. 115–123.

Frank, E., G. W. Paynter, I. H. Witten, C. Gutwin, and C. G. Nevill-Manning. 1999. Domain-specific keyphrase extraction. In *Proc. Sixteenth International Joint Conference on Artificial Intelligence*, Stockholm, Sweden. San Francisco: Morgan Kaufmann, pp. 668–673.

Freund, Y., and R. E. Schapire. 1996. Experiments with a new boosting algorithm. In Saitta, L., editor, *Proc. Thirteenth International Conference on Machine Learning*, Bari, Italy. San Francisco: Morgan Kaufmann, pp. 148–156.

———. 1998. Large margin classification using the perceptron algorithm. In Bartlett, P., and Y. Mansour, editors. *Proc. Eleventh Annual Conference on Computational Learning Theory*, Madison, WI. New York: ACM Press, pp. 209–217.

Friedman, J. H. 1999. *Greedy function approximation: A gradient boosting machine.* Technical report, Department of Statistics, Stanford University, Palo Alto, CA.

Friedman, J. H., T. Hastie, and R. Tibshirani. 1998. *Additive logistic regression: A statistical view of boosting.* Technical report, Department of Statistics, Stanford University, Palo Alto, CA.

Fulton, T., S. Kasif, and S. Salzberg. 1995. Efficient algorithms for finding multi-way splits for decision trees. In Prieditis, A., and S. Russell, editors, *Proc. Twelfth International Conference on Machine Learning*, Tahoe City, CA. San Francisco: Morgan Kaufmann, pp. 244–251.

Fürnkrantz, J., and G. Widmer. 1994. Incremental reduced error pruning. In Hirsh, H., and W. Cohen, editors, *Proc. Eleventh International Conference on Machine Learning*, New Brunswick, NJ. San Francisco: Morgan Kaufmann, pp. 70–77.

Gaines, B. R., and P. Compton. 1995. Induction of ripple-down rules applied to modeling large data bases. *Journal of Intelligent Information Systems* 5(3):211–228.

Genesereth, M. R., and N. J. Nilsson. 1987. *Logical foundations of artificial intelligence.* San Francisco: Morgan Kaufmann.

Gennari, J. H., P. Langley, and D. Fisher. 1990. Models of incremental concept formation. *Artificial Intelligence* 40:11–61.

Giraud-Carrier, C. 1996. FLARE: Induction with prior knowledge. In Nealon, J., and J. Hunt, editors, *Research and Development in Expert Systems XIII*. Cambridge, England: SGES Publications, pp. 11–24.

Gluck, M., and J. Corter. 1985. Information, uncertainty and the utility of categories. In *Proc. Annual Conference of the Cognitive Science Society*, Irvine, CA. Hillsdale, NJ: Lawrence Erlbaum, pp. 283–287.

Goldberg, D. E. 1989. *Genetic algorithms in search, optimization and machine learning*. Reading, MA: Addison-Wesley.

Groth, R. 1998. *Data mining: A hands-on approach for business professionals*. Upper Saddle River, NJ: Prentice Hall.

Hartigan, J. A. 1975. *Clustering algorithms*. New York: John Wiley.

Heckerman, D., D. Geiger, and D. M. Chickering. 1995. Learning Bayesian networks: The combination of knowledge and statistical data. *Machine Learning* 20(3):197–243.

Holmes, G., and C. G. Nevill-Manning. 1995. Feature selection via the discovery of simple classification rules. In Lasker, G. E., and X. Liu, editors, *Proc. International Symposium on Intelligent Data Analysis*. Baden-Baden, Germany: International Institute for Advanced Studies in Systems Research and Cybernetics, pp. 75–79.

Holte, R. C. 1993. Very simple classification rules perform well on most commonly used datasets. *Machine Learning* 11:63–91.

Humphrey, M., S. J. Cunningham, and I. H. Witten. 1998. Knowledge visualization techniques for machine learning. *Intelligent Data Analysis* 2(4).

Jabbour, K., J. F. V. Riveros, D. Landsbergen, and W. Meyer. 1988. ALFA: Automated load forecasting assistant. *IEEE Transactions on Power Systems* 3(3):908–914.

John, G. H. 1995. Robust decision trees: Removing outliers from databases. In Fayyad, U. M., and R. Uthurusamy, editors, *Proc. First International Conference on Knowledge Discovery and Data Mining*. Montreal, Canada. Menlo Park, CA: AAAI Press, pp. 174–179.

———. 1997. *Enhancements to the data mining process*. PhD Dissertation, Computer Science Department, Stanford University.

John, G. H., R. Kohavi, and P. Pfleger. 1994. Irrelevant features and the subset selection problem. In Hirsh, H., and W. Cohen, editors, *Proc. Eleventh Interna-*

tional Conference on Machine Learning, pp. 121–129. New Brunswick, NJ. San Francisco: Morgan Kaufmann.

John, G. H., and P. Langley. 1995. Estimating continuous distributions in Bayesian classifiers. In Besnard, P., and S. Hanks, editors, *Proc. Eleventh Conference on Uncertainty in Artificial Intelligence.* Montreal, Canada. San Francisco: Morgan Kaufmann, pp. 338–345.

Johns, M. V. 1961. An empirical Bayes approach to non-parametric two-way classification. In Solomon, H., editor, *Studies in item analysis and prediction.* Palo Alto, CA: Stanford University Press.

Kerber, R. 1992. Chimerge: Discretization of numeric attributes. In Swartout, W., editor, *Proc. Tenth National Conference on Artificial Intelligence,* San Jose, CA. Menlo Park, CA: AAAI Press, pp. 123–128.

Kibler, D., and D. W. Aha. 1987. Learning representative exemplars of concepts: An initial case study. In Langley, P., editor, *Proc. Fourth Machine Learning Workshop,* Irvine, CA. San Francisco: Morgan Kaufmann, pp. 24–30.

Kimball, R. 1996. *The data warehouse toolkit.* New York: John Wiley.

Kira, K., and L. Rendell. 1992. A practical approach to feature selection. In Sleeman, D., and P. Edwards, editors, *Proc. Ninth International Workshop on Machine Learning,* Aberdeen, Scotland. San Francisco: Morgan Kaufmann, pp. 249–258.

Kittler, J. 1978. Feature set search algorithms. In Chen, C. H., editor, *Pattern recognition and signal processing,* The Netherlands: Sijthoff an Noordhoff.

Koestler, A. 1964. *The act of creation.* London: Hutchinson.

Kohavi, R. 1995. A study of cross-validation and bootstrap for accuracy estimation and model selection. In *Proc. Fourteenth International Joint Conference on Artificial Intelligence,* Montreal, Canada. San Francisco: Morgan Kaufmann, pp. 1137–1143.

Kohavi, R., and G. H. John. 1997. Wrappers for feature subset selection. *Artificial Intelligence* 97(1-2):273–324.

Kohavi, R., and M. Sahami. 1996. Error-based and entropy-based discretization of continuous features. In Simoudis, E., Han, J. W., and Fayyad, U., *Proc. Second International Conference on Knowledge Discovery and Data Mining,* Portland, OR. Menlo Park, CA: AAAI Press, pp. 114–119.

Kohavi, R., and F. Provost, editors. 1998. Machine learning: Special issue on applications of machine learning and the knowledge discovery process. *Machine Learning* 30(2/3).

Kokar, M. M. 1986. Determining arguments of invariant functional descriptions. *Machine Learning* 1(4):403–422.

Kubat, M., R. C. Holte, and S. Matwin. 1998. Machine learning for the detection of oil spills in satellite radar images. *Machine Learning* 30:195–215.

Langley, P. 1996. *Elements of machine learning*. San Francisco: Morgan Kaufmann.

Langley, P., W. Iba, and K. Thompson. 1992. An analysis of Bayesian classifiers. In Swartout, W., editor, *Proc. Tenth National Conference on Artificial Intelligence*, San Jose, CA. Menlo Park, CA: AAAI Press, pp. 223–228.

Langley, P., and S. Sage. 1994. Induction of selective Bayesian classifiers. In de Mantaras, R. L., and D. Poole, editors, *Proc. Tenth Conference on Uncertainty in Artificial Intelligence*, Seattle, WA. San Francisco: Morgan Kaufmann, pp. 399–406.

Langley, P., and H. A. Simon. 1995. Applications of machine learning and rule induction. *Communications of the ACM* 38(11):55–64.

Lawson, C. L., and R. J. Hanson. 1995. *Solving least squares problems*. Philadelphia: SIAM Publications.

Li, M., and P. M. B. Vitanyi. 1992. Inductive reading and Kolmogorov complexity. *Journal Computer and System Sciences* 44:343–384.

Liu, H., and R. Setiono. 1996. A probabilistic approach to feature selection: A filter solution. In Saitta, L., editor, *Proc. Thirteenth International Conference on Machine Learning*, Bari, Italy. San Francisco: Morgan Kaufmann, pp. 319–327.

———. 1997. Feature selection via discretization. *IEEE Trans. Knowledge and Data Engineering* 9(4):642–645.

Madigan, D., A. E. Raftery, C. T. Volinsky, and J. Hoeting. 1996. Bayesian model averaging. In Chan, P., S. Stolfo, and D. Wolpert, editors, *Proc. AAAI Workshop on Integrating Multiple Learned Models*, Portland, OR, pp. 77–83.

Marill, T., and D. M. Green. 1963. On the effectiveness of receptors in recognition systems. *IEEE Trans. Information Theory* 9(11):11–17.

Martin, B. 1995. Instance-based learning: Nearest neighbour with generalisation. MSc Thesis, Department of Computer Science, University of Waikato, New Zealand.

Mehta, M., R. Agrawal, and J. Rissanen. 1996. SLIQ: A fast scalable classifier for data mining. In Apers, P., M. Bouzeghoub, and G. Gardarin, *Proc. Fifth International Conference on Extending Database Technology*, Avignon, France. New York: Springer-Verlag.

Michalski, R. S., and R. L. Chilausky. 1980. Learning by being told and learning from examples: An experimental comparison of the two methods of knowledge acquisition in the context of developing an expert system for soybean disease diagnosis. *International Journal of Policy Analysis and Information Systems* 4(2).

Michie, D. 1989. Problems of computer-aided concept formation. In Quinlan, J. R., editor, *Applications of expert systems, Vol. 2.* Wokingham, England: Addison-Wesley, pp. 310–333.

Minsky, M., and S. Papert. 1969. *Perceptrons.* Cambridge, MA: MIT Press.

Mitchell, T. M. 1997. *Machine Learning.* New York: McGraw Hill.

Moore, A., and M. S. Lee. 1998. Cached sufficient statistics for efficient machine learning with large datasets. *Journal Artificial Intelligence Research* 8: 67–91.

Nie, N. H., C. H. Hull, J. G. Jenkins, K. Steinbrenner, and D. H. Bent. 1970. *Statistical package for the social sciences.* New York: McGraw Hill.

Nilsson, N. J. 1965. *Learning machines.* New York: McGraw Hill.

Piatetsky-Shapiro, G., and W. J. Frawley, editors. 1991. *Knowledge discovery in databases.* Menlo Park, CA: AAAI Press/MIT Press.

Platt, J. 1998. Fast training of support vector machines using sequential minimal optimization. In Schölkopf, B., C. Burges, and A. Smola, editors, *Advances in Kernel Methods—Support Vector Learning.* Cambridge, MA: MIT Press.

Provost, F., and T. Fawcett. 1997. Analysis and visualization of classifier performance: Comparison under imprecise class and cost distributions. In Heckerman, D., H. Mannila, D. Pregibon, and R. Uthurusamy, editors, *Proc. Third International Conference on Knowledge Discovery and Data Mining*, Huntington Beach, CA. Menlo Park, CA: AAAI Press.

Quinlan, J. R. 1986. Induction of decision trees. *Machine Learning* 1(1):81–106.

———. 1992. Learning with continuous classes. In Adams, N., and L. Sterling, editors, *Proc. Fifth Australian Joint Conference on Artificial Intelligence*, Hobart, Tasmania. Singapore: World Scientific, pp. 343–348.

———. 1993. *C4.5: Programs for machine learning.* San Francisco: Morgan Kaufmann.

Ricci, F., and D. W. Aha. 1998. Error-correcting output codes for local learners. In Nedellec, C., and C. Rouveird, editors, *Proc. European Conference on Machine Learning*, Chemnitz, Germany. Berlin: Springer-Verlag, pp. 280–291.

Richards, D., and P. Compton. 1998. Taking up the situated cognition challenge with ripple-down rules. *International Journal of Human-Computer Studies* 49(6):895–926.

Rissanen, J. 1985. The minimum description length principle. In Kotz, S., and N. L. Johnson, editors, *Encylopedia of Statistical Sciences, Vol. 5*. New York: John Wiley, pp. 523–527.

Rousseeuw, P. J., and A. M. Leroy. 1987. *Robust regression and outlier detection*. New York: John Wiley.

Saitta, L., and F. Neri. 1998. Learning in the 'real world.' *Machine Learning* 30(2/3):133–163.

Salzberg, S. 1991. A nearest hyperrectangle learning method. *Machine Learning* 6(3):251–276.

Schapire, R. E., Y. Freund, P. Bartlett, and W. S. Lee. 1997. Boosting the margin: A new explanation for the effectiveness of voting methods. In Fisher, D. H., editor, *Proc. Fourteenth International Conference on Machine Learning*, Nashville, TN. San Francisco: Morgan Kaufmann, pp. 322–330.

Schölkopf, B., P. Bartlett, A. J. Smola, and R. Williamson. 1999. Shrinking the tube: A new support vector regression algorithm. *Advances in Neural Information Processing Systems*, Vol. 11. Cambridge, MA: MIT Press.

Shafer, R., R. Agrawal, and M. Metha. 1996. SPRINT: A scalable parallel classifier for data mining. In Vijayaraman, T. M., A. P. Buchmann, C. Mohan, and N. L. Sarda, editors, *Proc. Second International Conference on Very Large Databases*, Mumbai (Bombay), India. San Francisco: Morgan Kaufmann, pp. 544–555.

Stevens, S. S. 1946. On the theory of scales of measurement. *Science* 103:677–680.

Swayne, D. F., D. Cook, and A. Buja. 1998. XGobi: Interactive dynamic data visualization in the X window system. *Journal Computational and Graphical Statistics* 7(1):113–130.

Swets, J. 1988. Measuring the accuracy of diagnostic systems. *Science* 240:1285–1293.

Ting, K. M., and I. H. Witten. 1997a. Stacked generalization: When does it work? In *Proc. Fifteenth International Joint Conference on Artificial Intelligence*, Nagoya, Japan. San Francisco: Morgan Kaufmann, pp. 866–871.

————. 1997b. Stacking bagged and dagged models. In Fisher, D. H., editor, *Proc. Fourteenth International Conference on Machine Learning*, Nashville, TN. San Francisco: Morgan Kaufmann, pp. 367–375.

Turney, P. D. 1999. Learning to extract keyphrases from text. Technical Report ERB-1057, Institute for Information Technology, National Research Council of Canada, Ottawa.

Vafaie, H., and K. DeJong. 1992. Genetic algorithms as a tool for feature selection in machine learning. In *Proc. International Conference on Tools with Artificial Intelligence.* Arlington, VA: IEEE Computer Society Press, pp. 200–203.

van Rijsbergen, C. A. 1979. *Information retrieval.* London: Butterworths.

Vapnik, V. 1995. *The nature of statistical learning theory.* New York: Springer-Verlag.

Wang, Y. and I. H. Witten. 1997. Induction of model trees for predicting continuous classes. In van Someran, M., and G. Widmar, editors. *Proc. of the Poster Papers of the European Conference on Machine Learning,* University of Economics, Faculty of Informatics and Statistics, Prague, pp. 128–137.

Weiss, S. M., and N. Indurkhya. 1998. *Predictive data mining: A practical guide.* San Francisco: Morgan Kaufmann.

Wettschereck, D., and Dietterich, T. G. 1995. An experimental comparison of the nearest-neighbor and nearest-hyperrectangle algorithms. *Machine Learning* 19(1):5–28.

Wild, C. J., and G. A. F. Seber. 1995. *Introduction to probability and statistics.* Department of Statistics, University of Auckland, New Zealand.

Winston, P. H. 1992. *Artificial intelligence.* Reading, MA: Addison-Wesley.

Witten, I. H., Z. Bray, M. Mahoui, and W. Teahan. 1999. Text mining: A new frontier for lossless compression. In Storer, J. A., and M. Cohn, editors, *Proc. Data Compression Conference,* Snowbird, UT. Los Alamitos, CA: IEEE Press, pp. 198–207.

Witten, I. H., A. Moffat, and T. C. Bell. 1999. *Managing gigabytes: compressing and indexing documents and images,* second edition. San Francisco: Morgan Kaufmann.

Wolpert, D. H. 1992. Stacked generalization. *Neural Networks* 5:241–259.

Index

About the Authors

Ian Witten is professor of computer science at the University of Waikato in Hamilton, New Zealand. He has taught at Essex University and at the University of Calgary, where he was head of computer science from 1982 to 1985. He holds degrees in mathematics from Cambridge University, computer science from the University of Calgary, and a Ph.D. in electrical engineering from Essex University, England. He has published extensively in academic conferences and journals on machine learning.

The underlying theme of his current research is the exploitation of information about a user's past behavior to expedite interaction in the future. In pursuit of this theme, he has been drawn into machine learning, which seeks ways to summarize, restructure, and generalize past experience; adaptive text compression, that is, using information about past text to encode upcoming characters; and user modeling, which is the general area of characterizing user behavior.

He directs a large project at Waikato on machine learning and its application to agriculture and has also been active recently in the area of document compression, indexing, and retrieval. He has also written many books over the last 15 years, the most recent of which is *Managing Gigabytes: Compressing and Indexing Documents and Images, second edition* (Morgan Kaufmann 1999) with A. Moffat and T. C. Bell.

Eibe Frank is a Ph.D. candidate in computer science at the University of Waikato. His research focus is machine learning. He holds a degree in Computer Science from the University of Karlstruhe in Germany and is the author of several papers presented at machine learning conferences and published in journals.